P9-DBI-718

GILBERT HAVEN

Methodist Abolitionist

A Study in Race, Religion, and Reform, 1850-1880

William Gravely

Edited by

The Commission on Archives and History

of

The United Methodist Church

Published by

Abingdon Press
Nashville and New York

Library of Congress Cataloging in Publication Data

GRAVELY, WILLIAM B. 1939- Gilbert Haven, Methodist
Abolitionist. 1. Haven, Gilbert, Bp., 1821-1880. 2.
Slavery in the United States. 3. Church and race prob-
lems—United States. I. United Methodist Church
(United States). Commission on Archives and History.
BX8495.H28G7   287′.632′0924   [B]
72-14179

ISBN 0-687-14702-6

MANUFACTURED BY THE PARTHENON PRESS AT
NASHVILLE, TENNESSEE, UNITED STATES OF AMERICA

IN MEMORY

of
James McBride Dabbs
C. Jasper Smith
Artie H. Gravely
and
in honor
of
my father
who
each in his own way
shared the dream of
Gilbert Haven
and
taught it to me

G. Haven

Acknowledgements

Specific financial assistance for research and preparation of this manuscript has been provided by grants from the Center for Southern Studies at Duke University, the Dempster Graduate Fellowship of The United Methodist Church, the George E. Norman Fund and other scholarships through the graduate program in religion at Duke, a summer fellowship from the National Endowment for the Humanities, the Commission on Archives and History of The United Methodist Church, and the Faculty Research Fund of the University of Denver.

I am indebted to the staffs of the following institutions for their assistance in making available letters and/or other materials by and about Haven: Cornell, Denver, Drew, Duke, Ohio Wesleyan, Princeton, Southern Methodist, Emory, Syracuse, Wesleyan, Michigan, and Harvard university libraries; the Library of Congress; the libraries of Garrett Theological Seminary, the Interdenominational Theological Center, and the Historical Society of Pennsylvania; the Rutherford B. Hayes Library; the Arthur and Elizabeth Schlesinger Library at Radcliffe College; the New England Methodist Historical Society Library; the Boston, Malden, and Northampton public libraries; the Westfield Athenaeum in Massachusetts; the Boston Athenaeum; Michigan Historical Collections; Lovely Lane Museum, Baltimore; the State Historical Society of Wisconsin; the Christian Historical Commission of the Mother Bethel A. M. E. Church, Philadelphia; and the archives of the Philadelphia Conference Historical Society of The United Methodist Church.

Special recognition is due for particular contributions toward this book from the following persons: Ralph E. Morrow of Washington University, St. Louis, and Frederick Norwood of Garrett Theological Seminary for initial encouragement to undertake the project; to Dr. Jannette Newhall, retired librarian at the Boston University School of Theology, who kindly lent me her grandfather's journal and commonplace book; to Donn Michael Farris, librarian at Duke Divinity School, for purchasing microfilm that was essential for my work; to Ken Rowe of Drew, Lawrence O. Kline of Duke, and Ralph Luker of Allegheny College, for sharing leads and discoveries; to Mrs. John H. Warnick for digging out and sending materials from Southern Methodist University; to Mrs. Robert P. McMahon of Westfield, Massachusetts, for typing out a Haven sermon from a local newspaper; to Darryl W. Palmer of Australia, and Herman Thomas of Springfield College, for checking sources in Massachusetts; to John W. Spaeth, Jr., archivist at Wesleyan University, for materials on Haven's college years; to David Donald of Johns Hopkins University, for sharing information on Haven's relation to Charles Sumner; to Mrs. Alan J. Pethick for information on Haven's years at Wesleyan

Academy; to James E. Clark and his successor, Wilson N. Flemister, at the Interdenominational Theological Center Library in Atlanta, for access to materials not available elsewhere; to Elvin Strowd at Duke, for opening up stored library materials, and to Emerson Ford for assistance in interlibrary loans; to Mrs. Dorothy F. Kebker for lending important journals from the Methodist Historical Collection at Ohio Wesleyan University; to Mrs. Stanley R. McDaniel of Canton, Ohio, and Dr. Mattie Russell at Duke, for access to letters by Haven in the J. E. Bryant Papers; to Creighton Lacy of Duke, and Wendell D. Luke, Jr., of Wakefield, Massachusetts, for assistance in contacting surviving relatives in the Haven family; to Dr. and Mrs. Eric M. North, Dr. Jannette Newhall, and the libraries of Drew, Southern Methodist, and Wesleyan Universities, and The United Methodist Publishing House for providing illustrations; to Warren Carberg and Jonathan Saver of the Boston Wesleyan Association, in connection with Haven's editorial career; to Gerald McCulloh of the Board of Education of The United Methodist Church, for arranging for my summer's research in Atlanta in 1967; and to John H. Ness, Jr. and Mrs. Louise Queen of the Commission on Archives and History of The United Methodist Church, Lake Junaluska, North Carolina, for their aid in the technical matters of publication.

Contents

Illustrations

Jesse Lee Prize

of

The Commission on Archives and History

of

The United Methodist Church

1970

The plan for establishing an annual prize for a book length manuscript on some aspect of the history of American Methodism was developed in connection with the Bicentennial of American Methodism, celebrated at Baltimore, Maryland, in 1966. It was proposed by the Committee on Awards which first met at Garrett Theological Seminary on March 27, 1965. The name honors Jesse Lee (1758-1816), author (1810) of the first history of American Methodism.

Subsequently the program was modified in two ways: the prize was offered biennially instead of annually; and the money was committed directly to publication of the manuscript.

The first award went to Lewis M. Purifoy in 1967 for "Negro Slavery, the Moral Ordeal of Southern Methodism, 1844-1861." The prize was awarded in 1968 to Lester B. Scherer for "Ezekiel Cooper, an Early American Methodist Leader." The third award went to William B. Gravely in 1970 for "Gilbert Haven, Racial Equalitarian, a Study of His Career in Racial Reform, 1850-1880."

Other projects sponsored by the Committee on Awards include modest grants-in-aid for specific projects of research, a Seminary Award ($200 and $100 first and second prizes) for essays on Methodist history submitted by students in United Methodist seminaries, and the Sarah Dickey Award ($100) for essays by college or university students on black church history.

FREDERICK A. NORWOOD

Introduction

For most of American history an anti-Christian racism has corrupted the life and thought of the churches. American religion has more often accommodated to than it has effectively challenged the oppressive institutions of racial slavery and segregation. The Christian tradition, the most influential in the nation, has not usually been able to command sufficient moral resources to create significant interracial community. White and black churchmen continue to choose, for the most part, primary relations in their religious societies on a racially separate basis. This legacy of *racial* Christianity is one dimension of the malaise of contemporary American religion.

This book tells the story of Gilbert Haven, a churchman from the last century who was an authentic racial equalitarian and social reformer, who understood as well as any white American of his era the contradiction which racism posed to Christianity and to democratic values, who struggled valiantly for three decades to convince his fellow countrymen, and particularly his associates in the Methodist Episcopal Church, of the crisis in society and in religion that slavery and caste created.

While this study follows a general chronological scheme, it is not a comprehensive biography. The intent has been to analyze Haven's career by showing the essential correlation between his religious outlook, racial thought, and reform tactics. My analysis demonstrates the extent to which, despite Haven's own dedicated churchmanship, nineteenth-century American religion was unable to assist or lead the nation toward humane solutions for its racial dilemma. After the first, each chapter deals separately with sociopolitical and ecclesiastical developments affecting and expressing Haven's fundamental commitment to human freedom and interracial brotherhood.

In the text I have left quotations as they appeared in the original, despite inconsistencies in spelling and grammar, though the more obvious errors have been noted. Occasionally I have changed the tense of a verb in order to harmonize with the sense of my construction. When I have used the term "Negro" I have capitalized it, but the word often appears in the lower case in quoted material. I have sometimes used "black" as the proper antonym of "white."

In order to keep the notes from becoming unwieldy I have cited religious and secular newspapers by name and date, without, in most instances, giving the titles of articles. Despite the fact that the text tends to become awkward under these conditions, I have spelled out fully the names of the various branches of American Methodism. I have also occasionally referred to the Methodist Episcopal Church, South as Southern Methodism or the Southern Methodist Church, capitalized each time, because these synonyms, while not official titles, were employed interchangeably after 1846 with the proper name of the denomination. When I have used "northern Methodism" to refer to the Methodist Episcopal Church, however, I have left "northern" in the lower case. Strictly speaking, the term is inaccurate, except as a regional designation, apart from the period between 1844 and 1865. Following the latter date the denomination's missions into the South made it once more a national, rather than a sectional church.

Besides acknowledgments made in another place I wish to express appreciation to my graduate examining committee at Duke University, especially Frank Baker, I. B. Holley, and Stuart C. Henry, for encouragement and suggestions; to George A. Wood, Jr., of South Lincoln, Massachusetts, and Dr. and Mrs. Eric North of Chatham, New Jersey, for their assistance in providing materials which the Haven family had preserved; to Dean Edward A. Lindell of the University of Denver for making additional time available to me for writing; to James M. McPherson of Princeton University, H. Gordon Harland of Pennsylvania State University, John C. Livingston of the University of Denver, and H. Shelton Smith of Duke University, who read the earlier version of this study and offered many helpful criticisms for and during revision; and to my typists, Mrs. Jack K. Hallowell and Robert C. Sample. All stylistic errors, factual mistakes, and interpretations, of course, are my responsibility. My wife Lynn and daughter Julie, and other family and friends, especially Dr. and Mrs. W. H. Tibbals of Tavares, Florida, have been supportive in such ways as to have made possible the continuation and completion of this project which was begun in 1966.

An earlier version of this manuscript was a dissertation, "Gilbert Haven, Racial Equalitarian. A Study of His Career in Racial Reform, 1850-1880," completed at Duke University in 1969. I have used portions of this manuscript for two papers: one before the Western Jurisdictional Historical Society of The United Methodist Church, meeting in Denver, August, 1971; the other as an address delivered in Malden, Massachusetts, on September 19, 1971 to commemorate the 150th anniversary of Haven's birth.

W. B. G.

I
Birth of a Mission

When he died in 1880, Gilbert Haven was eulogized far and wide because of his commitment to racial justice. One editor wrote that "there was not another man in the American Church who spoke so vigorously, not simply for the freedom of the slave, but for the perfect equality in the state, in the Church, and in social life of the colored people." [1] Haven's reputation as a racial equalitarian, however, was established only during the last half of his life, beginning in 1850. Until that time what became his special mission was slowly evolving in a private search for religious assurance and vocational decision.

The event which transformed Gilbert Haven into an outspoken abolitionist was the passage by Congress of the Compromise of 1850 which included a tough fugitive slave law. Designed to alleviate sectional tensions, the legislation denied a defendant a jury trial, refused his right to testify in his own behalf, and prohibited the writ of *habeas corpus*. Special federal commissioners and marshals to enforce the law were appointed, and all citizens were required to assist in the arrest of potential fugitives. The legislation also threatened heavy fines upon police officers who refused to cooperate and upon citizens who aided in escapes or hid known runaways. The legal fee even conspired against the accused. Commissioners were paid ten dollars if the defendant was returned to slavery, five dollars if he was freed. These provisions posed sharply the central issue of the public controversy over the law, the morality and legality of the institution of chattel slavery. [2]

Two months after the compromise was passed, Haven joined the debate which spilled over from the halls of Congress into the press, the pulpit, and the public arena at large. He addressed the faculty and student body of Amenia Seminary, an academy in northeastern New York state where he taught and served as principal. [3] The sermon, which he called "The Higher Law," reiterated the theme which Senator William Henry Seward of New York had expressed in his famous speech during congressional debate the previous March. [4] "We cannot obey the law of the land and have a con-

---

1. *The Independent*, Jan. 8, 1880.
2. The text of the law, which is in *Statutes at Large of the United States . . . 1789-1873*, vol. IX (Boston, 1845-73), pp. 462-65, is summarized in Stanley W. Campbell, *The Slave Catchers, Enforcement of the Fugitive Slave Law 1850-1860* (Chapel Hill: University of North Carolina Press, 1970), pp. 23-25. See also Ralph Alan Keller, "Northern Protestant Churches and the Fugitive Slave Law of 1850" (Ph.D. dissertation, University of Wisconsin, 1969), ch. 3.
3. L. Wesley Norton erroneously makes Haven into a Methodist Episcopal bishop in New York state at the time of his speech. See "The Religious Press and the Compromise of 1850: A Study of the Relationship of the Methodist, Baptist, and Presbyterian Press to the Slavery Controversy 1846-1851" (Ph.D. dissertation, University of Illinois, 1959), p. 269.
4. George E. Baker, ed., *The Works of William H. Seward*, vol. I (New York, 1853), pp. 51-93; Glyndon G. Van Deusen, *William Henry Seward* (New York: Oxford University Press, 1967), pp. 122-24.

science void of offense toward God and toward man," Haven declared. "We should ever remember that there is a Law above the Constitution, a Lawgiver more exalted than Congress, obedience to whose will alone can make a people virtuous, prosperous, and happy." [5] The compromise had nationalized slavery, in the words of one of its authors, by obligating "every *man* in the Union . . . to assist in the recovery of a fugitive slave . . . who takes refuge in or escapes into one of the free States." [6] Hence, everyone was potentially implicated in the moral contradiction to American democracy which the system of human bondage presented. "The conflict between the eternal foes of freedom and slavery," Haven asserted, "has by this act changed us from unconcerned spectators . . . into actors, and requires every one to take his place under one of the hostile banners." [7]

The "higher law" sermon was representative of a new surge in antislavery sentiment that swept through the North during 1850, but it was significant in a much more personal sense to Gilbert Haven.[8] For nearly a decade he had been unable to decide whether he ought to become a Christian minister. Likewise, he had kept his antislavery views largely to himself. National political events in 1850, however, changed all that. His speech at Amenia, therefore, marked both the culmination of his vocational search and the inauguration of his distinctive mission in life. The following March, Haven left his post at the school where he had taught since 1846 to embark upon a career as a Methodist preacher and antislavery reformer.

I

Of the influences which shaped Haven's decision to commit himself actively in the moral crusade against Negro slavery and to become a clergyman, his regional heritage and his family had special significance. Visible symbols of New England's creative role in the American past filled Haven's environment. Reared in Malden, Massachusetts, a suburb of Boston, he grew to maturity surrounded by historic reminders of the colonial era and of the American Revolution. Atop Waitt's Mount, the tallest point near his home, he could spot the distant spire of Old North Church in Charlestown and the impressive dome of the historic state house five miles away. From the school yard in the village he saw, as well, the crest of Bunker Hill. In later years he recalled watching General Lafayette ride down Hanover Street in the capital city in

5. *National Sermons. Sermons, Speeches and Letters on Slavery and Its War: From the Passage of the Fugitive Slave Bill to the Election of President Grant* (Boston, 1869), pp. 26, 28.
6. From Henry Clay's speech in the Senate in February; see *Congressional Globe,* 31st Cong., 1st sess., 22, appendix, p. 122.
7. *National Sermons,* p. 2.
8. Stanley W. Campbell argues that northern attitudes were predominantly conservative and unionist so that dissenters against the Compromise of 1850 remained much in the minority, but Russell B. Nye's earlier study documents extensive hostility to the enactment. See Campbell, *The Slave Catchers,* ch. 3; and Nye, *Fettered Freedom. Civil Liberties and the Slavery Controversy 1830-1860* (East Lansing: Michigan State College Press, 1949), pp. 197, 202, 205-13, 216.

June, 1825, on the way to celebrate the fiftieth anniversary of the famous battle there.[9] Quite naturally Haven grew to associate the genius of the American system with New England origins.

On both sides Haven's family reached back to the Puritan and revolutionary eras. His father, "Squire" Gilbert Haven, was a sixth-generation American whose ancestor, Richard, had migrated from England about 1644. And his mother, Hannah, boasted that her father, John Burrill, had spent the terrible winter of 1777-78 with General George Washington at Valley Forge.[10] The Havens took especially seriously their family heritage. In 1844 they gathered at Framingham, Massachusetts, to celebrate the bicentennial of Richard Haven's arrival in the New World. The orator for the day drew upon a familiar theme in linking the colonial and revolutionary experiences to the present. He noted particularly "the evidence every where spread before us, that if ever there was a peculiar people, in whose behalf the finger of Providence was daily working out good, even as for the chosen tribes of Israel, it has been for these New England States." The reunion was such a grand success that it was repeated in five years.[11]

Since he left no written reference to these celebrations, the younger Gilbert Haven may not have attended either occasion, but other close relatives did participate, and he was certainly aware of the family heritage and regional tradition being honored. Furthermore, in 1849, when the town of Malden commemorated its bicentennial anniversary, over which Squire Haven presided, Gilbert, Junior, revealed publicly how the New England past was a significant dimension of his own consciousness. For the occasion he composed and delivered a lengthy epic poem that sketched the habits and customs of the Puritans. He joked about their propensity to name children for biblical heroes. He mused about the Puritans' disposition to wage unceasing "warfare" against "the Prince of Evil," who, they believed, threatened both their physical existence and their spiritual well-being. He observed as well the tendency of their strict morality to degenerate into a "cool indifference" to their own "faults." They were often "bigoted for trifles" and "free" in pardoning "sins" that agreed "with *their* lives," but they brought "atoning vengeance" down upon "those" who reminded them of their "sinful acts."[12]

The fundamental intention of the poem, however, was not merely to remi-

9. George Prentice, *The Life of Gilbert Haven, Bishop of the Methodist Episcopal Church* (New York, 1883), pp. 15-17; *Northwestern Christian Advocate*, Mar. 21, 1877; *Zion's Herald*, July 17, 1873; J. Bennett Nolan, *Lafayette in America Day by Day* (Baltimore: Johns Hopkins Press, 1934), p. 292.

10. Josiah Adams, *The Genealogy of the Descendants of Richard Haven, of Lynn* (Boston, 1849), pt. I, pp. 9-10, 13, 20, 39; pt. II, p. 25. William H. Daniels, ed., *Memorials of Gilbert Haven, Bishop of the Methodist Episcopal Church* (Boston, 1880), pp. 22-23.

11. John Cochran Park, *Address at a Meeting of the Descendants of Richard Haven, of Lynn, at Framingham, Mass., August 29, 1844* (Boston, 1844), p. 11. See the programs for the anniversaries and other related papers in the Malden, Massachusetts, public library.

12. "A Poem Delivered at Malden, on the Two Hundredth Anniversary of the Incorporation of the Town, May 23, 1849," *The Bi-Centennial Book of Malden* (Boston, 1850), pp. 66-72, 74.

nisce about the past or to criticize the Puritans. Haven wanted to delineate Puritan characteristics which had continued into the present—"To show how great resemblance there is still/Between those pioneers and us, who now/ Their faults and virtues readily allow." He depicted the traits of the Puritan become Yankee with his "keen eye for trade" and for "calculation, economic, shrewd," with a "ready boldness through all ills to wade" and a "bustling eagerness" that drove him into the future. But his focus was on the trait that made New Englanders "pioneers in every cause" which aimed "to introduce God's perfect laws."

> Seen in the burning zeal to consume
> All real or fancied ills in fiery doom,—
> That forms associations to suppress
> Intemperance, slavery, crime and wretchedness;
> That with a constant urgency of heart
> Would fain the world from its foundations start,
> And place it, whence nor time nor fate can move,
> On God's eternal laws of Truth and Love.[13]

The vision of progress and the duty of social responsibility which the poem portrayed pointed to one of the striking features of Haven's regional background. New England was the "home of 'isms' "—the center of American reform movements in the national period. The "improving spirit" of New Englanders was so vigorous that one historian has written of them: "Seldom has such a large proportion of citizens been so alert to measure the community against its best possibilities." Haven was deeply proud of this trait of his people. His poem wittily described how their "vitality of reform" even extended beyond the region's borders.[14]

> Hence they through danger bear the trembling slave
> To Freedom's home, from Slavery's living grave;
> Oppose polygamy in Hindostan,
> Preach toleration to the Vatican,
> Intrude their socialist advice on France,
> Bid modern Greece to ancient fame advance,
> On famished Ireland's cries place instant check,
> And strive to free from Britain's yoke her neck.
> And thus they see in every man, a brother,
> And will not let self-love such feelings smother.
> While some, to such extent this feeling cherish,
> That were all sin upon earth to perish,
> They would resort to other sin-struck spheres,
> Transferring thence the joy that here appears.[15]

13. *Ibid.*, pp. 78-79.
14. Daniel Boorstin, *The Americans: The National Experience* (New York: Random House, 1965), pp. 43-44.
15. "A Poem Delivered at Malden," pp. 80-81.

To a remarkable degree Haven's parents embodied the characteristics about which he wrote in this, the only verse which he ever composed for publication. Until the year of young Gilbert's birth, Squire Haven had belonged to the Congregational Church. Family tradition hallowed his association with the established church of Massachusetts, but in 1821, he joined the Methodist Episcopal Church, the local society of which at the time did not even have a meetinghouse in Malden. A decade earlier, before he married Hannah Burrill, he had read at her urging Phillip Doddridge's classic work on experiential Christianity, *Rise and Progress of Religion in the Soul of Man.* Thereafter the elder Gilbert Haven sympathized with evangelical piety, a fervent expression of which Methodist circuit riders preached. Shortly after he changed church relations, he organized a local Sunday school which he superintended for the next thirty-four years. Only in 1823 did Hannah Haven concede her own independence in religion and join the Methodists, from whose ranks there came a well-known itinerant named "Reformation" John Adams to baptize Gilbert, Junior.[16]

Squire Haven's religion was, to use his son's phrase, "a conglomerate of Puritan and Methodist," and it included a large sense of public responsibility and social concern. While bookkeeper at Barrett's dyehouse in Malden, he served the community as town clerk for fifteen years and as a justice of the peace for twenty-five. Contemporaries reported that he "healed many quarrels, adjusted many difficulties, settled many estates, and was known and beloved as the friend and protector of the widows and fatherless." In the later years of his life he held a position with the sub-treasury office of Boston. For nearly half a century he earnestly supported charitable causes and moral reforms. He belonged to the Methodist Missionary Society and the Methodist Historical Society and founded the first temperance organization in Malden. He was an early member and officer in the New England Education Society and a leader in cooperative Sunday school work among Protestants. For his "faith and good works" the elder Haven earned at his death tributes from a wide circle of coworkers in religious and reform associations, one of whom wrote that he was "the best specimen of a Christian gentleman that [he had] ever seen."[17]

In his extant writings the younger Haven gave little explicit testimony to the influence of his father upon the shaping of his own ideas, beliefs, and values.[18] Nonetheless, the senior Haven's character and style of life mediated

16. Daniels, *Memorials of Gilbert Haven,* pp. 21-22, 24. See the obituary, an editorial, for Gilbert Haven, Sr., in *Zion's Herald,* Mar. 18, 1863. His role in Malden church affairs is documented in "The Original Methodist Church of Malden Center. From the Papers of 'Squire Gilbert Haven," *Register of the Malden Historical Society,* vol. VI, pp. 30-46.

17. *Christian Advocate and Journal,* Dec. 12, 1861; *Zion's Herald,* Mar. 18, 1863; Prentice, *Life,* pp. 13-14; Daniels, *Memorials of Gilbert Haven,* p. 28. For a sample of 'Squire Haven's activities over a two-year period as reported in the area church paper, see *Zion's Herald,* May 12, June 2, Oct. 27, 1858; Mar. 9, Apr. 20, Nov. 2, 1859; June 6, 13, 1860.

18. He did honor the memory of his father in a dedication of one work in which he paid

family, regional, and religious traditions which he exemplified for his oldest son. As his nickname signified, Squire Haven had a "magisterial" personality. He was "of the old school of New England gentlemen, dignified, self-poised, courteous, with a dash of sternness in his nature." [19] He lived by a somewhat formal routine. He even channeled his moral activism into carefully regulated and socially acceptable benevolent institutions and organizations. Gilbert, Junior, had proper regard for his father, but their relation had few familiar ties. It was, however, precisely in consistent adherence to principle and in the authority which he commanded that lay the elder Haven's attraction and influence. He conveyed a sense of constancy and order, and he revealed his loyalty to eternal, unchanging absolutes that gave stability to life.

By lavishing generous affection upon young Gilbert, his mother compensated for what was absent in his paternal relationship. Hannah Haven was, in the words of her son's biographer, "a typical Puritan matron" who ruled the domestic realm with grace, dignity, and strength. She was, as well, a woman noted for extensive reading and for considerable interest in and knowledge about public affairs. In less than twenty years she bore ten children, one of whom died soon after birth. Two of her sons also died before reaching their teen-age years. As the eldest boy with four older sisters, young Gilbert demanded and received special attention from his mother, who said of him, "he gave me more trouble than all the rest of my family put together." [20] Despite the fact that there was another son who lived to maturity, she always referred to Gilbert as "my boy." [21] Whenever Haven left home, he regularly corresponded with her and sought her counsel on matters of importance. In later years son and mother grew even closer together, particularly after the deaths of Gilbert's wife in 1860 and of Squire Haven three years afterward.

Like parents of many religious and reform figures of the period, Haven's mother and father conditioned the lives of their children by providing in the home for religious observance and moral instruction. Near the close of Haven's collegiate career he recalled the rituals of devotion in the family circle of his childhood. He attributed the fact that he was "always homesick Sabbath nights" to "the memories of olden days" when all the family would sit and sing with Squire Haven until he went to "meeting." Hannah Haven would then instruct her children in reading from the Bible and direct their prayers. "You don't know how deeply those hours and acts are impressed on my life," Gilbert, Junior, wrote to his mother.[22]

special tribute to Squire Haven's churchmanship. See *Lay Representation in the Methodist Episcopan Church: Its Justice and Expediency* (Boston, 1864), p. iii.

19. Daniels, *Memorials of Gilbert Haven*, p. 22.
20. Quoted in *ibid.*, pp. 23, 25; Prentice, *Life*, p. 14.
21. See Haven's dedication to his mother in his book, *Our Next-Door Neighbor: A Winter in Mexico* (New York, 1875).
22. The letter is quoted in Prentice, *Life*, p. 19.

Both regional influences and Haven's family matrix inculcated religious precepts and ethical imperatives, social responsibility, and moral sensitivity. In such surroundings for him to have become, in time, a Methodist preacher and an antislavery reformer was no fortuitous development. That everyone influenced by similar forces and associations did not decide to be either an abolitionist or a minister merely attests to human diversity and the final inability to account for all the factors of human motivation.[23]

II

Two developments in 1839 had a special bearing upon Haven's future mission. Both were crucial to his maturation in the achievement of a personal identity and a sense of his place in the world. In the spring that year he left home for the first time to attend the Wesleyan Academy at Wilbraham, a small community in western Massachusetts. That fall a religious revival in the village church stirred a number of students from the Methodist school, including the new scholar from Malden.[24] In later years Haven referred to this experience as his religious conversion.

At the coeducational academy Haven was removed from the restraints of his home. He indulged his new freedom by learning to play cards and to drink intoxicants, by seeking out female company whenever possible, and by associating with those boys at the school who sometimes attended religious meetings with the sole intention of ridiculing the proceedings. Even as he adopted these new habits, Haven was aware that he was transgressing the moral code which his parents had taught him and upon which the school's administrators insisted. The religious atmosphere at the academy, with required daily attendance at both morning and evening prayers and weekly presence at two church services, enforced Haven's sense of guilt over the abuse of his time and opportunities.[25]

Just before his conversion Haven had become particularly morose over recent news that his sister, Bethiah, had a terminal illness. Three times the reality of death had already broken the family circle, including fatalities to younger brothers, Andrew Jackson Sprague Haven five years before and Benjamin Franklin Haven the previous October.[26] At home Bethiah had tutored Gilbert in French, and the two were deeply attached to each other. After he learned her fate he wrote to her, confessing his indifference toward

23. Bertram Wyatt-Brown has a perceptive analysis of the problem of motivation in the careers of social agitators in America in the 1830s and 1960s. A number of his observations apply to Haven's development. See "New Leftists and Abolitionists: A Comparison of American Radical Styles," *Wisconsin Magazine of History*, 54 (Summer, 1970), 258-61.

24. David Sherman, *The History of the Wesleyan Academy at Wilbraham, Mass. 1817-1890* (Boston, 1893), pp. 236-37.

25. Prentice, *Life*, pp. 28-31; Daniels, *Memorials of Gilbert Haven*, p. 32. See "Rules of the Wesleyan Academy, Wilbraham, Mass.," an undated pamphlet for the period, and *Catalogue of the Officers and Students of the Wesleyan Academy, for the Year, 1839-1840* on file at the school.

26. Prentice, *Life*, p. 14.

religion and promising that he would be more serious about the state of his own soul in the future.

Haven's religious conversion originated then in anxiety over his sister's condition and in guilt for having been threatened with expulsion from school. He admitted that he and another student, whom Haven designated "the wildest fellow here, except myself," would probably "have been sent home" if they had not undergone a moral and religious change. But he also acknowledged that he had been influenced by fear that "Bethiah might be taken suddenly away, and [he] never have the opportunity of informing her of the glorious news that [he had] some hopes of meeting her in heaven . . . [and] that [he] too [could] say, God is good." His description, contained in a letter to his parents, likewise referred, drawing upon New Testament imagery, to "the prodigal" who had "returned to his Father's arms." His account employed the familiar analogies used to portray evangelical conversion. "I feel," he wrote, "the blessed assurance of sins forgiven, that my sins, which were as scarlet, have become as white as snow through the blood of the Lamb." [27]

Not only did Haven date his religious awakening from his stay at Wesleyan Academy during the spring and fall terms of 1839, but he also traced his initial moral convictions about American slavery to his school experience. Until he went to Wilbraham, he had taken no special interest in the slavery question. Even Squire Haven, for all his involvement in moral reform, had not gone along with his brothers, Jotham and Kittredge, when they joined the antislavery movement in the 1830s.[28] Once in Malden's grammar school Gilbert, Junior, had angrily denounced the teacher for extreme punishment meted out to a black girl whose family lived in the town's poorhouse, but that incident revealed no special concern over the enslavement of Negroes in the South. When, on another occasion as a teen-ager, he ridiculed "Aunty" Knight, Malden's colored washerwoman, he reflected the same racial prejudices of most white Americans.[29]

In 1859 Haven recalled that twenty years earlier "the words of Whittier" fell upon his heart and awakened him from his "sinful slumbers." [30] Specifically he referred to some lines written by John Greenleaf Whittier in 1836, after the United States Congress had passed resolutions to bar antislavery literature from the mails. The poem attracted the young student with its call for the "men of the Northland" to renew "the old Pilgrim spirit" and to

27. Quoted in *ibid.*, pp. 32-33.
28. Kittredge Haven, pastor of a Congregational church in Shoreham, Vermont, signed a "declaration of sentiments" with 123 other clergymen in 1834, promoting the scheme of immediate emancipation. Jotham Haven, a Methodist local preacher and father of Erastus Otis Haven (see below), subscribed to William Lloyd Garrison's *The Liberator*, the reading of which prompted him to organize an abolition society in Weston, Massachusetts. See Amos A. Phelps, *Lectures on Slavery and Its Remedy* (Boston, 1834), pp. v-x; C. C. Stratton, ed., *Autobiography of Erastus O. Haven, D.D., LL.D., One of the Bishops of the Methodist Episcopal Church* (New York, 1883), pp. 22, 37.
29. Prentice, *Life*, pp. 21-24; Daniels, *Memorials of Gilbert Haven*, pp. 26-27.
30. *Zion's Herald*, July 20, 1859.

"put on the harness for the moral right." The militant Quaker bard accused "the statesman" and "the false jurist" of denying "human rights" and church-men of perverting "the pages of the hallowed Bible,/To sanction crime, and robbery, and blood." His condemnation fell sharpest upon those who took no stand, who, "Now, when our land to ruin's brink is verging," remained passive. "Silence is crime!" Whittier charged.[31]

Besides Whittier's poetry, other associations fed Haven's budding interest in antislavery before he left the academy. He joined the Reading Room Society whose members subscribed to and discussed abolitionist literature at weekly meetings. The topic grew so controversial that the board of trustees imposed a moratorium on discussion of slavery on the campus. The students rebelled, partly because they were jealous to maintain control over the Reading Room as their own organization. William Rice, Jr., a leader in the society, an avowed abolitionist and, ironically, son of a founder of and trustee at the school, called for a protest. He survived the threat of expulsion and later engaged in a public debate over slavery with Haven's roommate, Matthew Dooley. Though younger and less experienced, Rice made a persuasive case for his views and brought Haven under his influence. They began a friendship which had an important effect on Haven's view of anti-slavery reform and his vocational dilemma.[32]

On November 25, 1839 Haven gave the salutatory address in French at the exhibition of the Union Philosophical Society, which marked the end of the term at the academy.[33] He arrived home in time for the traditional New England feast day, Thanksgiving, to find Bethiah still alive, but lingering near death, which came a month later, just days prior to her twenty-first birth-day. That event and the developments at school over the previous year drew Haven into more somber and serious reflection. When the winter term commenced, he did not return to school. Instead, he began in March, 1840, the first of two years' experience in business.[34]

III

While he was working the first year as a clerk in Nichols' store on Tremont Street in Boston, Haven became even more pensive. Writings in his journal tended, according to his later description, to be characterized by "sadness, solitariness and religious sensibility." Daily entries charted progress or retrogression in the Christian life, the "novelty, solemnity, and grandeur" of which, in his words, "engaged my whole heart." His reading of the medieval mystic, Thomas a Kempis, and other devotional writers drove him "still

31. *The Poetical Works of John Greenleaf Whittier* (Boston, 1877), pp. 95-96.
32. Sherman, *History of the Wesleyan Academy*, pp. 343-44; Daniels, *Memorials of Gilbert Haven*, pp. 30-31, 34; [William North Rice and Charles Francis Rice], eds., *William Rice: A Memorial* (Cambridge, 1898), pp. 6, 19-20, 100.
33. The program for the exhibition is on file at the academy.
34. Prentice, *Life*, pp. 14, 36, 38.

further inward" in search of "peace and pleasure." He found "society and business" distasteful, and his work "under a disagreeable master in a disagreeable store" burdensome.[35] When the year's contract expired, he changed employers and took the position of clerk in the carpet store of Tenney and Company at the corner of Salem and Prince streets.

During the second year in Boston, Haven began to move out more and attend social meetings in the vicinity. Still, religion absorbed most of his attention. He worshiped regularly in the Bennet Street Methodist Episcopal Church, but he occasionally heard the pulpit celebrities of the city, including Edward Norris Kirk, a polished Congregational preacher, and Edward T. ("Father") Taylor, later a subject of Haven's literary effort and the model for Herman Melville's Father Mapple in *Moby Dick*.[36] In 1842 a religious revival, an established institution in evangelical Protestantism by this time, swept through Boston and afforded Haven an opportunity to observe the effect of powerful preaching. In his journal he recorded reactions to many of the sermons which he heard, reflecting perhaps his first serious interest in becoming a minister himself.[37]

His two terms at Wesleyan Academy had awakened "an intense thirst for knowledge," as Haven later put it, so that his leisure hours after work or during some of the duller periods on the job were spent in study. During the year at Nichols' he had begun to learn classical Greek under the direction of a fellow clerk, Elvin Pike. He read a great deal and on more diverse topics than before: a history of Greece in eight volumes, Edward Everett's orations, Thomas Chalmers' discourses, Joseph Butler's *Analogy,* volumes by famous essayists and poets.[38]

Despite his broader contacts and interests Haven continued primarily to seek for deeper religious experiences. His conscience, as his official biographer expressed it, appeared sometimes to be "morbidly exacting." A pious and somewhat moralistic disposition set him apart from the other clerks and some customers, whose jokes and language often vexed him and marred his "religious peace." [39] In most instances he apparently avoided controversial topics, but occasionally, by especially polite treatment of Negro customers or on account of some remark, he provoked a heated discussion on slavery and racial relations.[40] But the result was neither the conversion of his fellow employees nor any significant action on his part to become directly involved in the abolitionist cause. His religious introspection and moral sensitivity were focused narrowly in an individualistic, perfectionist frame of reference.

35. Quoted in *ibid.,* p. 38; see also, p. 43.
36. *Ibid.,* pp. 42-44, 48. See *Father Taylor, the Sailor Preacher. Incidents and Anecdotes of Rev. Edward T. Taylor, for over Forty Years Pastor of the Seaman's Bethel, Boston* (New York, 1871), written jointly by Haven and Thomas Russell.
37. See Haven's vivid account of the revival in *Zion's Herald,* Mar. 7, 1878.
38. Prentice, *Life,* pp. 38, 45-47.
39. *Ibid.,* pp. 44-45.
40. Daniels, *Memorials of Gilbert Haven,* p. 34.

In retrospect his last employer recollected that "the clerk's heart was set on books and religion." [41] That remark explained why, at the end of the year, Haven returned to Wesleyan Academy to finish preparation for entrance into college. Seven years afterward he looked back upon the conclusion of his brief career in business and candidly described his motives for resuming formal schooling. "Driven by dislike for my employment," he wrote, "intense hankering after knowledge, ambition to make a noise in the world, and perhaps a humble desire to be a preacher, though I almost doubt the humility of the desire, I escaped from Boston and business and buried myself in books." [42]

The fall of 1842 found Haven in Middletown, Connecticut, where he entered another Methodist institution, Wesleyan University. During his college years he engaged in continuing rigorous analysis of his religious life. He sought for a stronger sense of spiritual assurance and worried over the mixture of good and bad motives in his actions. [43] In religious matters he was undoubtedly affected by the sentiments of the president of the college, Stephen Olin, who one of Methodism's most eloquent preachers. Despite poor health during the years of Haven's attendance, Olin lectured and preached several times to the students, including an address in 1845 on the "Resources and Duties of Christian Young Men." In it he exhorted the students to "enter upon a high, holy career of virtue" and to draw "nearer to perfection in faith and love." [44] As Haven listened to the discourse, which he judged "a sublime, metaphysical, poetical, practical, pious" and "by far the ablest" production which he had heard from Olin, he was surely struck by the admonition concerning a vocational decision. [45] "Fear to move," the president advised, "in the grave matter of choosing your profession, and forming the more permanent plans and relations of life, before you assume your proper religious position, and are thus enabled to act under divine direction. You may not neglect this duty," Olin warned, "without incurring the entire forfeiture of God's promises and grace." [46]

In spite of a good academic record, which earned him selection to Phi Beta Kappa, and of continued interest in religion, Haven could not be sure of "divine direction" in the matter of choosing what he should do in life. He considered several possibilities but could not decide between them. Indecision about his future, however, did not stand in the way of a successful and enjoyable collegiate career. His major concentration of study was in the field of classical languages and literature, but, as before, he read broadly

41. Prentice, *Life*, p. 42.
42. Quoted in *ibid.*, p. 48.
43. For examples, see *ibid.*, pp. 56, 61, 73-74, 77-78.
44. *The Works of Stephen Olin, D.D., LL.D., Late President of Wesleyan University*, vol. II (New York, 1852), pp. 131-32.
45. Quoted in Prentice, *Life*, p. 55.
46. *Works of Olin*, vol. II, p. 158.

both ancient and modern history, literary criticism, biography, contemporary novels, and poetry.[47]

Wesleyan's commencement speaker in 1845, Ralph Waldo Emerson, also exerted an influence on Haven's intellectual growth. At Middletown the sage of Concord lectured on the "Function of the Scholar," which Haven called "the greatest treat" of the closing exercises of the school year.[48] The following December and January he attended Emerson's course of lectures in Boston on "Representative Men"—Plato, Swedenborg, Montaigne, Napoleon Bonaparte, Shakespeare, and Goethe.[49]

The students at Wesleyan knew Haven as a genial and popular classmate. Perhaps because he was older than many of his fellows, he drew others about him.[50] One of his colleagues remembered later that Haven was "apt in the use of sarcasm, loving to prick the bubble of sophistry or vanity"; that he spoke swiftly, loved debate, and engaged in "prodigious mental activity"; and that he hated "shams, hypocrisy, and oppression." By this time Haven had grown to be a man of medium frame with broad shoulders and a large head which was covered with "fiery red hair." He possessed, his contemporary reported, "a keen, flashing eye" and "a rosy, joyous face." [51]

By the time he was an upperclassman, Haven had achieved distinction as one of the best students in the college. In May, 1845, he appeared in the junior exhibition to deliver the "classical oration" on the topic, "The Adaptation of Grecian Genius to Universal Taste." A few weeks later he read Whittier's poem, "Fratricide," at the annual declamation contest between sophomores and juniors. The next year he stood third in his class of thirty-five, with which rank went the honor of delivering the philosophical oration at commencement.[52]

As he faced graduation, Haven had to deal more directly with the problem of his future vocation. He expressed his dilemma in a letter to his parents. "Would I could be driven into something I could engage in eagerly and delightfully!" he exclaimed. "You can form no idea of my indecision;

47. See a selection from his reading list for the year following May, 1845, as quoted in Prentice, *Life*, pp. 58-59.

48. Quoted in *ibid.*, pp. 64-65. Emerson's address was not published, but portions of what he said at Wesleyan appeared in a speech at Middlebury College in July, 1845. See Ralph L. Rusk, ed., *The Letters of Ralph Waldo Emerson*, vol. III (New York: Columbia University Press, 1939), pp. 294-96; James Eliot Cabot, *A Memoir of Ralph Waldo Emerson*, vol. II (Cambridge, 1899), p. 752.

49. Prentice, *Life*, pp. 65-68; Rusk, *Letters of Emerson*, vol. III, pp. 304-6.

50. Prentice, *Life*, p. 60. One of his letters near the close of his senior year illustrates the point. See Haven to Alexander Winchell, May 30, 1846, Winchell Papers, Michigan Historical Collections, University of Michigan, Ann Arbor.

51. The description came from one of Haven's classmates, Joseph E. King, as found in Erastus Wentworth, *Gilbert Haven: A Monograph* (New York, 1881), p. 10.

52. Prentice, *Life*, pp. 57, 77-78. See the commencement program for 1846, a sheet of autographs of the graduates and the manuscript of Haven's speech, "The Identity of Philosophy," in the archives of Wesleyan University.

it torments me day and night. Shall I be a merchant, lawyer, preacher, or teacher?" [53]

A growing antislavery commitment, nourished by contact with his friend from Wesleyan Academy, William Rice, complicated Haven's vocational planning. Before Haven began college, Rice had become a Methodist minister, joined the New England Conference, and accepted an appointment to the congregation at North Malden. There he renewed ties with his old classmate and the Haven family at Malden Centre. He appealed in such a convincing way in behalf of human rights on the question of slavery that he led Squire Haven to abandon his previous political association and in the election of 1842 to support, with seven of his townsmen, the new antislavery political movement, the Liberty Party. During his years at Middletown Haven visited Rice and discussed slavery and other vital topics of the day. They conferred, as well, on the matter of the unsure student's future. In his pastoral ministry Rice stood as a model for Haven's later decision.[54]

At the university Haven identified with a tiny minority of students who supported the antislavery cause. During the presidential campaign of 1844, in which he backed James G. Birney and the Liberty Party, for example, Haven observed: "A few, very few Birneyites are here." [55]

The Wesleyan faculty, from President Olin on down, were conservative on the slavery question. When he had earlier lived in the South, Olin had owned slaves. He publicly maintained that the church ought to preach and minister indiscriminately to both masters and slaves, and he deprecated the introduction of "exciting topics and engagements [like abolitionism] which do not come within the unquestionable scope of practical, saving Christianity." [56]

Several of Haven's fellow students, whom he tried to win to the antislavery cause, came from or had ties in the South. Even among New Englanders there were a number of students who defended slavery and expressed southern sentiments.[57] At Haven's request his family forwarded antislavery papers which he put in reading rooms on campus. He was known at the school as a lively debater and as "a pronounced abolitionist." [58] In a letter to his parents in 1845 he explained that because "anti-abolitionism" was "so strong" at the school, he was "accounted a ranting, fanatical Abolitionist by the students, and ranked with another Bay-State fellow as the most

53. Quoted in Prentice, *Life*, p. 75.
54. *Ibid.*, pp. 47-48, 62-63, 289; Daniels, *Memorials of Gilbert Haven*, p. 34; *Zion's Herald*, Mar. 18, 1863. See also Rice's letter in the *Daily Evening Traveller* (Boston), Jan. 6, 1880.
55. Quoted in Prentice, *Life*, p. 68.
56. For Olin's views on slavery, see *The Life and Letters of Stephen Olin, D.D., LL.D., Late President of Wesleyan University*, vol. II (New York, 1853), pp. 54-55, 64, 128, 216, 296-306, 313-14, 318-26, 343-44, 370.
57. Frank Nicholson, ed., *Alumni Record of Wesleyan University, Middletown, Conn.*, 4th ed. (New Haven, 1911), pp. 56-103. An example of the later views of three of Haven's friends from Wesleyan is contained in a letter to Alexander Winchell, Feb. 24, 1854, Winchell Papers.
58. Wentworth, *Gilbert Haven*, pp. 8-10.

fanatical students in college." He assured his mother that he would not yield to the proslavery tendencies of his associates.[59]

Like many abolitionists, Haven reacted intensely against the moral failure of the churches in America in permitting "that most grotesque of all marriages: Christianity and Slavery." [60] A decade after the antislavery reform emerged as a significant movement in northern society, most Protestant churchmen outside the South agreed with the conservative views of men like President Olin. They opposed alike the defenders of human bondage and abolitionist radicalism, but they effectively divorced religious concerns from the controversial issue, except when they argued that slavery and every social wrong would be corrected by changing individuals. The result was tacitly to accept the collective structure of slavery and to substitute a religious orientation which cultivated private piety and morality but disavowed social and political responsibility. A few ministers and laymen became committed abolitionists who challenged the individualistic social philosophy of mainstream American Protestantism and crusaded for the elimination of slavery from the churches and the national life.[61]

Developments which finally divided the Methodist Episcopal Church over the question of slavery twice in two years had particular bearing on Haven's attitudes and his vocational dilemma. The abolitionist minority in Methodism centered in New England and was led by Orange Scott. By 1842 these churchmen had fought a losing battle to be heard in the councils of the denomination, especially when they sought to enforce the prohibition of Christian fellowship with slaveholding Methodists. By the fall of Haven's first year of college the ecclesiastical withdrawal of Methodist abolitionists was underway. Protesting the complicity of the church in the sin of slavery, the secessionists organized a new denomination, the Wesleyan Methodist Connection of America, whose *Discipline* contained explicit antislavery principles. Two years later, partly because of the success of the Wesleyan movement, there was sufficient pressure in northern Methodism to force a sectional division of the church over the propriety of retaining a slaveholding bishop. In 1845 southern members organized the Methodist Episcopal Church, South. Even after the separation from the South, however, northern Methodist leadership remained decidedly unsympathetic toward abolitionism. Churchmen with strong antislavery views

59. The letter is quoted in Prentice, *Life*, p. 69.

60. The phrase is from Stuart B. James, "The Politics of Personal Salvation: The American Literary Record," *The Denver Quarterly*, 4 (Summer, 1969), 36. See Wyatt-Brown, "New Leftists and Abolitionists," pp. 262 ff.

61. There is no adequate single work on American Protestantism and slavery, and most denominational traditions need restudying with regard to the issue. Timothy L. Smith has two good chapters, (12 and 13), on the subject in his *Revivalism and Social Reform in Mid-Nineteenth Century America* (Nashville: Abingdon Press, 1957), but he seriously overstates the extent to which most evangelical Protestants were abolitionist. H. Shelton Smith's *In His Image But . . . : Racism in Southern Religion, 1780-1910* (Durham: Duke University Press, 1972) is not limited to the South, so that his first three chapters constitute the most comprehensive analysis yet of American religion and slavery.

who did not join the Wesleyans, like Haven's friend Rice, remained, therefore, a minority struggling to transform from within the Methodist Episcopal Church, which, after 1845, was a sectional denomination.[62]

The equivocating stance on slavery in the churches inclined Haven to entertain the perfectionist argument advanced by the antichurch segment of the abolitionist movement. The radicals censured the American churches severely for their compromises with slavery and insisted on secession from what one writer termed "the brotherhood of thieves."[63] During his college years Haven may have been attracted to the radical position, but he gave no evidence that he seriously considered withdrawing from his denomination. Four decades later, therefore, Erastus Otis Haven, Gilbert's cousin, probably overstated the case in recalling that "he was tempted . . . to accept the hatred of the Churches with what looked just then much like a hatred of Christianity itself, which tainted the writings and speeches of many of the abolitionist leaders." Otis was close to the mark, however, in saying that Gilbert saw "the necessity of defending [religious] orthodoxy while advocating radicalism . . . so that both as an abolitionist and as a Christian he belonged to 'the straitest sect.' "[64]

In his last year at Wesleyan Haven manifested his dissatisfaction over the moral compromise with slavery in American Christianity by attending and working in "the African Church" in Middletown's colony of free blacks. He became head teacher in the "Sabbath-school" at the church. In a note to his mother, he told of his new post and, to show what extreme sentiments he was willing to entertain, jested about racial intermarriage—a practice that was clearly a breach of social custom in the attitudes of most Americans at the time. "Isn't that Abolitionism enough?" he asked.

Harboring negroes and mingling with them. The class is a fine, large collection of ladies of various ages, colors, and faces. Some are handsome and some are not; of all shades, from the color of this ink to nearly that of this paper. I shouldn't wonder if I should bring one of them home with me next August as a bride. They think very much of me and I of them. Hope you will be prepared to receive her with great affection. Stranger things have happened.[65]

By this time Squire Haven shared some of his son's cynicism about the

62. The best study of the Wesleyan and southern divisions of episcopal Methodism is Donald G. Mathews, *Slavery and Methodism: A Chapter in American Morality 1780-1845* (Princeton: Princeton University Press, 1965), pp. 212 ff. See also William B. Gravely, "Methodist Preachers, Slavery and Caste: Types of Social Concern in Antebellum America," *The Duke Divinity School Review*, 34 (Autumn, 1969), 219-23. A contemporary analysis of the kinds of Methodist abolitionism found in the North after the sectional division is in the *Christian Advocate and Journal*, Aug. 30, 1848.

63. Stephen S. Foster, *The Brotherhood of Thieves; or a True Picture of the American Church and Clergy: A Letter to Nathaniel Barney of Nantucket* (Boston, 1844). See also Parker Pillsbury, *The Church As It Is: or the Forlorn Hope of Slavery*, 2nd ed. reprint (Concord, N.H., 1885) and [James G. Birney], *The American Churches: The Bulwarks of American Slavery. By an American*, enlarged ed. (Boston, 1843).

64. *Autobiography of Erastus O. Haven*, p. 80.

65. Quoted in Prentice, *Life*, p. 70.

response of the religious institutions of the country on the moral issue of slavery. In February, 1846, he joined with Wesleyan Methodists and other abolitionist churchmen to sponsor the "Religious Anti-Slavery Convention" in Boston. He belonged to the committee which issued the call for the meeting, asking for "united prayer and fraternal consultation" to inquire why the Christian gospel, "the great charter of human freedom and equal rights," had not abolished American slavery. The convention sought to assess the blame for the failure of the churches and to chart means and agencies which would end bondage "on Christian principles and by Christian influences." One of the leading black ministers in the North and a famous abolitionist orator, Henry Highland Garnet, addressed the group. Afterwards the participants drew up formal resolutions, sealing their convictions by pledging to labor "in the cause of Emancipation . . . , until the fetters are knocked from the limbs of the last slave in our country, and the honor of the Gospel is fully vindicated, as the remedy for slavery, and the charter of civil liberty as well as of eternal life." Even though antichurch radicals ridiculed the effort and, in effect, broke up the meeting after charging the churchmen with hypocrisy, the convention indicated increasing antislavery sentiment among some northern religious leaders.[66]

As his college days ended, Haven was trying to reconcile his continued regard for personal religion with his concern to choose a vocation that would do justice to his moral opposition to slavery. At times, when he thought of the importance of the "life of the soul," he was drawn toward the ministry, but he hesitated.[67] When he discussed the dilemma with his parents, he noted that his college work had not been "of a theological character" and that he was not really interested in a postgraduate "theological course." Nor did Haven feel competent "to teach Christians." He considered it "altogether too serious business" for him "to take charge of a church, to go to leading old men and women, young men and maidens, in the ways of holiness." In the same letter he commented sarcastically that should he go into the ministry, he would perhaps go South and be a "slave-holding preacher." [68]

At times Haven felt attracted to some other profession which would influence public opinion more directly and promote social change on great questions like slavery. Law and politics were the routes to a career as an influential statesman who would be a social reformer and a public servant. Doubtless his father's long and prominent career as a public official urged Haven in this direction. Perhaps he harbored a secret desire to surpass his father's local position and make a national impact. But the same alternatives

66. *The Declaration and Pledge Against Slavery, Adopted by the Religious Anti-Slavery Convention, Held at Marlboro' Chapel, Boston, February 23, 1846* (Boston, 1846). See the account of the meeting, with editorial comments, in *The Liberator,* Mar. 6, 1846, and later references, June 11, July 2 and 9, 1858.
67. Quoted in Prentice, *Life,* p. 95.
68. Quoted in *ibid.,* pp. 74-75.

kept forcing themselves upon him. When he thought of the opportunity "for the display of talent and the diffusion of righteous principles in the nation," he wanted to be a statesman. He even spoke of this desire as "the devouring propensity—to be a good, efficient, and great statesman." Yet when he considered "how greatly superior [were] the necessities and claims of the soul," he was "drawn" though not "inspired" to be a minister. He described his attraction to the ministry only as "a moral duty" which because of his "education or nature" appeared "less than the moral duty connected with politics." [69] This vocational predicament remained for Haven, but he was able to delay a final decision when he agreed to the offer of a job from his cousin, Otis, who was principal of Amenia Seminary. In the fall of 1846 he began teaching there in the field of ancient languages.

IV

In contrast to the "wide activity" which Haven was used to at college and in the Boston area, Amenia was, in his words, "a retired place," which would be "very delightful if it were only a little more active and prosperous." The natural beauty of the region Haven found most appealing, but he wished that the academy was not so isolated from the main currents of social and intellectual life.[70] Long walks through the meadows and forests surrounding the school became routine in his new schedule. Sometimes he went alone to read or to write or to ponder the scenery. More often than not, his cousin, Otis, or his classmate from Wesleyan, William Ingraham, or another faculty member went along.[71] The topic of conversation, particularly with Haven's more intimate confidants, was likely to be connected somehow with his search for what he should do with his life.

Gradually during more than four years at Amenia, Haven worked through his vocational dilemma, but he moved cautiously and indecision shadowed every step of his way. In November, 1846, he made his first attempt at preaching in the school chapel. Afterwards he considered the experiment unsuccessful. When he tried again a month later, he felt "lamentably deficient in soul." [72] Despite dissatisfaction over his efforts and perplexity about becoming a minister, he did obtain in June, 1847, a "local preacher's license" from the Methodist quarterly conference in the village. The move marked his first official step toward becoming a clergyman, but Haven described his feelings about it in a typically ambiguous fashion. "I felt it a very solemn time," he recorded in his journal, ". . . dreading, yet desiring the sacred duties I had drawn upon me." [73]

69. Quoted in *ibid.*, pp. 75-76.
70. Quoted in *ibid.*, p. 81.
71. For examples, see *ibid.*, pp. 82-86, 100-101.
72. Quoted in *ibid.*, pp. 97-98.
73. Quoted in *ibid.*, p. 99.

In the spring of 1848 his cousin resigned as principal at Amenia and the trustees chose Gilbert as his successor. Haven accepted "for an indefinite time," but he acknowledged in his journal that the office was "only useful as a passport, not as a permanency." The position usually did increase the reputation of its occupant, he recognized as well, and he saw it as a test to bring out whatever talents he possessed.[74] In the new post Haven spoke more and his style of public address improved, but doubts about himself did not vanish. He felt urged more and more to move into the pastoral ministry, but he held back from committing himself. Once he reflected, "I love to preach usually, better than others like to hear. Yet I shrink from taking the title Rev[erend]." [75] Frequent entries in his journal demonstrated the scrutiny to which he was subjecting himself. "The truth is," he wrote once, "my soul is not in the work. I do not love it as I ought." Each speaking occasion made him "shrink and stagger and dread" its responsibility. But Haven's difficulty was not a "lack of words, of ideas, of easy and ready expression and gesture" but the absence of "unction." He admitted that he was not even compelled by ambition to succeed as a preacher. "I lack the desire, the strong endeavor, the earnest fullness of soul which is the base, shaft, and capital of every pillar of fame or goodness left standing in the wastes of time," he concluded.[76]

By the time of his second year as principal, Haven had become restless in his job. He could count his administration a success. Except for an occasion when the trustees tried to prohibit a Negro girl from matriculating as a student, he maintained good relations with those who managed the school. In that case he dared the board to refuse her application by declaring that he would give the girl private instruction in his own room. The trustees backed down and gave reluctant approval to integrate the school.[77]

But Haven was not satisfied. Increased enrollment imposed extra duties upon him, especially in the area of discipline. More than once his patience wore thin. Near the end of his tenure he shared his irritation with a former member of the Amenia faculty. "It is strange," he wrote,

that Dante did not conceive of the punishment of pedagoguing in his discriptions [sic] of Purgatory. It seems to me, the governing of those who neither love nor respect you and whom you neither love nor respect, who are too young to be treated as Malefactors and too old to be indulged as children is a refinement of punishment that rather exceeds the fancy of the Italian, or of Grecian mythologists. . . . Teaching is endurable if the scholars be babies or dolls & agreeable when they are studious & thoughtful, but administration of discipline is only comfortable in the instructive affection of the nursery or the unmixed authority of the Prison.[78]

74. Journal entry for May 9, 1848, as quoted in *ibid.,* p. 89.
75. Quoted in *ibid.,* p. 100.
76. Quoted in *ibid.,* p. 98.
77. *Ibid.,* p. 290; see Haven's references to this situation in *Zion's Herald,* Apr. 24, 1867; Mar. 29, 1877.
78. Haven to Winchell, Feb. 4, 1851.

As early as 1849 Haven had decided that he "must engage in something more like [his] life-work" than teaching and administering an academy. "I must get away from this place," he wrote, "and then may God guide me." [79] The next year he offered his resignation to the trustees, but their commendation and a salary increase temporarily changed his mind.[80] That school year would be his last, however, for sometime in 1850 he declared his intention to join the ranks of the New England Methodist Conference the following April.

In his decision to leave teaching Haven was still driven more by a sense of duty than of confidence that preaching was his special calling. He had, however, come to see the relevance of his own New England religious tradition to his vocational dilemma. The distinction of that tradition, religiously speaking, was to insist on the church's role to be the conscience of the social order. Until 1833 in Massachusetts, the structural tie of religion to society was in an established church, but the conviction lingered on after disestablishment that it was the duty of the Christian community to influence law and shape social custom.

Haven was aware of the New England religious heritage whose "ministry," he wrote later, "from its origin, has been faithful in setting forth the relations of the Gospel to the laws and customs of man." [81] From the time of the Puritans, the practice of annual sermons before civil authorities had been one expression of this Christian social responsibility. [82] On fast days, Thanksgiving, and Independence Day in Haven's time, pulpit orators continued to make the connection of religion to "questions of civil and social import." [83] Clearly by July 4, 1847, when he preached a sermon at Amenia, "On Christian Politics, comparing the Passover of the Israelites with the Independence of our Nation," Haven had begun to grasp the connection.[84] His poem at Malden's bicentennial two years later praised the town's Puritan ministers "who stripped . . . all sin of its disguise" and the clergy of the Revolutionary era who were "inspirers of those struggling to be free." [85] With these models to draw upon, it is not surprising that Haven, during the national crisis over the Compromise of 1850, found a way to unite his two great concerns, religion and politics, in a conception of Christian ministry

79. Quoted in Daniels, *Memorials of Gilbert Haven*, p. 40.
80. Prentice, *Life*, p. 90.
81. *National Sermons*, p. v; see also p. 8.
82. The election sermon in Massachusetts began in 1634 and lasted for 250 years until 1884. See A. W. Plumstead, ed., *The Wall and the Garden. Selected Massachusetts Election Sermons 1670-1775* (Minneapolis: University of Minnesota Press, 1968), p. 6.
83. *National Sermons*, p. v.
84. Prentice, *Life*, p. 100. The sermon is not extant.
85. See Haven's praise for Michael Wigglesworth and Peter Thacher in "A Poem Delivered at Malden," pp. 75-76. Wigglesworth, who is known for his poetry, particularly "Day of Doom," preached the colony's election sermon in 1686 and the artillery election sermon ten years later. Thatcher was a political preacher of independence and defiance of King George during his ministry at Malden after 1770. See *The Bi-Centennial Book of Malden*, pp. 144-56, 162-66, 207-12; *National Sermons*, p. vi.

that was relevant to both individual concerns and social issues. His sermon on "The Higher Law" at Amenia, therefore, exemplified an updated version of the New England religious tradition that focused on the problems of slavery and sectionalism.

The years at Amenia had deepened Haven's perception of the moral and political crisis in American society which slavery precipitated. His views were sharply delineated in correspondence with his college friend and former faculty colleague at Amenia, Alexander Winchell, who had moved to Alabama. He warned Winchell against being influenced by the radical southern argument that held slavery to be "the Divine Institution." He noted how easily a man could move from accepting slavery as necessary "to the belief in the rightfulness of [the] practice." Thus, Haven rejected justifications of human bondage which emphasized the condition of the slaves and the difficulties accompanying emancipation. He explained the fundamental principle that lay beneath his opposition to black enslavement. "I am afraid these inherent elements of my soul," he told Winchell,

—the universal brotherhood of Man—white or black, savage or civilized—slave or free—righteous or ungodly—has [sic] become too much a part of my nature —planted years since & grown with every increase of thought & feeling for any casual visit to [the South] or long association with counter ideas to utterly annihilate or destroy—or even to essentially modify.

Haven concluded confidently, "I hope and expect a speedy overthrow of the Institution by the action of the Christian conscience under the guidance of the Christian Charity of the North." [86]

The clarity and forthrightness of Haven's abolitionism coincided with his commitment to the church's role in social reformation and shaped his choice to begin his pastoral ministry in the New England Conference, the official organization of Methodist preachers in Massachusetts. He was ready to identify with churchmen who composed the strongest antislavery contingent remaining in northern Methodism following the exodus of the Wesleyans. In the face of a conservative reaction in the denomination, these abolitionists buried the notion which some church officials entertained that, with the sectional division of 1844, agitation of the slavery question in the Northeast had ended. At its next session in 1845 the conference pressed for new action to "purge the church and the world" of slavery and "to restore our enslaved fellow men to the exercise and enjoyment of civil and religious liberty." The ministers also insisted on stronger measures to expel slaveholding members in the border states who adhered to the northern church.[87]

A year later Massachusetts Methodism officially protested "all efforts to

---

86. Haven to Winchell, Feb. 4, 1851.
87. *Minutes of the New England Conference of the Methodist Episcopal Church,* 1845, pp.12-13. The minutes were published annually. (Hereafter they are listed simply as *Minutes of the New England Conference* with the year.)

conciliate slave-holding friends and members of our church, who can free their slaves and will not," charging that denominational officials acted "to perpetuate slavery" by allowing "this evil to be retained, nursed and defended in the bosom of the church." [88] By 1847 a majority of the clergy adopted a sectarian abolitionist standard in stating, "We cannot recognize or fellowship as a Christian, any person who is guilty of this sin; nor can we acknowledge as a sister church any organization that clearly permits or sanctions this sin in its members." The preachers pledged to use their "influence and exertions as Christian ministers, philanthropists and citizens, to exterminate this sin from the church and from the nation." [89]

The General Conference of the Methodist Episcopal Church, which convened every four years, met in 1848 for the first time without southern delegates, but the session proved how little support New Englanders had for their effort to make the denomination's antislavery testimony "more explicit and decided." [90] Most northern Methodists did not even want to take credit for having forced Southerners out of the church over the issue of slavery. The annual conferences in the North repudiated a plan of separation to which leaders in both sections had agreed in 1844. The general conference, therefore, took the position that southern Methodists alone were responsible for the breakup of the national organization. By charging the South with secession, northern conservatives could claim that they had taken no new ground on the slavery question. At the same time antislavery churchmen could interpret the division of 1844 in terms of disciplining a slaveholding bishop. Because the action contemplated no change in the actual law in the church's *Book of Discipline,* conservatives could even join antislavery reformers to support a resolution that rescinded an interpretation of Methodist legislation on slavery given by the General Conference of 1840. It had read that "the simple holding of slaves, or the mere ownership of slave property . . . constitutes no legal barrier to the election and ordination of ministers to the various offices known in the ministry of the Methodist Episcopal Church." [91] Since that repeal was the only action on the issue of slavery taken at the general conference, New England delegates went home somewhat dejected that the church's highest legislative body had been content to remain silent.[92]

By 1850, when Haven decided to ask for conference membership, the fight against slavery took on new intensity. At the annual meeting in the spring the preachers rejoiced that slavery was not being considered chiefly "in political or fiscal connections, but that the moral sentiments of the nation

88. *Ibid.,* 1846, p. 13.
89. *Ibid.,* 1847, pp. 20-21.
90. *Ibid.,* 1848, p. 15.
91. *Journal of the General Conference of the Methodist Episcopal Church,* 1848, pp. 80-85, 125, 154-64.
92. Charles Baumer Swaney, *Episcopal Methodism and Slavery with Sidelights on Ecclesiastical Politics* (Boston, 1926), pp. 152-54; Lucius C. Matlack, *The Antislavery Struggle and Triumph in the Methodist Episcopal Church* (New York, 1881), pp. 189-97.

[were] being aroused against it, and the true principles of freedom with reference to the rights of all men [were] being rapidly and generally diffused." The conference formally avowed "that the glory of God and the good of mankind require the exclusion of Slaveholders from the Christian church." [93] Later the same year the Fugitive Slave Law aroused Methodists throughout the region to organize protest meetings and petition campaigns and to denounce "the black law" in the pulpit.[94] That November over at Amenia, just across the state line from western Massachusetts, Haven preached his "higher law" sermon in the same spirit of moral indignation which was still alive the next spring at the session of the New England Conference, during which he was admitted to membership on probation.[95]

In the oration Haven examined the nature of law, human and divine, and analyzed moral responsibility. Because it upheld human bondage, the fugitive slave legislation absolutely contradicted God's "moral law." He exclaimed that "any act which violates the instincts of our nature, clashes with the decisions of Conscience, deviates from the path of Providence, and disagrees with the Word of God, is clearly contrary to His will." When "tested . . . by all the means given us for discerning moral quality, slavery is condemned," Haven argued, for it "is the most extreme and terrible violation of human rights." [96]

On these grounds Haven dissented from the view that because "Slavery exists in society, and is recognized in the Constitution," opposition to it threatened "the preservation of the State and the Will of God." The Constitution recognized slavery, he admitted, but "it cannot trample on the rights which itself guarantees, nor can it justly command the violation of that higher law under which its own existence alone endures." Ultimate authority, he contended, resided "in Christ, not in the Constitution," with "the things that are God's," not with "the things that are Caesar's." The new law was a usurpation of that unconditional obedience owed to God, one aspect of which was the Christian duty to share the bonds of the enslaved. Therefore, Haven recommended non-compliance with what he always called, in order to deny its legitimacy, the "Fugitive Slave Bill." He even counseled active defiance of authority and civil disobedience of the law so as "to create a public sentiment which shall nullify its action and obtain its repeal." [97] Appropriately, for his first abolitionist sermon, he concluded the address by quoting "the mighty words of Freedom's Laureate," Whittier:

> But for us and for our children, the vow which we have given
> For freedom and humanity is registered in heaven;

93. *Minutes of the New England Conference*, 1850, p. 13.
94. For examples, see *Zion's Herald*, Oct. 9, 1850 to July 23, 1851.
95. *Minutes of the New England Conference*, 1851, pp. 7-9; *Zion's Herald*, May 7, 1851.
96. *National Sermons*, pp. 8-12, 16, 21.
97. *Ibid.*, pp. 8, 12-15, 22-24, 26-31.

No slave hunt in our borders, no pirates on our strand,
No fetters for our brethren, no slave upon our land.[98]

Four months later Haven bade farewell to his colleagues and students at Amenia, exhorting them, as he departed, about "the duty and excellency of mental and spiritual culture." He spoke of "the rise and progress of the great principles of Christianity that [were] removing or remodelling all the institutions of society, and working slowly but surely a complete and glorious transformation." There were evils in American society which threatened this evolutionary vision of progress, but Haven judged that there were not any which were "so inveterate as to be beyond cure, nor so terrible as to require revolutionary means for their extinction." [99] With such religious and social optimism Haven entered the ministry as "his true calling," confident "that he had something special to say to the Methodist Church and the world on the kindred sins of slavery and [racial] caste." [100]

98. *Ibid.*, p. 32; *The Poetical Works of John Greenleaf Whittier*, pp. 81-82.
99. *Education and Religion Essential to the Perfection of Character. A Discourse Delivered at Amenia Seminary, March 16th, 1851, on Resigning the Office of Principal* (New York, 1851), pp. 10, 29, 31.
100. Prentice, *Life*, p. 154.

II

Christian Abolitionism

Because Gilbert Haven believed that every reform, including the antislavery cause, was "but half perfect" until united with "the power of a Christian faith and a godly life," he expressed his abolitionism most naturally and creatively in and through the church.[1] After the spring of 1851 he served as a Methodist pastor in his native state, joining religion with reform to attack slavery and racial injustice. Following the denominational custom of the period, he changed parishes every two years, beginning at Northampton, and moving on to Wilbraham, Westfield, Roxbury, and Cambridge.

While the church was the primary base for Haven's advocacy of abolition, he did not hesitate to denounce the moral complacency which marked the American Protestant response to slavery. His antislavery career during the final decade before the Civil War was prompted by a concern to recover the zeal for reform that was characteristic in northern churches in the early years of the crusade against slavery, but which, during the 1840s, had waned considerably. The religious institutions of the land, Haven exclaimed in one sermon, had become so "dumb and paralyzed before great and general sins," that they were "the synagogue of Satan." He charged that slavery "polluted the sanctuary" and encroached upon "the sacred territory of the church," ranging in its influence "from her obscure layman and preacher to her pillars in pew and pulpit." American Christianity even had the dubious distinction of having slaveholders in "the high seats of the bishopric." Slavery, Haven explained, controlled the church's "organizations, and disciplined her discipline." [2]

For all of his criticism of the churches for their moral failure, however, Haven never reached such a crisis over the issue as to contemplate seriously a rupture with his own denomination. Nor did he in religious sentiment question the authenticity of the Christian faith, even though it had often been perverted to justify and sanction slavery. Because the church should set a moral example for society, he was convinced of the necessity of ecclesiastical reformation. Yet, he was clearly not a separatist, but a reformer from within the institution.

Church antislavery for Haven was not merely the sectarian purification of his own and other denominations. On the contrary, he viewed moral suasion, social agitation, and political action as crucial components of effective abolitionism. But virtually all that he did in support of abolitionism came through the instrumentality of the church, which, "with all her faults and failures," he once put it, remained "the best organization among men for the extirpation

1. *National Sermons*, p. 122.
2. *Ibid.*, pp. 48-49.

of national no less than individual sins." [3] He expected the church to be the conscience for the social order.[4] On this basis he urged his congregations to back antislavery political parties and candidates and to join in organized protest against sectional compromise which ignored the immorality of human bondage. His preaching was the chief medium of a social critique that damned both northern racism and southern slavery and that called churchmen to active engagement in the cause of justice and freedom. By joining social criticism and political involvement to religious reformation, therefore, Haven represented a distinctive antislavery and racially equalitarian position, designated by his contemporaries "Christian abolitionism." [5]

I

Christian abolitionists shared the major ideological principles and composed one faction of the larger antislavery movement which emerged after 1830. Since he had become active in the second generation of the reform, Haven inherited these tenets of a common faith. The initial article of abolitionist belief was the contention that chattel slavery was a sin per se, that the system of slavery and not merely its attendant evils was immoral. Haven maintained that slavery was "the essence of all sins" and "the perfection of iniquity," and he spoke of it as "the greatest sin of this or of any age." [6] More specifically he characterized slavery as an expression of inordinate, despotic power expressed by "the aribitrary will" of the white master whose "claim of Property in Man" deprived a black bondsman of the most precious of all freedoms—the "right to himself." [7] The real moral issue concerning slavery inhered not in the abuses within but the fundamental nature of the relation itself. Haven portrayed the system as "the taking of a human being, and selling him like a beast . . . the working of him without recompense; refusing his mind the light it seeks; refusing his soul the grace it needs; refusing his heart the affections it craves; making his conjugal, parental, and filial ties depend upon his master's pleasure." [8]

---

3. *Ibid.*, p. 48.

4. This viewpoint was implicit in Haven's reform philosophy. In a sermon published in *Zion's Herald*, June 27, 1860 he explicitly referred to "the world, whose conscience is the church."

5. Haven used the designation in *The Liberator*, Mar. 1, 1861 and the *Christian Advocate and Journal*, Feb. 20, May 1, 1862. See also William Goodell, *Slavery and Anti-Slavery: A History of the Struggle in Both Hemispheres: with a View of the Slavery Question in the United States*, 3rd ed. (New York, 1855), pp. 488-89, 492, 543; *The Minutes of the Christian Anti-Slavery Convention. Assembled April 17-20th, 1850, Cincinnati, Ohio* (Cincinnati, 1850), pp. 81-82; *The Independent*, Mar. 8, 1855; Clifton H. Johnson, "The American Missionary Association, 1846-1861: A Study in Christian Abolitionism" (Ph.D. dissertation, University of North Carolina, 1957), ch. I; William B. Gravely, "Christian Abolitionism: A Religio-Political Critique of Slavery and Caste in Antebellum America," paper presented at the Rocky Mountain-Great Plains regional meeting of the American Academy of Religion, Apr. 18, 1970.

6. Haven to Winchell, Feb. 24, 1854; *Westfield News Letter* (Mass.), July 2, 1856; *National Sermons*, pp. 89, 94-95.

7. *National Sermons*, pp. 16, 96, 160.

8. *Ibid.*, pp. 95, 157, 167; Aileen S. Kraditor, *Means and Ends in American Abolitionism. Garrison and His Critics on Strategy and Tactics, 1834-1850* (New York: Pantheon Books, 1967), p. 22.

In abolitionist ethical theory the duty of immediate emancipation followed from the assertion of the fundamental sinfulness of slavery. The analogy with the dynamics of religious conversion in evangelical Protestantism was obvious. When he debated the morality of slavery with Alexander Winchell, Haven developed his argument in terms of the guilt of slaveholding and the necessity of repentance. He declared, "I believe any thing held in violation of the law of God should be given up." When he acknowledged that there were distinctions between the various intentions of slaveholders, Haven seemed to compromise the principle of immediate emancipation. But the burden of proof was always upon the master to demonstrate that even as he deemed the system of slavery to be evil, he could not find a satisfactory way to extricate himself from the guilty relation and to manumit his bondsmen. "While I sympathize with the enlightened slaveholder who sees the wrong & knows not how to escape it," Haven conceded to Winchell, "while I can look with largest charity & with Christian regard upon such a soul—I cannot but detest the brute who knowingly abuses through this power all the rights of Manhood." [9] Throughout the decade, however, Haven remained convinced that there were penitent slaveholders who would respond to moral appeals against slavery and abolish the institution.[10]

As real as were the difficulties attending emancipation, Haven reiterated its claim and rebuked those who defended slavery on grounds of necessity "for the good of the black" or "because of the willingness of its embruted victims to endure it." He stated the matter firmly to Winchell, "I don't believe any degree of degradation would convince me of the necessity of perpetuating the causes of that degradation. I don't think any amount of helplessness on the part of the Master or Slave would show me the propriety or excellence of the state or its causes." [11] In his response, Winchell, then president of Masonic University in Selma, Alabama, inferred that it was probably not possible or even desirable to raise Negroes from the state of bondage. Haven answered by decrying "the barbarism" and "debased condition" of a society that allowed any man to "become so near a brute as to render . . . his elevation problematical." [12]

The moral scandal of American society in regard to slavery resided in the respectability, acceptance, and legal support which the institution commanded. Men of good character, in terms of private morality, were slaveholders and

9. Haven to Winchell, Feb. 4, 1851; Kraditor, *Means and Ends in American Abolitionism*, pp. 78-79.
10. For a discussion of his scheme to provide from the resources of northern philanthropy an inducement by financial compensation to owners who would free their slaves, see below, sect. 3.
11. Haven to Winchell, Feb. 4, 1851; Feb. 24, 1854.
12. Haven to Winchell, Mar. 29, 1853. On Winchell's later career as an important scientist and educator, see George P. Merrill's article in *The Dictionary of American Biography*, vol. XX, pp. 373-74. For his scientific defense of racial inferiority, see John S. Haller, Jr., *Outcasts from Evolution. Scientific Attitudes of Racial Inferiority, 1859-1900* (Urbana: University of Illinois Press, 1971), pp. 88-94. Winchell criticized Haven's racial views in his *Preadamites* (Chicago, 1888), pp. 81-82.

apologists for the system. Because they lent the sanction of religion, legality, and social status to the practice, they were the bulwarks of slavery. A black child "follows the condition of his mother," Haven asserted in a sermon at Westfield. If the mother was a slave, so would the child be, based on "sober and written *Law*" which "ministers and members of the professed Church of Christ, statesmen of the highest rank, judges of most rigid legal righteousness, and even philanthropists of tender hearts" enacted, advocated, and supported.[13] The implication was ominous. The overthrow of a socially accepted institution required radical surgery, beginning with the destruction of its ideological defense.

Religious pretensions were so ingrained in conceptions of slavery in America that any abolitionist attack had to encounter biblical arguments for its justification. Opponents of slavery first distinguished the institution in the Bible and in ancient history from its modern counterpart, which, they argued, was based primarily on the fact of race rather than on a division of labor or captivity in war. In answer to defenders of slavery who chose biblical examples to justify modern oppression of black men, Haven responded in a Fast Day sermon, "Scripture is stolen to deck a false idol. It is a new argument for an old sin, an argument without any antitype [*sic*] in history, or any authority in the Word of God." Like other abolitionists, Haven contended that the chief flaw in the biblical proslavery argument was its failure to find a justification for the racial nature of American slavery. "No doctor of diabolic divinity," he declared, "has ever picked from the sacred page any text for the enslavement of Indian, Mexican, Englishman, or Greek, though every argument which they wrest from the writings of Paul . . . must, on their principle, be applied chiefly to white persons, as these were almost the only slaves of Rome in the days of Paul." [14]

The most common hypothesis that upheld the racial character of modern slavery interpreted Noah's curse of Canaan, the son of Ham, in Genesis 9:25 as a prophecy for the subsequent enslavement of Africans. Proponents of the Hamitic myth overlooked the fact that the curse was not upon Ham. The entire argument presumed, as well, an uninterrupted continuity between Ham and the black race. Likewise, it involved a curious understanding of divine intent that employed the drunken profanity of Noah to account for the origin of races and their modern relations. Haven believed the prophecy, but he considered it "announced and completed four thousand years ago, when Joshua made the Gideonites his servants, and David ruled the whole of Canaan." [15] Beneath the use of the Hamitic argument, however, he detected the effort to represent slavery as "patriarchal, scriptural, domestic, respect-

13. *National Sermons*, pp. 96-97.
14. *Ibid.*, pp. 124-25; see also pp. 361-64.
15. *Ibid.*, p. 124. On the historical origins of the Hamitic myth, see Winthrop D. Jordan, *White over Black. American Attitudes Toward the Negro, 1550-1812* (Chapel Hill: University of North Carolina Press, 1968), pp. 17-20, 35-36, 41-43, 60, 62, 84, 111, 158, 200-201, 243-46, 308.

able, Christian," and nothing angered him more. "No sinner in all the Bible ever arrayed his wicked passions in such a cloak of holiness," he charged. "It was left for preachers and professors of the Gospel in this free and Christian America, in this nineteenth century after the coming of Christ, to weave such a garment of sanctity for the body of their death." [16]

Besides proclaiming the sinfulness of slavery, the duty of emancipation, and the rejection of social and religious justifications of the institution, abolitionists argued in behalf of racial equality. The underlying conviction of the entire critique of slavery was a belief in "the unity of the human race" as a component of the biblical doctrine of creation. Haven preached that "the Bible constantly proclaims the absolute oneness of the race of man, in Adam, Noah, and Christ." [17] At the time the theory of the unity of mankind had only religious grounding and little of the scientific proof which it has gained since. Scientists of Haven's generation attacked the Jewish-Christian view of creation generally and the concept of the unity of the human race specifically. Haven warned against this "false science" which he believed resulted from a "wave of infidelity," and he advised Christians to "cling to the central doctrine of the Word of God—one man, one Savior, one God." [18]

The Judeo-Christian understanding of human equality depended on the fundamental unity in creation. "We must acknowledge that every man, of every complexion," Haven asserted, "has in his genealogical chart, as Christ had in his, 'which was the son of Adam, which was the son of God.' " [19] The logic of Haven's religious outlook might well have led him to emphasize primarily, perhaps even exclusively, the doctrine of atonement as expressed in the particular Christian belief about the ubiquitous significance of the death of Jesus, "Christ died for all." He appealed instead to "the universal equality of all human souls" as created by God, and "the necessity of their universal elevation in intelligence, love, & purity, & the duty to love all & labor for all especially for those who are the farthest remove[d] from their true condition through their loss of all means & privileges of true and holy growth." [20] When Haven used christological categories, they were either an application of Matthew 25:31-46, as an appeal to see the image of Christ in the bonds-

16. *National Sermons*, pp. 94, 126.
17. *Ibid.*, p. 137. See also pp. 42, 53, 67-68, 72-73.
18. *Ibid.*, p. 137. The attempt to establish a separate origin for the Negroid race sparked a lively debate among biologists, theologians, philosophers, and natural scientists of the period. See William Stanton, *The Leopard's Spots. Scientific Attitudes Toward Race in America 1815-59* (Chicago: University of Chicago Press, Phoenix Books, 1966). See also Haven's comment in *Zion's Herald*, Sept. 19, 1872.
19. *Westfield News Letter*, June 18, 1856 (*National Sermons*, pp. 73-74). The quotation is from Luke 3:38.
20. Haven to Winchell, Mar. 29, 1853. The fundamental basis for Christian antiracism, Reinhold Niebuhr once pointed out, is the unity of mankind, "the unity of all men as they are created in the image of God." See " 'Let Love Be the Motive and Justice the Method,' " *Katallagete* (Winter, 1967-68). George D. Kelsey makes the same point in *Racism and the Christian Understanding of Man* (New York: Charles Scribner's Sons, 1965), pp. 86-89.

man, or an interpretation of Philippians 2:7 in which Christ is described as having taken the form of a slave.[21] Before his Westfield congregation he employed the former reference: "We selfishly let Christ be scourged and crucified in many of these His dear children in chains." In the same sermon he paraphrased lines from John Greenleaf Whittier's poem, "The Branded Hand."

> THOU must see HIM in the task-field, in the
> prison shadows dim,
> And thy mercy to the bondman, it is mercy
> unto Him.[22]

From the assertion of the unity of mankind Haven denied that human beings could be born into slavery. Human inequality, he maintained, had been the foundation for "all monarchies and aristocracies" and for "that chief of the doctrines of devils" of "the Southern Church and State . . .— that a man can be born the property of another man."[23] If the human race had no single origin, unity, and equality, racial slavery could be entirely justified; but, Haven believed, men could see in their "heart of hearts" the oneness of human kind. "Take away this conviction and we can trade in them as easily as in cattle or grain," he contended with reference to blacks. "The argument is simple and unanswerable. If essentially different and inferior, then they are and of right, ought to be servants, slaves, merchandise. There is but ONE race of men, and God has put all things under his feet. If the negro is a man, then he is the unquestioned equal in natural rights of every other man. If not an equal, not a man. If not a man, a merchantable thing."[24]

In all of Haven's parishes he faced some opposition on account of his public avowal of abolitionism, and because he put into practice his views on social equality between blacks and whites.[25] He made a special point to consider the Negro community of Northampton as part of his ministerial responsibility in his first appointment.[26] At Westfield, where a large portion of the members were racially conservative Democrats or Know-Nothings in political sentiment, he had several intense conflicts. The trustees even threatened to lock him out of the church building, but he rode out the storm and returned to the charge for a second year in spite of the controversy.[27] At Roxbury Haven preached so consistently about the sins of slavery and caste that when his successor

21. *National Sermons*, pp. 19-20, 26, 77.
22. *Westfield News Letter*, June 18, 1856 (*National Sermons*, pp. 71, 74). See *The Poetical Works of John Greenleaf Whittier*, pp. 83-84.
23. "Infant Baptism and Church Membership," *Methodist Quarterly Review*, 41 (1859), 8-9.
24. *Westfield News Letter*, June 18, 1856 (*National Sermons*, pp. 72-73).
25. Prentice, *Life*, p. 25; Daniels, *Memorials of Gilbert Haven*, pp. 46-49, 52-53.
26. See undated letter from Mary I. Haven to Elizabeth Vail as quoted in Prentice, *Life*, p. 124.
27. *Ibid.*, pp. 147-48; Daniels, *Memorials of Gilbert Haven*, pp. 55-57.

tried to continue in the same vein, he overheard parishioners complaining, *"Nigger again at our ch[urch]!"* [28]

To challenge the prejudices of his congregations, Haven depicted the accomplishments of the black race in ancient history and emphasized the admirable characteristics of American Negroes. He praised the "natural wit, pathos, and sublimity" of black preachers, paid tribute to the "style of music" of the Negro folk songs which had attained "national eminence," and commended the "courtesy of manners" that made black men America's "truest gentlemen." Likewise, Haven added, "in the culinary art" blacks had "no rivals." [29] When Haven spoke in this way, according to one historian, he romanticized black racial traits. A certain air of sentimentality does mark his description of "the gifts and graces" of the black race, but his basic intention was to counter the "inhuman and ungodly" prejudices which he found in his churches and in society generally. His polemic against anti-Negroism, therefore, was more than a white mind's "romantic racialism," because it was accompanied by ridicule that men would make so much of the superficial difference in skin color and by advocating amalgamation as the final answer to black-white relations. He considered that Shakespeare's "Othello" with its theme of interracial love taught a needed lesson to Americans. He reminded his audiences that Vice-President Richard M. Johnson had children by his black mistress, whom he would have legally married but for social pressure.[30]

Belief in the unity of mankind and the theory of racial equality were such fundamental elements in abolitionist ideology that Haven's perspective, except for his views on amalgamation, was not as unique as his first biographer claimed in designating him "the only man of his time . . . willing to accept the logical and necessary outcome of the doctrines of human liberty and equality." [31] From the opening of the nineteenth century black leaders had protested publicly the discrimination which they encountered throughout the country. They insured that opposition to racial caste had a central place in the organized antislavery drive after 1830. They warned white abolitionists, when prejudice against color cropped out even among the most faithful of the antislavery reformers, to "annihilate in their own bosoms the cord of caste." [32] As an heir to the insight of blacks whose experience gave birth to the struggle and of white abolitionists of an earlier generation, then, Haven himself made

28. Journal and Commonplace Book of Fales H. Newhall, entry for December 3, 1860, in the private possession of Dr. Jannette Newhall of Boston.

29. *National Sermons*, pp. 128-31.

30. *Ibid.*, pp. 131, 140, 145-49; George M. Fredrickson, *The Black Image in the White Mind. The Debate on Afro-American Character and Destiny*, 1817-1914 (New York: Harper & Row, 1971), pp. 102, 122, 173.

31. Daniels, *Memorials of Gilbert Haven*, pp. 47-48; see also p. 36.

32. Carter G. Woodson, ed., *Negro Orators and Their Orations* (Washington, 1925), pp. 32-41, 64-85, 87, 90-96; Benjamin Quarles, *Black Abolitionists* (New York: Oxford University Press, 1969), pp. 6-7, 54; Herbert Aptheker, ed., *A Documentary History of the Negro People in the United States* (New York: Citadel Press, 1951), pp. 70-71, 104-7.

no claim to originality in his attacks against caste. His distinctive and consistent support of racial equality, however, marked him as one of the very few white Americans of his time who recognized and combated the phenomenon of racism.

The abolitionist movement after 1830 provided a mixed legacy to Haven. Not only did he inherit its fundamental principles of antislavery and racial equality, but he was also influenced by its rifts and schisms. Those divisions explain why he never became a member of the most influential reform organization in the crusade, the American Anti-Slavery Society. He long admired and publicly defended the courageous course of the one whom he called "its originator, under God," the man with whom the Society was most readily associated.[33] In a sermon at Wilbraham in 1854, he predicted that "If ever freedom becomes the possession, as it is the birthright, of every man in this land, he who will be honored with the loftiest monument—a monument built by every hand that has ever been raised against him—will be that yet hated and proscribed, that somewhat error-led, but far more truth-led, man, William Lloyd Garrison." [34] The qualification that Haven imposed in his otherwise laudatory statement grew out of basic differences which prevented official connection between the two men and the factions which they represented in the antislavery movement. A thanksgiving sermon on the Republican presidential victory, which Haven preached at Cambridge in November, 1860, provided the occasion to air in public their separate viewpoints. Even though the debate came at the end of the decade and in the face of civil war, it symbolized a long-standing disagreement that dated back to Haven's entry into the abolitionist ranks.

Presenting a synopsis of antislavery progress in the sermon, Haven assailed the antipolitical views of the Garrisonians, which had been a major factor that triggered the secession of less radical abolitionists from the American Anti-Slavery Society in 1840. Furthermore, Haven rebuked Garrison for letting "his love of free speech" permit some of his associates to burden the antislavery cause "with gross infidelities and social absurdities." He also remarked with regret that Garrison had not, like the English abolitionist Christian, William Wilberforce, manifested more "prayer and piety" to accompany his philanthropic and reforming activities.[35] The charges were standard criticisms that abolitionist churchmen leveled against Garrison and fellow

33. *The Liberator*, Mar. 1, 1861; *National Sermons*, p. 38; *Zion's Herald*, June 27, 1860; *"Te Deum Laudamus." The Cause and the Consequence of the Election of Abraham Lincoln; A Thanksgiving Sermon Delivered in the Harvard St. M.E. Church, Cambridge, Sunday Evening, Nov. 11, 1860* (Boston, 1860), p. 18.

34. *National Sermons*, pp. 37-38.

35. *Election of Abraham Lincoln*, pp. 18-19. The latter remark reiterated the lament of Methodist editor and historian, Abel Stevens, that Garrison had failed to maintain "the Christian and prudent character of Wilberforce." See his essay, "American Slavery—Its Progress and Prospects," *Methodist Quarterly Review*, 39 (July, 1857), 442-43. See also Haven's private letter to Garrison, Jan. 31, 1861, Garrison Papers, Boston Public Library.

41

radicals. They represented an incompatibility in religious outlook, social philosophy, and reform strategy that destroyed unity and obstructed coordination in the antislavery cause.

The Garrisonians believed that antislavery societies should include a broad range of opinion on religious, social, and political questions not related to slavery. At the same time they tended to assume the more extreme viewpoints on these issues by supporting women's rights, nonresistance, pacificism, and the abolition of capital punishment and by disavowing political action because of the inevitable compromise of ideals involved. Their style of social agitation moved in the direction of revolution rather than reform, for they considered American society, North as well as South, to be "fundamentally immoral, with slavery only the worst of its many sins." As a remedy they worked toward "a thoroughgoing change in its institutional structure and ideology." [36] Moreover, several of the more prominent supporters of Garrison no longer accepted the religious outlook which had achieved something of a consensus in middle-class, Protestant America. They had passed through personal crises in belief which ended in the abandonment of traditional evangelical faith for "various modes of unbelief or a vague Religion of Humanity." [37] Nevertheless, they retained an intense moral passion along with a disposition to ridicule religious precepts and practices which they no longer found meaningful.

The exchange between Garrison and Haven early in 1861 echoed many another debate in *The Liberator* over the previous thirty years during which the famous Boston editor had obtained a well-earned reputation for confronting fearlessly all challengers. He chastised Haven for having criticized his associates, who, he said, had not "sought to burden [the antislavery cause] with any extraneous question." Their particular views on any issue, he insisted, were only held privately.[38] As Garrison saw it, Haven harbored a desire to squelch free speech and to enforce a test of religious orthodoxy upon members of the antislavery society. What dictated his position, Garrison charged, was ecclesiastical and theological conservatism. He complained that Haven had no right *"in the delivery of an anti-slavery discourse"* to impugn his "religious character" and to call him, in effect, "a heretic." Garrison wrote that Haven would never have introduced "a false and impertinent issue" like religious heresy, "if the priest had not mastery over the man, and his dogmatic theology a higher place in his estimation than the cause of bleeding humanity." [39]

The religious radicalism of the Garrisonian party, Haven claimed in response, deprived the abolitionist cause of the support of most evangelical

36. Kraditor, *Means and Ends in American Abolitionism*, p. 8.
37. Wyatt-Brown, "New Leftists and Abolitionists: A Comparison of American Radical Styles," p. 263; Kraditor, *Means and Ends in American Abolitionism*, ch. 4.
38. *The Liberator*, Jan. 18, 1861.
39. *Ibid.*, Mar. 1, 1861.

churchmen in the North. He contended that when the radicals raged "against the Church, the Bible, the Sabbath, the ordinance of perpetual marriage, and other sacred and blessed gifts of God to man," they needlessly alienated public opinion. By mixing several controversial reforms and by advocating heterodox religious sentiments, they distracted Northerners from confronting the greatest social wrong in the land, chattel slavery. On these grounds Haven denied that Garrison, or anyone else, could divorce his private views from his social role in the antislavery movement. He indicted Garrison and his colleagues for having gone beyond the boundaries of advocating abolition specifically to attack "that glorious, that divine, that eternal faith" of evangelical Protestantism. "I have read the *Liberator* many times, and I have rarely looked into its columns," he wrote, "that my faith as a Christian . . . has not been shocked by the profane skepticisms that were permitted to corrode its pages." [40]

Garrison's sympathy with the liberal theology of Theodore Parker especially offended Haven. After Parker's death in 1860, Haven preached in Cambridge that the deceased was "the first great American infidel" and "by far the ablest opponent that the Gospel has seen in this nation." [41] Parker's battle against what he called "the errors of the ecclesiastic theology" was, to Haven, a blatant denial of "the simple, fundamental truths of our holy religion: an inspired Bible, a divine Saviour, a helpless, sinful condition, that is in absolute need of that Saviour, a blessed salvation if we accept, a fearful doom if we refuse." [42] Haven particularly deplored Parker's statement, which Garrison seconded, that the widespread religious revival in 1857-58 was contrived.[43] "Voltaire assailed a dead and putrid form of Christianity; Paine struck at the Bible when French infidelity was tainting the Church with its rottenness," Haven asserted defensively. "Parker struck at the Church in her highest possible work; struck at her when God was prospering that work in a wonderful manner; struck at the work itself." [44]

The authenticity of the revival, by which Haven's Roxbury congregation was deeply affected, was, in his view, unquestionable.[45] It formed "one of the dearest and deepest convictions of the whole Evangelical Church, from the day of Pentecost until now." Attacks upon it and upon evangelical ideas

---

40. *Ibid.*
41. *Zion's Herald,* June 27, 1860, reprinted as "The Character and Career of Theodore Parker. A Sermon Preached in the Harvard Street Methodist Episcopal Church, Cambridge, Mass., June 10, 1860" in *Parkerism: Three Discourses Delivered on the Occasion of the Death of Theodore Parker* (New York, 1860), pp. 81, 113. Haven defined infidelity in its religious sense as "violent hostility to the express declarations of the Universal Church, and of the Bible itself" (*The Liberator,* Mar. 1, 1861). The charge was perennially made by evangelicals against rationalists, atheists, and "free-thinkers."
42. *Zion's Herald,* June 27, 1860 (*Parkerism,* p. 107).
43. *The Liberator,* Apr. 2, 9, 16, and 30, 1858; T. Smith, *Revivalism and Social Reform in Mid-Nineteenth Century America,* ch. 4.
44. *The Liberator,* Mar. 1, 1861.
45. Prentice, *Life,* pp. 177-79.

and practices in *The Liberator* were, he reasoned, surely not "essential to a defense of . . . antislavery, or even religious, consistency." "Is the article which precedes my letter," he asked Garrison, "opposing, with great harshness, the general opinion of Christians as to the right way of observing the Sabbath, essential to the prosperity of abolitionism?" Likewise, Haven took offense at an "advertisement" which had run "for nearly six months" in the paper, "entitled 'Self-Contradictions of the Bible,' and in which the Book is spoken of as 'the so-called Word of God.' " [46]

Throughout the debate Garrison excoriated Haven for an "assumption of religious superiority" which marked his argument and for being more interested in disparaging religious liberals than in laboring for "the success of the Anti-Slavery cause." [47] He vehemently rejected any possible interpretation of the recent religious awakening as efficacious. "That revival was manifestly not of God, but a device of the Adversary," he replied, "especially designed to draw off attention from the wrongs of the slave, to strengthen the tottering walls of an apostate church, and to subserve the purposes of a hireling priesthood." Thus, Parker "only exposed the hollowness of a trimming, time-serving, canting, spasmodic, pro-slavery revival, and therein did a noble work for true religion." Likewise, Garrison dissented from Haven's claim that it was "infidel" to say that " 'the Bible has settled nothing in theology, science, morality or religion, *beyond the prevailing opinions of the times'* . . . each individual being left free to interpret it for himself." [48] Such a relativistic understanding of the Scriptures, however, would endanger what Haven conceived to be clear biblical opposition to slavery. "For if that Word could be proved to indorse this crime," he declared on another occasion, "its sanctity and authority flee instantly and forever." [49]

The more moderate abolitionists like Haven did not fully appreciate the extent to which the Garrisonians were alienated from middle-class American religion, morals, and manners. *The Liberator,* its editor himself claimed, no longer limited its purpose narrowly to the promotion of abolition, but its columns were open on any subject which seemed "to help along the cause of human redemption in its broadest phase." To act otherwise, for Garrison, compromised "a free, impartial, independent" and "untrammelled press." [50] To other abolitionists, however, many of the causes Garrison espoused, or at least published for public consideration, threatened institutions in American life which, they believed, with the exception of slavery, only required improvement and reformation, not abandonment or eradication. For example, Haven became alarmed when he once understood Garrison to say in an address

46. *The Liberator,* Mar. 29, 1861. On the Sabbath question Charles K. Whipple, a Garrisonian, took Haven to task in *The Liberator,* Dec. 4, 1863.
47. *The Liberator,* Mar. 1, 29, 1861.
48. *Ibid.,* Mar. 1, 1861.
49. *National Sermons,* p. 125.
50. *The Liberator,* Mar. 29, 1861.

that "evangelical religion . . . was so bound up with the system of slavery, that the only way to destroy this monster was to destroy that faith." [51] But to Haven and to most abolitionist churchmen, the problem was not revivalist Protestantism, which he believed to be "historic, Biblical, vital Christianity," but with "false professors of a perfect religion," not with the churches and clergy per se, but with the corruption of their mission and calling.[52] That outlook in regard both to religion and politics characterized Christian abolitionism, which, in spite of its radical ideology in endorsing the principles of antislavery and racial equality, was in strategy more a commitment to reformation than revolution.[53]

For a time the American and Foreign Anti-Slavery Society, formed in 1840 as an alternative to Garrisonianism, tried to offer evangelical abolitionists an identity and a program of action. After a decade the society had compiled a rather spectacular record of failure, despite the valiant effort of its leading light, Lewis Tappan, to keep it alive. Before its founders closed operations in 1856, the society's successful projects were few—the publication of antislavery tracts and newspapers and a campaign to prevent the creation of an American branch of the European-based Evangelical Alliance in which slaveholding southern churchmen would have been accepted. With those exceptions the society did little more than provide an annual forum for conservative abolitionists to measure the progress of the cause.[54] Even though there was, after 1840, a broader diffusion of antislavery sentiment which could be found in the churches and in political parties, the society was even less effective than Garrison's organization in representing any considerable number of Americans who opposed slavery. But a more basic reason for the society's lack of success can be attributed to the attempt by its backers to reconcile abolitionism with accepted values and traditional institutions in American social and political life. The Tappanites, with Garrison and company, had inaugurated in the antislavery, anticaste crusade a more radical social revolution than they realized. Unlike the Garrisonians, however, their dissent from the American way of life did not extend fundamentally beyond a critique of slavery and white racism, the destruction of which would fulfill the grand destiny that awaited this democratic republic.[55]

With other Christian abolitionists Haven shared an ambivalence between a philosophical radicalism on slavery and racial caste and an otherwise conservative social and religious viewpoint. The combination was possible

51. As quoted in *ibid.*, Mar. 1, 1861.
52. *Ibid.*
53. Kraditor, *Means and Ends in American Abolitionism*, pp. 100-4.
54. Haven acknowledged as much in an article in *Zion's Herald*, Oct. 7, 1857.
55. Kraditor, *Means and Ends in American Abolitionism*, p. 8 and *passim*; Bertram Wyatt-Brown, *Lewis Tappan and the Evangelical War Against Slavery* (New York: Atheneum, 1971), pp. 198, 200, 249, 252, 279, 282, 310 ff., 332.

largely because he possessed a basic confidence in the American system of politics and in evangelical religion. Inherently, the nation and the church had failed to live up to their professions, but they had not entirely corrupted themselves. Haven did not consider it necessary, therefore, to go outside the established institutions of church and state in order to accomplish reformation. Perhaps if he had faced the scorn and rough handling of antiabolition mobs in the 1830s, which was the lot of the first generation of agitators, he would have appreciated the frustration of the radicals and understood Garrison's censure.

Officially Haven belonged neither to the ill-fated American and Foreign Anti-Slavery Society, nor its short-lived successor, the American Abolition Society. The one abolitionist reform association which he did join was a loosely organized and late-blooming movement called the Church Anti-Slavery Society, an interdenominational organization led by two brothers, George B. and Henry T. Cheever, who were Congregational clergymen. From its inception in 1859, the society coordinated efforts by abolitionist churchmen in the major denominations, but it had a small membership which extended little beyond New England. After the Civil War, it was phased out. At a Church Anti-Slavery Society meeting in the spring of 1859 Haven did hear and meet John Brown, who led the famous raid to free the slaves the following October. And Haven was active in the organization at least as late as 1863.[56] For the most part, however, his abolitionist activity found no other institutional expression than in political party and church, the latter of which he contended in a subsequent speech, "If it is truly the Church, it is also by necessity the Anti-Slavery Society." [57]

II

Christian abolitionism had two foci—the antislavery reformation of the churches and socio-political influence and action against slavery. For Haven both foci depended on the church as the institutional base for Christian social involvement. Throughout the decade he did not concentrate as much on changing the churches from within as he did later in his career, but antislavery developments in his denomination and his role in them were nonetheless significant aspects of what he called "Church purification." [58]

Haven participated in the dispute over slavery in northern Methodism through the New England Conference where the issue was debated each year and plans formed to strengthen the church's antislavery witness. Since he was not elected as a delegate to the quadrennial general conferences

56. *Zion's Herald*, June 1, 15, 1859; *Church Anti-Slavery Society. Proceedings of the Convention Which Met at Worcester, Mass. March 1, 1859* (New York, 1859); *The Independent*, June 3, 1863.
57. *National Sermons*, p. 361.
58. *Ibid.*, p. 49.

which authorized constitutional changes, he had no official opportunity to deal with the question at the highest denominational level. Even within his own annual conference, however, Haven played a minor and somewhat obscure role in the development of antislavery policy until after he moved east to Roxbury in 1857. By that time he had, as well, achieved some recognition as a vigorous and successful pastor.

The lack of more explicit and direct action in the church reform movement was due, in part, to Haven's optimism concerning the evolution of antislavery opinion. Because there was a new consciousness about slavery in northern Methodism during the 1850s, his belief in the progress of the cause seemed justified. But throughout the prewar period Haven persistently exaggerated the extent of past and contemporary antislavery sentiment among his fellow Methodists. He interpreted the sectional division of episcopal Methodism in 1844, for example, as a heroic demonstration of antislavery action by the northern conferences. Likewise, he viewed the northern general conference' refusal to agree to the plan of separation in 1848 as an abolitionist inspiration, a conviction not to recognize the Methodist Episcopal Church, South, as a Christian body "simply because of its submission to the Slave Power." [59] Only after he visited the border states in person at the beginning of the Civil War, did Haven face up fully to the extent and general acceptance of slaveholding in the congregations there which adhered to the northern church.

Furthermore, Haven did not permit himself to attack his denomination unreservedly because of strong institutional loyalties and a fervent devotion to Methodism, which he understood characteristically as "Christianity in earnest." He shared the perspective of most second-generation antislavery reformers in the churches who refused to countenance further ecclesiastical division over the issue. He stood with most Methodists in New England on a "policy of loyal abolitionism," rejecting both the conservative view that decried all antislavery agitation and the separatism of radical Garrisonianism.[60]

Finally, Haven's attitude toward church reform abolitionism was influenced by his fierce determination to succeed in his profession. This factor worked to keep his antislavery criticism of northern Methodism under wraps, if for

59. *The Liberator*, Mar. 29, 1861. The slave-power theme in Haven's thought is treated below, sec. 3.

60. *Zion's Herald*, July 20, 1859; Milton Bryan Powell, "The Abolitionist Controversy in the Methodist Episcopal Church, 1840-1864" (Ph.D. dissertation, State University of Iowa, 1963), pp. 174-78. Powell designated the New England Methodist antislavery position as "theocratic abolitionism," which insisted on the church's responsibility in its collective capacity to combat slavery not only within religious, but in social and political, life as well. He correctly distinguished this view from that of certain "sectarian" abolitionists in northern Methodism, especially in upper New York state, but he overlooked those conservatives among New England Methodists who failed to share the "theocratic" perspective. Likewise, Powell neglected to point out that Haven's racial equalitarianism, the mark of true abolitionism, separated him from most of his antislavery colleagues, even in New England.

no other reason than the kind of commitment required for success in the denominational system. Haven was first appointed to small churches which paid meager salaries and experienced perennial struggles just to stay alive. Despite the fact that he had to start his ministry in such situations, he threw himself with abandon into the most routine tasks of the pastorate and the conference. At Northampton, for example, he accepted an additional job on the school committee to earn an extra two hundred dollars for the year. The congregation there did not even own a parsonage, so that he and his young bride, the former Mary Ingraham of Amenia, began married life in the fall of 1851 in a local boarding house. Even with such problems to contend with, Haven managed to complete in half the regular time the conference course of study which the denomination required in the absence of more formal theological education.[61]

Since a prerequisite to clerical fame was to become a popular preacher, Haven was extremely self-conscious in his first appointments to develop a comfortable and effective pulpit style. At Wilbraham, where faculty and students from the Wesleyan Academy made up most of his congregation, he especially suffered the defects of his oratorical manner to trouble him. This source of anxiety continued with him at Westfield, where he once confided to his journal that he perhaps ought to quit the ministry because he "never had any great influence in the pulpit." [62] Only his abolitionist sermons seemed to communicate and evoke lively response, so that when he discoursed on slavery and the sectional controversy, a contemporary reported, he "knew well how to stir the embers." [63]

The major faults with Haven's preaching related to his inability to express ideas with clarity and syntactical precision, particularly when he spoke extemporaneously without adequate preparation. In order to remedy the flaws in his style and to keep a regular schedule for study, he formed in 1854, with two other young ministers in the conference, Fales H. Newhall and George M. Steele, a biweekly discussion group called "The Triangle." The members met to assist each other with exegetical study in the Hebrew Bible and with selections from classical Greek literature and mutually to criticize original essays and sermons. Several compositions, including Haven's first contributions to the denominational journal of religious thought, were worthy of publication.[64] In "The Triangle," which later included another member, Daniel Steele, Haven learned to express himself more cogently and to defend

61. For the list of readings on which Haven stood an eight-hour examination, see *Minutes of the New England Conference,* 1851, pp. 49-51; Prentice, *Life,* pp. 109, 130-31; Daniels, *Memorials of Gilbert Haven,* pp. 48-50; *Northampton Courier* (Mass.), Mar. 16, 1852.

62. Quoted in Prentice, *Life,* p. 152; see also pp. 133-35, 142, 151-54; and Journal of Fales H. Newhall, entries for Apr. 26, 1854; Jan. 20, 1856.

63. Sherman, *The History of the Wesleyan Academy at Wilbraham, Mass. 1817-1890,* p. 318; Daniels, *Memorials of Gilbert Haven,* p. 57.

64. See Haven's "Wordsworth," *Methodist Quarterly Review,* 39 (1857), 362-81; "Infant Baptism and Church Membership," *ibid.,* 41 (1859), 5-26; "John Ruskin," *ibid.,* 42 (1860), 533-54.

his views more persuasively. He also found its social fellowship most appealing. More than once during the six years of the group's existence an evening's study was laid aside for a jolly round of storytelling or for such reading as James Russell Lowell's satirical *Bigelow Papers.* During one such instance, the more scholarly and sober-minded Newhall recorded in his journal, "Gil [did] laughing enough for half a dozen, such companies." [65]

At the conference level among his fellow clergy Haven's drive for professional success displayed itself in a dedicated performance of varied responsibilities. Drawing upon his earlier experience as a teacher, he served first as a member of the general committee on education and on the examining board for the theological course of study. Later he was a founder of the Church Extension Aid Society which helped local congregations on building projects. He supported the Irish Mission in Boston, went on visitation committees to three schools which the conference assisted and worked on the Preacher's Aid and temperance committees. This extensive involvement in the institutional life of the church contributed to his growing reputation as a future conference leader.[66]

While he was working his way up in the conference, Haven played no prominent part in shaping antislavery legislation and strategy until late in the decade. With the majority of the preachers, he identified with the reform party in the denomination which sought to expel slaveowners from the church but by means of constitutional change. In his parishes he endorsed the antislavery positions taken by the Massachusetts Methodist clergy. In one sermon at Wilbraham, for example, he prayed for "the day when every Christian Church shall say to her slaveholding member, 'Repent, and forsake that sin. Let your oppressed go free, or release my hand from the grasp of Christian fellowship.' " [67] In 1855, when he was at Westfield, he also took a public stand against racial caste distinctions which the churches perpetuated. On that occasion Haven was responding to a published notice in *Zion's Herald,* the region's independent Methodist weekly, which warned area ministers against welcoming into their pulpits the famous black woman, Sojourner Truth, since she had associated with reformers "of the socialist, Garrisonian stamp." After chastising the author of the notice, Haven saluted the radicals for "being the first to fraternize with her on terms of perfect equality (in which great duty they have been teachers of Christ to this too prejudiced Church)." Through his earlier acquaintance with the Negro prophetess at her home in Northampton and later as a guest at his own house, Haven was confident, as well, that Sojourner Truth did not adhere to the religious heresies of the Garrisonians.[68]

---

65. Journal of Fales H. Newhall, Nov. 29, 1858; Jan. 26, Feb. 23, 1859; Prentice, *Life*, pp. 162-75.
66. *Minutes of the New England Conference,* 1852, p. 28; 1853, p. 22; 1855, p. 24; 1856, p. 26; 1857, pp. 17, 24, 29; 1859, pp. 20, 22-27; 1860, pp. 15, 23; 1861, pp. 29-32.
67. *National Sermons,* p. 49.
68. *Zion's Herald,* May 2, 16, 1855; *National Sermons,* p. 143; Daniels, *Memorials of Gilbert Haven,*

With these exceptions, however, Haven was content in his first appointments to let matters take their course within the churches. He concentrated more on the ethical implications of political developments connected with slavery than on antislavery reform of the churches, where he believed abolitionism would gradually but ultimately triumph. In 1854 he was in such a characteristically optimistic mood when he predicted of ecclesiastical antislavery, "Here comes an individual church and pastor, there a conference, or association, or synod of churches and pastors, until this act has shot, like a crystallizing force, through Church and ministry, transforming multitudes averse to agitation and abolitionism into the warmest friends of both." [69]

But antislavery reform in northern Methodism made slower progress than Haven admitted. If he and his New England colleagues had strictly interpreted their own declarations refusing fellowship with slaveholding churchmen, they would have withdrawn from the denomination. In the border states where Methodists were more numerous than anywhere else in the country, churchmen in at least eight northern conferences were guilty of owning and trading slaves.[70] Because of competition there with the Methodist Episcopal Church, South, the northern bishops to a man refused to enforce existing disciplinary legislation, which, though weak, admitted a more explicit antislavery interpretation than they chose to give it.

Throughout the decade a powerful conservative faction of editors, bishops, college presidents, and secretaries of denominational agencies opposed all agitation of the question, prevented antislavery liberals from achieving their objectives and forced them to compromise in order to keep the issue alive. At the General Conference of 1852 in Boston, for example, which Haven attended as a visitor, the delegates bowed to the conservative party by burying in committee the few memorials that were presented on the subject of slavery, one of which came from the New England Conference.[71] In addition they created a new conference in Kentucky that would potentially bring in more slaveholding'members on the border. The general conference also gave its approval to informal yearly meetings for "coloured local preachers," thus tacitly refusing to incorporate them into established church structures and

pp. 52-53; Prentice, *Life*, pp. 25, 124. See also Haven's recollection of a visit from Sojourner Truth in 1858 in *New York Christian Advocate*, Aug. 15, 1872.

69. *National Sermons*, p. 48.

70. The ratio of Methodists to the total population was 1 in 38 in New England, 1 in 20 in the middle states. See Norton, "The Religious Press and the Compromise of 1850," pp. 25-26; Swaney, *Episcopal Methodism and Slavery*, ch. 18, especially p. 241, n. 14; *The Liberator*, Feb. 1, 1861.

71. *Minutes of the New England Conference*, 1852, pp. 20-21; *Zion's Herald*, May 26, 1852; Apr. 27, 1853; *Journal of the General Conference of the Methodist Episcopal Church*, 1852, pp. 16, 22-23, 35, 37-40, 47, 54-55, 61, 68-69, 73-74, 103; George Peck, *The Life and Times of Rev. George Peck, D.D.* (New York, 1874), pp. 326-28, 333.

thereby sanctioning racial separation in the northern Methodist ministry.[72]

When the General Conference of 1852 so thoroughly refused to act against slavery in the church, a coalition of antislavery Methodists, drawing its main support from New England, central and western New York, and scattered sections of the Northwest, emerged to challenge the conservative denominational leadership. In the religious press and the annual conferences the reform party explored two basic options for constitutional revision to put some teeth into church law against slave-owning members and ministers. One strategy was to seek approval for a change in the General Rules, which as ethical prescriptions formed moral standards for Methodists. A General Rule on slavery originated as far back as 1789, but it was slightly altered in 1808 with a change of two conjunctions from "or" to "and." From that time on it forbade "The buying *and* selling of men, women *and* children, with an intention to enslave them." [73] Antislavery liberals wanted a more explicit reference not only to slave trading but to ownership as well. The New England Conference adopted one such version of the rule in 1854.[74]

Another strategy was to rewrite the chapter on slavery in the *Discipline*. Since 1824 it had ruled that a layman who held slaves was ineligible for official position in the church, but only "where the laws of the State in which he lives will admit of emancipation, and permit the liberated slave to enjoy freedom." It also required a slave-owning "travelling preacher" to free his bondsmen, "if it be practicable" and "legal." In addition, the section called on preachers to persuade members to teach their slaves to read the Bible and "to allow them time" for divine worship. The rest of the chapter dealt with special regulations to govern the employment of "coloured preachers." [75] The legislation was mild, but for more than thirty years there had been little disposition on the part of Methodist bishops to enforce or the general conferences to strengthen the disciplinary provisions. For this reason reformers insisted both on more explicit prohibitory standards and an executive commitment to carry out a stronger antislavery discipline.

In 1856 Haven's annual conference instructed its delegates to petition the approaching general conference for either disciplinary change, whichever could be put through. The actual memorial that they presented involved both strategies: a new rule forbidding "holding or selling a slave or slaves, or buying, except to emancipate," and a new chapter requiring within three years freedom of all slaves held by church members. The petition eliminated the qualification that required conformity to laws in the states.[76]

72. *Journal of the General Conference*, 1852, pp. 30, 34, 65, 69, 92; *Zion's Herald*, June 2, 9, 1852; Matlack, *The Antislavery Struggle*, pp. 209-16.
73. *Doctrines and Discipline of the Methodist Episcopal Church*, 1852, p. 27. Emphasis mine.
74. *Minutes of the New England Conference*, 1854, p. 30.
75. *Doctrines and Discipline of the Methodist Episcopal Church*, 1852, pp. 209-10.
76. *Minutes of the New England Conference*, 1856, p. 32. Memorials from the New England

Northern Methodists on the border objected vigorously to all new legislation on the question of slavery, so that a showdown at the general conference
was assured. In 1855 the powerful Baltimore Conference even threatened to
secede if there was a change in church law, and it repeated an ultimatum
first issued in 1846 which disfellowshipped abolitionists. Their commitment
"to stand by and maintain the Discipline as it is" was the watchword of the
conservative party.[77] Even in New England the conservatives had a few
allies. Under sponsorship of the denominational book agents, a veteran member of Haven's own conference, Gershom F. Cox, published a pamphlet
early in 1856 in which he protested against all antislavery reform in the
church. Cox contended that the modern church had no right to impose a
nonslaveholding restriction on members since there had been slave owners in
the primitive church and since Jesus made no specific rule against the practice.
Reiterating the views of proslavery Southerners, he denied that the church
had any legislative responsibility on the matter, claiming its only mission was
"to save souls." When he suggested that all reference to slavery should be
removed from the *Discipline,* he recommended, in fact, a position already
undertaken by the Methodist Episcopal Church, South, in 1854.[78]

The majority of Methodists in Massachusetts, however, disagreed with
Cox. At the annual conference in April, Haven's friend, William Rice, set
the tone for the session with a rousing speech before the missionary society
on "The Relation of Slavery to the Nation." The committee on slavery, which
Rice chaired, called for the church to cease apologizing for slavery, to
discipline slave owners and to witness to the "simple truth" of the sinfulness
of slavery by "straight-forward action." The report predicated the peace,
unity, and evangelical success of northern Methodism upon "decisive action"
to expel slavery from "her bosom." [79]

On the third day after the General Conference of 1856 convened, the
bishops struck a death blow to the hopes of the reform party by defending
the chief claims of the conservatives. The episcopal address, which Thomas A.
Morris wrote in behalf of his colleagues, contained no new admonitions
against slavery. On the other hand, Morris commended border Methodists for

---

Conference to the General Conference of 1856, in the papers of the conference at the New England
Methodist Historical Society Library, Boston.

77. Swaney, *Episcopal Methodism and Slavery*, pp. 196, 207. The viewpoint of Methodist conservatives is ably analyzed in Powell's "The Abolitionist Controversy," chs. 4 and 6.

78. *Matter for the Times. Three Questions Answered. What Is Slavery? Were Slaveholders Members of the Apostolic Church? Shall the Church Adopt the Apostolic Standard of Discipline, or
Make a New One?* (Boston, 1856). In 1854 Southern Methodists removed the disciplinary chapter
which they inherited at the time of the division of episcopal Methodism in 1844. See *Journal of the
General Conference of the Methodist Episcopal Church, South,* 1854, pp. 295 ff. Four years later
they rescinded the General Rule. See Ronald T. Takaki, *A Pro-Slavery Crusade. The Agitation to
Reopen the African Slave Trade* (New York: Free Press, 1971), pp. 134-45.

79. *Minutes of the New England Conference,* 1856, pp. 31-32; *Zion's Herald,* Apr. 9, 1856.

"their moral worth," "Christian excellence," "prudent conduct," "intelligence, piety and attachment to Methodist Discipline and economy." He concluded that the existence of northern conferences in slaveholding territory did not "tend to extend or perpetuate slavery." Furthermore, Morris insisted that the general conference was constitutionally powerless to alter the General Rule without *first* obtaining three-fourths approval in the annual conferences. Four separate proposals had been circulated throughout the church in the previous quadrennium, but no one received the required majority in the annual conferences.[80]

Although they were denied episcopal neutrality on the subject, antislavery liberals kept up the fight by flooding the conference with more than 150 petitions, which delayed regular business and provoked a number of counter-memorials from conservatives. After three weeks the general conference began a debate over new legislation that lasted eight days, but in the end the constitutional limits proved insurmountable, and the conservatives emerged victorious. The conference did vote 122 to 96 for an amended General Rule to prohibit "the buying, selling, or holding a human being as property," but the majority was short of the necessary two-thirds vote.[81] The reformers also succeeded in compiling the largest antislavery vote ever in a Methodist general conference, in getting approval to publish antislavery pamphlets through the denominational tract society, and in putting antislavery men into chief editorial positions for the *Methodist Quarterly Review* and the *Western Christian Advocate* in Cincinnati and for Sunday school literature.[82]

Antislavery success in 1856, however, was not as substantial as some reformers, including Haven, claimed.[83] The majority vote on the General Rule was a hollow victory since no change resulted in the church's official position. Although three proreform editors were elected, conservatives brought off a successful coup against William Hosmer, who was undoubtedly the most outspoken abolitionist editor in the denomination and who had been recommended for another term at the helm of the *Northern Advocate* both by its publication committee and by the sponsoring annual conferences

80. *Journal of the General Conference of the Methodist Episcopal Church*, 1856, pp. 199-200. John F. Marlay, *The Life of Rev. Thomas A. Morris, D.D., Late Senior Bishop of the Methodist Episcopal Church* (Cincinnati, 1875), p. 273.

81. Lucius C. Matlack, ed., *Proceedings and Debates of the M.E. General Conference, Held in Indianapolis, Ind., 1856* (Syracuse, 1856), pp. 119-22; *Zion's Herald*, June 4, 1856. For some unexplained reason the majority and minority reports on slavery were omitted from the regular general conference journal in 1856, but the next general conference corrected the deletion and published them in an appendix to the *Journal of the General Conference of the Methodist Episcopal Church*, 1860, pp. 475-80.

82. Daniel D. Whedon and Calvin Kingsley, respectively, were the new editors and Daniel Wise, former editor of *Zion's Herald*, the head of Sunday school publications. Earlier the secretary of the tract society, Abel Stevens, had printed John Wesley's *Thoughts on Slavery* and two moderately antislavery essays by Charles Elliott, but the executive committee had blocked their distribution. Matlack, *Proceedings and Debates*, pp. 355-61; *Zion's Herald*, Mar. 14, Dec. 19, 1855; Jan. 2, 23, Feb. 6, 1856; *Journal of the General Conference*, 1856, pp. 150-52, 157-59.

83. For Haven's retrospective comments, see *The Liberator*, Mar. 29, 1861.

in central and upper New York state.[84] Conservatives likewise continued control over four important editorial posts, including that of the *Christian Advocate and Journal,* which claimed the largest number of subscribers of any denominational paper. Border delegates maneuvered to get larger missionary appropriations for the new conferences in slaveholding territory. They, and conservatives from other areas, dominated committees which wrote in the pastoral address "that little or no mercenary slaveholding exists in the church," and that drew up the report on the state of "colored members" which declared that the privileges and rights of Negro Methodists depended on "the usages of the country." [85] Thus, in refusing to condemn Methodist slaveholding and by sanctioning racial segregation in the church, the action of the general conference was, to say the least, far from an unequivocal antislavery triumph.

In the spring of 1857, when Haven transferred from western Massachusetts to Roxbury, his role in the church struggle underwent a distinct change. From this time on he was more extensively involved in Methodist antislavery reform. In the Boston Methodist Preachers' Meeting, which met weekly to discuss social and political as well as religious and ecclesiastical topics, he promoted church abolitionism and interracial religious contacts. There he came to know Josiah ("Father") Henson, a black Methodist preacher who was an ex-slave and an active leader in the fugitive slave communities of Canada. By this time Henson had already achieved a considerable reputation both in England and in this country as having been the model which Harriet Beecher Stowe used for the chief character in her widely known antislavery novel, *Uncle Tom's Cabin.*[86]

In June, 1857, Haven took an active part in a discussion on whether the Preachers' Meeting should officially support Wilberforce University in Ohio, a school that was being formed exclusively for blacks. Even as he wanted to encourage every effort for wider educational opportunity for Negroes, Haven did not wish to endorse racially segregated schools. The year before, denomi-

84. Many of Hosmer's editorials were republished in *The Higher Law, In Its Relations to Civil Government: With Particular Reference to Slavery, and the Fugitive Slave Law* and in *Slavery and the Church* (Auburn, N.Y., 1852 and 1853, respectively). Both of Hosmer's books have been reprinted by Negro Universities Press, New York, 1969. *Journal of the General Conference,* 1856, pp. 159, 268-69; Matlack, *Proceedings and Debates,* appendix, pp. 1-21. After his defeat Hosmer began publication of the *Northern Independent* in which he continued to expound his abolitionist doctrines.

85. *Journal of the General Conference,* 1856, pp. 100, 162, 183, 297. The basis for classifying "conservatives" is an analysis of the votes on the General Rule and the motion to table the remainder of the majority report on slavery, correlated with membership of these committees. The *Christian Advocate* published in New York city was considered the official Methodist weekly.

86. A sketch of Henson's life and a critical discussion of the mythology that grew up around him is in the recent edition of *An Autobiography of the Reverend Josiah Henson,* with an introduction by Robin W. Winks (Reading, Mass.: Addison-Wesley Publishing Company, 1969). According to the Records of the Methodist Preachers' Meeting for Boston and Vicinity, in the New England Methodist Historical Society Library, Henson visited the weekly association Feb. 1, Mar. 1, 8, Apr. 5, and Nov. 8, 1858. The minutes for Feb. 21, 1859 also note the reception of a letter from Henson requesting financial assistance. See also *Zion's Herald,* Apr. 14, Sept. 29, Oct. 27, 1858.

national conservatives at the general conference had introduced the Wilberforce project with the acknowledged design "to make it emphatically the *colored people's college.*" [87] After debating the matter freely, a majority of the meeting finally approved a motion that backed the school, but with a provision calling on all Methodist institutions to admit Negro students without discrimination.[88]

Early in 1858 Haven found himself squarely in the middle of the denominational controversy when he introduced a series of resolutions at the Preachers' Meeting expressing sympathy for John D. Long, an abolitionist in the ultraconservative Philadelphia Conference. The previous year Long had sparked a violent reaction in his conference and an extensive debate in the church press when he published an exposé of slaveholding, slave trading, and proslavery sentiment among border Methodists.[89] The son of a slaveholder and once a master by inheritance himself, Long was due to stand trial in the conference on charges of misrepresentation. In pressing formal charges against Long, while refusing to discipline slave-owning churchmen, the Philadelphians were, in Haven's view, intolerably hypocritical. On March 15 he persuaded the Boston Methodist preachers to approve his resolutions and their publication in *Zion's Herald* and the *Christian Advocate.* They commended Long for "doing excellent service to our church and the cause of religion by his statements of facts proving the connection of our Church with the great sin of slavery." Furthermore, the resolves sought to convince Long's "opponents" to acknowledge "their error as Methodists and Christian Ministers in their silence on the great sin of slavery, their submission to the demands of slaveholding members and their opposition to those who speak for Christ and the Slave." Haven urged them "not only [to] abandon their efforts to ruin the ministerial character of their brother but [also to] become his assistants in the great work of purifying the Church from this sin." [90] A week later the meeting recalled the order to publish the document, which the officers, meanwhile, had refused to execute. When he could no longer command a majority vote on the issues of the controversy, Haven angrily but unsuccessfully attempted to censure the president and secretary for their failure to carry out the original directive.[91]

After the Philadelphia Conference passed through a turbulent session which involved heated charges and countercharges, Long came to New England to thank his supporters there and to tell his story in person. At the

87. *Journal of the General Conference,* 1856, pp. 270-72. Emphasis in the original.
88. Records of the Boston Methodist Preachers' Meeting, June 22, 1857.
89. John Dixon Long, *Pictures of Slavery in Church and State; Including Personal Reminiscences, Biographical Sketches, Anecdotes, etc. etc. with an Appendix, Containing the Views of John Wesley and Richard Watson on Slavery* (Philadelphia, 1857). Reprinted New York: Negro Universities Press, 1969.
90. Records of the Boston Methodist Preachers' Meeting, Mar. 15, 1858.
91. *Ibid.,* Mar. 22, 29, 1858.

anniversary of the New England Conference Anti-Slavery Society he revealed further the extent of slaveholding in border Methodism, after which "Father" Henson occupied the rest of the meeting, speaking about his life and work.[92] For backing Long, Haven was selected to chair the society for the ensuing year. In official conference action, Massachusetts Methodists praised Long and his book and greeted as "co-laborers in the anti-slavery work" other "newly found friends" on the border, one of whom was J. S. Lame, also from the Philadelphia Conference, who had published a series of letters in *Zion's Herald* that confirmed Long's findings.[93]

The growth of antislavery sentiment and the challenge which they had to face from Long, Lame, and others in the border conferences posed the most formidable opposition which Methodist conservatives had confronted since the Wesleyan abolitionist movement flowered twenty years earlier. Their only hope to block new legislation lay in preventing a single strategy from developing among the reformers. Antislavery churchmen in the conferences in New York state unwittingly aided the conservative cause by refusing to support a move to alter the General Rule. Claiming that they wanted to redeem the antislavery reputation of early Methodism, they argued that the present rule was sufficient, if properly interpreted and enforced. The clamor to change it only conceded the conservative argument that liberals were trying to impose a new standard of membership. Moreover, it was practically impossible on any one version of the rule to get a two-thirds vote in the general conference along with a confirmation by three-fourths of the members of the annual conferences. Instead, the New York faction insisted on a new section on slavery in place of the old chapter in the *Discipline*.[94]

In order to capitalize on the difficulties which constitutional change placed upon liberals, the conservative wing organized for the ensuing confrontation in 1860. An antireform minority in the New York East Conference established the Ministers' and Laymen's Union, with the aging denominational statesman, Nathan Bangs, as president. In circulars mailed to influential laymen the union warned of the danger of new division in the church and sent out its

---

92. *Zion's Herald*, Apr. 14, 1858; *The Liberator*, Apr. 23, 1858.

93. *Minutes of the New England Conference*, 1858, pp. 16, 23-24; *Zion's Herald*, Mar. 31, Apr. 7, 21, 1858; J. S. Lame, *Maryland Slavery and Maryland Chivalry. Containing the Letters of "Junius," Originally Published in Zion's Herald* . . . (Philadelphia, 1858); J. Mayland M'Carter, *Border Methodism and Border Slavery* . . . (Philadelphia, 1858). After the Civil War Long operated the Bedford Street Mission in Philadelphia which had a racially integrated Sunday school. Haven saluted his old friend in *Zion's Herald*, June 26, 1867; Apr. 16, 1868; Jan. 9, 1873.

94. Hiram Mattison, *The Impending Crisis of 1860; Or the Present Connection of the Methodist Episcopal Church with Slavery, and Our Duty in Regard to It*, 4th ed. rev. (New York, 1859), pp. 5-17, 22, 86 ff., 120 ff. and *"What of the Night?" or a Glance at the Recent History, Present Condition, and Future Prospects of the Great Anti-Slavery Struggle in the Methodist Episcopal Church* (New York, 1860), pp. 8-13, 15-24. See also Daniel DeVinné, *The Methodist Episcopal Church and Slavery. A Historical Survey of the Relation of the Early Methodists to Slavery* (New York, 1857). On the sectarian style of reform of New York Methodist abolitionists, see Powell, "The Abolitionist Controversy," ch. 8.

agents to contact other conservatives.[95] There were also new threats from the border. In October, 1858, the *Baltimore Christian Advocate* began publication with the explicit purpose to defend the conferences of the region. Just before the general conference met in 1860, the Maryland clergy floated new rumors of secession and repeated their refusal to fellowship churches which made nonslaveholding a basis for membership.[96] The editor of the *Christian Advocate and Journal* in New York, Abel Stevens, also sided with the border and aligned himself with the new union. Contradicting his earlier antislavery advocacy when he was editor of *Zion's Herald,* Stevens reasoned that the present *Discipline* should not be tampered with, since it permitted northern Methodism to be "slaveholding" though "antislavery," to maintain a general standard against slavery while ministering to both masters and bondsmen. Because Stevens' view had the familiar ring of the southern proslavery religious apologetic, Haven ridiculed it as "that most original of all the original ideas of this century." [97]

Right up until the time of the general conference, New England Methodists hoped that some version of a new General Rule would get enough support to meet constitutional demands, but the campaign was doomed. Nonetheless, Haven and his colleagues continued to work for a change. He helped to write antislavery circulars which the Boston Methodist Preachers' Meeting issued to counter the attempt by the Ministers' and Laymen's Union "to control the Church at the next General Conf[erence] on the Subject of Slavery." [98] In *Zion's Herald* Haven also argued in behalf of an amendment to the General Rule which the New England Conference settled upon in 1859, proposing the insertion of the word "slaveholding" as a prefix to the traditional rule. "It is easily read, easily understood," he wrote. "It has no qualifying words, no *mercenary* or other style of slaveholding, excluded or included. It simply *takes for granted* that slaveholding and slavery are one, and leaves it to the Jesuit Methodist, if such there be, to manufacture his qualifying exception, or allows the offender and his appointed judges to adjust their action to their sense of justice and mercy, under the singleness of eye with which it looks upon them." [99]

The intent of Haven's essay was to find common ground on which Methodists of all shades of antislavery opinion could unite. Some of his remarks about "the fanatical conservatives of Maryland and vicinage," and their new paper, the *Baltimore Advocate,* however, touched off a debate which proved the border party's absolute hostility to any new legislation on slavery. The

95. *Zion's Herald*, Sept. 21, Oct. 5, 19, Nov. 2, Dec. 7, 14, 21, 28, 1859.

96. *Ibid.*, Oct. 20, 1858, Mar. 14, 21, 1860.

97. *Ibid.*, June 8, 1859. Stevens' views appeared in numerous editorials, but his basic position can be found in *An Appeal to the Methodist Episcopal Church Concerning What Its Next General Conference Should Do on the Question of Slavery* (New York, 1859).

98. Records of the Boston Methodist Preachers' Meeting, Sept. 19, Oct. 3, Nov. 28, 1859; Jan. 2, 1860.

99. *Zion's Herald*, June 8, 1859; *Minutes of the New England Conference*, 1859, p. 19.

Advocate's editor, Thomas E. Bond, Jr., responded with some satirical remarks about Haven's style, but the real difficulty was over what had been written, not how it was constructed. In his reply Haven assailed Bond for always ridiculing the foes of slavery while remaining silent before its advocates. He warned of divine judgment upon the entire church unless it removed slavery. Admonishing Bond that the climate of agitation forced him to make a choice, Haven asserted, "You cannot be stationary in this matter. . . . You must drift with the current, if you do not vigorously resist it. It sets southward in your quarter—Beware, lest you go over the dam into the bottomless gulf which has swallowed up the Southern Church." [100]

Even though Haven and other antislavery Methodists represented more power in 1860 than ever before, the conservative strategy to divide and conquer prevailed again. When the New England Conference met in April, it acknowledged "the humiliating fact that there [was] . . . no effectual bar to the admission of slaveholders to membership" in the church. Since antislavery forces could never agree on any one proposal to present to the whole church, William Rice's slavery committee could only recommend that the general conference draw up a plan and submit it to the annual conferences for ratification.[101] After the movement for change had failed at the annual conference level, the reform party tried to make its point with a deluge of petitions to the general conference—811 from 33 conferences signed by 45,857 members of the church, forming an unprecedented mandate for change. Conservatives countered with 137 separate memorials representing 3,999 members opposed to new laws on slavery. For the entire month of May, the conference received petitions on the subject.[102] With few alterations the story of 1856 repeated itself. A new version of the General Rule to outlaw "the buying, selling, or holding of men, women, or children, with an intention to enslave them," was favored by vote of 138 to 74, but again the action failed to obtain the necessary two-thirds majority.[103]

The attempt to write a new chapter for the *Discipline* was only slightly more successful. The antislavery majority rounded up enough support (155 to 58) to replace the old chapter which had been in the *Discipline* unchanged for thirty-six years, a period which antedated the rise of the modern abolitionist movement. The substitution was immediately annulled, however, when conservatives got through a resolution (130 to 55) to express the sense of the general conference that the new chapter had only "declarative and advisory," and not prohibitory, power. Unlike the old section it did apply to all Methodists, laity and clergy alike, and it did condemn slaveholding as well as buying and selling. But without specific disciplinary guidelines to

100. *Zion's Herald*, July 13, 20, 1859. Bond became a member of the Methodist Episcopal Church, South, after the war and continued, until his death, a running battle with Haven in the religious press.
101. *Minutes of the New England Conference*, 1860, p. 18.
102. *Journal of the General Conference*, 1860, pp. 251, 425-26.
103. *Ibid.*, pp. 244-45.

enforce the sentiment and with an episcopal board that would not interpret strictly such controversial legislation, the declaration was more symbolic than productive of effective action against slaveholding Methodists.[104]

Just as in 1856, there were many signs of the continuing power of Methodist conservatism. The bishops in their address discouraged new action on slavery by repeating their praise of border Methodists from four years before. The majority report on slavery itself was far from an abolitionist document. The committee stated baldly: "We do not affirm that the holding of a slave is, under all circumstances, sinful; nor is the buying or selling." The minority report, like that of 1856, warned of the dangers of disunion in new antislavery legislation. The pastoral address emphasized that the new chapter on slavery was only "a declaration of principles" whose application necessitated "due regard" for the laws on slavery in the states. The general conference also continued its policy of exclusion against black Methodists. The church refused to grant regular powers, including the right to elect and ordain ministers, to the informal yearly conferences for Negroes. When they failed to act on a petition "to admit Colored Preachers to membership in our Annual Conferences," white Methodists made clear that they were not willing to provide any equal place for blacks in the church.[105] Behind the scenes various committees quietly disposed of abolitionist efforts to deal in specific cases of breach of discipline by slaveholding local and traveling preachers and of illegal administration by Bishop Edward R. Ames at the Philadelphia Conference in 1858 which tried John D. Long.[106]

There was, as before, a great surge of antislavery spirit evident at the general conference. When Haven evaluated the outcome, he pointed to the progress which had been made, but again he overestimated the actual degree of abolitionism in the denomination. Of the new chapter in the *Discipline,* he asserted that northern Methodism "has by an immense majority, publicly expelled the fiend [of slavery] from her midst." [107] When *The Liberator* called him to account by quoting a host of testimony on the extent of actual slaveholding in the church, he attempted to set aside the evidence by claiming defensively that "there are thousands of Methodist preachers [who are] as good and true Abolitionists as any" who never earned a line of recognition from Garrison and his followers.[108]

Haven could not deny, of course, that many Methodist abolitionists in New York state seceded in 1860 because the general conference action on slavery continued to be so weak. Some of them formed the Free Methodist Church, which, like the Wesleyans, wrote antislavery standards into its con-

104. *Ibid.,* pp. 258-62.
105. *Ibid.,* pp. 308, 319, 404-17, 469.
106. *Ibid.,* pp. 131, 158, 160, 191, 277.
107. *Zion's Herald,* June 27, 1860; see also *The Liberator,* Mar. 29, 1861.
108. *The Liberator,* Feb. 1, Mar. 1, 1861.

stitution.[109] Nor could Haven overlook the border's local nullification of antislavery principles which had been clearly stated, if only as an admonition, by the general conference. A sizeable contingency of the Baltimore and East Baltimore conferences was making good the threat to repudiate any action on slavery by withdrawing from the denomination to establish an independent organization, which, after the war, united with the Methodist Episcopal Church, South. When Bishop Levi Scott tried to pacify border churchmen and prevent division by construing the provisions of the new disciplinary chapter as inapplicable there, his action further demonstrated how mild was the official Methodist antislavery commitment. Haven tried in vain to get the New England Conference to reprimand Scott for his decision, since, in his view, it was not consistent with northern Methodism's stronger "public posture" on slavery in 1860. The very belligerency of "the Maryland conferences" was proof to Haven that antislavery forces had come to power in the denomination. "The conscience of the slaveholders," he wrote, "makes them interpret our words and deeds according to their real intent." [110]

Whatever antislavery progress had been made, however, the Methodist Episcopal Church had not become abolitionist. When pressed on the matter, Haven could only resort to the excuse that the church, being a voluntary society, was often "helpless for a season against the disobedience of some of her subjects." Then he went to the heart of his difference with Garrison and the contrast between their abolitionist strategies, applied in this case to church antislavery reform. When Garrison demanded separation from "a Church thus contaminated," Haven claimed that no other denomination had as good an antislavery record as his own. He refused to "come out" of the church, because "the world [was] far more identified with this iniquity, as well as with every other, than any branch of the real Church of Christ." If he withdrew from his present ecclesiastical relation, moreover, he would be compelled to join or found another church. For an analogy, Haven turned to politics. In desperation over the proslavery corruption of national principles and parties, the Garrisonians had renounced the American political process as corrupt, and they refused to vote or campaign during elections. To Haven, however, such separation was finally impossible, because its logic, "to leave the State," would lead finally to "the utter barbarism of no civil society." Since separation was not possible, some compromise was inevitable, and because, with its imperfections, the Methodist Episcopal Church was "greatly in advance" of the nation in "antislavery action," he would not abandon it.[111]

109. Powell, "The Abolitionist Controversy," pp. 215-19.

110. *Ibid.*, p. 191; *Christian Advocate and Journal*, Mar. 21, May 2, 1861; *Minutes of the New England Conference*, 1861, pp. 25-26; "Protest of the Baltimore Annual Conference of the Methodist Episcopal Church," a broadside against the "new chapter on slavery" in the New England Methodist Historical Society Library; Robert D. Clark, "Methodist Debates and Union Sentiment on the Border, 1860-1861," in J. Jeffery Auer, ed., *Antislavery and Disunion, 1858-1861: Studies in the Rhetoric of Compromise and Conflict* (New York: Harper & Row, 1963), pp. 168-70.

111. *The Liberator*, Mar. 29, 1861.

By reminding Garrison that all men compromise at some point in order to accomplish any partial good, Haven sought to vindicate his own course of action in the church struggle. Earlier he wrote a similar caveat by observing that Garrison implicated himself in the abhorrent system of slavery even when he purchased a slave to free him from his master. That act compromised the abstract principle, that slaves deserved their liberty without paying owners, by tacitly acknowledging the claim to human property.[112] In time, however, Haven would come to see how much more accurate than his own was Garrison's estimate of northern Methodist complicity with slavery and to appreciate the editor's final statement in their debate—"But let us all be uncompromising in the cause of liberty." For the present Haven was content to have wrung out of Garrison grudging recognition and even a reluctant greeting for the "earnest minority of ministers and lay members . . . zealously laboring to make [Methodism] wholly and actively on the side of the oppressed." [113]

III

The radical nature of Haven's views on slavery and caste was not as apparent in his position regarding the reform of northern Methodism as it was in his social and political outlook. Since his style of ecclesiastical abolitionism was gradualist in strategy, there were fundamental compromises in his position. He faced similar problems in the effort to translate his theory into social and political practice. He wished to reform church and state, to free American society from the scandal of ownership in human beings and from the racist presuppositions which upheld that system. The language of reform and of moral suasion, which he continued to echo throughout the decade, was inadequate for the social and political realities of which he was also increasingly aware. He did not resolve those tensions, however, until civil war provided its own solution, proving that slavery would not be abolished peaceably. Up to that time Haven sought to utilize the influence of the church to mold the nation's social norms and political morality. But, as in the case of ecclesiastical reform, he was dependent on the growth of public opinion over which he had little control.

From the occasion of his first official association with the annual conference in April, 1851, Haven found that New England Methodists were aware of the church's social and political responsibility. During that session he witnessed the revival of the previously defunct Conference Anti-Slavery Society, which had been the central organization for Methodist abolitionism in New England in the 1830s.[114] On April 24 the Society turned its anniversary meeting into a rally against the Fugitive Slave Law. On the same day the preachers greeted

112. *Ibid.*, Mar. 1, 1861.
113. *Ibid.*, April 5, 1861.
114. See Haven's dedication and introduction to *National Sermons*, pp. iii, vi.

with loud "amens" the news that Free Soil candidate Charles Sumner had been elected to the United States Senate. They were relieved that the election, after twenty-six ballots in the state house of representatives, was finally settled, but they also rejoiced that an antislavery politician was to occupy the seat of Daniel Webster (now secretary of state) who had angered his constituency for having led northern support of the Compromise of 1850.[115]

In keeping with the mood of the conference that year Massachusetts Methodism publicly opposed the recent deportations of two blacks from Boston to the South, which acts, in the clergymen's eyes, had made local magistrates and police authorities into accomplices with slave-catchers. More than a hundred members of the conference, including Haven, formally memorialized the state senate against the local execution of the objectionable law. Besides endangering "the liberty of many of their colored Christian brethren," the petitioners declared, "this oppressive statute" led "to the demoralization of the public mind," injured "the humanity and moral sense of the people," and threatened "the popular reverence for the law and the officers of justice." As "public teachers of religion," they implored the legislature "to prevent further harm to the moral sense and ancient honor of the State of Massachusetts" by doing whatever it could to correct the abuses which the law entailed. The preachers also defended themselves against "the charge of meddling with subjects foreign to their sacred calling," thereby confirming Haven's own commitment to a ministry which guarded "the moral sentiments of the people." [116]

Three years later, when the congressional debate triggered new outbursts in the sectional controversy, Haven and his conference associates again took a public stand, joining more than three thousand other clergy in New England, and, before the excitement subsided, another five hundred ministers from the Northwest. Senator Stephen A. Douglas' Kansas and Nebraska Bill proposed to nullify the provision of the Missouri Compromise of 1820, which prevented the extension of slavery north of a line running $36°30''$ latitude. The village of Wilbraham, Haven's parish, was a microcosm of New England reaction. On April 19, while Haven was away at annual conference, the citizens joined the faculty and students at Fisk Hall on the campus of the Wesleyan Academy to denounce the bill. The mass meeting featured "an array of nine inflammable speakers" from the student body to whom the audience responded enthusiastically. A month later, just as the bill was coming up for final vote, the rendition in Boston of Anthony Burns, a fugitive slave, aroused the community to new protest. The townspeople mourned their "dead liberties" as the bells of the academy and of local churches tolled the whole day on which

---

115. *Minutes of the New England Conference,* 1851, pp. 7-9; *Zion's Herald,* May 7, 1851; *Northampton Courier,* Apr. 29, 1851; David Donald, *Charles Sumner and the Coming of the Civil War* (New York: Alfred A. Knopf, 1960), pp. 183-204.

116. *Minutes of the New England Conference,* 1851, pp. 38-40; *Zion's Herald,* May 7, 1851. On the exodus of black churchmen from Boston after passage of the Fugitive Slave Law, see Quarles, *Black Abolitionists,* pp. 199-200.

Burns was deported. On the following Sunday, Jonathan D. Bridge, Haven's presiding elder, preached in the Methodist church on Jeremiah 5:30—"A wonderful and horrible thing is committed in the land." The citizenry responded by hanging on an elm tree in town an effigy of the commissioner who surrendered Burns to his captors. Six weeks of excitement reached a climax on the Sunday following the passage of Douglas' legislation when Haven delivered an oration on "The Death of Freedom." [117]

At the regular session of the New England Conference that spring, Methodists joined area ministers in a "united clerical protest" to the United States Senate which Harriet Beecher Stowe organized and financed from the royalties of her *Uncle Tom's Cabin*.[118] The petition in the form of a scroll two hundred feet long had already been presented to the Senate in March, and the debate over its reception heard Douglas indict the memorialists with having "desecrated the pulpit, and sacred desk to the miserable and corrupting influence of party politics." [119] Such remarks helped keep the campaign alive, and New England Methodists were part of the renewed effort. Their memorial was the standard text that other clergymen had signed. It condemned the repeal of "existing legal prohibitions of slavery" in the territories and called Douglas' bill "a great moral wrong," "a breach of faith," and "a measure full of danger to the peace and even to the existence of our beloved Union, and exposing us to the righteous judgments of the Almighty." [120] Late in May, Senator Sumner reintroduced the memorial with new support, but the majority of the body again blocked its consideration and adopted the legislation, though not before the Massachusetts representative issued his final protest against the bill along with a defense of the New England clergy.[121]

The clerical protests of 1851 and of 1854 were only the more dramatic examples of responses made during the decade by the New England Conference to national developments affecting slavery. In 1857 the preachers condemned the Dred Scott Decision of the Supreme Court which effectively denied that Negroes possessed the same birthright to citizenship as other Americans. They dissented as well from Governor Henry J. Gardner's fast day proclamation that year asking the clergy to "abstain from political discussions and secular considerations" of "national transgressions," and instead "to address the spiritual wants of the individual heart." It was obvious to the

---

117. Sherman, *History of the Wesleyan Academy*, pp. 318-19; *Zion's Herald*, May 3, 1854; *National Sermons*, pp. 33-56.

118. Donald, *Charles Sumner* (1960), pp. 259-60; Forrest Wilson, *Crusader in Crinoline. The Life of Harriet Beecher Stowe* (Philadelphia: J. B. Lippincott Co., 1941), pp. 400-401.

119. *Congressional Globe*, 33rd Cong., 1st sess., 28, pp. 617-23.

120. *Minutes of the New England Conference*, 1854, p. 31. Methodism's official weekly, *Christian Advocate and Journal* in New York, refused to print the petition despite the conference's request. *Zion's Herald*, June 14, 1854.

121. *Appendix to the Congressional Globe*, 33rd Cong., 1st sess., 31, pp. 653-61, 836-40, 883; *Zion's Herald*, June 7, 14, 1854; *National Sermons*, pp. ix, 104.

ministers that the governor wished to silence the clerical voice against slavery, so that they were all the more determined to fulfill their "duty" by bringing "the whole moral power of the pulpit to bear against this great evil." [122] The next year the conference commended the congressional delegation from the state for its antislavery consistency. In 1859 the preachers stated their "deep indignation" over new efforts to reopen the African slave trade and expressed their great regret "that the sentiment prevails to any extent in the nation that territories, as such, are open to the existence of Slavery." [123]

As in the case of antislavery church reform, Haven's views coincided with the conference majority on these issues. Of the court decision which said Negroes had "no rights which white men are bound to respect," he exclaimed, "My God, what a decree! Let us obey God rather than man, and hold in higher respect their natural and divine rights." [124] From the pulpit he answered politicians like Douglas and Gardner who wanted the clergy to refrain from meddling in state affairs. He cited biblical examples of prophetic and apostolic chastisement of political authorities. "What is this 'consecrated politics' that is beyond the reach of the Word of God?," he asked indignantly. "Away with all such blasphemous folly. We ask no pardon for entering this arena. The greatest crimes that ever broke away from hell, and emerged on this fair earth, are being defiantly committed by the rulers of this nation. . . . God forbid that I should keep silence." [125]

In contrast, Haven charged those preachers who confined "their discourse to the abstract nature of God, or sin, or holiness" and sought to be neutral regarding slavery with responsibility for American Christianity's "oppressed gospel, oppressed in its preaching, in its discipline, in its literature, in its whole character and claim." [126] What was needed was a ministry to "give deliverance to the captive, and open the prison door to the bound," "to preach a full salvation, salvation from all sin, personal, social, national," and to plead "for God and humanity against the contemptible prejudices of this age and nation." [127] Such a ministry of social reform Haven envisioned for himself. By the end of the decade through an independent course of action in his writing and preaching he had come to represent a more extreme social and political position than any of his Methodist contemporaries. His views even earned some notice outside his own conference as well as within the region.[128]

122. *Minutes of the New England Conference*, 1857, pp. 25-27; *The Liberator*, Mar. 27, Apr. 3, 1857.
123. *Minutes of the New England Conference*, 1858, p. 23; 1859, p. 19.
124. *Daily Evening Traveller*, Nov. 15, 1859 (*National Sermons*, p. 167). See also *Zion's Herald*, Oct. 14, 1857; and *National Sermons*, pp. 505-6.
125. *National Sermons*, pp. 88-90, 104.
126. *Ibid.*, p. 90; *Westfield News Letter*, June 18, 1856 (*National Sermons*, p. 72).
127. *National Sermons*, pp. 49, 88-89, 147.
128. See the review of his sermon on Lincoln's election in the *Methodist Quarterly Review*, 43 (1861), 352-53. His sermon on John Brown's raid in 1859 was published in an anthology of responses to the event edited by James Redpath and entitled *Echoes of Harper's* [sic] *Ferry* (Boston, 1860). Arno Press and the *New York Times* reprinted this volume in 1969 in the series, "The Anti-Slavery Crusade in America."

All but one of Haven's antebellum sermons which are extant responded to specific crises in the sectional controversy over slavery. Another address that does not survive alluded to the divisions that resulted from the Compromise of 1850. That discourse he delivered on the State Fast Day in the First Church (Congregational) of Northampton, and he later described it as "half-way antislavery in language, and wholly so in tendency, to the great joy of the Abolitionists, and the great rage of the Websterian portion of the audience." [129] Two years after his sermon on the Kansas-Nebraska Bill he eulogized Charles Sumner, who had been brutally beaten on the floor of the United States Senate by Congressman Preston Brooks of South Carolina. Before his Westfield congregation he identified the senator with all the martyrs for truth in history. After the elections of 1856 Haven called the Democratic victory "the national midnight." In 1859 he considered John Brown's ill-fated raid on Harpers Ferry, Virginia, to be "the beginning of the end of American Slavery," which title he gave to a discourse in Cambridge. On Brown's day of execution in December he also prepared, but was not permitted to deliver, a further endorsement of the heroism of the insurrectionists. In a sermon whose title he prefaced with *"Te Deum Laudamus,"* Haven told his Cambridge congregation that Abraham Lincoln's victory in 1860 clinched the fate of slavery and began to restore America's reputation for freedom among the nations of the world.[130]

Haven's abolitionist preaching traced out the pattern of tensions that finally led to civil war, but he did not offer a narrowly sectional interpretation of the national dilemma. He intended not to array "the North against the South, but the whole nation, North and South, against this sin" of slavery.[131] The American crisis, he believed, was rooted preeminently in moral factors, the difference over which subverted and finally "disrupted peaceful sectional relations." [132] His sermons, therefore, emphasized national complicity in the sins of slavery and racial caste, the necessity for national repentance and the hope for national salvation.

In his effort to develop a collective conscience on the evil of slavery and to

129. Quoted in a letter to his father, undated, in Prentice, *Life,* pp. 109-10.

130. All these sermons, including the address which was not given in December, 1859 (though Haven claimed that it was published in *Zion's Herald*), are in *National Sermons,* pp. 1-212. His reference is on p. 169, note at the bottom, but there is no evidence that the Dec. 8, 1859 issue of *Herald* contained the sermon, either in its regular columns or as a supplement. Three of the sermons, were published separately after they were delivered: "The State Struck Down," preached June 8, 1856 (not June 11, as Haven reported in *National Sermons,* p. 57), and published under the heading "Sermon for the Times" in the *Westfield News Letter,* June 18, 1856; "The Beginning of the End of American Slavery," preached on Nov. 6, 1859 and published first in the *Daily Evening Traveller,* Nov. 15, 1859, and reprinted in Redpath, *Echoes of Harper's Ferry,* pp. 125-40; and "The Cause and the Consequence of the Election of Abraham Lincoln" delivered Nov. 11, 1860, and printed in pamphlet form late that year, with extracts appearing in *Zion's Herald,* Feb. 6, 1861 and *The Liberator,* Jan. 18, 1861.

131. *Daily Evening Traveller,* Nov. 15, 1859 (*Echoes of Harper's Ferry,* pp. 135-36; *National Sermons,* p. 164).

132. Louis Filler, *The Crusade Against Slavery 1830-1860* (New York: Harper Torchbooks, 1963), p. 276.

win a commitment to social reformation, Haven drew once again upon his New England religious heritage. His homiletic style resembled the Puritan jeremiad in which the logic of the covenant theology spelled out a fallen people's need of repentance and warned of divine retribution for their sins. According to Perry Miller's reading of the covenant tradition in colonial and early nineteenth century America, the jeremiad, changed beyond recognition by 1850, survived "only as a species of utilitarian exhortation" because there was no longer "any living sense of a specific bond between the nation and God." [133] But Haven certainly had not abandoned the idea of a national bond with God. He invoked the "higher law" theme against "the wicked lie of popular sovereignty" on the basis of a covenant relation which subsumed national destiny and political authority to divine sovereignty. Moreover, he assumed that Americans were as "a people, the peculiar people of God" and that uniquely in this land God had given to man "the principles of His government and attributes of His nature." [134] The "abolitionist jeremiad" [135] was a species of utilitarian exhortation only if one were willing, as Haven never was, to maintain an ethical neutrality toward Negro bondage or to ignore the racist perversion of American democracy. In an important sense, then, the jeremiad was neither inoperative nor ineffective, but transformed to relate to new national sins, it was an accustomed formula by which Haven engaged in the ritual of the moral condemnation of society.[136]

Haven employed the jeremiad in his critique of a political system which was erected upon compromises over slavery and of a national economy which heavily depended upon cotton production and slave labor. By 1857 he could write without extensive explanation as to his meaning about "that solid mass of pro-slavery power that has petrified itself in all the offices and legislation of the Union." [137] He was convinced as well "that slavery would not die bloodlessly, unless the monied power was brought to bear against it." [138] Not only the operative forms of government and commerce, but the slogans and symbols of national identity and ideology were also contradicted by a way of life that apathetically accepted human enslavement. After the passage of the Kansas-Nebraska Bill, for example, Haven lamented that the nation had given up "the Declaration of Independence," "the Constitution," "the names of our Pilgrim and Puritan ancestry, our hopes and prospects, our morals and

133. "From the Covenant to the Revival," in James Ward Smith and A. Leland Jamison, eds., *The Shaping of American Religion* (Princeton: Princeton University Press, 1961), p. 361.

134. *National Sermons*, pp. 86, 93.

135. David Brion Davis uses the designation in his *The Slave Power Conspiracy and the Paranoid Style* (Baton Rouge: Louisiana State University Press, 1969), pp. 79-82.

136. William Gribbin suggests that the covenant tradition "not only developed into evangelical revivalism but also was transformed . . . into rationale for fervid, and continuing, reform," but he stops short of showing how the jeremiad related to the moral and sectional crises over slavery. See "The Covenant Transformed: The Jeremiad Tradition and the War of 1812," *Church History*, 40 (September, 1971), 297-305.

137. *Zion's Herald*, Sept. 30, 1857, where Haven uses the pseudonym "Voluntary Compensationist."

138. *Ibid.*, Jan. 2, 1861.

religion" to lay "at the feet of Slavery." In the same oration he proclaimed that "there should be no more Fourth of July," for "its celebration [was] a mockery" where "the human auction-block, the whipping-post, the branding-iron, the bloodhound, the gallows-tree, and the stake" were "the true elements of a nation's growth and glory." [139]

One of the ways that Haven dramatized how national sins were incarnated in American life was to use the common refrain of a slave power threat. The thesis was based on the claim that "southern slaveholders, organized politically as a Slave Power, were conspiring to dominate the national government, reverse the policy of the founding fathers, and make slavery the ruling interest of the republic." [140] The roots of the slave power theme lay in the rhetoric of antislavery politics during the 1840s, but beginning with heightened fears which the Compromise of 1850 provoked, the charge of subversion had a more convincing ring to it than ever before. Those who adopted it, including Haven, read national history from the perspective of an internal conspiracy that endangered the vitals of American democracy.[141]

Though the word itself was omitted from the national compact, initial concessions to slavery occurred in the Constitution "in its representative basis" and "in its fugitive clause," opening the way for proslaveryites to insist that slavery was "a co-heir with Liberty, of the great inheritance just won from Britain." Prior to the passage of the Constitution, Haven noted, the Ordinance of 1787 had already permitted slavery into the country south of Ohio, a territory which later comprised four large and influential slave states. The Fugitive Slave Law of 1793, which he described as "the ancestor of our present accursed Fugitive Slave Bill," became the first national embodiment of slavery in a legislative statute. Then, in 1820 the famous compromise between the sections over rights to the territories brought Missouri, Arkansas, and Louisiana into the Union "under the pirate flag" of "the slave power." The progress of that power proceeded apace to bar antislavery petitions and debates in the congress and to refuse the use of the mails to abolitionist publications. Because slave power advocates manifested the same spirit of expansion shared by other Americans of the era, they asserted their rights to carry chattels, as property, into the new territories. Subsequently, from Haven's point of view, they won the annexation of Texas, provoked the Mexican War, and forced the terms for the Compromise of 1850. The adoption of the Kansas-Nebraska Act and the election of James Buchanan to the presidency were but the latest in the series of slave power victories. The culminating result made America "of all Christian, of all heathen lands" into "the propa-

139. *National Sermons*, pp. 34-35, 45.
140. Eric Foner, *Free Soil, Free Labor, Free Men. The Ideology of the Republican Party before the Civil War* (London: Oxford University Press, 1970), p. 73.
141. *Ibid.*, ch. 3; and Davis, *The Slave Power Conspiracy*, pp. 18-19.

gandist of slavery, the advocate and practicer of the dogma that man can, and should, and shall own his fellow-man." [142]

The conspiracy thesis always implied that aggression and expansion were essential to slavocratic designs, or as Haven put it, "the slave power must advance or die." On several occasions he predicted the awful results that would befall the nation if the slave power was successful in prostrating "the whole country under [its] hoof." In a dark picture of the end of free society and the dawn of universal tyranny and repression, he forecasted that Kansas would become a slave state; that slavery would be accepted in all territories and perhaps carried into Central and South America; that the African slave trade would be resumed; that antislavery statesmen, preachers, and editors would be silenced; and that slave pens would appear in New York and Boston as the institution expanded into all parts of the land.[143] Sufficient numbers of Northerners came to believe, with Haven, in such a plot to nationalize slavery that the Free Soil and Republican parties were able to make effective political capital out of the doctrine of nonextension.[144]

When Haven contended that there were but "two parties in this land, the Slave and the Free" struggling for the control of the country, he was identifying the more basic ideological battle of antagonistic principles with the sectional conflict.[145] It was natural enough to draw that conclusion if one believed, as did Haven, that the northern states "more than any other Nationalities in the world" represented "the Christianity of the Nineteenth Century" and that they embodied more of "the fruits of Christianity" within "a higher state of culture than any other people." [146] Since he assumed that the North possessed a superior civilization, Haven was tempted at times of crisis to employ "the ultimate symbols of polarization" to the sectional dispute.[147] The most extreme example when he yielded to this temptation appeared in his sermon of June, 1856, on the caning of Sumner by Brooks. The two men personified the sectional conflict—Sumner as the noble martyr in the cause of liberty, Brooks as the prototype of the degenerate slaveholder. But the contrasting pair also represented the eternal antagonism between good and evil, giving to Haven's description a quasi-cosmic, apocalyptic quality. Sumner had received "the blows of Arch-Iniquity" from Brooks.

It was Anarchy assaulting Order; deepest Ignorance the highest Learning; savage Habits, the finest Culture; coarse Speech, exquisite Style; foul Declamation, perfect Oratory. It was Barbarism beating Civilization; diabolic Passions, the self

142. *National Sermons*, pp. 36-37, 44-45, 92-93; *Westfield News Letter*, June 18, 1856 (*National Sermons*, pp. 63-64).
143. *National Sermons*, pp. 50, 100-106; *Westfield News Letter*, June 18, 1856 (*National Sermons*, pp. 79-82); *Zion's Herald*, Sept. 30, 1857.
144. Nye, *Fettered Freedom*, pp. 229-32.
145. *Westfield News Letter*, June 18, 1856 (*National Sermons*, pp. 78-79).
146. *Westfield News Letter*, July 2, 1856; see also *Election of Abraham Lincoln*, pp. 34-36.
147. Davis, *The Slave Power Conspiracy*, p. 61.

control and purity of a Perfect Man—grossest Irreligion, most spiritual Christianity. It was Idleness murdering Industry; Piracy, honorable Trade; Disunion. the confederacy of Free and Sovereign States—Slavery, Freedom; progressive debasement in every work and want of man, cleaving down progressive enlightenment in every walk of the soul. It was, *in fine*, every Vice throttling every Virtue; Satan attacking God.[148]

The symbol of the slave power abetted sectional polarization and oversimplified complex social forces and political realities in both the North and the South. Sometimes it took absurd forms. Occasionally Haven even equated the symbol with the number of slaveholders—fifty thousand in one reference, a quarter million in another.[149] Nonetheless, the conspiracy argument contained much truth. Throughout the decade Southerners were shaping the rudiments of a separate nation whose cornerstone was Negro bondage. Dixie politicians in Washington used the secession threat to good effect, working to control the national administrations of Millard Fillmore, Franklin Pierce, and Buchanan. In the structure of southern society and in the collective consciousness of regional identity slavery was wedded to the way of life, expressing itself simultaneously as an economic institution, a method of racial control, a political ideology, and a religious mission. The South had become a closed society, defensive of its moral position in the modern world and aggressive of its rights in the nation. Southern proponents also had their own version of ultimate polarization, in which "the parties," according to one prominent proslavery religious leader, were "not merely abolitionists and slaveholders" but "atheists, socialists, communists, red republicans, jacobins, on the one side, and the friends of order and regulated freedom on the other." [150]

Fundamentally Haven used the slave power thesis to symbolize the extent to which the interests of slavery were dominant in political and economic life and to urge a "complete conversion of the Government from Slavery to Freedom in all its ideas and acts, in every branch and office of its power." [151] Therefore, he subordinated the sectional conflict to the moral and ideological clash which was being contested not only between North and South but within his own region as well. For twenty-five years the moral struggle against slavery had been championed by abolitionists, whom Haven described as national prophets who "lifted up their voice like a trumpet, and told the house of Israel its transgressions, and the house of Judah its sins." But the nation, North and South, spurned "the new apostles of Jesus Christ." Their message of "sym-

148. *Westfield News Letter*, June 18, 1856 (a slightly altered version of the quotation is in *National Sermons*, p. 61).

149. *National Sermons*, p. 106; *Daily Evening Traveller*, Nov. 15, 1859 (*Echoes of Harper's Ferry*, p. 133; *National Sermons*, p. 161); Davis, *The Slave Power Conspiracy*, pp. 7-10.

150. James Henley Thornwell, "Slavery and the Religious Instruction of the Coloured Population," *Southern Presbyterian Review*, 4 (1850), 114; Foner, *Free Soil*, pp. 99-100.

151. *Westfield News Letter*, June 18, 1856 (*National Sermons*, p. 75; see also p. 50).

pathy with the slave as a son of man and a son of God, an heir of heaven, a joint heir with Jesus Christ," no church dared "fully and faithfully" to preach. From Boston to "the shores of the Mississippi" these agitators endured mob violence for trying to awaken the public conscience "to the dreadful character and workings of slavery." [152]

As a counterattack against continuing antiabolitionism Haven was willing to align the moral cause of emancipation with the defense of northern liberties, but he made clear that no protection of sectional interests could ignore what slavery did to its victims. Before his Westfield congregation he maintained with reference to enslaved blacks, "You are, you must be if a defender of your own rights, a defender of theirs. Abolitionist, Negro worshiper, Black Republican, whatever name is attached, honorably or contemptuously to the upholder of the great sentiment of perfect human equality and brotherhood must be your title." [153] However much slavery had polarized sectional politics, its greatest cost was in terms of human suffering through the systematic oppression of black people. In 1856 Haven argued that the new Republican party's slogan should not have been slavery's peril to "Free Labor" but its destruction of "the rights of our brethren." He concluded, "It is their wrongs and not ours that are shaking this land." [154]

Racial oppression in America appeared in its most extreme form in the southern institution of perpetual servitude, but the plight of free Negroes who were everywhere plagued with a system of racial segregation revealed that injustice to blacks was a national and not a regional phenomenon.[155] Because of its racial character Haven's condemnation of slavery was in itself a critique of national attitudes and practices. But he and other abolitionists also turned their philosophy of human equality into a direct attack upon caste, or white racism, which, in his view, was the special sin of the North as slavery was of the South.[156]

"The cornerstone of this system is prejudice against color," Haven proclaimed in a sermon linking slavery and caste that he preached at Wilbraham and at Roxbury and in which he developed most fully his antebellum racial views.[157] He assailed the more obvious manifestations of "colorphobia" and attributed to the "sinful aversion" of caste the failure of the "Free North" to show southern slaveholders that whites could accept the idea of a society in

152. *Westfield News Letter*, June 18, 1856 (*National Sermons*, pp. 65-66); *Election of Abraham Lincoln*, pp. 12, 18 ff.; *National Sermons*, pp. 37-38.

153. *Westfield News Letter*, June 18, 1856 (*National Sermons*, p. 72).

154. *Westfield News Letter*, June 18, 1856 (*National Sermons*, p. 74); *National Sermons*, pp. 39-42, 95-97, 107, 110; *Daily Evening Traveller*, Nov. 15, 1859 (*Echoes of Harper's Ferry*, pp. 138-39; *National Sermons*, p. 167).

155. The standard account of racial discrimination in the antebellum North is Leon F. Litwack, *North of Slavery: The Negro in the Free States, 1790-1860* (Chicago: University of Chicago Press, 1961).

156. *National Sermons*, p. 126.

157. *Ibid.*, pp. 123 ff.

which both races could live on terms of equality and justice. "When they observe," he admonished, "with all our abolitionism, no recognition of the unity of man; when they see these, our brethren, set apart in churches and schools, . . . when they behold every avenue of honorable effort shut against them,—that no clerk of this complexion is endured in our stores, no apprentice in our workshops, no teacher in our schools, no physician at our sick-beds, no minister in our pulpits,—how can we reproach them for their sins, or urge them to repentance?" [158] Northerners who believed "the dogma of necessary segregation" sanctioned southern slavery, Haven insisted. All who cherished "a pride of caste" and made "complexion a Heaven-appointed barrier of separation" were apologists and defenders of "the system of slavery, commending the graces of the masters, the submission, contentment, and even happiness of the slave." [159]

To end slavery and cure its source, racial caste, Haven called for a spirit of national repentance that would transform attitudes and, in turn, affect social practice. He asked his parishioners to identify with the suffering of the bondsman, to feel within themselves the psychic meaning of the loss of one's freedom, "to pray for the slave as one with him." [160] Likewise he enjoined his hearers to "feel the brotherhood of man" and to extirpate "the great sin of this nation," caste, from themselves and from "every heart" which they could influence.[161]

As he preached, Haven condemned and admonished, but he also sought to create an incentive to envision what could be. He dreamed of a future American society "where civil and social equality and fraternity, where the humanity of man, is the passport to every station," and he wanted others to share that vision.[162] Haven often began his sermons with dismal prophecies of gloom, but in the end he reaffirmed his hope in the eventual realization of that dream. The Kansas-Nebraska Act might have been "the death of freedom," but the hope for resurrection kept the struggle alive.[163] Buchanan's election was "the national midnight," but "a brighter day" and "the salvation of this nation" would come. In the same discourse he drew upon the Hebraic covenant symbols of the Flood and the Exodus to lift up the promise that "this enslaved nation . . . all of us, black and white, North and South," would yet be led "into the land of holy liberty." [164]

As important as were general appeals to conscience, empathy, and brother-

---

158. *Ibid.*, pp. 42, 139-40; *The Liberator*, Nov. 6, 1857; *Westfield News Letter*, June 18, 1856 (*National Sermons*, p. 73).

159. *National Sermons*, p. 42.

160. *Westfield News Letter*, June 18, 1856 (*National Sermons*, pp. 71-75); *National Sermons*, pp. 52-56, 107-14, 142-44, 151-52; *Election of Abraham Lincoln*, p. 34. On the abolitionists' use of empathy, dramatized in various ways, see Kraditor, *Means and Ends in American Abolitionism*, ch. 8.

161. *National Sermons*, pp. 142, 149; *Daily Evening Traveller*, Nov. 15, 1859 (*Echoes of Harper's Ferry*, pp. 133-35; *National Sermons*, pp. 162-63).

162. *National Sermons*, p. 151; *Election of Abraham Lincoln*, pp. 10, 14-15.

163. *National Sermons*, pp. 55-56.

164. *Ibid.*, pp. 121-22.

hood, however, there remained the question of how relevant Haven's preaching and writing were in proposing specific solutions and in defining concrete duties for antislavery and racial reform. In the political struggle to free Washington from the slave power, Haven promoted the cause of the Free Soil and Republican parties. He recognized that the Republican antislavery position was so mild that it represented only "the least of the claims and duties of abolitionists." But, he acknowledged as well, that in 1856, for "the first time in national history . . . the cause of Anti-Slavery [had] prevailed, openly and avowedly, in a single State." [165] At Westfield during the campaign that year Haven conducted "election prayer-meetings" to invoke divine aid in behalf of John C. Frémont's presidential aspirations. The meetings were poorly attended, but he made the effort because he thought, as he put it later, that "Christians of all sects should have met together on the morning of the election, and marched from the prayer-meeting to the ballot-box." Such a demonstration would have been consistent with Haven's exhortations that churchmen ought to "labor in the closet, at the family altar, in the community, at the polls, with prayer, and speech, and purse, and vote" in order to defeat the social and political power of slavery in the nation.[166]

In the prewar decade Haven apparently did not become active in any organized protest or legislative reform affecting civil rights, but he did declare himself publicly in favor of "social, business, and political equality." He advocated the removal of all laws forbidding interracial marriage, creating racially separate schools, and denying political participation to blacks. In addition he urged employers to end discriminatory hiring practices and to encourage "industry and enterprise" among Negroes by just treatment of black employees.[167] Massachusetts was one of the few states where black citizens had full exercise of voting rights. In 1855 colored schools were also abolished in the commonwealth.[168] But the spirit of caste had not been crushed out. Formal civil equality was no guarantee of social acceptance. Even those who affirmed racial equality in principle, Haven realized, often failed to "fraternize" with black people by inviting them to their own "houses and tables," by sharing religious fellowship and worship and by working under or beside them. [169]

Of the more specific solutions that were offered to the American racial dilemma, the one which had been thoroughly debated before Haven identified himself with the abolitionist cause, was the African colonization scheme. He disapproved of the idea because "the Blacks have as good right to this

165. *Ibid.,* pp. 118-20; see also pp. 53-54, 537.
166. *Ibid.,* pp. 56, 110-11; see also pp. 22-23, 32, 53-54, 78 ff.
167. *Ibid.,* pp. 142-45, 149.
168. *The Liberator,* Sept. 14, 1855.
169. *National Sermons,* pp. 141, 149; *Daily Evening Traveller,* Nov. 15, 1859 (*Echoes of Harper's Ferry,* pp. 133-34; *National Sermons,* p. 162).

country as we." [170] The plan, moreover, was impracticable due to the numbers of people involved and morally unthinkable without the uncoerced consent of Negroes to leave the land of their birth. There was renewed interest in colonization among blacks at the time, especially following the Dred Scott Decision of 1857, but Haven would not agree to the fundamental presupposition of inevitable racial hostility which lay beneath every emigration scheme involving Negroes. [171] Ultimately he resorted to a theological rationale by finding a providential aspect to American race relations. "They must abide with us," he declared, "till we acknowledge by word and act that they are one with us. And when we confess and embrace them as brothers, we shall never listen to their expatriation. . . . God will keep them with us till He has cured us of our sins." [172]

Even though he rejected the idea of an exodus of Negroes to Africa, or to some other foreign location, Haven did support a modified domestic colonization program as part of an emancipation plan. It included the voluntary resettlement of newly manumitted slaves "where they could possess freedom & in such a pecuniary condition as would be needed to make that freedom valuable." From the time he first considered the idea in private correspondence in 1854 until he publicly presented the scheme, in 1857 and again in 1860, Haven was seeking some way to accomplish the "peaceful removal" of slavery.[173] Among the objections which southern whites had to emancipation, he acknowledged, was an "unwillingness to have so many millions of an abhorred race dwelling among them" in the state of freedom. "This aversion is the corner-stone upon which slavery is supported among non-slaveholders," Haven argued. If there could be no "manumission on the soil" due to the curse of caste, he considered it an insignificant concession for the sake of a higher good to combine freedom of slaves with their "transportation" to free areas of the North and West.[174] One of the Garrisonians, Charles K. Whipple, immediately took Haven to task for giving in to the Colonization Society's "false and wicked fundamental principle, that black and white men cannot dwell together, peaceably, in the enjoyment of equal rights." But Haven claimed that his plan intended to provide "a home for these Americans in America," "a home among ourselves," and that it was not at all the same as "the unchristian and inhuman and unbrotherly idea of colonization." [175] Yet he could continue to support the idea only at the

170. Haven to Winchell, Feb. 4, 1851.
171. See Hollis R. Lynch, "Pan-Negro Nationalism in the New World, Before 1862," in August Meier and Elliott Rudwick, eds., *The Making of Black America: Essays in Negro Life and History* (New York: Atheneum, 1969), vol. I, pp. 42-65.
172. *National Sermons*, pp. 150-51.
173. Haven to Gerrit Smith, Dec. 16, 1854, Gerrit Smith Papers, George Arents Research Library, Syracuse University.
174. *Zion's Herald*, Sept. 30, 1857, under pseudonym, "Voluntary Compensationalist"; *The Liberator*, Nov. 6, 1857, under signature "H."
175. *The Liberator*, Nov. 6, 13, 1857.

expense of refusing to face up fully to several difficulties in the scheme, not the least of which was the ugly anti-Negro spirit in many areas of the North that would effectively confine black migration.

The domestic colonization component of Haven's plan, however, was secondary to his fundamental concern, which was to find a way to end slavery, even if it was necessary to compensate owners and move freedmen out of the South. Just as his critique of the sins of slavery and caste was national in scope, he searched for a national solution to the problem. He was willing to compromise with the principle that owners do not deserve payment for their slave property, if bondsmen could be freed. His plan was to form "a Manumission Aid Society" in which "the charities of Abolitionists" would be brought "into a general treasury" for the purpose of redeeming slaves from bondage. In this sense he sought only to organize nationally what had been done on a case by case basis, but he also wanted to prove to Southerners that "our talking is of the heart & not the lip," that Northerners would contribute some of their wealth to bring about the freedom of slaves. He was confident that "the conscientious among them" would cooperate with such an effort.[176] "Let us make this call," he wrote in defense of his plan, "not in that Pharisaic spirit of self-righteousness and parsimony which binds on these men's shoulders burdens grievous to be borne, while we touch them not with so much as one of our fingers, but with a liberality that shall compel the respect of the basest, and the love of the best, let us melt away the chains of indifferentism, procrastination, and love of ease and honor which now bind them to this system, and make them unwilling approvers of its myriad crimes." [177]

Some of the features in Haven's proposal were similar to a program which the Quaker blacksmith, Elihu Burritt, inaugurated in 1857. In fact Haven first publicly discussed the idea in response to Burritt's call for a convention that year to organize a National Compensation Society.[178] There were, however, major differences in the two schemes. Haven was concerned, as Burritt by and large was not, to offer not only compensation to the master but some remuneration to the slave as well in token of his unrequited labor and as initial capital with which to begin free life. Haven also dissented from Burritt's method, which was modeled after the British emancipation program in the West Indies. The Quaker reformer asked the Congress to provide revenue for the purchase of slaves at an average rate of $250 from the sale of public lands. Haven's Manumission Aid Society was to be a voluntary charity, not only because he was sensitive to the improbability of getting

176. Haven to Smith, Dec. 16, 1854.
177. *Zion's Herald*, Nov. 25, 1857, signed "H."
178. Burritt, *A Plan of Brotherly Copartnership of the North and South, for the Peaceful Extinction of Slavery* (New York, 1856). Haven's essays were three letters addressed to Burritt and published in *Zion's Herald*.

74

a compensation bill through the radically divided Congress, but especially because he believed that the appeal to the conscience of the masters required Northerners to make sacrifices in order to provide for the freedom of the slaves. That requirement was especially incumbent, as Haven put it, "because we have become enriched by our connection with them in this sin." [179]

Although nothing concrete came of it, Haven's proposition illustrated the dilemma of finding a realistic national resolution to slavery. Haven hoped that his program could combine Americans of diverse outlooks in "an open, united, large-hearted, liberal-handed movement." [180] But the sentiment which he thought would prevent passage of congressional legislation also stood in the way of public support for his voluntary charity. He rightly read the difficulty which Burritt's proposal would have in persuading white Americans to incur an $875 million debt to free black slaves, but he failed to see that his own idea likewise presupposed a willingness to contribute voluntarily to pay owners for their bondsmen.[181] He recognized that many slaveholders would not sell their slaves for a price three or four times less than the market value, but again his plan contained the same hindrance. He warned Burritt that the "southern slaveholding conscience" was not universal. "Too many sad and fearful facts prove that the mass of slaveholders and all their leaders, ecclesiastical and political, are without conscience in this matter." [182] Yet, as Whipple repeatedly pointed out, Haven assumed that there were "penitent masters" waiting for northern assistance to extirpate the institution of slavery.[183] He generalized too widely the example of James G. Birney, Cassius Clay, William Henry Brisbane, and other southern slaveholders who did free their chattels on grounds of conscience. He could not believe that "the moral sense of the slaveholding South" was *universally* in favor of slavery." [184] He refused to surrender faith in a latent southern antislavery conscience, even though the belief contrasted with his assessment of the designs and power of a slavocratic South bent on dominating national policy or destroying the Union.[185]

The idea of a manumission aid society lay dormant in Haven's mind after 1857, until December, 1860, when he resurrected it in a public letter sent to a meeting in Boston to commemorate the first anniversary of the death of John Brown. Meanwhile, Burritt's National Compensation Society had turned out to be a dismal failure, despite the support of Gerrit Smith, Henry Wadsworth Longfellow, Ralph Waldo Emerson, and a number of northern educa-

179. *Zion's Herald*, Sept. 30, Oct. 7 and 14, 1857.
180. *Ibid.*, Oct. 7, 1857.
181. *Ibid.*, Sept. 30, 1857.
182. *Ibid.*
183. *The Liberator*, Oct. 23, Nov. 6, 13, 1857; *Zion's Herald*, Nov. 11, Dec. 16, 1857.
184. Haven to Smith, Dec. 16, 1854; *Zion's Herald*, Oct. 7, 1857.
185. *Daily Evening Traveller*, Nov. 15, 1859 (*Echoes of Harper's Ferry*, pp. 129-30); *Election of Abraham Lincoln*, pp. 24 ff.; *National Sermons*, pp. 50-51, 119.

tors.[186] The sectional impasse had been reached, and the nation was on the brink of war. Hence, the proposition of compensated emancipation was a weak palliative. The mere fact that Haven tried to find a peaceful, national solution to slavery during the secession winter, however, signified that he at least had no desire to plunge the country headlong into a bloody war.[187]

It would not have been inconsistent in December, 1860, for Haven to have commended a violent solution for the problem of slavery. Earlier he had approved of force to prevent slaveholders from taking over Kansas, calling for ten thousand armed settlers to occupy the territory in the summer of 1856.[188] After the Harpers Ferry invasion of 1859, he vindicated Brown's action by comparing overt and covert violence, contrasting the raid with "the violent enslavement of forty hundreds of thousands of our kindred in the flesh and in the Lord, in Adam and in Christ." [189] In this way he reversed the responsibility for the violence from the invading liberators to the oppressive slaveholders. Americans could not consistently glorify the deeds of their "*revolutionary* fathers" and damn Brown's raid. Slaves had an unquestioned right to fight for their freedom so that "their uprising," as he designated Brown's rebellion, was not "to be condemned," rather "the *resistance* to that uprising." In the choice of "freedom through blood, or perpetual slavery," Haven insisted, "as men or as Christians" no one had the right "to decide for the latter." [190] When he eulogized Brown, he disclaimed that Christians were bound to "the doctrine of non-resistance." A year later he likewise declared that "the gospel of Peace does not always require of its disciples non-resistance to every form of revolting oppression." [191]

Despite his avowed willingness to employ force as a means to end the injustice of slavery, Haven did not advise precipitant action against the seceded southern states in the winter of 1860-61. He was loath to believe his own analysis of the sectional crisis, which included, in 1856, a forecast that civil war was imminent unless a "political reformation" took place that year.[192] That reformation came in 1860, as far as Haven was concerned, but it only served to divide further rather than to unite the nation. Late in December, when he wrote the preface for the pamphlet version of his sermon on the recent election, he observed that the Union was in danger, but as-

186. Peter Tolis, "Elihu Burritt: Crusader for Brotherhood" (Ph.D. dissertation, Columbia University, 1965), pp. 291-310.

187. His public letter to James Redpath appeared in *Zion's Herald*, Jan. 2, 1861, and a defense of it two weeks later, Jan. 16. See also *Douglass' Monthly*, 3 (January, 1861), 394; *Christian Advocate and Journal*, Jan. 17, 1861. Haven also appended the letter in a note to his sermon on Lincoln's election when he published it in December. See *Election of Abraham Lincoln*, pp. 39-44.

188. *Westfield News Letter*, June 18, 1856 (*National Sermons*, pp. 74-78).

189. *Daily Evening Traveller*, Nov. 15, 1859 (*Echoes of Harper's Ferry*, p. 125; *National Sermons*, p. 154).

190. *Daily Evening Traveller*, Nov. 15, 1859 (*Echoes of Harper's Ferry*, pp. 131, 133, 138; *National Sermons*, pp. 159-61, 167).

191. *National Sermons*, p. 172; *Election of Abraham Lincoln*, p. 26.

192. *Westfield News Letter*, June 18, 1856 (*National Sermons*, p. 83).

sured himself that secession would neither be generally supported nor last long.[193] He believed that Union sentiment went too deep with Americans of both sections for a successful rebellion to occur. In January, 1861, he wrote: "I trust in my country. I doubt not its perpetuity; I doubt not in its liberty; Union and liberty more than ever before shall be our glory and our joy." [194]

To the end, therefore, Haven spoke the confident language of progress and reform, while facing what he, at other times at least by instinct, knew to be a revolutionary situation. He even referred once to the antislavery conflict as a "revolution" which, because it was "for the political and social salvation of all men," had "far greater objects" and, "if successful, results far greater than that of 1776." The American Revolution had been only "for the political salvation of the white race over the world." [195] Civil war, however, lay ahead, and with it the fulfillment of the tragic prophecy of Gerrit Smith, who wrote to Haven in 1854 about voluntary compensation, saying that he feared there was "not virtue enough in the American people to accomplish" it and that "American Slavery" would "die a bloody death." [196] Such portents threatened Haven's reformist strategies, but he was prepared to sanction the war, particularly after it became overtly a crusade for black freedom. An assertion in his discourse on Harpers Ferry anticipated as much. "There will be no war nor bloodshed, thanks to the great Northern, the great Christian sentiment," he predicted; "but if there were, God has often blessed it, and might again." [197]

193. *Election of Abraham Lincoln*, p. 4.

194. *Christian Advocate and Journal*, Jan. 24, 1861.

195. *Westfield News Letter*, June 18, 1856 (*National Sermons*, p. 72). In the original version of this passage Haven referred to "the highest of the races of men" and to "the lowest of the races," but he altered the quotations in the 1869 edition of the *National Sermons*.

196. Smith to Haven, Dec. 19, 1854. Haven quoted this letter as a warning in *The Liberator*, Nov. 6, 1857, and in *Zion's Herald*, Nov. 25, 1857.

197. *Daily Evening Traveller*, Nov. 15, 1859 (*Echoes of Harper's Ferry*, p. 133). Haven altered the quotation in *National Sermons*, p. 161.

III

From Slavery to Freedom

For the year preceding the Civil War, Gilbert Haven was not only absorbed in the exciting events of national politics and the sectional controversy, but he was also facing the most serious personal crisis of his life. At midday on April 3, 1860, his young wife Mary died, five days after she gave birth to their fourth child. The baby, a son whom they named Bertie, survived only three days after his mother's death. The tragedy seemed more than Haven could bear. He sought comfort in the classic hopes of Christian faith in immortality and heaven, remembering, as he wrote of his feelings five weeks later to William Rice, "how blessed is her condition." But, in the words of the same letter, he could "feel no relief." [1] To his private journal and intimate family associates Haven confessed that he searched in vain for the divine purpose in the event and that he longed to be united with Mary in death. His intense grief, combined with physical illness the next winter, almost induced an emotional breakdown.[2]

As a tonic for his general health Haven thought about making a trip to Europe. Temporarily, he moved his children, Willie who was four and Mamie, two years old, to the family home in Malden while he finished out the year at Cambridge.[3] He was ill so much of the time, however, that preaching substitutes, especially his cousin Otis who was now editor of *Zion's Herald,* were frequently required. Because of his health and anticipated travel, when the New England Conference met in the spring of 1861, he was left without an appointment.[4]

That April the firing on Fort Sumter disrupted Haven's travel plans and posed the question of how he would respond to the attack on his nation's flag. He decided immediately to volunteer for service, perhaps as much to leave behind for a time the familiar scenes of home and region which evoked memories of his beloved Mary, as to express his patriotism and loyalty to the Union. On April 18 he went to see Governor John A. Andrew and offered his "services as Chaplain." The governor sent Haven to General Benjamin Butler who assigned him to the Eighth Massachusetts Regiment. On the next day— which, Haven remembered, was the anniversary of Paul Revere's famous ride in 1775—he took the oath from his father, a justice of the peace, and went

1. Haven to Rice, May 11, 1860, as quoted in Prentice, *Life,* p. 194. For Mary's obituary see *Zion's Herald,* May 2, 1860.
2. Prentice, *Life,* pp. 190-218.
3. The first child, Georgie, died at Wilbraham in 1854 before he was eight months old. *Ibid.,* p. 143.
4. *Ibid.,* p. 195. See comments by Fales H. Newhall, expressing concern over Haven's condition in his Journal, entries for Sept. and Oct. 10, 1860; Feb. 25, 1861; Harvard Street Methodist Church Cambridge-Watertown Station Ebenezar Church Quarterly Conference Records Nov. 21, 1845-Mar. 22, 1869, entries for June 30, Sept. 25, Nov. 30, 1860; Mar. 7, 1861, New England Methodist Historical Society Library.

off to war.[5] By the last day of the month he had joined his regiment in Maryland and was officially mustered into service with the "three months' army" of volunteers. In addition to his duties as chaplain, Haven corresponded regularly with two Methodist weeklies—his cousin's paper in Boston and the *Christian Advocate and Journal* in New York, whose new editor, Edward Thomson, had made him a regional contributor the previous January.[6]

I

Even though his first reaction to the prospect of war was to think of "its horrid nature," Haven concluded that it would not be "the worst evil that could happen to the land." To the "many things worse than war" with its "short though severe distresses," he contrasted "the shames and agonies" which "the millions of our enslaved brethren for these many years" had endured.[7] Haven continued to hope, however, that slavery, the fundamental cause of the national crisis, "would pass out of our body politic," as he put it, "without any bloodier struggles than powder and paving stones can get up."[8]

At least theoretically, the problem of a proper justification for the Union cause worried Haven initially. He pondered the question whether a democratic nation could justify force against a portion of its people who elected not to live under its government. It was no simple matter, he recognized, to enforce obedience to the Union against the free will of the people of the South. American democracy was based on the right of revolution and upon government by the consent of the governed. As he pursued the logic of these considerations, Haven argued in May, "If, therefore, the South shall persist in choosing secession and a new Confederation, if the majority of her citizens, fairly appealed to, shall so decide, it will not be consistent with our national idea to subjugate her."[9]

On the other hand, Haven realized that the North could hardly permit peaceable secession. Thus, he stated that the initial issue at stake in the conflict was "the dignity and sovereignty of the United States" and that the confrontation was "a war of defense—the defense of all that is vital and glorious in our heritage." There was no way to grant freedom to the rebellious states and let them go their way. Haven was sure that the leaders of the

5. For Haven's own account, see his manuscript journal, May 1, 1861, in the private possession of Mr. George A. Wood, Jr. of South Lincoln, Mass. (Hereafter the journal will be referred to as "War Journal.") See also Commonwealth of Massachusetts, Adjutant General's Office, *Massachusetts Soldiers, Sailors and Marines in the Civil War* (Norwood, Mass., 1931-37), vol. I, p. 517.

6. The series in *Zion's Herald* was called "Letters from the Camp," and the articles in the *Advocate* were entitled "Correspondence from the Seat of War."

7. *Christian Advocate and Journal*, May 2, 1861.

8. *Zion's Herald*, May 8, 1861.

9. *Ibid.*, May 15, 1861. The northern clergy in the early months of the war discussed fully the question whether the right of revolution could rightly be claimed by the South. See Stuart W. Chapman, "The Protestant Campaign for the Union. A Study of the Reactions of Several Denominations to the Civil War" (Ph.D. Dissertation, Yale University, 1939), pp. 49 ff.

slave power would demand more. "We must let them have New Mexico," he claimed.

We must promise not to interfere with their projected occupation of Mexico and the West India Islands. We must not seek to suppress their foreign slave trade. We must offer no facilities to their fugitives, and no opposition to their use of our ports for the transportation of their hellish merchandize [*sic*]. In a word, we must consent to be a weak and rotten power, more despised by them than their own slaves are.[10]

Peaceful separation was impossible under such conditions. The only hope was in the triumph of "Union sentiment" among the people of the South in opposition to their leaders. [11]

By June, Haven had overcome whatever reservations he had felt earlier so that he could give unqualified approval to President Abraham Lincoln's strategy. He saw that since the rebellion had attracted wide popular support in the South, the federal government had to impose its authority, suppress the revolution and restore the disaffected states to the Union. "We shall have to occupy every rebellious commonwealth with our armies," he wrote on June 24, "until the Union sentiment can be made powerful, and *all-powerful*." [12] The ambivalence in Haven's position remained, but he did not bother to reconcile his earlier belief in the South's right to revolution with his support of Lincoln's determined effort to prevent the dissolution of the Union.

Even though Haven first claimed that the war was not against slavery per se, but for the perpetuation of national sovereignty, he understood that it was not possible to think of the protection and defense of the Union without facing the issue of slavery. Dixie's peculiar institution was inextricably tied to the secession of the slaveholding states. Confederate Vice-President Alexander Stephens of Georgia gave the clearest explication of that relation when in March, 1861, he boldly stated that the defense of "African slavery . . . —the proper *status* of the negro in our form of civilization" was "the immediate cause of the late rupture and present revolution." Criticizing Thomas Jefferson and the founding fathers for their belief in human equality and in the evil of slavery, Stephens announced that the "new government" of the Confederacy was founded "upon the great truth, that the negro is not equal to the white man; that slavery—subordination to the superior race—is his natural and normal condition." He was proud to claim that the new nation was "the first, in the history of the world, based on this great physical, philosophical, and moral truth." [13]

10. *Zion's Herald*, May 15, 1861.
11. Several Protestant ministers in the North held the view that the majority of Southerners opposed secession. See Chapman, "The Protestant Campaign," pp. 119-20, 133-34.
12. *Christian Advocate and Journal*, July 4, 1861.
13. There are several versions of this speech and of this particular quotation, but the text used here is the authoritative volume, Henry Cleveland, *Alexander Stephens, in Public and Private. With*

Despite the Confederate position as avowed by Stephens, the national government emphatically denied that it sought the death of slavery. Haven understood the strategic value of Lincoln's move to unite all the North behind the defense of the Union and the Constitution without obtruding the controversial question of slavery into the picture. But he believed that the administration could not long delay taking a stand against slavery. Even before he left for his army post in Maryland in April, 1861, he wrote, "The war, though directly for the salvation or destruction of the Union, is indirectly for the salvation or destruction of slavery. It cannot be waged a great while without coming to this head." [14] Though he was not at all certain by what means emancipation would be achieved, Haven tried to anticipate some possible moves which would insure slavery's end. "It may be by military necessity on the part of the Government," he wrote in May, "or, as is not unlikely, if the war is long, on the part of the slave masters . . . [who if] compelled to choose between emancipation and submission . . . may prefer to make their slaves their allies by making them free." If neither of those alternatives prevailed and the Confederacy maintained itself, Haven reasoned, slavery was still "certain to die" through "insurrections aided by arms of avenging abolitionists." [15]

During these early weeks of the war Haven persisted in his hope of a peaceful resolution. As late as June he reiterated his plan for compensated emancipation. On the one hand, he thought that slaveowners deserved no payment for their so-called property and that the "country ought to decree the slaves their liberty" and grant them funds for their labor and suffering. On the other hand, Haven realized that such benevolent action was not forthcoming. At this point he would have gladly settled for any practical move by the government against slavery. He estimated that "the most it can do is to extinguish this legal title of property in man. It can do this most easily, most speedily, most peaceably, most cheaply, by purchase." [16] But as Haven hoped for political action which would prevent fraternal war while ending slavery, he saw the necessity to prepare for the conflict that lay ahead. He concluded that perhaps the rebellion and slavery would be overthrown only by force. "The legion of devils [slavery] shall be cast out of our body politic

---

Letters and Speeches, Before, During, and Since the War (Philadelphia, 1866), p. 721. Haven referred to this quotation in a sermon in March, 1862 and in a letter published in the *London Watchman* during the summer of 1862. See *National Sermons*, pp. 272, 296.

14. *Christian Advocate and Journal,* May 2, 1861. Most abolitionists shared Haven's confidence that despite the reluctance of the Lincoln government to make emancipation a war aim, the end of slavery was imminent. See James M. McPherson, *The Struggle for Equality. Abolitionists and the Negro in the Civil War and Reconstruction* (Princeton: Princeton University Press, 1964), p. 48.

15. *Zion's Herald,* May 15, 1861. Earlier the same year William Goodell had argued that the government had the right under the war power to abolish slavery outright. The Church Anti-Slavery Society, meeting in New York in January, adopted Goodell's position. See McPherson, *Struggle for Equality,* p. 39.

16. *Christian Advocate and Journal,* July 4, 1861.

without much bloodshed, I trust; with much blood, freely and gladly shed, if that is the only way in which we can be saved." [17]

In his ninety days of military service Haven was involved in none of the early battles of the war. Responding to the first flurry of excitement in the North when rumors spread that the national capital was in danger, his regiment, among others, rushed South. For a time these units were the center of attention as they protected and assured free access to Washington. Haven's regiment stayed in the capital only a few days, but long enough for him to attend a reception for officers at the White House at which President and Mrs. Lincoln, Secretary of State William H. Seward and his wife, and Major Robert Anderson of Fort Sumter fame were present. The unit soon moved to the Relay House near Baltimore where the troops guarded the junction of the Baltimore and Ohio and the Washington railroads. In camp the soldiers had little to do except for the daily drills of military routine.[18]

The inaction of his unit gave Haven several opportunities to visit in the countryside of Maryland and northern Virginia. There he had his first empirical impressions of the South. The whole pattern of life which he observed was contrary to his Yankee instincts. There was too little enterprise and too much idleness which amounted to a "slip-shod style of existence." Haven attributed southern laziness and lack of industry to the system of slavery which cursed the entire country. In one of his letters to the *Herald* he commented that "the whole region would be alive with business and covered with factories, stores and dwellings, if it were anywhere else than in 'Dixie's Land.' " [19] His accounts often drew the familiar contrast between the aristocratic South, based on landed wealth and slave labor, and the democratic North, which had an industrialized, free-labor economy. Haven implied that the war was in some sense a conflict of these two civilizations or cultures. The future of the South lay with an influx of "Northern ideas," he believed, and that required a "crusade of the North into the South." [20]

Occasionally, despite himself, Haven had to confess that southern life did have its attractions. He especially appreciated the overwhelming physical beauty of the upper South with its fertile fields and great plantations, its "silent forests and farms," its "valleys slumbering in the lap of spring." Once he spoke of it as an "earthly paradise." [21] He admitted that he "could easily

17. *Ibid.*, May 23, 1861. Earlier he wrote: "If it [the rebellion] is not quenched without blood, I have no doubt that the thousands of soldiers here will readily pour out theirs upon the flames" (*Zion's Herald*, May 8, 1861).

18. "War Journal," May 20, 1861; *Zion's Herald*, May 15, 1861; *Christian Advocate and Journal*, May 16, June 6, 1861. See also Haven's detailed account of military life, "Camp Life at the Relay," *Harper's New Monthly Magazine*, 34 (1862), 628-33, and compare it with the original manuscript of the article (in the private possession of Mr. George A. Wood, Jr.), from which the editors of *Harper's* excised the many references to slavery. See Prentice, *Life*, p. 321.

19. *Zion's Herald*, May 22, 1861; see also *Christian Advocate and Journal*, May 30, 1861.

20. *Zion's Herald*, May 1, July 3, 1861.

21. *Ibid.*, May 22, June 19, 1861; *Christian Advocate and Journal*, May 30, July 4, 1861.

waste [his] days on these pleasant farms and in this nerveless lassitude of being." The thought inspired a further reflection which revealed one of the roots for his abolitionism and which permitted a momentary doubt that Yankee activism was the epitome of human existence. "I have often thought my sympathy for the slaves may have arisen from this disinclination to work," he confessed, "and . . . I have instinctively felt that that forced service was about the hardest part of bondage. It is sweetened with us by the rewards thereof; but it is none the less disagreeable. 'In the sweat of thy brow shalt thou eat thy bread' was pronounced as a curse, not a blessing; but the promises of Heaven are all bathed in that blessed idea of rest." His musing then gave rise to the question, "Does not the very idleness of man here, the dreamy, yet thoughtless ecstacy of his daily life, give us one of the foci of the soul's eternal orbit, as much as the sharp and intense activity of his Northern counterpart supplies the other?" [22]

For all of his appreciation of the physical beauty of the region and the subtle attraction of aristocratic culture, however, the one dominant characteristic of southern life to Haven was slavery. His weekly contributions to the *Advocate* and the *Herald* never strayed far from that subject. The first southern slave whom he saw was a twelve-year old girl in Annapolis, where he was visiting his former teacher at Wesleyan University, Professor A. W. Smith who had become a member of the faculty at the Naval Academy.[23] Before he left the border, Haven had many other contacts with slaves when he visited the homes of Methodist preachers and laymen and plantations like the residence of John H. B. Latrobe, president of the American Colonization Society; Carrolton Manor, owned by the descendants of the signer of the Declaration of Independence and famous Maryland Catholic, Charles Carroll; and the Robert E. Lee home in Arlington, Virginia.[24]

In order to satisfy his curiosity Haven tested the constant claim made by southern whites that "the slaves were better off than the free blacks" and that they did not desire liberty. He personally interviewed Negroes for their own responses and reported the conversations in his editorial correspondence. He was deeply touched by the life stories of free blacks who had bought themselves from out of slavery, and he learned to sympathize with their difficulties. A Negro waiter in Washington, whose wife and children were still enslaved in Tennessee, particularly impressed Haven with his answer to a query about why he worked so hard "to buy himself." He replied, "I wanted to lie down massa and get up massa!" An old black man named John Diggs, who told of

22. *Zion's Herald,* May 22, 1861. Haven expressed similar sentiments in the *New York Christian Advocate,* June 25, 1874.

23. Haven found it significant that the first slave he met was named Mary, which was both his late wife's name and that of the mother of Jesus. See "War Journal," May 1, 1861; quoted in Prentice, *Life,* p. 222. See also *Zion's Herald,* June 5, 1861; *The Liberator,* June 14, 1861.

24. "War Journal," May 21, June 19, 1861; *Zion's Herald,* May 22, July 3, 1861; *Christian Advocate and Journal,* Aug. 1, 1861.

the problems free Negroes had in getting employment, echoed similar senti-ments. "Why, sir," he said to Haven, "you know when a boy's about thirteen years old, he feels as he'd like to be his own master, and the feeling don't grow any less as he grows older." [25]

In his accounts of talks with slaves Haven never failed to employ a story either to disprove the argument of "the superior condition of the slaves to the free blacks" or, more often, to inject some satirical comment on white atti-tudes. He remarked, for example, that since the slave quarters were "about half-way between their master and his other cattle," the location was consistent with "the idea that they are a kind of distinct order of beings"—"a sort of half-way house between a white man and a fine horse." [26]

Haven was keenly sarcastic about southern proslavery apologists, but in-stead of attacking their defense of servitude directly, he criticized the failure of the whites to use their slaves to the best advantage. He based his argument on the consensus of southern churchmen like Virginia theologians, William A. Smith and Albert T. Bledsoe, that Negroes, though inferior to white men, were endowed with reason.[27] Haven satirically suggested that Southerners had not begun to exhaust the uses of blacks. "This 'strange beast' that can think, and feel, and talk, just like a human being," he wrote, "should not be confined to works that a steam-plow and reaper, a mere ox and horse, can do as well as he." He predicted that with "the right kind of culture" and "the right sort of feed" slaves would "relieve the divine Caucasian of much of the drud-gery which he has to undergo, and which is so hard in this hot country and so degrading to that dignified head of creation." Blacks could learn, Haven advised, to be doctors, lawyers, merchants, editors, legislators, and clergymen and thus free white men from the responsibilities which these professions as-sumed.[28] His intention was obvious. He wanted to expose one of the many contradictions in the proslavery apologetic—the disjunction between the claim that the Negro in slavery had made wonderful intellectual and moral im-provement and the assertion that no black had the capacity to acquire an education and advance out of slavery into freedom.[29]

One of the readers of the *Advocate,* James Goodling of Hillsboro, Mary-land, saw what Haven intended, and he scorned "the discovery that the negro

25. *Zion's Herald,* June 5, 1861. For Haven's notes on this conversation see "War Journal," May 21, 1861.

26. *Christian Advocate and Journal,* May 30, 1861. For similar comments see issues for June 27, Aug. 1.

27. Haven specifically named these two educators and authors in his article which appeared on July 4, 1861 in the *Christian Advocate and Journal.* Smith, the president of Randolph-Macon Col-lege, was the leading Methodist proslavery apologist. See his *Lectures on the Philosophy and Practice of Slavery* (Nashville, 1857). Bledsoe, a member of the faculty at the state university, was an Episcopalian, but he transferred into the Methodist Episcopal Church, South, after the war. See his *An Essay on Liberty and Slavery* (Philadelphia, 1857).

28. *Christian Advocate and Journal,* July 4, 1861.

29. An editorial by Edward Thomson lists a dozen such contradictions. See *Christian Advocate and Journal,* July 18, 1861.

is fully equal if not superior to the white, giving him the advantage of education and training." [30] Again in satire, Haven denied that he had advocated an equality between blacks and whites. "I was only describing a species of property I had found down here," he explained, "and suggesting the admirable uses to which it could be applied. Though it might reason, and write, and speak, and fight as well as man, it does not follow by any means that it is the equal of man." He kept up the pretense. "There is a certain something which separates him from man, who is of one blood, salvation, and destiny. The difference is precisely the same as separates some somebodies I have seen here in colored churches from white people. What it is I know not." [31]

Haven did not confine his conversations on slavery to interviews with Negroes. He also discussed the question openly with slaveholders. Even though he had little success in converting anyone to abolitionism, his direct confrontation with men who controlled the system of human bondage had an impact on his own views.[32] From his visit at the Latrobe house he found that the famous colonizationalist "honestly entertained" the view that "the Black race must inevitably die out of this country—and can only flourish in Africa." Haven called it an "absurd opinion." He also complained over Latrobe's expression of a common sentiment "about the blacks not being able to take care of themselves—not desiring freedom—not being as well off when free as when enslaved, and much other white trash, which goes for good common sense in this section of the country." The whites were "regular Aristotelians on this subject of inquiry," he charged. "They shut themselves up in their own exclusive Caucasian conceit, and theorize as to the state of feeling in their neighbors, whom they never honestly converse with." [33]

The fundamental explanation for the views of southern whites was clear to Haven. They, like most other Americans, did not believe in the human equality of the races. Occasionally Haven had come across someone who frankly admitted he could not think of blacks "as of the same order of beings with himself." More often the belief in black inferiority was more subtle and less explicitly stated. The widespread bitter anti-Negro prejudice on the border, however, far exceeded Haven's expectations. He was particularly surprised by the feelings which he found among white women in Maryland. To New England readers he reported having "heard frequent and bitter denunciations of their brethren and sisters, from the lips of elegant and excellent Christian ladies," not unlike what he had heard from "Massachusetts and New York ladies" except for "the ferocious intensity of contempt and hatred which marked these speakers." Haven commented that he now understood "how

30. The letter is contained in Thomson's editorial, *ibid.*
31. *Ibid.*, Aug. 8, 1861.
32. Accounts of visits with slaveholders appear in *Zion's Herald*, May 8, June 5, 1861; and in his "War Journal," May 1, 20, 21, 27; June 10 and 15, 1861. Some of these journal entries are quoted in Prentice, *Life*, pp. 222, 230-32.
33. "War Journal," May 21, 1861; *Zion's Herald*, May 22, June 5, 1861.

the secession feeling [raged] the hottest with the female part of the community, from Baltimore to New Orleans." [34]

But a greater shock was in store. Haven saw for himself how deeply implicated in the system of black servitude were the leading churchmen of Maryland and Virginia. Violent hostility against abolitionism and prejudice against blacks among his fellow Methodists were more common than he was prepared to accept. "The name of abolitionist they dread now worse than a Hebrew that of a leper," he wrote of his Methodist colleagues. "Their hearts are very hard on the rights, especially the equality of the negro. They hate & fear him. I haven't heard a single man talking as though they [sic] really felt that they were brethren." [35]

Slaveholders, Haven soon realized, were the leading men in the churches as well as in the community at large. At a Methodist quarterly conference he witnessed the election of a slaveowner to the office of steward. The minister in charge nominated the man, and there was no objection to his selection. Afterwards Haven offered to congratulate the member on his honor, if he would free his slave. The other churchmen present laughed at the suggestion and refused to take Haven seriously.[36]

Such experiences confirmed Haven's judgment that border Methodism had largely become captive to the power of slavery within its own membership. He came across a few Methodists, like a Brother Beals and David Creamer (a pioneer hymnologist in America), who were antislavery, but these men usually kept their sentiments "on the vexed question" to themselves. But, Haven found out, there was no timidity in expressing antiabolition and secession on the part of border churchmen like the intrepid editor of the *Baltimore Advocate,* Thomas Bond. Twice the two argued over slavery and "the life & death of the nation." Haven came away from the last encounter calling the doctor "disagreeable," "insolent," "a disappointed man, and ugly withal." [37]

Haven saw no hope for antislavery success until churchmen began to speak out against "the rotten and hideous system . . . which they have allowed to creep into the Church" and to cease "elevating these holders and breeders of Christian flesh to be classleaders, stewards and trustees." He damned Maryland Methodists who had seceded over the legislation on slavery at the General Conference of 1860, but he discovered that the "loyal" churchmen in the region were only a little less rabid in their opposition to a strong antislavery witness. They nullified the new rules and ceased to support the official church

---

34. *Zion's Herald,* June 5, July 31, 1861.

35. *Christian Advocate and Journal,* May 30, 1861; "War Journal," July 11, 1861. The quotation, slightly altered, appears in Prentice, *Life,* p. 233.

36. *Zion's Herald,* June 5, 1861; "War Journal," June 15, 1861; Prentice, *Life,* p. 232.

37. "War Journal," June 10, July 6, 19, 25, 28, 1861; Prentice, *Life,* pp. 232, 234, 236.

paper in New York because of its new editorial stance against slavery.[38]

The most trenchant criticism in Haven's war correspondence developed this theme of the captivity of religion to slavery. He recounted the story of a successful farmer in the area, who, despite his secessionist sympathies, provided milk for the Union Army, including Haven's regiment. On Sundays, however, he refused to send milk because of his scrupulous Sabbath observance. The same man had made his fortune from slave labor, and had once refused $1,300 for a female servant when her father offered to buy her from bondage. His moral inconsistency became Haven's subject for a sermonic commentary developed around Jesus' saying to the scribes and Pharisees, "You blind guides, straining out a gnat and swallowing a camel" (Matt. 23:24 RSV). "Wont [sic] that do for a modern illustration of the ancient text?" Haven asked rhetorically. "A man who wouldn't sell milk on Sundays and wouldn't sell a father his own daughter, would sell a score or two of his brothers and sisters into hopeless bondage, and with their blood and bones live in elegance and abundance! Did he not strain at a gnat and swallow a whole herd of camels?" Haven climaxed the narrative by noting that though "this conscientious soul-trader and soul-holder" was "a minister of our Lord and Saviour Jesus Christ," no one in the community objected to his conduct.[39]

As a conclusion to the story Haven described a visit to the Sunday service conducted by the slaveholding rector. The account focused on his eminent personal qualities—his ability to read the beautiful Episcopal service of common prayer and his instructive sermon on the trials of the Christian. Haven recognized that the portrait contrasted with what his readers anticipated. "You expect a hard-featured, hard-voiced, hard-mannered man, with tones like the snapping of a slave-whip, and the manners of Haley and Legree combined," he wrote. "You don't know human nature." [40] The observation dramatized the great contradiction of antebellum southern religion—a fact which abolitionists like Haven did not miss. He saw what he had long theorized about from a distance, that good men, like this rector, were the bulwarks of the system of slavery. His realization of how moral men became implicated in an evil social structure was profound ethical realism. Far from being "morally simplistic" about slaveholding—a common charge levied against abolitionists—reformers like Haven expanded the dimensions of ethical responsibility beyond the bounds of a private morality and diagnosed the cor-

38. *Christian Advocate and Journal,* June 6, 1861; William Warren Sweet, *The Methodist Episcopal Church and the Civil War* (Cincinnati, n.d.), pp. 49-50; see successive issues of the *Advocate,* February through May, 1861; and *The Methodist,* an independent weekly published in New York by dissident denominational conservatives, from July, 1860, through March, 1862.

39. *Christian Advocate and Journal,* July 25, 1861. Haven referred to "the hypocrisy of the slave-holding piety" in *Zion's Herald,* Nov. 4, 1863.

40. *Christian Advocate and Journal,* July 25, 1861. Haley and Legree are a slave trader and a cruel slaveholder, respectively, in Harriet Beecher Stowe's famous antislavery novel, *Uncle Tom's Cabin.*

porate character of evil and the complicity of good men in social wrong.[41]

Defeats to the Union Army in Virginia in the summer of 1861 drew Haven's attention away from southern life and perspectives on slavery to more somber reflections on the war. After the Battle of Big Bethel on June 10, he commented that the war had ceased to be a "holiday pastime," for it had become a serious struggle for national existence. Haven sought to assure himself that the progress of the Union cause could not be expected to proceed without interruptions and defeats. But he feared that the Confederacy might ultimately triumph, resulting in the end of America's democratic experiment and hence, the death of republicanism in the New World.[42]

With the Union cause being frustrated on the battlefield, Haven proposed as a remedy a more comprehensive war aim. "Something more than Union makes that a live word through the Free States," he wrote just before the disaster at Bull Run on July 21. "Liberty is the name." [43] Three weeks earlier he had been more explicit when he insisted that the government must not merely deliberate on the extinction of slavery, but "it must *act.*" He declared, "Slavery is the cause, the only cause of rebellion." Reunification of the country was impossible as long as the North refused to face up to the true issue. "The army of the republic can never leave the [southern] soil if it leaves the slave there. If it does it will find all its labor lost." [44] A visit, with his college classmate Samuel Beach, to the slave market in Alexandria in July increased Haven's conviction that the war had to extinguish slavery. There he prayed that the conflict would not end until every slave mart was closed and all slaves "standing in the fulness of their long sought liberty." [45]

The position which Haven took on the relation of slavery to the war did not go unchallenged. Another Union chaplain, writing from Baltimore under the pen name, "Hanover," launched a direct blow against it in a letter to *The Methodist,* the paper which denominational conservatives had begun the previous summer in New York. After noting the disapproval in Maryland of Haven's remarks on slavery in the *Advocate,* "Hanover" demanded that there be "no more such letters as 'H.' writes." "There are men here candid enough to say that God may design the entire overthrow of slavery as a consequence of this rebellion," he asserted. "But once let the Administration avow such a purpose, and you will transfer the conflict to the northern side of Mason and Dixon's line." [46] Although Haven dismissed the attack by predicting that "Hanover" would change his views before the war was over, his opponent came back with a longer tirade against northern "ultraists" on whom he

41. See Donald G. Mathews, "The Abolitionists on Slavery: The Critique Behind the Social Movement," *Journal of Southern History,* 33 (1967), 163 ff. In *Our Next-Door Neighbor,* Haven wrote: "Good men have been connected with every controlling evil that the world has ever seen" (p. 128).
42. *Christian Advocate and Journal,* June 27, 1861.
43. *Ibid.,* Aug. 1, 1861 (letter dated July 17).
44. *Ibid.,* July 4, 1861.
45. *Zion's Herald,* Aug. 14, 1861; "War Journal," July 6, 1861.
46. *The Methodist,* July 13, 1861.

blamed the war. Twice he repeated the warning that the government dare not touch the institution of slavery, and he charged Haven and other emancipationists with treasonous sentiments which aided the South.[47] Similar criticism appeared in *Zion's Herald* whose New York correspondent wrote that he could agree with Haven's plan for "compensation to the owners of the blacks" but not with the view "that the war is to continue till slavery is abolished." [48]

Despite opposition, Haven's insistence on the necessity of emancipation grew more pronounced. By the time he mustered out of service in August, he was convinced that the North could gain no real victories until slavery was ended. He saw the recent reverses as divine judgment upon the country. "He who made us of one blood is leading this nation, stuffed with pride and insolence, into the fires that shall humiliate and purify," he wrote.[49] Once he reflected soberly that the nation would perhaps have to endure greater suffering before the conflict was over. "Could you see what I have, and hear what I have," he declared, "you would feel that we deserve a deeper baptism of blood than God in his mercy we trust will require." [50] The defeat at Bull Run gave further evidence of the divine intention in the war. Afterwards, Haven wrote, "The object of God is to liberate these children of his who have cried day and night unto him for these many generations." Addressing New England Methodists, he compared the "poverty" and "the agony now rending a great multitude of Rachels, North and South, . . . with the poverty and distress of the hundreds of thousands, of the millions upon millions of God's dear children in this fair land for these centuries of bondage!" He went on, "The cup is being commended to our own lips of which they have drank [sic] so constantly and so deeply." [51]

As the first phase of the war drew to a close and Haven returned to civilian life, he summarized the nation's progress since Fort Sumter in his final war report to the *Advocate*. The recent failures in Virginia to the contrary, the North had developed a remarkable sense of unity and determination to put down the rebellion. There had been a slow evolution in public opinion at first, but after three months things were different. Clearly, there would be no peaceful secession. There would be no compromise with the South, since there were only two sides to the great question of national sovereignty. The war had become a war of national survival, and the question whether the slave power would succeed remained yet unanswered.[52]

The period after Bull Run, in Haven's view, was a state of transition during which the government would demonstrate whether it possessed the "courage to meet the demands of the hour." The primary obligation upon the adminis-

47. *Christian Advocate and Journal*, Aug. 8, 1861; *The Methodist*, Aug. 31, 1861.
48. *Zion's Herald*, July 17, 1861.
49. *Ibid.*, July 31, 1861.
50. *Ibid.*, July 3, 1861.
51. *Ibid.*, July 31, 1861.
52. *Christian Advocate and Journal*, Aug. 8, 1861.

tration was to use all means to subjugate the South. In this context, to refuse to face the issue of slavery was unrealistic and perhaps fatal. Haven recommended that "no quarter . . . be shown to slavery. That or we must die." In a letter to the *Herald* he was more concrete. He favored a declaration of emancipation under the war powers of the President and the Congress as a military necessity. Senator Lyman Trumbull of Illinois had anticipated that strategy in a speech in the Senate at the end of July.[53] Other abolitionists, including Frederick Douglass, William Goodell, and Moncure Conway, advocated a similar plan. Another year passed, however, before the chief executive of the country accepted the idea and embodied it in his proclamation of emancipation.[54]

II

A month before Haven's term of military service was up, he wrote in his journal that he planned to go home, after which he would "perhaps return to the war" because he liked what he was doing "about as well as anything" and since he thought he was "doing as much good as in any other way." [55] Later the same month he rejected offers to go to Virginia as a traveling correspondent and to take the presidency of Lawrence University in Wisconsin. In early August he returned to Malden.[56] Though he never publicly explained the decision, Haven chose not to reenlist in the army. He remained at the family home for nearly three months, reflecting upon his stay in Maryland and northern Virginia and especially about his firsthand contact with slavery. What he had observed about the relation of his own church to the institution troubled him deeply. As he mulled the problem over, he recorded his feelings in an "Affectionate Admonition to the Members of the Baltimore Conferences," which he published in the church press.[57]

From the outset Haven took pains to clarify his rationale for issuing such a public letter. He recalled "many pleasant acquaintances" and "many precious religious communions" during his time in the region, and he commended the dedication and energy of churchmen there. Then, he explained, "I could not therefore approach this duty with any envyings or strife in my heart, but solely under the impulse of an honest regard at once for you, for the slave, for the Church, and for Christ." He hoped that his "fathers and brethren" in Maryland Methodism would receive the appeal as written "in no spirit of

53. *Ibid.; Zion's Herald,* July 31, 1861. An account of Trumbull's speech is in Frank Moore, ed., *The Rebellion Record* (New York, 1862), vol. II, pp. 436-37, documents section.
54. McPherson, *Struggle for Equality,* pp. 62-64; John Hope Franklin, *The Emancipation Proclamation* (Garden City, N.Y.: Doubleday Anchor Books, 1965).
55. "War Journal," July 6, 1861.
56. *Ibid.,* July 25 and 28, 1861.
57. The address, divided in two parts, appeared simultaneously, in *Zion's Herald,* Sept. 4, 11, 1861; and *Christian Advocate and Journal,* Sept. 5, 12, 1861.

bitter criticism," but as an incentive to change their course of action toward slavery.

In discussing the relation of the denomination to slavery on the border, Haven was careful to make an accurate analysis. He agreed that there were relatively few slaveholders in the church compared to the total membership and that the slaveowning members were more numerous in the country churches and in the southern portions of the conferences. At the same time he noted that the influence of slavery was dominant in the church. The chief local officials in border Methodism owned slaves. There was a bar to membership for "the winebibber and rum-seller," but none against slaveholders. Slavery had "sovereignty over the Church," Haven frankly observed, and "the slave power" was its "archbishop." "It is everywhere, and everywhere powerful," he wrote. "It makes appointments, dictates conference reports, compels the vote of its members, presides over every pulpit, and forbids any investigation into any of its iniquitous acts." [58]

In the second part of the "Admonition" Haven pointed to the duties of Maryland churchmen on the great question. First, he urged the preachers to overcome their fears and end their silence in the pulpit. "You may be ever so earnest in other really Christian duties, ever so able expounders of much of the truth as it is in Jesus," he warned, "but if you falter in a double sense when you approach this theme, if you dare not say a word in public upon it to God or your fellow-man, all these virtues avail you nothing." In like manner, Haven advised that the border conferences speak in their official capacity against slavery and put an end to the nullification of the antislavery spirit and action of the denomination.[59] "Cease to complain of the Christian utterance of your Northern brethren," he admonished. "Cease to charge the present existence of slavery among you to that agitation." A third duty which Haven recommended would abolish racial caste, at least in the church. "Cease to foster the wicked prejudice against your colored brethren," he declared, "from which we are far from free, but which with you is carried to such a pitch that even their little children cannot attend the same Sunday-school with your own, much less be members of the same class." [60]

Moving forcefully to a conclusion, Haven expressed confidence that slavery was doomed and that, despite the great upheaval in the nation, the true churches of the land would emerge "abolitionized." "Through the Methodist Church or over it will the great reform be carried forward," he exclaimed.

The idea is preposterous that slavery is to go down in some imperceptible way, without the least agitation in Church or State, with the silent or active acquiescence

58. *Zion's Herald*, Sept. 4, 1861; *Christian Advocate and Journal*, Sept. 5, 1861.

59. Here Haven reminded his border associates of the early Methodist testimony against slavery. He admitted that the Methodist "fathers" compromised in their legislation on the subject, but he insisted that they, unlike their descendants, never justified and approved of slavery.

60. *Zion's Herald*, Sept. 11, 1861; *Christian Advocate and Journal*, Sept. 12, 1861.

of Church and State in its continuance. The fearful struggle in which this country is now engaged to deliver herself from its deadly folds proves this to be an awful deception.

With the triumph of antislavery Haven predicted that the "apostate" southern church—"established on the corner-stone of property in human flesh"—would be blotted out. "It shall not much longer feed the fires of infidelity in the North by its miserable caricature of Christianity," he contended.

It shall not much longer entangle the feeble kneed with us in its meshes by professions of pious care for its servile population, while it leaves them in hopeless bondage without one cheering word; while it helps to force them into the dungeons and seals the watch with diabolical quotations from the word of God, and more diabolic assumptions of the name and dignity of the Christian Church and ministry.

The contrast between true and false Christianity precluded any middle ground. "Think not," Haven warned Maryland Methodists, "that you are to be a chosen and prosperous Church of Jesus Christ and remain with folded arms in this tremendous war." [61]

The "Admonition" did not go unanswered. "A more injurious or unjust attack upon true men . . . can hardly be imagined," George R. Crooks of *The Methodist* charged. His defense of the loyal Methodists of the border conceded, however, that about a dozen ministers in one conference and as many as a majority of the preachers in another were "pro slavery in morals and secession in politics." Nonetheless, Crooks was anxious to vindicate those who were "true to their Church principles" and loyal to the Union, regardless of their views on the question of slavery.[62]

Because Crooks would not publish it, Haven's response appeared in the *Advocate,* where he defended his analysis of Methodism in Maryland and his own course of action while there. He agreed with Crooks that there were loyal men in both conferences who hated slavery, but he justified his admonition precisely on the ground that these very men ought to be encouraged to speak out and demonstrate their position. Since Crooks identified these men with the antislavery cause, Haven disputed the claim. He denied that "there could be real, active opposition to slavery which rested short of its extirpation." The Maryland conferences could best show their loyal intentions and antislavery sentiment, he suggested, by affirming the statement against slavery made by early Methodists at a meeting in Baltimore in 1780. That declaration was the strongest antislavery position within the denomination until the rise of the "new" abolitionism in the 1830s. Its clarity demonstrated to Haven that latter-day border Methodism had fallen away considerably from

61. *Ibid.*
62. *The Methodist,* Oct. 5, 1861.

the high standard of its founders. He had recognized as much during his military tour when he told one of the proslavery Baltimore preachers that "every stone he threw at New England Abolitionism shied off & hit the graves of their [sic] fathers." [63]

A shift in Haven's evaluation of the role of the churches in the antislavery crusade was going on during this controversy. Six months before, just prior to the outbreak of the war, he had vigorously defended the course of the Methodist Episcopal Church against the attacks of William Lloyd Garrison and Charles K. Whipple. He was confident that slavery had died "elsewhere" and was "dying here, through the life of the Church more than through all other instrumentalities." [64] After he returned from Maryland, however, Haven wondered whether he had not overstated the accomplishments of organized religion in the antislavery reform. In his defense of his admonition, he wrote that "the privilege of regenerating Maryland may not be given to the Church" because of "her long complicity" with and "long silence" concerning slavery.[65] During the ensuing months Haven came to realize more fully the failure of the churches when political events outdistanced religious action and influence in bringing emancipation.

In the fall of 1861 Haven remained undecided about his future role, both in the church and in the national conflict. After more than a year of mourning he still had not fully resolved the problem of accepting the death of his wife. He did not see how he could return to the parish ministry without a mother for his young children.[66] As deeply concerned as he was with the Civil War, he did not know where best to invest his energies in that effort. Postponing a final decision about the future for a time, Haven agreed in October to take a temporary position as pastor of the Clinton Avenue Methodist Episcopal Church in Newark, New Jersey.[67]

Because of the conservative political sentiments of most of his congregation, Haven had serious questions about his prospects for success in this interim pastorate. But he entered the work enthusiastically, generated new interest, and mobilized broad participation among the members.[68] In addition to his pastoral responsibilities, he began again his editorial contributions.

63. *Christian Advocate and Journal*, Oct. 31, 1861; "War Journal," July 6, 1861; Prentice, *Life*, p. 233. Haven had become newly aware of the early Methodist antislavery movement and the denomination's subsequent compromise on the question because he had been given a copy of the *Minutes of the Methodist Conferences, annually held in America; From 1773 to 1813, Inclusive* (New York, 1813) while he was in Maryland in July, 1861. The author has Haven's copy of these minutes with an inscription from its donor. Haven referred to the book in the second part of the "Admonition," *Christian Advocate and Journal*, Sept. 12, 1861; *Zion's Herald*, Sept. 11, 1861.

64. *The Liberator*, Mar. 29, 1861.

65. *Christian Advocate and Journal*, Oct. 31, 1861.

66. See a comment in his "War Journal," July 6, 1861. During the fall Fales Newhall observed in his Journal how unsettled Haven was about his future (Oct. 22, 1861).

67. *Zion's Herald*, Oct. 23, 1861; *Christian Advocate and Journal*, Nov. 7, 1861.

68. Prentice, *Life*, pp. 241-42.

Simultaneously he was the Boston correspondent for the *Advocate,* and the anonymous New York contributor for *Zion's Herald.*[69]

For six months Haven had the opportunity of observing the war spirit amid "the intense activity of New York." He fully expected antiwar sentiment to reign, since the stock market had suffered immense economic losses from secession. The decline of cotton investments had created a financial crisis, but, by late 1861, the Lincoln administration had repaired most of the machinery in New York's economic operations. Hence, there was wider support for the Union than Haven anticipated, and he even heard occasional appeals for abolition.[70] There was enough diverse opinion to make him believe that many of the people were "ready for one war-cry—Emancipation!"[71] He admitted that antislavery sentiment was often inspired by expediency rather than high principle, but he commended the movement just the same, urging "Emancipation for the Union, if we cannot say the bigger word, emancipation for the sake of the slave, for the sake of humanity, for the sake of God."[72]

During the fall and winter of 1861-62 Haven grew more critical of the government's reluctance to strike at slavery as the South's most vulnerable point. In his first article for the *Advocate* after he moved to Newark, he called Lincoln's government "an antislavery administration [which] is afraid of being antislavery."[73] Earlier he had supported General John C. Frémont's proclamation which sought to free the slaves of all rebels in Missouri. When the President revoked the act, Haven and many other abolitionists altered the enthusiastic endorsement which they had given the administration since the war began.[74] Though Haven did not abandon his general support of Lincoln, he became a loyal critic for the remainder of the war. At the same time most abolitionists resumed their role as agitators by organizing a propaganda campaign to convince public opinion and the President that slavery was "the fundamental cause and basic issue of the war." Apparently Haven did not

69. He continued to write under the pen name "Once-in-a-While" for the *Advocate*. He signed his articles "X." and "&c." for the *Herald*. See Prentice, *Life*, p. 245; Daniels, *Memorials of Gilbert Haven*, p. 260.

70. *Zion's Herald*, Nov. 6, 1861; see also Haven's earlier comments on New York's financial problems, *ibid.*, May 15, 1861.

71. In an undated letter from Haven to his family written from Newark, quoted in Prentice, *Life*, p. 242.

72. *Zion's Herald*, Nov. 6, 1861.

73. *Christian Advocate and Journal*, Oct. 31, 1861.

74. *Zion's Herald*, Nov. 6, 1861; *Christian Advocate and Journal*, Dec. 5, 1861. Lincoln forced Frémont to modify the unauthorized order and bring it within the lines of congressional legislation on the confiscation of enemy property. An act, passed Aug. 6, 1861, permitted only the confiscation of those slaves who aided the Confederacy in a military way. See McPherson, *Struggle for Equality*, pp. 72-73; Moore, *Rebellion Record*, vol. II, pp. 475-76, documents section; Roy P. Basler, ed., *The Collected Works of Abraham Lincoln* (New Brunswick, N.J.: Rutgers University Press, 1953), vol. IV pp. 506-7, 517-18. When Frémont was dismissed from his post in the West, Haven charged that "his proclamation, not his pride or extravagance" caused his removal. *Christian Advocate and Journal*, Oct. 31, 1861.

join any specific movement of this kind, but the positions which he took on the main questions coincided with the goals of the organized campaign.[75]

The abolitionist drive got a major boost in October when at the Massachusetts State Republican Convention in Worcester, Charles Sumner called "the overthrow of slavery" the best method to "make an end of the war." He recommended "a simple declaration, that all men within the lines of the United States troops are freemen." [76] Though there was widespread opposition, even in Massachusetts, to Sumner's position, Haven was enthusiastic about the address. "It is full of thanksgiving and of hope," he wrote. "It rejoices over that greatest of emancipations, the liberation of our government from the yoke of slavery. It summons the nation to its grandest privilege and duty, the destruction of the accursed system that is striving to destroy it." Sumner's plan was "constitutional," Haven believed, and it would be "practical, bloodless, and effectual in breaking up the rebellion." But to his surprise and chagrin, he found that the New York press gave greater support to Sumner than the Boston papers. Massachusetts Republicans were apparently afraid of the political consequences of criticizing the President's policy, so that the convention itself refused to back Sumner's advocacy of emancipation as a war strategy.[77]

In his Worcester speech Sumner dealt with another controversial issue which had repercussions during the winter of 1861. He suggested, rather obliquely, the use of Negro troops in the Union Army, recommending that "we carry Africa into the war . . . in any form, any quantity, any way." [78] Haven did not comment on that reference, but he did praise the effort by the secretary of war, Simon Cameron, to get approval for arming black soldiers. The attempt was "an improvement on the famous [Frémont] proclamation, in fact, though far below it in feeling and expression." [79] Haven called Cameron's position "a fine show of our progress" toward "immediate and unconditional emancipation." "To arm and uniform the slaves, even those of loyalists, for this is the intent of the order," he wrote, "is a wonderful stride toward the goal." Boston would welcome enthusiastically a "regiment of Carolina slaves," for they would "redeem at once themselves, the nation, and democratic institutions, and true Christianity from an infamous yoke." [80] But again President Lincoln delayed. In this instance, he reprimanded Cameron for recommending in his annual report to Congress the freeing and

75. McPherson, *Struggle for Equality*, p. 61.

76. *Charles Sumner. His Complete Works*, Statesman ed. (Boston, 1900), vol. VII, pp. 252, 256.

77. *Christian Advocate and Journal*, Oct. 31, 1861; *Zion's Herald*, Dec. 18, 1861; McPherson, *Struggle for Equality*, p. 77; Sumner, *Works*, vol. VII, pp. 273-304. No Boston daily supported the senator, but Horace Greeley's *New York Tribune* published the speech in its weekly edition, which reached as many as a million readers. In November, 1863, Haven referred to these developments in a sermon; see *National Sermons*, p. 385.

78. Sumner, *Works*, vol. VII, p. 253.

79. *Zion's Herald*, Nov. 6, 1861.

80. *Christian Advocate and Journal*, Nov. 28, 1861.

arming of all slaves of rebels who were capable of military service as soon as they came into Union lines.[81]

In early December, 1861, the President's own annual message further disillusioned abolitionists like Haven. Instead of taking steps toward emancipation, Lincoln reiterated his conservative policy that the war continued only to suppress the insurrection and not to emancipate slaves. Guarding lest the conflict "degenerate into a violent and remorseless revolutionary struggle," as he put it, Lincoln discussed only how to provide for those ex-slaves who had been freed under the confiscation act of the previous August. He asked Congress to acquire territory for the colonization of former bondsmen and other "free colored people already in the United States . . . so far as individuals may desire."[82] Understandably, Haven regretted the President's position. He wrote of Lincoln, "Within the near future it is to be seen whether we have only a moral improvement on Mr. Buchanan, or one who can see and grasp the right in spite of all the impediments of darkness and fear."[83]

At times Haven despaired over the President's refusal to sound the note of freedom and about the failure of the military, especially General George McClellan's Army of the Potomac, to advance. Occasionally, he took consolation in believing that the public in its sentiment was ahead of the national leadership. "The people are crying out for leaders," he wrote once, "men who will lead, not for fort-builders, to protect their party or their antiquated professions. There is no safety like advance and victory."[84] At other times, Haven was completely exasperated. In February, 1862, he complained: "Congress is timid, the President is timid, M'Clellan [sic] is timid, the people are full of fear of doing their duty, and we shall have to be scourged into the work or destroyed from being a nation." Above all, Haven believed the greatest failure to be the national war aim and the reluctance of the government to call for a crusade against slavery. "Our hope," he wrote in the *Advocate,* "is in no girdlings of the South, or marches upon their batteries when the great word 'Freedom' has ceased to be spoken, when we have for our national policy that weakest of war cries, 'The Constitution, the Union, and the Enforcement of Laws.' 'God and Liberty' are the only cries that will win us the victory."[85]

The appointment of Edwin M. Stanton in January, 1862, as the new secretary of war gave Haven some hope that a more aggressive leadership was emerging. The need of the hour, he sensed, was victory "on the Potomac

---

81. McPherson, *Struggle for Equality,* p. 194. Benjmain P. Thomas and Harold Hyman, *Stanton. The Life and Times of Lincoln's Secretary of War* (New York: Alfred A. Knopf, 1962), p. 134, n. 7.

82. Basler, *Works of Lincoln,* vol. V, pp. 48-49; McPherson, *Struggle for Equality,* p. 94.

83. *Zion's Herald,* Dec. 18, 1861.

84. *Christian Advocate and Journal,* Oct. 31, 1861; *Zion's Herald,* Mar. 5, 1862. Confidence in an advancing public opinion was common among abolitionists. See McPherson, *Struggle for Equality,* pp. 95-96.

85. *Christian Advocate and Journal,* Feb. 20, 1862.

and in the halls of Congress." [86] The military victories which Haven looked for came in early 1862, not on the Potomac but in the West where Ulysses S. Grant won his first fame by capturing a Confederate stronghold, Fort Donelson, taking more than fourteen thousand rebels as prisoners. In the aftermath of victory Haven was confident that some move toward emancipation was imminent. In late February, he wrote: "Whether Congress wishes it or not, emancipation is in the near future." Secretly, Haven feared that military victory would come so quickly that emancipation might not be enacted. That eventuality was not nearly as probable as he thought.[87]

But another development soon gave Haven something about which to rejoice. On March 6, 1862, President Lincoln took a first major step toward ending slavery by asking Congress to pass a joint resolution which offered federal compensation to any state that would initiate gradual emancipation.[88] The resolution was couched in "old and conservative words," Haven noted, but the meaning was clear. The government had set out toward the goal of emancipation. "It may be long before we reach it, but we shall never lose it from our eyes," Haven announced jubilantly. "It is the first glimpse we have had of it. We walked by faith, now we shall walk by sight." [89]

The indication that the President was slowly accepting the necessity for emancipation encouraged Haven more than any event since Lincoln's election in 1860. In a sermon at Newark on March 9, he praised the presidential message as "the most important word spoken in this land since the Declaration of Independence." [90] He emphasized that the act would give "clearness and tone to the national mind as to the character of slavery." Haven's outlook was exuberant. Henceforth, everyone would see "the great evil of slavery, and the necessity of its extirpation." He did not think it would be possible any longer for a scriptural or political defense of slavery to stand. "No man here, no man elsewhere in our land, can again say . . . ," he exclaimed optimistically, "Slavery is right, is divine, is for the best good of the African, though he be an American of ten generations, and nine tenths of him be Caucasian." [91] Other consequences would follow. Haven predicted that Lincoln's move would hasten the downfall of the rebellion by ending European sympathy for the Confederacy, by uniting the diverse political factions of the North, and by encouraging the slaves. This step toward freedom, moreover, would restore the moral prestige of the American republic among the nations of the world.[92]

86. *Zion's Herald,* Mar. 5, 1862.
87. *Ibid.*
88. Basler, *Works of Abraham Lincoln,* vol. V, pp. 144-46.
89. *Zion's Herald,* Mar. 26, 1862.
90. *National Sermons,* p. 276. Haven probably borrowed this comparison from Greeley's *New York Tribune* of Mar. 8. See William Ghormley Cochrane, "Freedom Without Equality: A Study of Northern Opinion and the Negro Issue, 1861-1870" (Ph.D. dissertation, University of Minnesota, 1957), p. 19.
91. *National Sermons,* pp. 276, 279.
92. *Ibid.,* pp. 280-84, 287.

Since the first act toward ultimate emancipation had been taken, Haven began to consider what was necessary to reunite and reconstruct the nation after the war. One event above all others shaped his perspective. On March 3, he stood in New York harbor and watched the embarkation of the first shipload of missionary teachers and farmers headed for the sea islands off South Carolina to conduct the Port Royal experiment among ex-slaves as a model for reconstruction.[93] Haven saluted the group of emigrants who called themselves the "Gideonites," referring to them as the new "Pilgrim Fathers" who "assured a New South after the Puritan and perfect pattern." Their plan for the reconstruction of the South immediately appealed to him. It was a colonization scheme based on New England principles and designed to create a "new society and civilization." Half in jest, half seriously, Haven suggested that South Carolina be renamed New Massachusetts after the war.[94]

What he understood at this early date was the necessity to overturn the antebellum aristocratic southern social order. In his thanksgiving sermon on Lincoln's emancipation message to Congress Haven spoke of subduing the entire region, "the richest and most beautiful in America." "The waves of liberty, a Nile of wealth, must fertilize this American Sahara," he declared. "Churches, schools, workshops and farms, must be filled with free worshipers, students, toilers." [95] The regeneration of the South would be so thorough that no segment of the society would be untouched. In the economic sphere "the great fundamental idea of free labor, of the dignity of labor, of the rights of labor" would replace the ownership of labor. Even northern religion must replace a southern orthodoxy whose "one dogma" was "a doctrine of the devils" which began, "I believe in slavery." [96] The revolutionary scheme required that retributive justice fall heavily upon the slave masters. "The voice of those who are defrauded of their wages cries to God," Haven preached at Newark, reinterpreting one of Jesus' parables, "and He has come down to see if it be according to their cry. He finds they told the truth. Therefore will He destroy those husbandmen, and give that vineyard to others?" As they replaced the old slavocracy, the downtrodden blacks and poor whites would rise to new manhood and with European and northern immigrants create a new social order in the South.[97]

Because most whites doubted that blacks could manage their freedom, the Port Royal experiment, Haven hoped, would also prove that the ex-slaves could take responsibility and work toward prosperity. They would

93. See Willie Lee Rose, *Rehearsal for Reconstruction. The Port Royal Experiment* (Indianapolis: Bobbs-Merrill, 1964).

94. *Zion's Herald*, Mar. 19, 1862; *National Sermons*, p. 286, note; McPherson, *Struggle for Equality*, pp. 162-69.

95. *National Sermons*, pp. 284-85.

96. *Ibid.*, pp. 283-84.

97. *Ibid.*, p. 285. The parable of the vineyard which Haven uses for his analogy is found in all three synoptic gospels: Matt. 21, Mark 12, Luke 20.

prove "their fitness for freedom," he declared, and give a fatal blow to the "mean and wicked prejudice" which insisted that whites and Negroes could not live together peaceably where both races had liberty and equality. Because white supremacist beliefs were so widespread, Haven thought that it would be ironic should Port Royal and the postwar experience show "that the superior race is the enslaved race." [98] At the time he had little idea of the magnitude of the problems which general emancipation would bring. For a long time abolitionists had exposed the dehumanizing character of chattel slavery and its dire effects upon the personality, morality, and intelligence of its victims. In light of those factors, and especially the recalcitrance of white racism, the transition from slavery to freedom promised to be extremely difficult. But in 1862, Haven was so absorbed in the promising future which lay ahead that he did not consider the practical problems which would challenge every prospect for success.[99]

Lincoln's first move toward emancipation in March, 1862, further convinced Haven to reevaluate the role of the churches in antislavery reform. The initiative for emancipation no longer lay with the moral influence of religion but within the political sphere. Haven blamed the churches not only for their inability to expel slaveholders from their constituencies, but for their failure as well to speak effectively as the conscience of the society on the question. He wrote in March that the war was in one sense the result of the "fatal mistake" of churchmen, like the early Methodists, who ceased to preach emancipation as part of the Christian gospel at a time when abolition could have been peacefully accomplished. "The cause of truth and righteousness, which is the cause of God," he admitted soberly, "requires us to say what future ages *will* say, that our church, in common with all other forms of religion, quailed before and compromised with that terrible foe of God and man." [100]

One significant aspect of Haven's growing realism about the church's role in the antislavery crusade was his new appreciation for the prophetic work of William Lloyd Garrison. The first sign of Haven's modification of his religious strictures against Garrison came out in a report on the anniversary meeting of the Massachusetts Antislavery Society early in 1862. Writing for the *Advocate,* Haven did not ignore Garrison's unorthodox "views on evangelical religion and the Bible" which he had attacked so fervently the year before, but he offered a new explanation for them. "The criminal conduct of the Churches of Christ" regarding slavery was the real cause for Garrison's infidelity. Haven put the matter bluntly: "No Church, as a Church, has yet stood by him. The Presbyterian, and the Methodist, and the Episcopalian, and the Unitarian, all, for years, bowed the knee to Baal, and persecuted

98. *Ibid.,* p. 286.
99. McPherson, *Struggle for Equality,* pp. 172-73.
100. *Zion's Herald,* Mar. 5, 1862; *National Sermons,* p. 270.

the prophet of the most high God who came preaching the Gospel of Liberty."
Then, Haven made his challenge. "They cannot, therefore, find fault with him
if he sometimes forgot the blood that redeemed him and the blessed book that
is a light shining in a dark place," he declared. "His sin was no greater, was
far less than theirs; for he refused to *believe* the whole truth as it is in Jesus,
they to *practice* it." [101]

Two weeks later, the editor of the *Advocate,* Edward Thomson, reacted
strongly to Haven's attack on the churches and his defense of Garrison.
Ironically, he used many of the same arguments which Haven had employed
against Garrison early in 1861. He asserted that the churches generally had
played a significant part in arousing the public conscience against slavery;
that the Bible should be believed whether or not some churchmen failed
to practice its teachings; and that Garrison had made a great mistake in
denouncing established religious institutions. "It takes time to educate the
Church to duty in regard to established social evils," he wrote. Yet Thomson
did advise Methodists to try to understand Garrison more sympathetically and
to take "higher ground" on reforms, but he still dissented from Haven's viewpoint. [102]

In response, Haven exhorted his friend, Thomson, not to fret over his
"chatterings." "If they are thoughtless," he wrote, "they will die in a day
and be forgotten; if they are true, they can do no harm." Then he explained
his rationale for criticizing Methodism. He believed that "truth never yet
harmed the Church, though many are often afraid that it will." Those churchmen who think the Church "must be handled as carefully as Sevres china"
become offended when someone speaks "a plain truth about its defects."
"You must keep saying," they insist, "that it is without spot, or wrinkle,
or any such thing, and then it will be." Inevitably, Haven claimed, the
"Church militant" will be afflicted with "faults and defects, and those who
love it most will be most anxious to tell it its faults that it may be healed."
Then, he cited biblical examples of "divine rebuke" of the people of God.

Moses, Isaiah, Paul, John in the Apocalypse, would have fared ill with our modern
Church nurses. They did not cease to lift their voice and tell the house of Jacob
their transgressions and Israel her sins. So ought every member of the Church
to-day, especially those in authority, to search out in a spirit of love her short-
comings, and to seek to lift her up to a higher plane of holy living. [103]

To defend his earlier interpretation, Haven stated again that the future
historian would have very little basis on which to commend the churches

101. *Christian Advocate and Journal,* Feb. 20, 1862; *National Sermons,* pp. 271, 276.
102. *Christian Advocate and Journal,* Mar. 6, 1862. A more caustic criticism of Haven on these
same issues appeared in a letter by James M. Edgerton of Massachusetts, which came out in the
Advocate, May 15, 1862. Since Haven was out of the country when the letter was published, he
did not reply.
103. *Christian Advocate and Journal,* May 1, 1862.

for their role in the abolition of slavery. He acknowledged that members and ministers in the churches had taken part in the reform from the beginning, but he distinguished between the faithfulness of the prophetic minority of churchmen and the "limping support" for abolition given by most church organizations. "Where are the brave words of a general convocation, synod, association, or conference against this sin?" he asked. "Where the word that demands its instant and utter extirpation?" After praising the emancipationist position of early Methodists, Haven showed the subsequent compromise and reversal of sentiment in the next half-century. "Only one speech the Church ought to have uttered," he argued, "and that was for immediate and unconditional and universal emancipation. She did say that in 1784. But she backed down the next year, and never rallied again." Abolition was revived among New England Methodists during the 1830s, Haven acknowledged, "and for thirty years we have labored to make that truth sovereign." But, despite gradual progress toward the goal, he admitted reluctantly "that as a Church we have not earnestly and ceaselessly labored in this cause." The poor antislavery record of the Methodist and other major denominations left them no ground on which to condemn Garrison for his "error in faith." Only when the churches proclaimed universal emancipation, "the great word which Mr. Garrison revived," would they obtain the right to censure the fiery abolitionist editor.[104]

Even as he issued his strongest criticism of the church, Haven did not abandon his faith in the influence and power of Christianity to advance the cause of humanity. He blamed the church for past failures, but he called as well for new commitment to future responsibilities. The same article which harshly condemned the church for its ineffective moral witness regarding slavery called it to take the lead in regenerating the South. "May our zeal in the future palliate our timidity in the past," Haven prayed. "May the Church spread itself zealously, purely, successfully over the South . . . and so seek the salvation and elevation of the oppressed that our Saviour shall remember no more our lukewarmness and hostility in the penitence and activity that we shall henceforth exhibit." [105]

The basic aspects of what Haven saw as a new social mission for the church had occurred to him earlier. In January, addressing the Methodist Tract Society, he called attention to the church's emerging duty to instruct the southern freedmen.[106] A month later he challenged the denomination's missionary society and the episcopal leadership to send men South on ventures like the Port Royal expedition in order to build "a true and pure Methodist Church out of the unconverted masses, whose consciences have been too scrupulous to accept of a pro-slavery religion." [107] In April, Haven

104. *Ibid.*
105. *Ibid.*
106. *Zion's Herald*, Feb. 5, 1862; *Christian Advocate and Journal*, Feb. 13, 1862.
107. *Zion's Herald*, Mar. 19, 1862.

joined his fellow ministers in the New England Conference to ask church authorities to plan a northern Methodist reoccupation of the South. These New Englanders recognized that more than "the defeat of treason with the bayonet" was essential to reunite the nation. They recommended preparations for "the Christian educator" to follow "the footsteps of the victorious soldier" and engage in a "Christian bloodless warfare, in behalf of Christian civilization in America." [108] When Haven enthusiastically reported the conference action for the *Advocate,* he was hopeful that his church, by such moves, would keep step with the nation's progress and meet the demands of the fast changing era.[109] By the time his report appeared in print, however, Haven had left the work of the church in other hands for a season.

III

The spring of 1862 was a time of considerable optimism about the national situation throughout the North. Secretary Stanton ceased recruiting for the army, and the New York press began to write that the war was about over.[110] Haven shared this rosy outlook. "It looks as if the backbone of the rebellion were broken," he wrote to Major Ben Perley Poore of his old regiment, "and if McClellan does what his friends expect of him Jeff[erson Davis] and Co[mpany] will soon be making tracks for the allied armies off Mexico." [111] Because "the times" were "so auspicious," Haven felt free to renew plans for his trip to Europe. "If they had been dark & desperate," he explained, "I should have gone into Frémont's department." [112]

The proposed European trip was apparently quite important to Haven. He looked upon it as an opportunity to rest and gain perspective on his life. He was still struggling to resolve the tragic death of his wife. A foreign tour was the customary way many people of the time sought to overcome emotional depression and poor health. That he chose such a time for travel is curious, retrospectively, but he justified, at least to himself, his decision to leave the country. On April 30 he departed from Boston on the ship *Canada* for what was to be a journey of nine months through England, Scotland, France, Holland, Germany, Switzerland, Italy, Greece, Egypt, and

108. *Minutes of the New England Conference,* 1862, pp. 19-20, 22-24.

109. *Christian Advocate and Journal,* May 1, 1862.

110. Cochrane, "Freedom Without Equality," p. 33.

111. Haven to Major Ben Perley Poore, Newark, N. J., Mar. 18, 1862, Gratz Collection, Historical Society of Pennsylvania. His satirical reference to "the allied armies" concerns the move by the French emperor, Louis Napoleon, to install Maximilian as ruler of Mexico and unite with the Confederacy against the United States. See Clement Eaton, *A History of the Southern Confederacy* (New York: Collier, 1961), pp. 82-83.

112. He added: "But I don't think he's going to have much to do." Haven to Poore, Mar. 18, 1862. On March 11, President Lincoln had given General John C. Frémont a new command, the Mountain Department of western Virginia and eastern Tennessee. See Bruce Catton, *Terrible Swift Sword* (Garden City, N.Y.: Doubleday & Co., 1963), p. 201.

the Holy Land. Throughout the trip he composed essays and letters on his travels, which he sent back to the *Advocate* and the *Herald* and to two periodicals for which he had never written, a Methodist monthly, the *Ladies' Repository,* and *The Independent,* unquestionably the most important religious weekly in the country.[113] Most of the articles described places, people, and customs which Haven observed as he hiked and rode over Europe. After the war he republished the accounts of his experiences in England, France, and Germany in his first book, *The Pilgrim's Wallet,* which he dedicated to Isaac Rich, a wealthy Bostonian, who paid part of the cost of the trip.[114]

The trip abroad in 1862 forced Haven to reflect on the American Civil War in a broader perspective. For its first year he had concentrated on the conflict almost entirely in its national aspects. He was concerned whether the nation could permit or withstand the secession of a major portion of its territory and citizens and whether slavery could be abolished in the struggle. From abroad his interpretation of the war began to take on a new dimension, shaped by his recognition of its international significance.[115]

In world perspective the Civil War was, to Haven, an irrepressible conflict between democracy and all decadent forms of European government and social organization: monarchies, oligarchies, aristocracies. "If American political ideas prevail," he wrote in 1861, "then must European ones die. They cannot live together for ages in a progressive Christian civilization. They are radically different. One is on the rock of ages, one on the sands of time." [116] He linked the southern slavocracy to these antidemocratic ideas in order to account for the fundamental impulse behind the rebellion. European nobility and royalty sympathized with the Confederacy because they wished to see American democracy fail. "The haughty aristocracy of Europe [would love to say] republicanism is a failure," he contended. "Then this everlasting prating about rights of man, liberty, equality, and fraternity will cease." [117] The war, therefore, was a test to prove that, as Lincoln said in his eloquent Gettysburg Address, this nation "conceived in Liberty, and dedicated to the proposition that all men are created equal" with "government of the people,

---

113. Henry Ward Beecher was editor-in-chief of this New York paper at the time, but Theodore Tilton carried most of the responsibility for its operation. Haven's association with *The Independent* began in June, 1862 and continued until his death eighteen years later.

114. The full title is *The Pilgrim's Wallet; or, Scraps of Travel gathered in England, France, and Germany* (Boston, 1866). Rich was later a benefactor of Boston University. See Haven's article, "Isaac Rich," *Ladies' Repository,* 28 (1868), 321-24 and a memorial tribute in *The Independent,* Jan. 25, 1872. See also *Zion's Herald,* Apr. 18, 1866.

115. Occasionally during 1861 Haven had thought about the war in world perspective, but the European trip provided an opportunity to develop this view more extensively. See *Christian Advocate and Journal,* June 27, July 4, 1861. He wrote to Newhall, for example, that the North's success would make the nation greater and thus demonstrate to Europe American invincibility. See Journal of Fales H. Newhall, May 27, 1861.

116. *Christian Advocate and Journal,* June 27, 1861.

117. *Ibid.; Zion's Herald,* June 11, Sept. 10, 1862; "Pictures of Travel. Lake Geneva," *Ladies' Repository,* 23 (1863), p. 29. On this topic see *National Sermons,* pp. 439-72.

by the people, for the people, shall not perish from the earth." [118] With that test, in Haven's view, lay not only America's destiny, but the future of mankind. He did not hesitate to say, "We are fighting the battle for the peoples the world over." [119]

Of all the European powers, England drew Haven's most stinging criticism for its aristocratic social system and government. Before he went abroad, he had damned the British government as "a perfect system of inequality" controlled by an oligarchy which "more than all others . . . [respects] rank and caste." [120] Doubtless, England's official neutral position toward the Civil War added to Haven's anglophobia. He was certainly offended by the sympathy for the South which he found among British passengers on his voyage to Europe, among leaders in Parliament and in the London press, and among colonial officials in Alexandria and Cairo.[121]

While he was in England, Haven undertook to enlighten the British public about the real questions in dispute in the American war. In July, responding to an invitation from the editor of the Methodist weekly, the *London Watchman,* he composed a long letter on the issues of the conflict. Only the first half of the essay appeared, however, because the publication committee of the paper decided not to print the remainder due to Haven's criticism of the English government and his prophecy of an imminent democratic revolution against it. Even the incomplete essay aroused considerable controversy which went on in the *Watchman* while Haven was traveling on the continent. When he returned to England in January, 1863, he discovered that the second half of his article had never been issued and that a contributor, "Amicus," had spent four months answering the first part.[122]

The essay which Haven wrote for the *Watchman* contained his most complete statement on the Civil War in its world perspective. "The rebellion began," he wrote, "and has been waged, solely in the interests of Slavery." The basic cause of the war was beyond the "need of any argument in America" for "no man nor woman, North or South, bond or free, white or black" denied it. But, Haven complained, "the rebels, and their allies of the press, and of Parliament . . . have had the effrontery to say that Slavery was not involved in the struggle; that other interests caused the revolt—the tariff, or national alienation of the people, or oppression of minorities." Contrariwise, Haven contended that Americans were "one people, far more than England and Scotland, by marriage, emigration, language, interest, and feel-

118. Basler, *Works of Abraham Lincoln,* vol. VII, pp. 17-23.
119. *Christian Advocate and Journal,* June 27, July 4, 1861; *Zion's Herald,* Sept. 10, 1862. The view was not an uncommon sentiment. See Chapman, "The Protestant Campaign for the Union," p. 91.
120. *Christian Advocate and Journal,* June 27, 1861.
121. *Ibid.,* June 12, Aug. 7, 1862; *Zion's Herald,* June 11, Sept. 10, 1862; Feb. 4, 1863.
122. The entire essay is in *National Sermons,* pp. 291-316, and note, pp. 641-42. Haven published the second half when he returned home, along with a letter written in London on Jan. 14, 1863, to *The Watchman* about the earlier censorship. See *Zion's Herald,* Feb. 25, Apr. 1, and 8, 1863; *The Methodist,* Aug. 9, 1862; *The Independent,* Aug. 21, 1862.

ing." When he insisted that "Slavery, and slavery alone" was the cause of the war, however, he represented his own view more than he gave an accurate account of American opinion. There was no one view of the relation of slavery to the war among Americans at home, North or South. At the same time Haven did have some evidence for his interpretation, particularly in the constitution of the Confederate States, which had special provisions to protect domestic slavery, and in the famous "corner-stone" speech by Alexander Stephens.[123]

The obvious difficulty with Haven's description was the timidity of the North to strike at slavery which he had often condemned at home. For his purposes in England, however, Haven softened his criticism of the Lincoln government and defended its strategy to reunite the nation without acting directly against slavery. "What the government must do," he wrote, "is, not first to abolish slavery, but to re-possess itself of its property, re-assume its authority, and destroy the insurrectionary armies." Haven's views were contradictory, but he apparently intended only to defend the North and win broader English support for the Lincoln government, which, he claimed, was "actually, earnestly, entirely on the side of freedom." As proof, Haven cited the abolition of slavery in the District of Columbia, the liberation of slaves by the Union armies, federal support of schools and jobs for freedmen, and the exclusion of slavery from the national territories.[124]

Despite the evidences of antislavery progress Haven admitted in the originally unpublished part of the essay that America still had a great unfinished work to do. His statement summarized the American dilemma, the unfaithful practice of the nation's democratic principles with reference to "the relation of the African race to the Caucassian [sic]—the white to the black. Our fundamental and most vital theories," he declared, "require that we make no distinction; that we be as unmindful of the accident of color as that of birth or tongue. But our feelings are powerfully averse to the conclusions to which we are thus driven. We cannot deny the foundation principles; we cannot instantly overcome the repugnance of ages and ages." [125] The war, Haven believed, was forcing the nation to extend liberty and equality to, and thus assimilate, the American Negro in the same way that the "races" of Europe had mixed in the country's melting pot. "Nothing but the danger of losing her own liberties could have made her grant the African his," he wrote of America. "Nothing but the sacrifice of his own equality would make a white citizen admit the black as a sharer." [126]

Besides his public discussion of the American conflict in England, Haven

123. *National Sermons*, pp. 294, 296. On the Confederate constitution see Moore, *Rebellion Record*, vol. II, document 97 1/2, pp. 321-27, documents section.

124. *National Sermons*, pp. 298-300; *Zion's Herald*, Apr. 1, 1863.

125. *Zion's Herald*, Apr. 1, 1863. The quotation, slightly revised, appears in *National Sermons*, p. 307.

126. *Zion's Herald*, Apr. 1, 1863; *National Sermons*, p. 308.

further developed his perspective on the war in his travels, especially in France, Italy, and Greece. In each country he analyzed for his readers back home the prospects for democracy, seen always, of course, through the lens of its supreme expression in America. As a desirable outcome of democratic political movements on the continent, he projected a kind of European union of national states, which, like the American union, would be a forerunner to a "World Republic" or a "world Congress." [127] Since he was not really interested in providing political blueprints for Europe, however, Haven only suggested the idea without developing it. His major concern was with American responsibility in the world scene. The United States must emerge from the Civil War more than ever "the Model Republic," purged from slavery and truly representative of civil equality.[128] For this reason, Haven never lost interest in the political and military developments at home. He followed events, as best he could, firmly convinced that the American war was "the battle for the world." Because he was sure that the North was "struggling for the rights of mankind," the outcome of the war determined the future of Europe as well as of the American republic.[129]

As Haven looked on events from abroad, he was more than ever distressed about the timidity and inaction of the Lincoln administration on emancipation. His enthusiasm about the government's antislavery commitment in March, 1862, turned to despair by July and August. In a letter from England, he warned that the military reverses which the Union army suffered that summer would continue until the "white banner of Emancipation" was unfurled.[130] Writing from Switzerland in August, he focused his criticism more directly on Lincoln. "Twice has our President suppressed the great word as it burst forth from the lips of his authorized representatives," he complained, referring to the Frémont proclamation in the summer of 1861, and a similar edict of emancipation issued by General David Hunter for South Carolina, Georgia, and Florida in May, 1862, which Lincoln also revoked.[131] In a small room in his hotel in Lucerne, Haven joined five other American clergymen to pray for their country and for Lincoln "that God would give [him] courage to speak the great word, EMANCIPATION." When he reported the prayer meeting, Haven likewise beseeched his American readers to "hear the word of the Lord." "Trample under foot the accursed prejudice against your brother because of his complexion," he pleaded. "Give him his liberty. Give him the rights and privileges which God and our civil principles alike de-

127. *Christian Advocate and Journal*, Aug. 7, 1862; *Zion's Herald*, Apr. 1, 1863; *The Independent*, Jan. 15, Mar. 19, 26, 1863; *National Sermons*, pp. 305-6.

128. *Zion's Herald*, Apr. 1, 1863; *National Sermons*, p. 306.

129. *National Sermons*, pp. 302-4; *The Independent*, Feb. 26, 1863.

130. *Zion's Herald*, July 16, 1862.

131. *The Independent*, Sept. 25, 1862. The article was dated Aug. 10, and it appeared, ironically, in the issue announcing Lincoln's projected emancipation proclamation. See McPherson, *Struggle for Equality*, pp. 107-8; Basler, *Works of Abraham Lincoln*, vol. V, pp. 222-24.

mand." Then, Haven predicted, "out of the dark and stormy night of blood and death and anguish," the nation would "be led in triumph, and the timbrels of the emancipated . . . ring forth the notes of thanksgiving, for their salvation and for the salvation of our common country." [132]

As he had done publicly for more than a decade, Haven was calling for a social revolution that would transform American racial attitudes and practices. He wanted desperately for the nation to vindicate its own democratic idealism. In the fall of 1862, he asked in one article, "Will the country take this Satan [slavery] for its sovereign, or will it stand by the principles of [Thomas] Jefferson's youth, and faithfully apply them to the duties of the hour? Will it proclaim all its men free, and treat them as equal?" [133]

In Haven's view the two democratic principles, liberty and equality, had to complement each other. Thus, he believed, emancipation coupled with colonization, forced or voluntary, would be nearly as wicked as slavery. Lincoln's continued commitment to colonization, therefore, received a blistering attack in Haven's correspondence from abroad. "The President seeks to expatriate five millions of his fellow-countrymen, and refuses to let them defend and re-establish the flag under which they and their fathers were born for two hundred years," he wrote from Germany.

It does not look very rational for a rail-splitter and a scow-boat navigator to be saying this people cannot live and work with us, but must be hustled off to some ungenial and unoccupied climate, where there are no civilized and organized institutions. He has worked beside them in the days of his humiliation; he should not despise them in the days of his exaltation. He should remember the hole of the pit from which he was dug.

To conclude his blast against Lincoln, Haven inferred that the President's "connection with the poor white trash," made him "afraid to take the rebel slaveholder by the throat and the slave by the hand." [134]

On October 1, from Florence, Haven gave one of his most emphatic appeals to national duty regarding slavery and the Negro. "The hour is come when the principles of the Declaration must be applied in our nation, or no independence is ours," he wrote. "No faint utterances will answer for this hour. No expatriating projects, joined with declarations that white and black cannot live together with us, when they have lived together for two hundred years. There must be no backing into the right. Arm the slaves, and call them *men*—call them brethren." [135] As he composed this imperative, Haven

132. *Zion's Herald*, Sept. 17, 1862.

133. *The Independent*, Dec. 18, 1862 (article dated Oct. 1).

134. *Christian Advocate and Journal*, Oct. 9, 1862 (article dated Sept. 1). For similar sentiments against colonization see *Zion's Herald*, Aug. 13, 1862; *Christian Advocate and Journal*, Aug. 28, 1862; *The Independent*, Sept. 25, 1862. On the debate over colonization during the war see James M. McPherson, "Abolitionist and Negro Opposition to Colonization During the Civil War," *Phylon*, 26 (1965), 391-99.

135. *The Independent*, Dec. 18, 1862.

did not know that Lincoln had issued ten days before, a preliminary proclamation of freedom to take effect on the first day of 1863.[136] But three weeks afterwards from Rome, Haven responded to the edict. "The Proclamation is as life from the dead," he exclaimed. "To leave America the greatest of slaveholding nations—to find it on our return after a brief absence almost universally free,—it seems well nigh miraculous. It is miraculous!" [137]

Either because he had not seen the entire document, or because he thought criticism inappropriate, Haven made no comment on Lincoln's announced intention to push forward Negro colonization. He was silent as well about the limitations which the proclamation contained. He interpreted the decree to be "immediate and unconditional emancipation" for the whole nation, but Lincoln had carefully designed the proclamation as a war measure which applied only to those states in rebellion. What mattered most to Haven, however, was the glorious declaration that the slaves were to be "forever free." Whatever the intent, the North had a new war aim. The war for the Union had become also a war for emancipation.[138]

Even though he was jubilant over the proclamation, Haven was aware that "the work [had] not ended." The war was not over. The struggle for equality to accompany the liberty of the freedmen still had to be endured. There would be moves to dissuade the nation from following through with its commitment to universal freedom. Before Haven returned home, the congressional elections in November, 1862, showed strong reaction against Lincoln. During the campaign the Democrats used white racial antagonism against blacks to oppose the proclamation, which they called "unconstitutional, dictatorial, and ruinous." [139] The results of the elections reached Haven while he was in Egypt, and his earlier despair returned. "Slavery is burning our children, our liberties, our national being in its fiery embraces, and we still fall down and worship it," he lamented. "We still say, It shall not be touched. We fight those who seek its overthrow, and call it a victory for right; right when traitors go free, even if the enemies thunder at our gates." Damning peace Democrats who were trying to end the war by compromising with the South, Haven prayed that God would not permit that kind of "a re-united, re-enslaved, debauched, accursed America!" [140]

Just as his agitation over the latest renewal of the struggle for black freedom reached an emotional peak, Haven turned his attention to the biblical region of Palestine and Egypt which surrounded him as he wrote. He recalled the history of faith and promise, and of judgment which emerged from the past.

136. See Basler, *Works of Abraham Lincoln*, vol. V, pp. 433-36.
137. *Zion's Herald*, Dec. 31, 1862 (article dated Oct. 20). An extract from it appears in *The Liberator*, Jan. 9, 1863.
138. *Zion's Herald*, Dec. 31, 1862.
139. *Ibid.*; McPherson, *Struggle for Equality*, p. 119; Cochrane, "Freedom Without Equality," pp. 41, 45 ff., 50-51.
140. *Christian Advocate and Journal*, Feb. 12, 1863.

The hills seemed to teach him, he remembered later, "the depth of the goodness and severity of God," and invite him to mediate on the divine rule in history. His vision of the divine kingdom relieved his anxiety and confirmed his faith. He wrote of "a society that is eternal, a country where prejudice, selfishness, and sin shall never enter. It can," he continued, "be seen above America as easily as from this rocking deck. It can be entered from thence first by faith, then by the unfettered feet of the emancipated soul. The glory of God doth lighten it, and the Lamb is the light thereof. May we," Haven prayed, "follow that light, streaming as it does upon our every pathway, even if our country, and all countries, should in their willful blindness refuse it, and dwell finally and forever in its ineffable fullness of glory and of joy." [141] Upheld by this religious conviction and renewed in body and spirit, he was ready to return home to a war-weary America and assume new responsibilities in its future struggles.

141. *Ibid.*

IV

Beyond Emancipation

Late in May, 1863, scarcely four months after he arrived home from his foreign tour, Gilbert Haven addressed the annual Church Anti-Slavery Society meeting in Boston's Tremont Temple. Flanked by eminent abolitionists like George Cheever and Frederick Douglass and one of his state's antislavery senators, Henry Wilson, he argued that emancipation was not the climax to the crusade for Negro freedom. The end of slavery was only the necessary first step toward overcoming all forms of racial injustice. "The slave is gone, the negro remains," he declared. "Many abolitionists, and all mere Unionists and partisans, have fancied their sole work was to liberate the slaves. It is their least work." Haven acknowledged that there remained the more difficult task of purging American life of racism and of moving toward the ideal of human brotherhood, toward "one family" as a nation. "The basis of slavery is caste," he insisted. "That feeling of caste yet prevails exceedingly over all the land. The blackness covers our hearts deeper than it does the faces of our brethren. It must be removed." [1]

This important address signified the continuity in Haven's abolitionism from prewar protest against slavery to an even more active leadership in the struggle for racial justice after emancipation. At the time he gave it, he was settled again in the parish ministry, indicating that the church would still be, as it had been in the antebellum decade, the channel of his reforming activity. He was pastor of North Russell Street Methodist Episcopal Church in Boston, a position to which he was assigned in April. For the next two and a half years he commuted to his new job from the family home in Malden, where, after his father's death in February, 1863, he had become the man of the house. [2]

Haven soon was known as the most radical Methodist minister in the city, as he had already become in his denomination, and his views were widely disseminated on the public platform, in the pulpit, and in writing. When the black community of Boston held January anniversaries of the Emancipation Proclamation in 1864 and 1865, Haven spoke as the lone white Methodist representative in the company of such eminent Negro leaders as the lecturer and writer, William Wells Brown, and Joshua B. Smith, a caterer (both former slaves), and of white abolitionists like William Lloyd Garrison and the British antislavery leader, George Thompson. [3] He preached

---

1. *Zion's Herald*, June 10, 1863. The speech, "The Church and the Negro," was reprinted in *National Sermons*, pp. 361-72. The date of delivery was May 25, not June 10 as Haven stated in a note on p. 361. See *Daily Evening Traveller*, May 27, 1863; *The Liberator*, May 29, 1863; *Zion's Herald*, June 3, 1863; *The Independent*, June 4, 1863.

2. *Zion's Herald*, Mar. 18, 1863; Prentice, *Life*, pp. 266, 274-75.

3. *The Liberator*, Dec. 25, 1863; Jan. 8, 1864; Jan. 6, 1865. Haven also spoke at a public meeting on the condition of the colored people of Georgia in the fall of 1865. See *ibid.*, Oct. 6, 1865. On Brown and Smith, see Quarles, *Black Abolitionists* pp. 35, 61-63, 231-32.

regularly on developments in the war and in politics, and he kept up his correspondence in the Methodist press and in *The Independent*. At least one daily paper covered his sermons for the national thanksgiving following General W. T. Sherman's capture of Atlanta in September, 1864, and for the annual state fast day in 1865.[4] Three other addresses, which commemorated the battles of Lookout Mountain and Missionary Ridge, the advance on Richmond, and the fall of Charleston, apparently received no contemporary publication or coverage, but Haven included them in his postwar collection of *National Sermons*.[5]

Denominational publications likewise presented Haven's sermons to their readers. The *Christian Advocate and Journal*, Methodism's official weekly, printed his Independence Day address of 1864 in which he compared the Civil War with the American Revolution.[6] In August of the same year *The Methodist*, competitor with the *Advocate* in New York, reported on his national fast day sermon, "The Crisis Hour." [7] Haven's speech, "The Wonderful Year," delivered on January 1, 1865, to celebrate Abraham Lincoln's reelection, was published in the succeeding issue of the *Methodist Quarterly Review*, marking the first time that the denominational journal fully aired his radical racial sentiments.[8] His sermon on the assassination of Lincoln that April was distributed afterwards as a pamphlet, as was the report on church reconstruction in the South, which he wrote in behalf of a committee for the New England Conference.[9]

Through all these media Haven called upon the nation and the church to take responsibility for achieving racial justice and equality and for building a new interracial social order. He dealt with these matters beginning in the

4. Both the thanksgiving sermon, entitled "The End Near," and the fast day address on "Jefferson Davis and Pharaoh," were covered in the *Daily Evening Traveller*, Sept. 12, 1864, Apr. 14, 1865. They were included in *National Sermons*, pp. 473-88, 529-50. The annual fast day sermon of 1864 was apparently preached the previous year to Haven's own congregation. The *Traveller* reported rather fully an address, "The Conflict of America with the Crowns of Europe," on May 6, 1863, which was the same sermon, under the title "The World War: Aristocracy and Democracy," that appeared in *National Sermons* (pp. 439-72) as the state fast day oration, April 4, 1864.

5. "The War and the Millennium," Nov. 26, 1863, pp. 373-92; "Why Grant Will Succeed," national fast day, May 15, 1864, pp. 393-406; "The Vial Poured Out on the Seat of the Beast," Mar. 5, 1865, pp. 517-28. John L. Thomas has extracted part of the sermon on the millennium in his *Slavery Attacked: The Abolitionist Crusade* (Englewood Cliffs, N.J.: Prentice-Hall, 1965), pp. 172-74.

6. "Three Summers of War: The Revolution and the Rebellion," in the issues of Sept. 8 and 15, 1864; reprinted in *National Sermons*, pp. 407-20.

7. Aug. 20, 1864. The text is in *National Sermons*, pp. 421-38.

8. Haven used the title, "The Great Election," 47 (April, 1865), 253-75, for the *Review*. It is reprinted in *National Sermons*, pp. 489-516. He had published several pieces previously in the *Review*, including "Exegesis of Romans IX, 3," 45 (July, 1863), 420-34, but no one prior to this article so clearly delineated his abolitionism and racially equalitarian views.

9. *The Uniter and Liberator of America. A Memorial Discourse on the Character and Career of Abraham Lincoln: Delivered in the North Russell Street M.E. Church, Boston, Sunday, April 23, 1865* (Boston, 1865); Prentice, *Life*, p. 269; *The Independent*, May 4, 1865. See also Haven to Charles M. Hart, Dec. 27, 1866, from Malden, Mass., Library of the Boston Athenaeum. The report is in the *Minutes of the New England Conference*, 1865, pp. 42-45, and as a manuscript in Haven's handwriting, in the New England Conference Papers. The pamphlet version, which has not been located, was reviewed in the *Methodist Quarterly Review*, 47 (July, 1865), 479-83.

state fast day sermon, "The Mission of America," which he preached on April 2, 1863, to his colleagues of the New England Conference. The burden of the address was to spell out two distinctive features of the national mission of the American republic. They were to proclaim "universal toleration of religion, with the acknowledged supremacy of Christianity," and to establish "the universal equality and fraternity of the human race." Haven typically called the latter challenge "the question of the age" as it appeared in the form of racial caste. But he defined as "the greatest problem" of the nation how "to preserve the utmost liberty of worship and the utmost liberty of no worship, with a pure society and a predominant Christianity." [10]

Haven's diagnosis of the role of religion in American society related directly to the problem of implementation for his moral commitment against racism. If the nation was to overcome its racial problems, a fundamental transformation of social beliefs and habits was necessary. It was imperative that the churches of the country not abdicate the responsibility to initiate and carry through this transformation. But, Haven had come to acknowledge, religion in a democracy had no coercive influence, only the power to persuade people toward certain views and actions.

The American tradition of religious liberty was rooted in a desire to protect "the inviolable sanctity of conscience." That protection Haven wished to uphold, but he was alarmed over the trend for religious toleration to become latitudinarianism which put "all faiths and non-faiths on the same basis as Christianity." Inevitably, he believed, the tendency was to sever the connection between religion and the public sphere, and thereby, in his view, to destroy the moral foundation of American freedom. He detected "licentiousness," for example, in the practice "to carefully abstain, in every presidential message and proclamation of fasting or thanksgiving, from mentioning the name of the Saviour of the world." He likewise doubted whether the attempt "to build up and make mighty in the earth, a nation that is Christian in reality and not in name" could be successful. This outlook led him finally to support a move to amend the Constitution so as to give official legal recognition of Christianity as the dominant religion of the nation.[11]

In his understanding of America Haven assumed a necessary interrelation between Christianity and national identity and destiny. He shared a "socio-religious faith" in "America as God's empire," which was the latter-day version of the New England Puritan portrayal of the Christian commonwealth that was to be the model society for all the world. "It was," one

10. *The Mission of America; A Discourse Delivered Before the New England M.E. Conference, at the High Street Church, Charlestown, Ms., on the Occasion of the Annual State Fast, April 2d, 1863* (Boston, 1863), pp. 6-7, 25, 37. In a revised form under the title, "The State, A Christian Brotherhood," Haven republished this address in his *National Sermons*, pp. 317-60.

11. *Mission of America*, pp. 9, 13-14; *National Sermons*, pp. 427-28, 590-91. The General Conference of 1864 recommended constitutional change along these lines. See the *Journal of the General Conference of the Methodist Episcopal Church*, 1864, pp. 264, 381.

writer has aptly put it, "a buoyant faith, born of the assurance of the adequacy of all things here and hereafter of the union of the evangelical gospel with republican institutions." Its dynamics lay in the energies of revivalism joined to the vast network of voluntary societies for reform through which the spreading of Christian civilization would be accomplished. The goal was the creation of "a great Christian democracy," but it was not to be achieved by formal religious establishment but through voluntary association, persuasion, and a crusading "evangelical moralism." [12]

That goal, Haven was confident, could never be realized, if religion was relegated exclusively to a private concern and context. The result, which he had already seen in the antiabolitionist reaction of northern politicians, was to contend "that religion and the State, being divorced, ministers, the teachers and representatives of true religion, must not meddle with politics or the affairs of the state." Such a divorce, made in the compromise over slavery, had produced "a more shameful prostitution of the ministry and the church than in any country in modern history." Methodist experience proved the point. "We have seen in its brief life," he asserted, "a large portion of its clergy in the presence of an enormous sin refusing to confront it; declaring that to say aught against it was to preach politics, and for this cause they were not sent." The apostasy was more visible in the South where slaveholding "deacons, vestrymen, and class-leaders, ministers and bishops" in every branch of "the professed Church of Jesus Christ" were always "opposed to meddling with political and social sins." [13]

If the church was to fulfill its "chief mission," Haven explained, its ministers had to proclaim a gospel that was "not confined to a repentance and faith that has no connection with social or civil duties." Those churchmen who opted for religion merely as a private matter abetted the nation's "chief peril . . . in refusing to avow [itself] Christian, and in excluding the appointed ambassadors for Christ from the questions that agitate society." Behind this conception lay the prophetic heritage of the Bible and the protest tradition in church history. "Isaiah, Ezekiel, Jeremiah, Hosea, Amos;—all preachers of righteousness—dwelt on social and civil sins," Haven argued. "They dwelt

12. Haven uses the phrase, "a great Christian democracy," in *The Methodist*, Sept. 10, 1864, and in his *Lay Representation in the Methodist Episcopal Church*, p. 48. "Evangelical moralism" is Gordon Harland's effective designation of the social philosophy of mainstream American Protestantism in the national period. See his article, from which the extended quotation above is taken, "The American Protestant Heritage and the Theological Task," *The Drew Gateway*, 32 (1962), 71-93. For further treatments of this development in American religion, see Sidney E. Mead, *The Lively Experiment: The Shaping of Christianity in America* (New York: Harper & Row, 1963); Perry Miller, *The Life of the Mind in America: From the Revolution to the Civil War* (New York: Harcourt, Brace & World, 1965), Bk. I; James Fulton Maclear, " 'The True American Union' of Church and State: The Reconstruction of the Theocratic Tradition," *Church History*, 28 (1959), 41-62.

13. *Mission of America*, pp. 17, 22-23; "The Great Election," p. 255 (*National Sermons*, p. 495). Haven in the last reference mentioned specifically Episcopal bishop and Civil War general Leonidas Polk, Methodist bishop George Pierce, the eminent Presbyterian preacher Benjamin M. Palmer, and Southern Baptist Basil Manly.

on hardly anything else. . . . The whole history of the church since has been a history of its conflict with the world and the rulers of the world." Ministers, therefore, had a duty to condemn "popular and powerful sin," "preach against usury," attack "social vices" and censure "a wicked system of government." [14]

When the church failed in its social responsibility, as in the case of "the church of America" refusing "the mission of abolishing slavery," Haven's biblical theology and national faith taught him, God used other agencies than the church to accomplish his purpose. "The red right arm of God is achieving the redemption which He would fain have wrought through his church," he told a Boston gathering in May, 1863. "He has poured out upon us the plague of war and its abounding miseries, because his church would not testify and toil for the salvation of their brethren." [15] This conviction led Haven to give expression to a distinctive theology of national experience that probed the divine purpose in America's fraternal conflict.

I

The primary category for Haven's discussion of the significance of America in the context of God's sovereign rule was the idea of the millennium which signified the fulfillment of divine will either within, or at the end of, human history. Before 1863 he had often made passing references to the millennium in his preaching and writing, but the idea was not fully developed until he sought to speak of the Civil War's ultimate meaning.[16] From a millennial perspective he clarified the religious dimensions of his dream of racial equality and brotherhood.

Two meanings for the idea of the kingdom, or rule of God, which were operative in the period affected Haven's conception of the millennium. In mid-nineteenth-century American Protestantism the idea of the kingdom commonly meant "the reign of Christ" as expressed in the lives of regenerate men and extended through individuals into society. The additional notion of the coming "kingdom on earth," which was more characteristic of the later social gospel movement, also had its roots in the reform ethos of Haven's generation. It emphasized human responsibility to bring society into harmony with the will and purpose of God.[17] In its basic character as the reign of Christ, then, the millennium involved the regeneration of individual and society. Haven defined it as "the triumph of Christ over Satan in the hearts and lives, the laws and institutions of man. . . . It is," he continued,

---

14. *Mission of America*, pp. 19-25.

15. *Zion's Herald*, June 10, 1863 (*National Sermons*, pp. 365, 367).

16. For millennial references prior to 1863, see *Christian Advocate and Journal*, May 2, July 25, 1861; Feb. 13, 1862; *Zion's Herald*, Feb. 5, 1862; *National Sermons*, pp. 85-86, 121-22, 210-12, 269.

17. The distinction here is derived from H. Richard Niebuhr, *The Kingdom of God in America* (New York: Harper Torchbooks, 1959).

"a struggle as to whether man shall be saved from sin, or kept in sin. It is an attempt to make the earth a heaven or a hell." The "war . . . between Christ and anti-Christ," between the good and the evil, Haven explained, "all hearts that know themselves, too painfully understand." Beginning in the "moral nature, and in the sovereign head of that nature, the free will," he asserted, "it extends through every emotion, sensibility, intellect, appetite, habit, custom, law, or institution, whether of the individual or society."[18]

Already the millennial vision implied the second motif, the coming kingdom on earth. Its signs were to be seen both in societal trends and cosmically, in "the whole creation," but it depended initially on "the restoration of man." "His new creation can alone renew the face of the earth," Haven contended. "As is the fall, so must the rising be. As the struggle, so the triumph. The plunge was through Satan unto sin, the deliverance must be through Christ unto holiness. The perfected deliverance is the Millennium."[19]

Fundamentally, Haven had little interest in the details of a classical theological treatment of the millennium as an eschatological doctrine or a philosophy of history. He allowed for the possibility of postmillennialism, the coming reign of Christ on earth "gradually, and by the operation of laws that have been molding and transforming men for ages," as well as of the more pessimistic premillennial emphasis on an apocalyptic "breaking up of the present order and institution of a new earth and a new man" with Christ's return. In any event, he declared, "the end is sure and the same. The Millennium is a world of men, equal, brotherly, united, and holy. Every approach to that state now renders its violent introduction less necessary. If it can be effected by natural causes there will be no need of the supernatural. It is being effected." Haven appeared not to choose between the two outlooks, but his basic propensity was toward the former. He could say that "the millennial day [may] break upon the world . . . in a day," but he followed with the assertion that "events [were] hastening it forward." In the end he always implied human responsibility to inaugurate the new era in history.[20]

As a historical development, the millennium, in Haven's conception, was the working out of the overarching sovereign purpose of God in the earth. Neither blind fate nor mere human initiative ultimately shaped the world. "He is pushing us forward to His, not our Millennium," Haven explained. "He is using and blessing us if we choose to work with Him. If not, He is none the less using us, while also chastising, for the advancement of mankind to

18. *National Sermons*, p. 374.
19. *Ibid.*, pp. 374-75.
20. *Ibid.*, pp. 374, 384, 387. One basic issue, according to Ira V. Brown, which millennialists debated, was the mode by which the kingdom would come—whether "by gradual stages and through human instrumentalities or in consequence of cataclysmic action by the Almighty." See "Watchers for the Second Coming: The Millenarian Tradition in America," *Mississippi Valley Historical Review*, 39 (1952-53), 441.

the same goal. He maketh our wrath or righteousness alike to praise and prosper Him." [21]

A symbol for a new order in the world, the millennium signified the overcoming of "man's hostility to man" in various "civil and social forms." French democracy's liberty, equality, and fraternity became for Haven the social and political principles of the millennium. But they were divinely bestowed endowments, natural rights not subject to man's control to be given or taken away. "You did not create the doctrine of human fraternity," he told his Boston congregation. "You may have fancied that you did; that it was your patent, and could be limited and controlled at your pleasure. So did the Athenian democrats . . . [and] the Southern slavemongers. Where are they? God, my friends, not you, made man, of one father, that all might be brethren." [22]

With the coming of the millennial reign, Haven believed, there would be freedom from "all artificial social barriers" and the unity and equality of man would be universally recognized. "Whatever opposes this consummation—blood, language, color, caste—must give way, that Christ may be all in all." [23] All three principles of the millennium complemented each other to overcome "the last of the mountains interposed that have made enemies of nations and of men." The vision was of a universal equality of "the sons of Adam at peace with themselves and with their God. They speak one language," Haven proclaimed. "They feel the pulsations of a common brotherhood. While they have all the distinctions of a family in taste and action . . . , they will rejoice in this diversity of gifts, but the same spirit." [24] The portrait was obviously eschatological. Yet, Haven believed, the millennium was not just a "golden dream," but "scriptural, rational, inevitable. It is hardly now a prophetic vision," he said, "so much of it has been accomplished." [25]

In Haven's understanding, the coming millennium had particular reference to the American nation. "We are the depository of the civil principles of the millennium," he boldly declared. "There is nothing more theoretically perfect in the secrets of Divine Wisdom for the construction of human society than has been offered to us." [26] According to Haven, "the divine doctrine of democracy" had already been realized more fully in America than

---

21. *National Sermons*, p. 384.

22. *Ibid.*, pp. 379, 384.

23. *Ibid.*, pp. 380-81.

24. *Mission of America*, pp. 30-31.

25. *National Sermons*, pp. 387-88.

26. *Christian Advocate and Journal*, Sept. 15, 1864 (slightly altered in *National Sermons*, pp. 419-20); *Mission of America*, p. 28. The relation of millennial thought to the national character and mission has been inadequately studied, but see James Fulton Maclear's very suggestive essay, "The Republic and the Millennium," in Elwyn A. Smith, ed., *The Religion of the Republic* (Philadelphia: Fortress Press, 1971), pp. 183-216; and Ernest Lee Tuveson, *Redeemer Nation. The Idea of America's Millennial Role* (Chicago: University of Chicago Press, 1968). Timothy L. Smith employs Haven's millennial statements to establish the basic thesis of his book that locates the beginnings of the social gospel in the evangelical revivalist tradition of prewar American Protestantism. See *Revivalism and Social Reform*, ch. 14.

anywhere in the world. He viewed the development as part of "that gospel scheme [God] is seeking to establish in the earth." [27]

In spite of his confidence in the destiny of the nation, however, Haven clearly saw that American racism was the great contradiction to all three social principles of the millennium. The racial meaning of American democracy had been "at the worst, equality of white people, and the slavery of all other complexions; at the best, equality of the whites, and the liberty, but not fraternity, of the blacks" or "the oneness of man as man." [28] Haven maintained that a major aspect of the American national mission was to prove "that the utmost liberty and equality of all men can co-exist with a stable and prosperous government." His challenge was not directed against the basic tenets of the democratic creed but toward the nation's failure to extend its full meaning to every man. "Here we have as our foundation-stone the European democrat's triad," he wrote. "We have it elevated and consecrated by universal education and the fullest expression of Christianity. There we stop. To apply these to ALL our people—aye, there's the rub." [29]

The unique feature of Haven's egalitarian interpretation of the national mission was the way he conceived the principle of equality in relation to his millennial vision. "As the world is approaching its ultimate paradisiacal estate, it must approach the condition of the primitive abode," he observed. "There must be one language and one family." America was bringing in this new world by spreading the English language everywhere and by providing a model of democracy which would demonstrate "the solidarity of the human race." However much the unity and brotherhood of man appeared to be only a "dubious and seemingly remote" possibility, Haven prophesied, "America seems to be the spot where this divine purpose is to be first accomplished." [30]

Gradually Haven came to believe that the Civil War was God's way of inaugurating brotherhood in America. In the prewar period he had often warned of an imminent divine judgment upon the nation because of slavery and racial caste. When the war came, he was confident that the divine purpose in the conflict was to abolish slavery, even if the South succeeded in obtaining independence.[31] Thus, in 1862, he associated Lincoln's first move against slavery "with the coming of the kingdom of God." After emancipation, he stated that slavery had died "BY THE VISITATION OF GOD." In

27. *National Sermons*, pp. 384, 590; *Mission of America*, p. 27.

28. *National Sermons*, p. 384.

29. *Mission of America*, pp. 26-28. Compare the transracial character of this conception of the national mission with the views of Bishop Matthew Simpson, the most eminent Methodist of the time, who, as late as 1870, was still recommending the colonization of American Negroes. See James E. Kirby, "Matthew Simpson and the Mission of America," *Church History*, 36 (1967), 299-307 and "The Social and Ecclesiastical Thought of Matthew Simpson" (Ph.D. dissertation, Drew University, 1963), pp. 273-303.

30. *Mission of America*, pp. 27-28; see also *Zion's Herald*, Aug. 12, 1863.

31. *Christian Advocate and Journal*, May 2, 1861; *Zion's Herald*, May 15, 1861; *National Sermons*, p. 434.

time he claimed that God's ultimate purpose in the war was not merely emancipation, but interracial brotherhood.[32]

Since Haven was a sensitive man, he was certainly aware of the tragedy and suffering which the war brought. Yet he affirmed that God was working out his intent, even through such means. He stated that the seeming "waste of life and treasure" in the war was both "for purposes of punishment . . . [and] for purposes of mercy." No matter what chastisement God had brought, he argued, it was "far less than" what the nation deserved. "He has compelled North and South, alike guilty, if not equally, to scourge each other with bloody rods," Haven exclaimed. "He has arrayed millions against millions, and made the whole land rock with His thunders. In the midst of our sufferings, He has wrought salvation for His sufferers." The surprising thing to Haven was "not that the land is deluged with the blood of the race that has oppressed, despoiled and despised" black men, "but that the God of heaven endured with much long suffering such awful iniquities for so many years." [33]

The ultimate test facing the American nation in the war was whether its people would cooperate with God "in carrying out His designs on the earth." But no matter how the nation responded, there was no way to prevent the divine consummation of "the brotherhood of man in Christ." Haven put the alternatives sharply. "If we cooperate with Him, He will make us His vanguard," he declared. "If we refuse, He will do with us as He did with His more chosen and more beloved people—cast us off, and raise up another people who shall follow His guidance." [34]

As the war went on, Haven contended that sacrifice and mutual suffering were necessary to develop a sense of interracial brotherhood. "A common baptism of sorrow and death will make us, at last, one people," he preached hopefully, "and thus prepare the way for a universal family." [35] In a memorial address on "The Christian Soldier," he spoke of the Union war dead as those who gave "their lives . . . to save this nation from destruction . . . [and] to inaugurate the era of human brotherhood." This millennial hope overshadowed the tragedy of death so much that Haven ended the funeral sermon with a call to duty.

Let us dedicate ourselves to the great ideas for which they laid down their lives. Let us carry forward this truth—the brotherhood of man in Christ. It may be

---

32. *National Sermons*, pp. 269, 435, 542, 547-49.

33. *Ibid.*, p. 434; *Zion's Herald*, Nov. 4, 1863. For examples of Haven's portrayal of "horrid war," see *Zion's Herald*, Aug. 12, 1863; "The Great Election," pp. 254-55, 260-61; *National Sermons*, pp. 381, 393-94, 421-22, 493-94 and in his postwar sermon, "Peace: Her Gifts and Demands," preached in Boston, July 9, 1865, pp. 583-85. In Aug. 1864, Haven spoke of the providential coincidence that the war had required almost the exact number of soldiers as there were slaves. *National Sermons*, p. 422.

34. *National Sermons*, p. 405.

35. *Mission of America*, p. 32.

that many a bloody hour shall pour its rain on us before that blessed morning shines. It may be that we shall be called to follow them into the conflict and the consummation. Let us not fear to follow where these lead. Let us, too, be willing to die for the salvation of this land, which is the salvation of all lands.[36]

If the divine purpose of the war was to be realized, then, a national commitment to interracial brotherhood had to accompany a northern victory. Racism, no less than slavery had to be overcome. Only then could Haven's dream of America as a land of "universal liberty and universal brotherhood, supported by universal law and sanctified by universal piety," be fulfilled. That goal might require, Haven surmised, "all our sons, all our treasure, all our generation" in order "to destroy the enemy [of slavery] that is seeking to prevent this consummation." The deeper enemy of racism "may take a longer time and greater struggles to destroy," but, he promised, "triumph over both" if the nation was faithful to its principles and its God.[37]

II

When, in the fall of 1864, Haven analyzed progress toward racial justice in the North, he saw hopeful "evidences that a true and glorious day [was] breaking; a day that no night shall follow, and in which peace shall be one with brotherhood; in which true democracy, the rights and fraternity of all men, shall be universally recognized and practiced." [38] He had in mind anti-slavery and civil rights legislation which Congress passed in 1863 and 1864. The Fugitive Slave Law had been abolished. Legislation requiring the colonization of all slaves freed in the District of Columbia was repealed. The coastwise slave trade had ended. There were new laws to equalize educational opportunity for Negroes in the District, to prohibit exclusion of witnesses in

36. William I. Haven, ed., *Christus Consolator or Comfortable Words for Burdened Hearts* (New York, 1893), pp. 230-33. This undated sermon may have been the same address which Haven mentioned in his journal sometime in 1865 after the end of the war, and delivered for Rev. Daniel E. Chapin's son. See Prentice, *Life*, pp. 269-70. On the theme of an impending millennium of brotherhood emerging out of the war see George M. Fredrickson, *The Inner Civil War. Northern Intellectuals and the Crisis of the Union* (New York: Harper Torchbooks, 1968), pp. 82, 118-19.

37. *Mission of America*, p. 39. The consistency of Haven's polemic against racism makes it impossible to accept Robert T. Handy's judgment that his views on the Civil War simply "identified the old theme of America's destiny with northern success." See *A Christian America. Protestant Hopes and Historical Realities* (New York: Oxford University Press, 1971), p. 66. The religious dimension of the Civil War needs fresh study. Neither the biased analysis of Chester F. Dunham, *The Attitude of the Northern Clergy Toward the South, 1860-1865* (Toledo, Ohio: Gray Co., 1942), which Handy uncritically accepts, nor Stuart W. Chapman's "The Protestant Campaign for the Union," is adequate. What William A. Clebsch began, in his "Baptism of Blood: A Study of Christian Contributions to the Interpretation of the Civil War in American History" (Th.D. dissertation, Union Theological Seminary, New York, 1957), ought to be extended if a more nearly comprehensive understanding of the theology of the war is to be had. The chapter, "To the Bitter End," in H. Shelton Smith's *In His Image, But . . .* is a significant step toward that goal, as was James W. Silver's earlier study, *Confederate Morale and Church Propaganda* (Tuscaloosa, Ala.: Confederate Publishing Co., 1957).

38. *National Sermons*, pp. 483-84. But in July Haven had commented that the public conscience on the Negro question had grown more rapidly than the public resolution to do anything about the problem. See *National Sermons*, pp. 412-13.

court on account of race, and to end segregation on railroad cars in the capital.[39]

Not all signs, however, pointed to a coming millennium of racial harmony in America. Bitter reaction marked every step forward. Antiblack sentiment from legislators of both parties emerged during congressional debates on controversial issues like the question of Negro suffrage. In 1864 Congress rejected a move to grant Negroes the right to vote in the first election held in the Montana Territory. The legislators also refused to extend suffrage in the District of Columbia to all citizens regardless of race who met certain literacy and tax requirements. Because of Democratic opposition, the campaign for a constitutional amendment against slavery, which had presidential support, failed in the summer of 1864.[40]

As he had done during the first two years of the war, Haven observed the American political scene carefully and analyzed particular questions for their bearing on racial justice and equality. On most issues he agreed with other abolitionists, though he refused to follow Wendell Phillips' effort to prevent the reelection of President Lincoln in 1864.[41]

The arming of Negro soldiers, which Haven advocated as early as December, 1861, was one of the major war-time questions on which he concentrated. The enrollment of blacks for military service had an important positive effect upon northern racial attitudes, but opposition to the move was vigorous at the time.[42] Even in Massachusetts, sentiment against the first Negro regiment, which Governor John A. Andrew raised in 1863, was intense. As Haven recalled later, "It was almost as great a deed to organize a colored regiment in Boston as it was in Richmond." [43] During the controversial recruitment campaign Haven publicly supported the governor's action in an address before the New England Conference. "They [Negro soldiers] are the true Copperheads that will save the Republic," he exclaimed. "They will go into this war, as Frederic Douglas [sic] says, not as hewers of wood and drawers of water, but as men. They will come out of it, our recognized equals and associates." [44]

Even after Negro troops were in action, Haven and other abolitionists had to continue their attack upon discrimination in the army. The permission

39. Cochrane, "Freedom Without Equality," pp. 91-92.

40. *Ibid.*, pp. 92-103, 174-216. The Thirteenth Amendment passed and was ratified in 1865.

41. *National Sermons*, pp. 479-82; *Christian Advocate and Journal*, Oct. 6, 1864. See McPherson, *Struggle for Equality*, pp. 260-86.

42. Cochrane, "Freedom Without Equality," pp. 60-66. McPherson calls the action "one of the most revolutionary features of the war," in *Struggle for Equality*, p. 219.

43. *National Sermons*, pp. 385-86, 544, 598-99. See also *Christian Advocate and Journal*, Aug. 27, 1863, for Haven's review of a tract on the military service which blacks performed in the Revolutionary Army.

44. *Mission of America*, p. 32. Haven's entertaining account of the parade of the black 54th Massachusetts Regiment through Boston is in *Christian Advocate and Journal*, June 25, 1863. See also *National Sermons*, pp. 369, 642-44.

to arm black soldiers had been won partly through racist appeals to let them die in place of whites, partly because of the military necessities of an all-out war. The army segregated Negro soldiers, placed only white officers over them, and paid them less than half the basic salary which whites of the same rank received.[45] In the summer of 1863, Haven praised Senator Henry Wilson's bill to enroll soldiers and commission officers without distinction of color. Later in the year he called for full integration of the army.[46]

The controversy over equal pay for blacks went on until the end of the war. In the spring and summer of 1864, Haven strongly criticized Lincoln for refusing to pay the two Negro regiments from Massachusetts on an equal basis with other soldiers and for neglecting to appoint able black lieutenants.[47] In September, 1864, and again in January, 1865, he repeated his call for an end to the racial segregation of troops. "The idea of color or origin should be as far from the mind of the provost marshal as is that of nationality or name," Haven argued. "We shall then cease to read of the valor of white or colored troops as separate bodies, but of men and patriots, whose complexion may be various, but whose blood and bravery are one." [48] Finally, Congress did grant retroactive pay to all Negroes who were promised equal wages when they enlisted. Less obvious forms of discrimination, however, continued throughout the military.[49]

Another major political question which concerned Haven was Negro suffrage, the controversial subject which would be a main issue in southern reconstruction after the war. For Haven, suffrage was a basic right of citizenship. To grant the franchise impartially would overturn the racist perversion of the American democratic system, which, in acts like the Dred Scott Decision of the Supreme Court in 1857, virtually denied national citizenship to black people.

The refusal to permit at least limited suffrage to loyal blacks in the restoration of the southern states was Haven's primary objection to Lincoln's plan of Reconstruction. In his annual message to Congress in December, 1863, the President outlined what the basic conditions were for those in rebellion "to resume their allegiance to the United States, and to reinaugurate loyal State governments within and for their respective States." Whenever there were loyal white voters equal to 10 percent of the total votes cast in the state in 1860, Lincoln promised to recognize the right of that state to reestablish its government. Though he did not require it, the President suggested that the state legislatures, when reorganized, "recognize and declare"

45. White privates were paid $13 per month, plus a clothing allowance of $3.50. Negroes were paid $10 per month, with a deduction of $3 for clothing. See McPherson, *Struggle for Equality*, pp. 212-13; Cochrane, "Freedom Without Equality," p. 64.
46. *Christian Advocate and Journal*, June 25, 1863; *National Sermons*, p. 386.
47. *National Sermons*, pp. 404, 431, 544.
48. *Ibid.*, p. 484; "The Great Election," p. 269 (*National Sermons*, p. 510).
49. McPherson, *Struggle for Equality*, p. 219.

the "permanent freedom" of the slaves, "provide for their education," and do whatever else would temporarily aid their plight "as a laboring, landless, and homeless class." [50] The President was silent on the question of Negro voting. Late in the war, Haven joined the abolitionist attack against Lincoln's failure to provide for the political participation of the freedmen. "Let not those rebellious states be reorganized," he insisted, "without conferring the right of suffrage on every loyal man." [51]

In 1864, Haven expressed definite opinions concerning the first test of the presidential reconstruction policy in Louisiana. General Nathaniel P. Banks, who was in charge of the operation, by-passed an already existing Unionist political organization which favored limited Negro suffrage, and authorized elections in which only whites could vote. With Banks' support, Michael Hahn, who opposed black voting, won the gubernatorial election in February, 1864. In a sermon the following May, Haven charged that Banks had "disfranchised two thirds of the Union men of the State, and compelled the election of a rebel in heart over an honest lover of union, liberty, and the rights of man." [52] A year later, when the franchise was still being denied Louisiana blacks, Haven complained, "Twelve thousand half loyal whites . . . refuse the petition of six thousand thoroughly loyal colored men to give them equal suffrage." [53] Because of this discrimination, he supported the refusal to admit to Congress Louisiana's representatives who had been elected under Lincoln's plan and Banks' supervision.[54]

During the Louisiana controversy, Lincoln moved toward a position favoring selective suffrage for Negroes. After a group of educated black property owners from New Orleans petitioned for the vote, he wrote privately to Governor Hahn, suggesting that "some of the colored people"—particularly "the very intelligent" and the soldiers—be allowed to vote. Actually, the President did not come out publicly for even a limited suffrage for Negroes until April 11, 1865, three days before his death.[55] He did not intend to complicate the reconstruction of the South by making impartial suffrage a condition for the resumption of normal relations. Moreover, he already had his hands full with congressional "radicals" who considered his terms for national reunion much too lenient. Surprisingly, they failed to include even limited suffrage for Negroes in the Wade-Davis Bill, their original plan for reconstruction which Lincoln left unsigned in the summer of 1864.[56]

50. Basler, *Works of Abraham Lincoln*, vol. VII, pp. 49-56.
51. *National Sermons*, p. 550.
52. *Ibid.*, p. 403. Haven also criticized Banks because of the labor system which he had forced upon Louisiana freedmen. Banks' regulations were not unlike the antebellum slave codes. McPherson, *Struggle for Equality*, pp. 289-93.
53. *National Sermons*, p. 550.
54. *Christian Advocate and Journal*, May 25, 1865.
55. Basler, *Works of Abraham Lincoln*, vol. VII, p. 243; vol. VIII, pp. 399-405. In antebellum New Orleans, 18,000 free Negroes owned $15 million worth of property. John Hope Franklin, *Reconstruction After the Civil War* (Chicago: University of Chicago, 1961), pp. 22-24.
56. For the full text of the bill, see Harold M. Hyman, ed., *The Radical Republicans and Recon-*

Lincoln's reconstruction program, even with some Negro suffrage, was, in Haven's words, a "mistaken policy." [57] He insisted that black voters were necessary in the South to insure loyalty to the national government. In his sermon on January 1, 1865, he pointed to an imminent danger after the war, predicting that ex-Confederates would seek "to re-establish themselves in more than their former power." He recognized that there would be more southern congressmen because emancipation would end the practice of counting the slave population on a three-fifths basis for representation. "These once active rebels . . . will outnumber their loyal neighbors," Haven warned, "and snatch again the scepter after having thrown down the sword with which they had sought the murder of the very government they will then represent." The situation required a coalition of "loyal whites" and "their like loyal colored fellow-citizens" to counteract "the voting of their Secession neighbors." [58] Shortly after the war, Haven reasserted his belief that "the enfranchisement of the negro alone can renew that land."

It is impossible to hang, banish, or disfranchise the half a million former aristocrats of the South. Neither confiscation of their lands nor emancipation of their slaves can annihilate their power. They cannot thus be prevented from vaulting into authority again. The white serfs who have so faithfully fought their battles will assuredly honor their military commanders with civic power. What can make them and keep them powerless? Negro suffrage. Nothing less, nothing more.[59]

A more important reason for impartial suffrage was the duty of the nation to its black citizens, particularly those who had fought in the defense of the country. Haven saw how inconsistent it was to permit the "foreigner" to vote, while denying Negroes, born on American soil, the same right.[60] Claiming the enfranchisement of every loyal citizen as a national duty, he declared "shame" on the nation, "if having won its triumphs by the valor of men of color, it shall refuse those men that franchise which it bestows on any Northern traitor who has done his uttermost to oppose the government, and even upon the Southern rebel, on his taking the oath of allegiance." [61] The ultimate solution, Haven argued, was not merely to permit a few selected Negroes to vote, but to break down all barriers to universal suffrage. "Manhood suffrage is the *only* basis of democracy," he wrote, "and manhood does not depend on complexion, or outward marks of physical distinction." [62]

struction, 1861-1870 (Indianapolis: Bobbs-Merrill, 1967), pp. 128-34. Hyman also includes the Wade-Davis Manifesto, which was the response by congressional Republicans to Lincoln's pocket veto (see pp. 137-47). Lincoln's message on the bill is in Basler, *Works of Abraham Lincoln*, vol. VII, pp. 433-34.

57. *National Sermons*, pp. 549-50.
58. "The Great Election," pp. 270-71 (*National Sermons*, pp. 511-12).
59. *The Uniter and Liberator of America*, pp. 23-24 (*National Sermons*, pp. 571-72).
60. Haven decried this practice especially in relation to Roman Catholic immigrants. See "The Great Election," p. 271 (*National Sermons*, p. 512).
61. *National Sermons*, p. 550.
62. *Christian Advocate and Journal*, Sept. 28, 1865. The article, signed "G." and entitled "Con-

Clearly Haven did not support Negro suffrage just to punish the South. To be sure, he sometimes depicted the meaning of Reconstruction in terms of a revolutionary reversal of social roles, slaves and masters exchanging places. He made his most radical statement of this kind in his memorial sermon on Lincoln, when he commended "No citizenship for the rebel leader; perfect citizenship for his slave. No land for the chiefs of the rebellion, homesteads for his loyal bondmen. Expatriation," he continued the comparison,

which was urged upon the negro, not three years ago, must be enforced upon his master. The African had no rights these would respect. These must have none the nation will respect. Outlawed, homeless, exiled, let these once mighty rulers of the land thus expiate their crime of treason, while their victims take their homes and their crowns. The first shall be last, and the last, first.[63]

Even when Haven seemed especially harsh toward the white South, however, he was still motivated by his dream of racial brotherhood. Three months after Lincoln's assassination, in a more reflective and less vindictive mood, he defined what he meant by "a complete overturn in . . . [southern] society." He explained that "the South must admit the black, not to the supremacy, but to equality. Their blood must mingle as freely in the channels of social unity as it has on the fields of carnage." This vision of social and political equality implied a fierce struggle. Haven anticipated as much when he stated that "no party holding such power [as the ex-Confederates] ever yet abandoned it gratuitously." [64]

The campaign for equal suffrage, therefore, had its particular southern application, but it was basically national in scope. Haven did not limit its focus to the South, for he was committed to political equality throughout the country. Of racial restrictions generally, and of voting particularly, he said,

Our Declaration is read every Fourth of July, and broken every other day of the year, and that also. Our friends and neighbors, who have dwelt in this land as long as we, nine tenths of whom have English blood in their veins, and one half of whom have more of that blood than of their original African, all of whom, if entirely and directly from the lowest tribe of Africa, are included in our national creed,—these fellow-citizens and fellow-men, born of our blood and on our soil, are shut out of the legitimate workings of that creed. They are disfranchised in thirty States of this Union. They are despised in them all.[65]

---

necticut and Impartial Suffrage," was identified as Haven's contribution in a note by the editor in the next issue.

63. *The Uniter and Liberator of America*, p. 23. When Haven republished this sermon in 1869, he modified the passage, substituting "may" for "must," in each case. (*National Sermons*, p. 571). Normally Haven was not especially vindictive toward the defeated South, so that the desire to revenge Lincoln's death probably accounted for the bitter tone of the statement. A similar example was his sermon on the capture of Charleston. See *National Sermons*, pp. 517-28.

64. *National Sermons*, pp. 599-600.

65. *Ibid.*, p. 429.

To counteract "this cruel disability," Haven called on Congress "to decree the right of suffrage for national officers to be without respect of color."[66]

The most important immediate postwar test of progress against racism in the North was the vote on a state constitutional amendment in Connecticut, which proposed to remove racial restrictions from the franchise. To Haven, the election was crucial both as a symbolic step toward political equality for northern Negroes and as a measure of the nation's integrity involving a basic question in southern Reconstruction. He warned that there would be no consistent way to "demand equal rights for the colored people in South Carolina, if we will not give it to that fraction of our population here."[67] After the election Haven regretfully reported that Connecticut had refused to give the ballot to its black populace. The action, he exclaimed, "made every rebel heart leap for joy" and imperilled "the whole work of reconstruction." He asked, "With what face can Connecticut refuse South Carolina admission to the Union?," and he answered:

Her beam is like Connecticut's mote, of the very same timber, and of the very same size. "This is a white man's government," she infamously says; and Connecticut more infamously (for she sins against far greater light) responds Amen! The majority of the citizens of Mississipppi and South Carolina are disfranchised by this sin of a Puritan commonwealth. It supports the West in their iniquitous prejudice, and casts the party of Union and liberty into peril, if not into destruction.[68]

When Haven turned to national leadership for promoting Negro political and civil rights, he was likewise disappointed, especially in Lincoln's successor, Andrew Johnson. At first, he spoke of Johnson as "the new Jefferson" raised up especially to guide the country toward a "consistent and complete democracy." As Lincoln's special work was to defend and unify the nation and to emancipate the slaves, so Johnson's mission was to become the "regenerator" of the land by effecting a true reconstruction.[69] It was not long, however, before Haven began to question the policies of the new chief executive, who pursued Lincoln's plan of Reconstruction and ignored pleas for Negro suffrage. In late August, 1865, Haven attacked the administration's program for permitting the South to "reorganize the region after its former likeness and image."[70] Before Congress convened in the winter, Haven had already sided with the radical Republicans against Johnson. He fully expected the national legislature to correct the presidential reconstruction program.[71]

66. "The Great Election," pp. 270-71 (National Sermons, pp. 511-12).
67. Christian Advocate and Journal, Sept. 28, 1865.
68. Ibid., Oct. 12, 1865.
69. National Sermons, pp. 549-50; The Uniter and Liberator of America, pp. 23-24 (National Sermons, pp. 571-72).
70. See his unsigned editorial, "Beware," Christian Advocate and Journal, Aug. 31, 1865. Proof that Haven wrote this piece can be found in an editorial note in the issue for October 5, and in articles on November 23 and 30.
71. Ibid., Aug. 31, 1865; The Independent, Jan. 18, 1866.

In the end the changing racial situation in America after 1863 hardly fulfilled Haven's millennial expectations. Slavery had ended, but the drive for racial equality was not achieving immediate success in any part of the land. The conversion of the whole nation from racism was an even more formidable task than that which the early antislavery reformers realized. The stakes were high. Haven thought that racial justice was essential if a true and lasting national peace was to occur after military hostilities ceased. He even predicted that unless interracial brotherhood developed with the reunion of the nation, America would face "another war . . . a war of races and of extermination." [72] If the racial situation forced him to be realistic, Haven did not surrender his millennial vision for postwar America nor cease laboring for its realization. He maintained this perspective of hope for the remainder of his life, believing that interracial brotherhood was necessary for the "consummation of the divine desire in Christ with respect to man." [73]

When Haven contemplated the arrival of the millennium, he conceived a "grand future" for America in which blacks would rise to posts of honor and authority in Congress, in state politics, in the church, in business, and in social life. He anticipated that future by recommending that New York send the able black leader from Rochester, Frederick Douglass, as one of its representatives to Congress; by arguing that Robert Smalls, a Negro hero in the Civil War, was as qualified for the governorship of South Carolina as Michael Hahn was of Louisiana; by nominating a black attorney from Boston, Dr. John S. Rock, for chief justice of the Supreme Court; by portraying John Sella Martin, a talented Negro preacher, as pastor of a congregation "of many complexions" but "of one Lord, one faith, one baptism." [74] As a step in this direction Haven undertook the organization, in cooperation with Governor Andrew, of a movement that nearly succeeded in electing Leonard A. Grimes, an ex-slave and prominent black Baptist minister in Boston, to the chaplaincy of the Massachusetts legislature. He lobbied senators, spoke out at abolitionist rallies, wrote in the press, and formally petitioned the senate in behalf of Grimes' candidacy. He entreated the legislators at "the inauguration of a new era of our national life" to expel "the unnatural, undemocratic, and unchristian prejudice on account of African descent," that was the "one barrier" preventing the realization of "a pure and perfect democracy." [75]

72. *National Sermons*, pp. 485-86.
73. "The Great Election," p. 259 (*National Sermons*, p. 499).
74. *Ibid.*, pp. 271-74 (*National Sermons*, pp. 512-15); *New York Christian Advocate*, Oct. 4, 1866; *National Sermons*, p. 601; *Mission of America*, p. 36.
75. Extracts from Haven's petition are in Prentice, *Life*, pp. 310-11. When he first endorsed the move, he referred to the chaplaincy of the house of representatives. See *The Liberator*, Jan. 8, 1864, and his letter to Governor John A. Andrew, Jan. 2, 1864, as reprinted in Mrs. W. S. Robinson, ed., *"Warrington" Pen-Portraits: A Collection of the Personal and Political Reminiscences from 1848 to 1876, from the Writings of William S. Robinson* (Boston, 1877), pp. 493-94. A year later he made the same effort in the senate, *The Liberator*, Dec. 30, 1864; *Christian Advocate and Journal*, Jan. 19, 1865. On Grimes' leadership in the black community of Boston, see Quarles, *Black Abolitionists*, pp. 82, 146, 206, 208-9.

Despite the failure of the campaign, the attempt was a token of what Haven insisted must happen throughout the land—to abolish *"from the national heart all distinctions arising from color or origin"* and thus bring in the coming millennium through "the unification, the liberation, the fraternization of America." [76]

III

Haven's millennial vision of freedom, equality, and brotherhood necessarily included a specific program of racial reform for the churches. Characteristically, he was engaged more practically in trying to end racism in and through the church than by any other means. The conversion of America from racial discrimination required that the church and the nation move together, as Haven put it, "to erase from our statutes, our tongues, our hearts, every recognition of color as a badge of distinction or separation between man and man." [77]

The special social task of the church in America, after emancipation, was to become a racially inclusive community and to prod the nation to move toward a racially integrated and just society. Haven looked upon racial separation in the Christian church as "a scandal and offence, a stench in the nostrils of the Almighty." Medical and legal fraternal organizations and the army were better examples of interracial community, he reluctantly admitted, than any "Conference, association or synod." [78] The only remedy for the church was a recovery of the Pauline standard of Christian equality. "In that oneness, there shall be neither Greek nor Jew, barbarian nor Scythian, bond nor free," Haven reminded his fellow preachers, quoting "the apostle's bold declaration to the proud Greeks of Colosse."

He [Paul] did not add "white or black," because there are no whites, as we call them, in that dusky clime. He touched the marrow of their sensitive prejudice, in putting Scythian and barbarian on a level with themselves. His equally bold declaration to the most fastidious Athenians, that God made of one blood all the nations of men, must yet be verified in the earth.[79]

In essence, Haven was asking the white religious community of the nation to become a "servant" church to blacks—to "take up this race, in the infancy of its freedom, in its arms amd bless them." The church had a new opportunity to champion the cause of the lowly. "As our Master gained a name

76. "The Great Election," pp. 268, 273 (*National Sermons*, pp. 509, 515).

77. *National Sermons*, pp. 592-93; see also pp. 433, 440; "The Great Election," pp. 268-69 (*National Sermons*, p. 509); *The Independent*, Nov. 19, 1863.

78. *National Sermons*, pp. 600-602; *Zion's Herald*, June 10, 1863 (*National Sermons*, pp. 369-71); "The Great Election," pp. 272-73 (*National Sermons*, pp. 513-15).

79. *Mission of America*, p. 28 (*National Sermons*, pp. 345-46); "The Great Election," pp. 272-73; *National Sermons*, pp. 513-14, 600. The biblical texts to which Haven refers are Galatians 3:28 and Acts 17:26.

that is above every name by humbling himself to us outcasts of the universe," Haven maintained, "so will the church be uplifted by descending to these its brethren." [80] If the church accepted the challenge to become a social pioneer, he believed, the nation would follow, and racial caste would be destroyed. "The hour is propitious," he told the Church Anti-Slavery Society in 1863. "The great deeps of social pride are breaking up. The church can take the lead in these divine movements if she will. She can drive this spirit of caste from the temple of Christ." He urged its expulsion "out of our stores, our shops, our families, our pews and our pulpits, yea and first of all, out of our own hearts." By blotting caste out of the land, "the church, redeemed by her valor and faithfulness from her shame and sin" in her antislavery failure, would "[win] and [transform] the whole world." [81]

Haven particularly hoped that the New England Conference would lead Methodism, as it had done in antislavery reform in the 1830s, denounce the sin of caste and be an example of Christian brotherhood. He urged his colleagues, to "build on the corner stone of Jesus Christ—the brother alike to all men—the brother especially of the poor, the oppressed, and the despised." In calling for a return to "first principles" in the church, Haven was not content to give a general exhortation. He listed practical duties. He ridiculed the custom of distinguishing church members according to race in ecclesiastical records and in the religious press. The practice, he said, was as "unchristian and inhuman" as it would be to refer to people on the basis of other physical characteristics. Haven also called for an end to segregated seating at worship and at the communion table. He recommended further the abolition of "the iniquity known only to Protestant America, the colored Church," and pleaded that racial distinctions in the ministry, which prohibited black preachers from pastorates over white parishioners, cease.[82]

Long before race became an issue in the ecclesiastical reconstruction of the South, Haven was busy trying to achieve some measure of integration in New England Methodism. In Boston he first worked to develop fraternal relations between black and white clergymen and ecclesiastical bodies. In the spring of 1864, he led the Boston Methodist Preachers' Meeting to a session of an annual conference of the African Methodist Episcopal Church. Frequently Haven brought black ministers as his guests to the weekly sessions of the Preachers' Meeting.[83]

One of Haven's close associates was John N. Mars, a well-known Negro

80. *Zion's Herald*, June 10, 1863 (*National Sermons*, p. 371); *The Independent*, Nov. 19, 1863.

81. *Zion's Herald*, June 10, 1863 (altered in *National Sermons*, pp. 367, 371-72). Haven once wrote: "When the church gets converted the world will speedily follow." *Christian Advocate and Journal*, June 25, 1863.

82. *Mission of America*, pp. 33 ff.; "The Great Election," pp. 272-74 (*National Sermons*, 352-56, 513-15).

83. Records of the Methodist Preachers' Meeting for Boston and Vicinity, Mar. 27, June 20 and 27, 1864; February 13, 1865.

in church
ssion work
ion by ex-
al Church
delegates
ded privi-
ccupation

action on
quest the
Among
ervatives,
had even
rt of the
of setting
onference
people"
pattern,
inisters.
nces," it
readily
mpatible
rom the
eception
y when
mission
Western
Dela-
Con-

strated
dercut
most
racial
ght of
d the
ention

official
pp. 58,

as a chaplain in the Union Army and as a
n.[84] His story illustrated one of Haven's at-
in the North. For several years New England
ed this popular black preacher as a revivalist
lthough he had been a "local preacher" in the
not been permitted to join the regular clerical
and Conference. Racial prejudice was too great
ar appointment unless it was to a black congre-
before Mars went South to work with the
the Conference Anti-Slavery Society where, a
hard blows at the prejudice against color which
t the conference session the next year, Haven
ars' membership, and the body received him al-
the time among the freedmen in North Carolina
rican Missionary Association. The significance of
y symbolic at the time, but the experiment later
erable controversy for Haven, who made it a test
northern Methodism.[87]

after "Father" Mars had joined the New England
Conference of the Methodist Episcopal Church
An alternate delegate, Haven did not share in the
e conference, but he followed carefully what took
twin issues of slavery and caste. The first question
he conference followed the suggestion of the bishops
07 to 9, to alter the General Rule and exclude all
ch fellowship.[88] Since this antislavery action came
he Emancipation Proclamation, the move was hardly
d. But most of his fellow Methodists considered the
r freedom. In a national fast day sermon the following
ir self-congratulatory spirit. "We had many jubilations
cil," he remarked sarcastically, "because we concluded
a certain class of sinners, when there were no more
arbored." [89]

dead issue in 1864, Haven was concerned more about

, and 22, 1863. In response to the Fugitive Slave Law of 1850, Mars
tee to aid escaped bondsmen. See *The Liberator*, Oct. 4, 1850.
1865.
Records of the Boston Methodist Preacher's Meeting, April 27, 1863.
ngland Conference, 1864, p. 8.
eral Conference of the Methodist Episcopal Church, 1864, pp. 165-67,

p. 429-30. His cousin Otis made a similar observation in a letter to Gilbert,
Haven papers, Michigan Historical Collections, University of Michigan,

the church's response to what were live problems—racial caste
and society, the plight of the freedmen, the church's policy for mi
in the South. The general conference did take a progressive acti
changing fraternal greetings with the African Methodist Episcop
conference, which was also in session at the time in the city.[90] Th
also endorsed the idea of a national freedmen's bureau, recommen
leges of citizenship for ex-slaves, and planned the ecclesiastical re
of the South.[91]

More crucial to Haven's immediate concern, however, was the
the status of Negro members and ministers. At the bishops' re
general conference appointed a "Committee on the State of Wor
People of Color," but all members of the committee were racial cons
mostly from the border conferences. Two of the seven members
voted with the minority against the new rule on slavery.[92] The rep
committee clearly indicated that most Methodists had no intention
racially integrated standards for the church in the North. The c
adopted the paper which called for "colored pastorates for colored
and for racially separate annual conferences. To justify the segregated
the committee stated the policy on conference membership for black
"To propose their incorporation with the existing Annual Confere
said, "will be attended with difficulties too formidable every way to b
disposed of, and the delay incident to such a proposition is inco
with the urgent requirements of the times." A separate report f
committee added that there was, however, no *"legal* obstacle to the r
of colored preachers in our Annual Conferences."[93] On the same d
these measures passed, the general conference provided for two '
conferences" for blacks only—the Washington Conference (for "
Maryland, the District of Columbia, and the territory south") and th
ware Conference (for "the territory north and west of the Washingt
ference").[94]

The authorization of further racial separation in the church fr
Haven. The official segregation of black Methodists in the North u
whatever progressive moves the general conference had taken. Th
galling aspect of the new arrangement was not merely the implicit
discrimination, but the general conference went on to deny the r
representation to these new colored conferences. Haven first criticiz
action in his occasional column in the *Christian Advocate*. He called at

90. The Methodist Episcopal conference did not take action, however, on a request to ope
correspondence with the black denomination. See *Journal of the General Conference*, 1864,
150-51.
91. *Ibid.*, pp. 278-79, 382, 440-42.
92. *Ibid.*, pp. 58, 97, 167.
93. *Ibid.*, pp. 252-53, 485-88.
94. *Ibid.*, p. 263.

to the fact that the New England Conference delegation had gone to Phila-delphia instructed to expunge entirely "the doctrine of caste" from the church.[95] Late in the summer he attacked the general conference more forcefully, complaining that, "when the question was asked whether there was any objection to admitting a colored brother to our Conferences, it was answered . . . that 'there was no *legal* objection'—as if there were moral; thus elevating their prejudices into the dignity of divine law." [96]

An event in late October impressed upon Haven the full significance of the church's new policy. The bishops transferred "Father" Mars from the New England to the newly formed Washington Conference and appointed him to "Sharp-street" Church, a prominent Negro parish in Baltimore. Im-mediately, Haven protested in writing to the *Advocate*. He argued that Mars had not requested the transfer and that the bishops took the step only because they thought it would be difficult to give him "suitable appointments" in New England. He then explained that Mars had been admitted to the New England Conference "in order that he might be employed as a missionary in the vast openings of the South" where "he had had marked success." For that reason his brethren in the conference

felt assured that he would be an honor to their body, and an important instrument in the renewal at once of the Church in the South and in the North. In his union with them they saw the dawning of that diviner sun than that of the Union, or even that of liberty, the sun of true righteousness, the brotherhood of man. These anticipations have been destroyed by his untimely removal from their ranks.

The transfer by "our chief pastors," Haven admonished, would not be required by public sentiment or "allowed by the Church" in any other country but America. It, and the organization of colored conferences, proved "that the work of our national regeneration is not yet completed." In con-clusion Haven asked that Mars be restored to his former relations in New England and that the colored conferences be integrated with existing annual conferences which overlapped the same geographical region.[97]

In reply, the editor of the *Advocate,* Daniel Curry, vindicated Bishops Levi Scott and Edward R. Ames, who had arranged the transfer, and pointed out that Mars had consented to the appointment. Moreover, he argued, the bishops could not properly appoint Mars to work outside the specific con-ference to which he belonged, especially since his missionary labors had not been connected with the Methodist Episcopal Church. Answering Haven's more fundamental points, Curry stated that he likewise detested "anti-negro prejudice," but he believed that caste would end when it was left "to die

95. *Christian Advocate and Journal,* June 23, 1864; *Minutes of the New England Conference,* 1864, p. 24.
96. *National Sermons,* p. 430.
97. *Christian Advocate and Journal,* Nov. 17, 1864.

of the contempt it merits and is bound to receive." He pleaded with Haven to have patience with those who did not share his racial views.[98]

Not surprisingly, Curry's reply did not satisfy Haven. He wrote an immediate defense of his protest in which he disputed every one of his colleague's contentions, arguing "that the Church had power to send missionaries to the South who held their connections with northern conferences; that it was the desire of Brother Mars, . . . to be so employed; that the Church had not been as faithful as she ought in the work of extirpating slavery, and that she should not fail to see and embrace the new and higher openings of this hour." Furthermore, Haven reiterated his attack on "colored conferences," demanding that black Methodists "be admitted to our [regular] conferences." He acknowledged that they were "subject to the impediment . . . that arises from their color," but racial separation was not the way to cure caste nor aid their rise "to the real height of Christian *manhood*."

Then Haven analyzed the practical bearing which an anticaste policy would have in the racial reform of Methodism. "Abolish as fast as possible colored Churches, and let the members find homes in the neighboring Churches," he requested, letting "them take such seats as they please." If compromise "between policy and duty" was necessary, he continued, "at least refuse to organize another colored Church." In the South "all worthy applicants" to church membership ought to be admitted "without regard to color." Black as well as white missionaries should be sent there, putting "the black man of capacity beside his white brother in as good a Church with as high authority." The two independent Negro Methodist bodies, the African Methodist Episcopal and the African Methodist Episcopal Zion churches, should be invited "not to unite with each other," Haven contended, but with the mother denomination from which both had seceded over the issue of caste.[99] Practically, he was more willing for the integration to be from black into white than vice versa. Obviously he was not sufficiently sensitive to the outlook of Negroes, who, dedicated to their own separate institutions, were reluctant to surrender autonomy in order to assume subordinate roles in white-controlled organizations. But Haven was addressing a predominantly white readership whom he wished to convince of the necessity to overcome caste. Therefore, he was willing to concede in an integrated church that bishops in the two black denominations could become "presiding elders" until "new vacancies occur in our board." Then they could compete for the openings and, if "more fit for the post than their whiter rivals," be elected and "preside with [their] peers at the General Conference" and "over the annual

---

98. *Ibid.*
99. On the independent black Methodist congregations in Philadelphia and New York, out of which grew the African Methodist Episcopal Church as a denomination in 1816 and the African Methodist Episcopal Zion Church in 1820, see Daniel A. Payne, *History of the African Methodist Episcopal Church* (Nashville, 1891), pp. 1-18; Christopher Rush, *A Short Account of the Rise and Progress of the African M. E.* [Zion] *Church* (New York, [1843], 1866).

Gilbert Haven, Jr.
by John P. Soule
Boston

Chaplain Gilbert Haven
by Black & Batchelder
Boston

The Rev. Gilbert Haven, D.D.
engraved by F. E. Jones
for the Ladies' Repository

Bishop Haven
by Warren
Cambridgeport, Mass.

Bishop Haven
by Rockwood
New York

Gilbert Haven, Sr. ("Squire" Haven)
father of Bishop Haven

Mary Ingraham Haven
wife of Bishop Haven

Children of Gilbert and Mary Haven
William Ingraham Haven
Mary Michelle Haven

Birthplace of Bishop Haven at Malden, Mass.

Wesleyan Academy, Wilbraham, Mass.

Daniel Curry

Randolph S. Foster

E. O. Haven

E. R. Ames

B. T. Tanner

George Prentice

Matthew Simpson

Fales Henry Newhall

138

conference." In this way, Haven remarked, the church would "teach the nation the true application of its central doctrine of the unity, equality, and fraternity of man." [100]

The controversy over Mars' removal from mission work continued on into 1865. As chairman of the Committee on the Reconstruction of the Church at the New England Conference in April, Haven included several references to the transfer in the report.[101] In May, the *Northwestern Christian Advocate* in Chicago renewed the debate with a note which read, "We are authorized to say that the transfer of Rev. Mr. Mars, (colored) from the New England Conference to one of the colored conferences was understood by the bishops to be according to his wishes and judgment." [102] Responding in *Zion's Herald*, Haven recounted the whole story with more complete details. In effect, he charged the bishops and the missionary board with refusing to authorize Mars' ministry in the South, even though he had obtained conference membership in New England in order to meet the official requirements for a missionary assignment. The decision by Mars to accept the post in Baltimore was not, Haven insisted, his personal preference, but only obedience to duty that was required of all Methodist ministers when appointed by a bishop. Moreover, Haven reported, the New England Conference had at its last session passed a resolution of regret over Mars' removal, with a respectful petition that the bishops return him to his former conference relation and assign him, like white missionaries, to the South.[103]

Before the controversy over Mars ended, Haven had alienated himself from Methodist episcopal and missionary leadership. Throughout the dispute he condemned Bishops Scott and Ames. In an article in January, 1865, he invited further hostility when he took to task the best known Methodist leader in the country, Bishop Matthew Simpson. A highly popular orator, Simpson had just given his famous "war speech" on the providential mission of America which had excited audiences all across the North.[104] Haven paid proper tribute to Simpson's talents, saying "Boston joined the rest of the country in crowning him with the laurels of oratory." But he could not let pass Simpson's recommendation that American Negroes be voluntarily colonized—a suggestion, Haven wrote, which "was received *cum grano salis*" in Boston. Then, in his own unique way, he chastised the bishop.

His treatment of the negro question generally it took a good many grains of his best oratoric salt to make palatable. Colonization has been a theme unheard in a popular audience here for more than ten years; it never was believed and never will be. This defect in his grand accumulation of our providential aids in the great war for humanity and God caused one somewhat sarcastic listener of the outside

100. *Christian Advocate and Journal*, Dec. 8, 1864.
101. *Minutes of the New England Conference*, 1865, pp. 42-45.
102. Quoted in *Zion's Herald*, June 7, 1865.
103. *Ibid.*, July 5, 1865. The resolution which Haven quoted did not appear in the official *Minutes of the New England Conference* for 1865.
104. Kirby, "Matthew Simpson and the Mission of America," pp. 300-301.

Church to remark that "the bishop believed in all kinds of force but *moral force.*" But we can't expect a Philadelphian, where a captain [*sic*] in the United States Navy is ejected from the cars because of his complexion, to rise to the heights of Boston radicalism in a moment. When he does get his eyes and his lips open, with what eloquence will the great doctrine of human and Christian brotherhood find utterance. The Lord hasten that blessed day![105]

Methodism's agitation over race, for which Haven was in large part responsible, reached a climax in the spring of 1865. At that time he took two steps which led ultimately to an open breach with Methodist officialdom. In late May and early June, he published essays in the *Christian Advocate* which criticized severely the failure of the bishops and the missionary board to move effectively and with a proper racial policy in the South. In the first article he asked, "How shall our Church go South?" and he concluded, "The only right and successful way is *to entirely ignore the idea of color in the organization of our Churches and conferences throughout the whole land.*" Haven warned that in granting equal rights to Negroes the nation was moving faster than the church. He attacked the slow pace of northern Methodist reoccupation of the South, and he pointed out what he considered the greatest failure—the absence of an official policy which declared that blacks would be received on equal terms with whites.

One reason for the failure lay in the sentiment of some northern Methodists who looked forward to a postwar reunion with the Methodist Episcopal Church, South. At this time the reunion movement made little tangible progress, but its supporters influenced the northern church's southern program. Haven chided them for concentrating more on the national unification of white Methodism than on the plight of the freedmen. "We are half inclined to their masters, and half declining them," he wrote satirically. "In our perplexity as how to save both them and their less loyal and less Christian brethren, without abandoning our own sinful pride of race, and more sinful prejudice against race, we are standing all the day idle." Explicitly he damned whites, North and South, for "the great and deplorable blunder, nay sin, of organizing conferences" and churches "after the old God-accursed and God-chastised pattern" of racial segregation.[106] A few weeks later, Haven editorialized against reunion with Southern Methodism, which he described as "a body so deeply implicated in secession, treason, slavery, and war; and that is without the least contrition for its dread and awful sins." In the end he opposed discussion of the idea of merger because it would paralyze the northern Methodist mission into southern territory.[107]

105. *Christian Advocate and Journal,* Jan. 26, 1865. In the Matthew Simpson Papers at the Library of Congress there is a letter dated November 7, 1864, from a local preacher in Philadelphia, C. C. Leigh, who was an officer in the National Freedmen's Relief Association, powerfully protesting the bishop's racial views.
106. *Christian Advocate and Journal,* May 25, 1865. In the same issue Abel Stevens called for "Christian fraternization" with Southern Methodists. See also *The Methodist,* June 24, 1865.
107. *Christian Advocate and Journal,* Aug. 31, Nov. 23, 1865.

In the second of his essays in the spring, Haven anticipated the concrete results of an ecclesiastical policy of racial inclusiveness. He asked again that the two colored conferences, Washington and Delaware, be allowed to die and their members and ministers be received in the regular conferences of the areas involved. Then he recommended that the church employ her most able men for southern mission work, which, in organizing conferences in the South, ought to have "no colored or white Churches as such." If ecclesiastical reconstruction in the South was operated on a transracial basis, it "would insure not alone the salvation of the South, but of the North." Of the sin of racial caste, Haven confessed, "we are as guilty as they." In racially segregated worship "New York is more unclean . . . than New Orleans, Philadelphia than Richmond." Haven also renewed his call for the union of the two Negro denominations with the Methodist Episcopal Church. In an interracial national denomination, he predicted, Bishop Jabez P. Campbell of the African Methodist Episcopal Church would become as popular as Bishop Simpson.[108]

A debate of Haven's arguments went on in the *Advocate* for most of the summer, but by the time his original articles appeared, he had taken another bold step to challenge the church's racial policy.[109] In May he sent copies of the report which he had composed for the New England Conference on the reconstruction of the church to several Methodist leaders, including John P. Durbin, the missionary secretary, and Bishop Ames.[110] The report dissented from any plan to make the Methodist Episcopal Church, South, the agency of ecclesiastical reconstruction. It also stated that there should be no recognition of race in the membership and ministry of the church, and that the bishops ought to send their best men to the South, including black preachers. As a challenge to the missionary board, Haven cited the large financial support for southern work raised by the American Missionary Association. He called for Methodists to match the Congregationalists financially and by setting the same no-caste policy. The national reconstruction of the church would be successful, he promised, only if carried out with the right racial policy that fulfilled "the perfect gospel of human and heavenly brotherhood in Christ Jesus." [111]

In sending the report to Bishop Ames, Haven apparently hoped to influence a principal figure in the council of bishops to adopt his position. The year

108. *Christian Advocate and Journal,* June 1, 1865. Campbell was one of the delegates, with Willis R. Revels and M. M. Clark, from the African Methodist Episcopal Church to the Methodist Episcopal General Conference in 1864. See *Journal of the General Conference,* 1864, pp. 150-51.

109. See issues for May 25, June 1, 8, 15, July 20, Aug. 10, 1865.

110. Prentice, *Life,* p. 277.

111. *Minutes of the New England Conference,* 1865, pp. 42-45. The editor of the *Methodist Quarterly Review,* D. D. Whedon, opposed the "fast philanthropy" of the report, saying, "We do not take share in the zeal for an immediate inauguration of a Church without regard to distinctions of races, as races at present stand related" [47 (1865), 482-83]. On May 30, J. P. Newman in New Orleans criticized the report for "sentiments which are not well-founded" and "theories which are impracticable." *Christian Advocate and Journal,* July 29, 1865.

before, Ames had been favorably impressed with Haven's carefully researched report on temperance to the New England Conference.[112] Perhaps in 1865, he thought he could build upon Ames' confidence and win a hearing for the report on church reconstruction. With it he enclosed a personal note in which he reviewed his basic arguments and showed that leading Methodists in his own, and majorities in the Maine and New Hampshire conferences, had endorsed the paper. He apologized for intruding upon the bishop's time and attention, but insisted that "the greatness of the cause . . . impels it." If Ames would lead, Haven stated, "the whole Church [would] gladly follow [him]" to "break up this unchristian line of separation in the yet-unoccupied territory." [113]

Before he responded, the bishop was likely already convinced by Haven's agitation over the case of "Father" Mars and his writing in the denominational press that he was dealing with "an unexperienced and, therefore, unpractical theorist." [114] Nearly six weeks after Haven's letter Ames replied without mentioning that he had received the report with its accompanying note. His brief answer was an order for Haven to report to Vicksburg, Mississippi as a missionary. The only information which he provided was a brief description of the situation. "There are many colored people in the city and vicinity," he wrote to Haven, "to whom your presence and influence will, I trust, be of service in many ways." He spoke of a forthcoming constitutional convention for the state, expressing the "good hope" that Haven could influence "the public men of the State . . . in securing some constitutional protection for the colored people." Since on this assignment Haven would be the only Methodist Episcopal minister in the state, Ames reminded him of the "responsibility" which rested upon him.[115]

The new appointment came as a great surprise to Haven. Clearly, part of the bishop's intent was to force Haven to apply his racial theories in the South or cease agitating the church on the subject. Several factors complicated Haven's decision on how to respond. He had already been thinking about whether or not to volunteer for southern missions. He had, moreover, to consider his responsibility for his elderly mother and his two children. In addition, a building project with the North Russell Street congregation in Boston was incomplete. He had promised church officials to raise the remaining funds to finish the work.[116]

While Haven weighed the various aspects of his decision, the announcement of the appointment spread through the church press. Nelson Cobleigh, editor of *Zion's Herald*, gave out the news on June 28, with a comment, "This is

112. *Minutes of the New England Conference*, 1864, pp. 9, 33-38.
113. Haven to Bishop [Edward R.] Ames, May 10, 1865, quoted in Prentice, *Life*, pp. 277-78.
114. This is the view of Prentice in *Life*, p. 279.
115. Ames to Haven, June 21, 1865, from Indianapolis, as quoted in *ibid.*, p. 279. See Haven's articles after visiting Vicksburg in 1873, *Zion's Herald*, June 19, 26, July 3, 1873.
116. Prentice, *Life*, pp. 280-81; *Central Christian Advocate* in St. Louis, Jan. 9, 1867.

a suitable appointment, and we have no doubt that the new missionary will be serviceable to the cause of God in laying the right foundations for our church in the valley of the Lower Mississippi." [117] The same week, the two Methodist papers in New York passed along the word. Everyone assumed that Haven was headed right away to Mississippi.[118]

In his initial reaction to Bishop Ames, Haven expressed his surprise at the unexpected appointment, but said that he was not unwilling to accept. He did point out that his congregation was writing to ask 'the bishop to defer the transfer until the remodeled church building opened in the fall. He made it quite clear that he could go only according to the Pauline standard for church organization that made no distinction of classes or colors. Regarding the bishop's comments on the political climate in Mississippi, Haven expressed doubt whether he could affect that situation immediately. In closing, he requested a delay before departing, but stated that he would go "instantly" if Ames so ordered him.[119]

Bishop Ames' letter of July 13 again failed to respond directly to Haven's primary concerns. He expressed satisfaction that there was no "serious objection" to the appointment, inquiring if Haven could start for Vicksburg by August 1. There was one reference to Haven's fundamental condition for taking the assignment. "I have no direction to give you touching your duties," he remarked. " 'We be brethren,' ministers in the same Church, having the same Discipline to guide us. I have neither the authority nor inclination to make laws. . . ." Appealing anew to Haven's reform interests, the bishop referred again to the Mississippi constitutional convention and to Haven's possible influence in it.[120]

The correspondence continued with a lengthy reply from Haven. He clarified the meaning of his consent to the appointment, calling it not a voluntary choice but obedience to orders. He knew that he could not decline without risking a church trial for a breach of ordination vows. Once more he sought to induce the bishop to respond to the basic condition which he had set for accepting the work—equal rights and no distinction of race in the church. He disagreed that an abolitionist like himself without contacts in local politics, could accomplish much at the constitutional convention. The real work of reconstruction for which he was trained, Haven maintained, was the reform and reconstitution of the church on a proper foundation. He asked whether the bishops would support his campaign against racial separation in Methodism. Ames closed the discussion with the impatient answer that he had "never failed to sustain a brother minister," whom he had appointed, "in

117. *Zion's Herald*, June 28, 1865. Cobleigh editorialized on "Self-Denial for the Sake of the South," perhaps with an eye to Haven, in the issue of July 5, 1865.

118. *Christian Advocate and Journal*, June 29, 1865; *The Methodist*, July 1, 1865.

119. This letter is included only as a summary in Prentice, *Life*, p. 281. It is not extant otherwise.

120. Ames to Haven, written from Iowa City, Ia., July 13, 1865 (erroneously dated 1863) as quoted in *ibid.*, pp. 281-82. The full text of the letter does not appear, and the letter is not extant.

a responsible and trying position." He promised to give official sanction to pastoral work based on the refusal to regard color among the members, and he commented that he personally favored the admission of black ministers to annual conferences to be formed in the South.[121]

Since Ames did not repeat his order that Haven go to Vicksburg immediately, the would-be missionary remained in Boston until his new church opened in the early fall. Meanwhile he wrote at least two letters to Bishop Simpson, requesting how to get "letters of introduction" to be presented to "leading men in Miss[issippi]." In an assessment of his forthcoming "mission" he told Simpson "it [was] a difficult & probably dangerous work . . . for Christ & his Church . . . & one that [he engaged] in at great personal sacrifice." If it was to be done properly and as Haven was "willing to do it," he looked for the task to require "a labor of years, of men, of money, of obloquy, but of righteousness & ultimate success." [122]

Meanwhile, the appointment, and the issues surrounding it, became an occasion for editorial controversy between Nelson Cobleigh of *Zion's Herald* and Daniel Curry of the *Advocate* in New York. Curiously, the latter instead of the former supported Haven. After he called the appointment "eminently a fitting one," Curry said candidly that he hoped Haven would not go South. "There are a hundred men within the reach of the Episcopal authority who can do that work as well as he," he wrote, "while there is no other that can do the work in which he has been so efficiently occupied for more than a year." Haven was needed more to vindicate "the interests of the southern freedmen" in the North than he was for "practical missionary work at the South." [123]

A few days later Cobleigh admonished Curry for taking a position against the bishops of the church. It was inconsistent, he wrote, for Curry to attack the mission board and the bishops "for not acting more promptly and doing more for the South," and then oppose them when they assigned a man for southern missions. Cobleigh insinuated his personal disagreement with Haven into the course of the discussion.[124] His sarcastic reply to Curry was directed as well against Haven.

121. *Ibid.*, pp. 282-83. Neither of these letters appears in full in Prentice's biography, nor is either extant.

122. Haven to Simpson, July 22, 1865, written from Brooklyn, Simpson Papers, Library of Congress. This letter refers to an earlier note "from Boston a few days ago" which made the original appeal for letters of introduction.

123. *Christian Advocate and Journal,* July 20, 1865. Curry may well have written this piece at Haven's request, or perhaps after talking with him about the matter. In the days immediately preceding this editorial Haven was in Brooklyn visiting relatives. It would have been quite customary for him to go to the Methodist Book Room in Manhattan to confer with Curry.

124. For Cobleigh's earlier defense of the bishops, see *Zion's Herald,* June 7, 1865. Haven had virtually ceased to write for the *Herald* after Cobleigh became editor in 1863. Cobleigh's view of southern missions clashed with Haven's main contentions, so that it is not too much to surmise that their vigorous opposition contained some personal hostility.

If the church needs an *agitator,* as Dr. Curry thinks, he himself is the proper man to agitate, and his friends put him into that office for that very work. . . . If he needs the assistance of the present *appointee* to Vicksburg, we know of no better place for obtaining the thunder with which to shake the church, than the place to which Mr. Haven has been assigned. We do not see why he cannot write as good letters for the *Advocate* or any other journal from the Mississippi Valley as from the "Hub of the Universe." We think it very important for the good of the cause and especially for its moral effect upon others who may be needed and appointed hereafter to the work, for Bro. Haven to go in good faith to the place and to the work, ascertain how things are, and report to us in the North. We all feel the need of light from that very region, and Bro. Haven is the best man we know of to give us that light. We say to him, Go, by all means go; and if he cannot succeed—if they are not ready for him—he can return.[125]

In his next issue Curry emphasized anew "that Mr. Haven can do more for our Southern work where he now is than he can do in Vicksburgh." Explaining what he meant in his former editorial, Curry declared that "it [was] not as an 'agitator,' in the sense that the term is commonly used, that Mr. Haven's services [were] needed," because he was doing "a good deal besides 'agitating.' "

He is of that very small class of men whose mission is to lead public opinion by clear and cogent arguments, and to *conserve* right sentiment in the community on the great living questions of the day. And that he may effectively do this work his presence is needed at the centers of public opinion . . . such rare material should not be used in a work that might be done by others, . . . Dr. Cobleigh to the contrary notwithstanding.[126]

The editor of the *Herald* ended the dispute, claiming that "so many in this [New England] region" agreed with him that he concluded again that Curry was mistaken. He implied that there was much sentiment in the church against Haven in Boston, but he only said, "As the subject involves delicate points, it may not be wise to ventilate it before the public." [127]

In the *Advocate* of the same week an anonymous correspondent from Boston challenged Cobleigh's claim that many New England Methodists would be happy to see Haven leave the area. "If Brother Haven's friends here think he ought to go," he wrote, "it is because they believe in obedience to episcopal orders, even when they come unheralded by a previous hint." He continued:

There seems to be something ungenerous in the *Herald's* emphasized hint about an *agitator.* Brother Haven agitates well and wisely, striking when the iron is hot. Some men who can agitate seem never to do so until the time to effect anything has gone past, then they smite the crude and hardened mass till their sledges are

125. *Zion's Herald,* Aug. 2, 1865.
126. *Christian Advocate and Journal,* Aug. 10, 1865.
127. *Zion's Herald,* Aug. 16, 1865.

broken in their grasp; whereupon they cry, See what comes of this wretched agitation! [128]

While controversy continued among Haven's friends and foes, he was busy bringing his work in Boston to a close and planning for his southern adventure. The *Western Christian Advocate* in Cincinnati reported in August that Bishop Ames had said that Haven was proceeding South "at once" via that city and Cairo, Illinois.[129] Because of that report Haven's delay was subject to further misrepresentation in the church. On October 18, 1865, the North Russell Street Church finally celebrated its opening as a "free church" with open sittings and no sale or rental of pews to members. Governor John A. Andrew attended the dedication of the refurbished building, which was preceded by Haven's successful effort to raise the remaining two thousand dollars' debt on the project.[130] Thus, Haven ended his pastorate of two and a half years and in early November left for the South, going first to New York to meet Bishop Ames at the annual meeting of the missionary board.[131]

If there was any question whether Haven had compromised his racial stance on Methodist reconstruction by agreeing to go South, he summarized his views another time in the *Advocate* just before he left Boston. His remarks were directed in two letters to Leroy M. Lee, an eminent minister and editor in the Methodist Episcopal Church, South. The correspondence was not, however, a diatribe against the southern church, for Haven was trying to be impartial in arraigning "the whole body of white believers" for the sin of caste. He even suggested a plan of union between the two sectional bodies, if they would agree to honor "the absolute oneness of believers, or no distinction in the Church on account of color or condition." Southern Methodism could become "the first Church in the land" if it would "*disregard caste.*" "Ours will be proud to solicit her fellowship," Haven confessed, "for we, with our colored conferences, Churches, and social separations, are far, very far, from that divine and only grace of man." [132]

The two letters appeared in print just as the missionary board convened in New York. At the meeting a debate occurred when Haven stated that he could not conscientiously go to Vicksburg under Methodism's racial

128. *Christian Advocate and Journal,* Aug. 17, 1865.

129. Quoted in *Zion's Herald,* Aug. 9, 1865.

130. *Zion's Herald,* August 24, 1864; Oct. 25, Dec. 13, 1865; *The Methodist,* July 9, 1864; *Christian Advocate and Journal,* Nov. 2, 1865; Prentice, *Life,* pp. 272, 309. According to the Records of the Boston Methodist Preachers' Meeting, July 11, 1864, Haven's congregation sold their former church building at another location to a parish of the African Methodist Episcopal Zion Church, and relocated near the state capital.

131. Prentice, *Life,* pp. 3, 283.

132. *Christian Advocate and Journal,* Nov. 23, 30, 1865. For extracts from Lee's original attack on Haven, see *Zion's Herald,* Oct. 11, 1865.

policy for mission. His account of the entire controversy several months later recalled the confrontation.

The Missionary Board was in session and in its appropriations constantly made distinction on account of color; appropriating moneys to build colored churches alone, and for colored ministers and schools and white superintendents. Members of the Board of the highest standing told me I could not consistently go South on the basis of that action. I still offered to go if my views would be supported by the church, and that endorsement, I was told, had been overruled by the action of the Board. Under these circumstances a decent regard for my own reputation, if no higher motive, compelled me to request a release from the appointment.[133]

Anxious to vindicate himself in some way, Haven offered to Bishop Davis W. Clark to go to Tennessee and begin a racially integrated college for which Lee Claflin, a leading New England Methodist layman who had chaired the board of trustees at the North Russell Street Church, had offered support. The bishop declined because the proposed college would be only "for blacks, but not for students without distinction of color." When Haven reported these negotiations to Bishop Ames, he put his position clearly: "As the Bishops seem to feel that, in some sort, this distinction must be kept up, I must conscientiously decline to aid its perpetuation." Bishop Edward Thomson, with whom Haven had had a pleasant association when Thomson was editor of the *Christian Advocate,* invited him to become a presiding elder in Mississippi for work among blacks. Since the basis of the work remained racially separate, Haven again regretfully refused.[134]

Before he left New York, Haven provided the substance of an article on Methodist racial policy for Theodore Tilton, editor of *The Independent.* The story, which appeared as an editorial, used the Methodist situation as an opportunity to criticize caste in any form in the church. Tilton urged the Methodist Episcopal Church to take its liberal endowment for southern missions, four hundred thousand dollars for 1866, and become the "divine model" for other churches and for the nation by establishing schools, churches, and conferences on racially equalitarian grounds.[135]

Methodist leaders promptly protested what they thought, at first, was a Congregationalist attack upon their church. Bishop Simpson provided a quasi-official reply, which Tilton published with a note identifying, by inference, Haven as the source of the original article. In defense, Simpson denied that there was any "distinction as to color recognized in the discipline" for "membership in a church, or in an annual conference, or for any official position whatever in the church." Besides explaining away the disciplinary provision for colored conferences, Simpson's argument, as Tilton pointed

133. *Central Christian Advocate,* Jan. 9, 1867.
134. *Ibid.;* Haven's letter to Ames is quoted in Prentice, *Life,* p. 284.
135. *The Independent,* Dec. 14, 1865. Congregationalists were the founders and major supporters of *The Independent,* but it was not an official denominational paper.

out, blatantly ignored the very real de facto segregation that existed through-out the denomination. The editor's response, for which Haven again provided the information, rehearsed the arguments of the original charge with further evidence.[136]

The Methodist press uniformly condemned the articles in *The Independent* and Haven's role in their production. In the *Advocate* in New York, Daniel Curry also took the position that northern Methodism was not guilty, but he argued differently from Bishop Simpson. The church, he claimed, *"no where discriminates to the disadvantage of any one on account of race or color."* Then he directed some slurs against the Congregationalists, who, he claimed, talked more than they actually did regarding Negro equality.[137] A week later Curry turned his guns on Haven, confessing "to a most sincere regret to see our Church assailed in this wise by a Methodist, and especially by one whom we so much esteem." He would not concede that the denomination needed "apology" or "defense," for "her position is the right one." Then he sought to put Haven in his place.

> The real question at issue is, whether the Church shall so conduct a crusade against the crime of *caste* as to forego all else that pertains to the preaching of the Gospel, or, while protesting boldly and unmistakably against that iniquity, to enter every open door, even where *caste* prevails, there to denounce *caste,* and to preach Christ to all. Our Church has taken the latter alternative, and we rejoice that she has. If others wish to devote themselves *wholly* to the removal of a single evil, we will not revile them, but we pray them not to make us offenders for not agreeing with them.[138]

Under the guise of discussing the issues without reference to personalities, Nelson Cobleigh gave still another defense in *Zion's Herald.* He acknowledged that a racially integrated church, locally and nationally, was the right ideal, and he looked forward to a time "when it may be put into practice without friction, without opposition, and without even social or ecclesiastical convulsions." Until the idea could be accepted, he urged all churchmen to support those who try to do their best "for the colored man." Covertly, Cobleigh was lecturing Haven for needless agitation. "It is hardly modest for a few men," he wrote, "on whom the providence of God and the church have not placed the responsibilities of administering affairs, to presume that all the practical wisdom of the age is with them." Haven was not only one of the "radical theorists," and hence "impracticable," but his "theories [were] far in advance of [his] own practice." What black people in the South required, Cobleigh summed up, was immediate help—"a heart to pity, a hand to relieve

136. *Ibid.,* Jan. 4, 1866; Prentice, *Life,* p. 286.
137. *New York Christian Advocate,* Jan. 4, 1866.
138. *New York Christian Advocate,* Jan. 11, 1866. Curry wrote a sarcastic piece on Haven in the issue of Feb. 1, 1866.

present necessities—practical working more than abstract theorizing." [139]

Still another line of reasoning on Methodist policy came from two other editors, Benjamin F. Crary of the *Central Christian Advocate* and George R. Crooks of *The Methodist*. More than others, their papers represented the sentiment of border Methodists and racial conservatives throughout the denomination. Crooks admitted that there might be a better way to organize mission work, but he insisted that the church had to be practical. Both men based their arguments on a familiar half-truth regarding black-white relations. Crary wrote that "it is a fact that our colored brethren prefer their own house and their own colored preacher." Their desire for ecclesiastical separation was so strong, he asserted, that he knew of no black congregation in Missouri which "would be willing to go in with a white congregation and be served by a white pastor." Crooks recalled a statement made by one of the fraternal delegates from the African Methodist Episcopal Church, who, at the General Conference of 1864, said that Negroes wanted racially separate churches.[140]

While his attack upon the mission board was being debated, Haven was at home in Malden, stricken physically with a fever and drained emotionally from the strain of the past months of controversy.[141] Desperately he tried to sort out the various aspects of his dilemma. Until the annual conference met in April, he would be without a specific assignment. At that time the presiding bishop could seek further to embarrass him by an ecclesiastical trial for refusing an appointment. In such an event Haven thought his conference would stand by him. Even if nothing of this nature occurred, he was still in a most awkward situation with church authorities. In their view Haven's decision not to go South virtually destroyed the credibility of his racially equalitarian program of church reconstruction. But Haven never wavered, in public or privately, in his conviction that their position, and not his own, was in error. "I am right, as every Bishop and every Christian knows," he recorded in his journal. "The Church has yielded. She must come to the only true path." Even should his conference fail to support him, Haven believed that divine aid would uphold him because "the Master . . . will not faint nor be discouraged till he has made us ignore one's skin as we have already his condition. . . . With the Saviour's help," he wrote, "I hope to be faithful to him. For I know he is Judge. May he say unto me in that day, 'Inasmuch as ye have done it unto one of the least of these my brethren, ye have done it unto me.' " [142]

139. *Zion's Herald*, Jan. 24, 1866. John M. Reid, editor of the *Western Christian Advocate*, defended the church's policy along similar lines in the Jan. 10, 1866 issue.

140. Crary's editorial is extracted in *Zion's Herald*, Feb. 14, 1866; *The Methodist*, Jan. 13, 1866.

141. Haven's journal had an account of his trip home from New York and of an attack on Dec. 30, 1865 of what he called "typhoid and brain" fever. He wrote that he "was dangerously sick for a week," with "a tendency to apoplexy." Quoted in Prentice, *Life*, p. 285.

142. Quoted in *ibid.*, p. 286. See also p. 287. The biblical citation is Matt. 25:40.

As his physical condition improved, Haven wrote out an answer to his critics. He also made plans to go South on his own. He especially wanted to observe the mission work in South Carolina where New England Methodists, T. Willard Lewis and Alonzo Webster, were forming schools and churches on a racially integrated basis.[143] Some of his friends raised six hundred dollars to finance the trip, and the Charleston missionaries wrote that they were anxious to have Haven come.[144] But he got only as far as Brooklyn, where his brother-in-law, a physician, forbade the journey. He returned home to begin more than a year of recuperation during which time he did little work.[145]

In late February after the Charleston trip had been cancelled, Haven's defense against opponents of his racial views appeared in a two-part essay in the New York *Advocate*. He called the paper, "The More Excellent Way," and it was a superb effort. Though he spoke of "the three general forms" of racial caste—the civil, the social, and the ecclesiastical—he focused on segregation in the church. He gave a passionate statement of his commitment to the church's social role in the crusade for racial equality.

Every person clothed with [the Negro's] complexion is under the unrighteous curse of society. How shall the Church regard them? Out of their depths they cry to us to lift from them this unspeakable load. . . . Shall the Church disregard it, despise it, oppose it, remove it from her pale, and as fast as she can from society? What else is her mission? Is the servant above his master? Is the Church greater than God? And did not God come down to earth that he might undo the heavy burdens, make men brothers, abolish pride and all its cruel train, and bring soul to soul in an eternal oneness of life and love? [146]

The second installment was Haven's direct answer to his critics. First, he dealt with the claim that blacks desired separation rather than union with whites. He admitted that though the argument was partly true, "it is far from being entirely so, and that because the whites will not treat them as equals." Yet he denied that either the hostility of the whites or the separatist wishes of the blacks was sufficient cause for racial segregation in the church which ought to unite diverse elements to make them one "people of God."

Another argument to which Haven replied was the assertion that northern Methodism could make no progress in the South except on the basis of expediency, yielding to the local customs of its constituency. Here he pointedly admonished Crooks who had declared, "It may be argued that there is theoretically a better way of organization; but a great Church *must deal*

143. See Lewis' reports in *Christian Advocate and Journal*, June 8, Sept. 7, 1865.
144. *New York Christian Advocate*, Mar. 1, 1866.
145. See his journal entry for Mar. 25, 1866, as quoted in Prentice, *Life*, pp. 286-87. The Boston Methodist clergy expressed their grave concern over Haven's "perilous illness." See Records of the Methodist Preachers' Meeting, Feb. 19, 1866.
146. *New York Christian Advocate*, Feb. 22, 1866.

with facts as it finds them." [147] Haven warned of the implications of this line of reasoning. "Do we find this maxim in the Bible?" he asked. "Did our Church conquer sin by yielding to it? Where she yielded, as in the matter of slavery, was she not weakened and well-nigh ruined by the complicity? Is this the mission of the Church of God?" Ending the rhetorical flourish, Haven refuted Crooks' rationale: "[The Church] must deal with facts that are wrong to rectify them. Righteousness is her only corner-stone, her only cap-stone. We must oppose evil with good."

Haven's final retort was directed against Curry's justification of the church's equivocating policy to "enter every open door even where caste prevails, there to denounce caste and preach Christ to all." Haven was indignant over Curry's pious camouflage of hard facts. "I beg to ask," he exclaimed, "where have we denounced caste? Have the Baltimore and Philadelphia Conferences . . . the Holston or Mississippi Conference denounced it? Has the General Conference or the Missionary Board? Could they have done it with consistency? Nay, rather we establish it. We are going thither not to denounce but to practice it . . . in New Orleans as truly as in Baltimore." [148]

To conclude his long but eloquent appeal, Haven stressed the positive nature of "this more excellent way." He showed how the church could complement the work of leading statesmen who were seeking "to make true democracy prevail in all the land." The church, he contended, had its own unique task—to carry out interracial brotherhood in its own sphere. If that mission was fulfilled, it would have its own effect upon society. Entreating the church to do what was right, whatever the consequence, Haven portrayed the meaning of his millennial vision of interracial harmony with reference to the divine opportunities which lay before his own denomination. He expressed the hope that before long New England Methodism's protest against caste would be "reechoed from Mississippi and the Gulf"; that "the next General Conference [would] behold the iniquity of colored conferences washed away"; that "Bishop [Daniel A.] Payne's prayer on the reception of [the Methodist Episcopal] delegates [at the African Methodist Episcopal General Conference in 1864 would] be answered, 'that men should not recognize men by the color of the skin' "; and that Daniel Curry's wish to keep "our colored people with us" instead of in "separate organizations" would be fulfilled. Recent disappointment over the inability of church leaders to share his hope prepared Haven for the possibility of temporary, but not ultimate, defeat. "But if this vision does not soon gladden our eyes," he wrote,

147. *The Methodist*, Jan. 13, 1866.

148. *New York Christian Advocate*, Mar. 1, 1866. Haven quotes from Curry's article of Jan. 11, 1866. For reports by missionaries on the failure of "mixed congregations in the South," see *Zion's Herald*, Aug. 16, 1865; *The Methodist*, Feb. 17, 1866; *New York Christian Advocate*, Mar. 15, 1866.

if weary years, back-slidings, and bloody battles intervene, it will assuredly appear: for the mouth of the Lord hath spoken it. Every letter of his word
breathes a common and a burning flame against all such distinctions among
brethren. From lid to lid it declares the oneness of his people on earth as in
heaven. Through it, by his Spirit, he will yet subdue the Church to himself, and
she shall prove by her love for her brother whom she hath seen, how truly and
ardently she loves her God whom she hath not seen.[149]

By the time this essay appeared in print, Haven had undergone a psycho-
physical collapse. For three years of intense effort he had tried to convince
others to share his vision of the millennial future of racial equality and
brotherhood and to see its social and political implications in the nation and
its crucial religious bearing for the church, particularly his own denomination.
It was not, however, the failure to have accomplished more tangible achievements toward the millennial goal that brought on Haven's personal crisis.
He could accept the necessity of gradual progress, even of temporary defeat,
and he was prepared for conflict. What threatened to undo him was the
agonizing realization that most other Americans, and especially that most
Methodists, would not basically share his dream. When Haven faced that
hard reality, he was jolted to the roots.[150]

In April, 1866, he retired from the New England Conference because of
"nervous prostration." One of his journal entries a few days prior to the
conference contained the revealing statement, "My feelings are the cause of
my sickness, they only." His doctor prohibited "any participation whatever
in exciting or wearing thought and labor." [151]

Haven's retirement came at a particularly unfortunate time. Besides his
breach with the Methodist establishment which damaged his ecclesiastical
standing and reputation, there was the more important loss of his prophetic
influence for much of 1866, the centennial year for the denomination. His
fellow Methodists were less disposed than ever to engage in critical reflection
about the "form of Protestantism" which, according to *Harper's Weekly*,
had become "the predominant ecclesiastical fact of the nation." [152] Everyone
was too involved in calling attention to the providential aspects of American
Methodism's phenomenal success.[153] Isolated in his illness and alienated

149. *New York Christian Advocate*, Mar. 1, 1866. At Haven's insistence Cobleigh published "The
More Excellent Way," in *Zion's Herald*, Mar. 14, 21, 1866. See also issues for Jan. 31, Feb. 21, 28,
Mar. 7, 1866.
150. In light of the failure of Haven's denomination to support his racial policy, it is questionable
whether his views ought to be considered as representative, among northern Methodists, as does
Donald Gene Jones in his excellent analysis of "The Moral, Social, and Political Ideas of the
Methodist Episcopal Church from the Closing Years of the Civil War Through Reconstruction
1864-1876" (Ph.D. dissertation, Drew University, 1969).
151. *Minutes of the New England Conference*, 1866, p. 13; *New York Christian Advocate*, Apr.
12, 1866; journal entry for Mar. 25 as quoted in Prentice, *Life*, p. 287.
152. Oct. 6, 1866.
153. In addition to numerous articles in the church press, see an excellent example in Abel
Stevens, *The Centenary of American Methodism: A Sketch of Its History, Theology, Practical
System, and Success* (New York, 1866).

from many of his associates because of the recent controversy, Haven had reason to despair. No one seemed willing to assume his mantle as prophet for social reform and interracial brotherhood.

IV

By the fall of 1866, Haven began slowly to return to public life. From Malden he journeyed over to Amenia, New York, where he spent a month with his late wife's relatives. From there he went West, pausing to see friends and relations along the way. On his return he stopped off in Missouri, Kentucky, and Tennessee to visit Methodist schools and churches and to tour scenic spots like Lookout Mountain. After making a hurried call on friends in New York, he rejoined his family for Thanksgiving.[154]

At the close of the year Haven's health had improved considerably, but he was still bothered by the effects of his breakdown. Likewise he was not at all sure when, whether or how to resume his place in the church. Even after his trip to the Midwest, he did no preaching, and he still had to refrain from all physically taxing work. He had been encouraged, however, by the moral support which some of the New England Methodist brethren had provided by endorsing his anticaste views for church reconstruction.[155] At his leisure he did resume his favorite avocation, writing for the religious press. In his first essays he showed that he had not lost touch, despite his illness, with political and ecclesiastical developments. Before long he was back into the thick of the debate over reconstruction.[156]

There was certainly no indication that the controversy with church officials had intimidated Haven. He was as outspoken as ever in criticizing all forms of racial separation in Methodism. Because of the implied separatism he even attacked the name of and rationale for a new agency, the Freedmen's Aid Society of the Methodist Episcopal Church.[157] He insisted that existing boards in the church could direct the southern work. To form a special organization insured institutional racial distinctions.[158]

154. Prentice, *Life*, pp. 287-88. See articles he wrote on the trip in *New York Christian Advocate*, Oct. 18, Nov. 1, 22, 1866; *The Independent*, Nov. 22, 1866; *Western Christian Advocate*, Nov. 21, 1866.

155. In 1866 the New England Conference, after a brisk debate between "the conservative and radical" elements of the body, adopted a Report on the Reconstruction of our Church in the South which contained many of the sentiments which Haven had written again and again during 1864, 1865, and 1866. See *Minutes of the New England Conference*, 1866, pp. 7, 12, 41-45, and a manuscript copy of the report, signed by L. R. Thayer, chairman; papers of the New England Conference.

156. *New York Christian Advocate*, Nov. 29, 1866; Prentice, *Life*, p. 288.

157. The society was organized in Cincinnati in August, 1866, "to labor for the relief and education of the Freedmen, especially in co-operation with the Missionary and Church Extension Societies of the Methodist Episcopal Church." Previously, northern Methodists had worked with interdenominational programs for the freedmen. For an account of the organization's beginnings see *Reports of the Freedmen's Aid Society of the Methodist Episcopal Church, 1866-1875* (Cincinnati [1893]), pp. 3-15.

158. *New York Christian Advocate*, Aug. 30, 1866. Later Haven supported the new society enthusiastically for its practical aid to black churches and schools in the South.

While he was on his midwestern jaunt, Haven published an appeal to the members of the missionary board, asking again that they officially adopt a policy against racial caste in all church agencies in the South. He praised the pioneering efforts in this direction being undertaken by New England Methodist abolitionists in the new South Carolina Conference. The church's failure to have a single policy, however, fortified an "antibiblical, anti-christian prejudice." Furthermore, where racial separation had occurred in colleges, local churches, and district organizations, he contended, the denomination was wasting money by duplicating facilities. What was even more serious was the hesitancy of the largest Protestant body in the land to take an anti-caste stand. That failure hindered the work of national unification, for the church ought to "give Congress the key-note it hesitates to strike;—the key-note it must yet strike—the political equality of all citizens." [159]

Undoubtedly before he wrote and published his appeal, Haven measured the likelihood of renewing the debate of the year before. If so, he did not have to wait long before he heard the charge that because he had refused to go South as a missionary, he had no right to speak about the church's racial policy. The editor of the *Central Advocate* and one of the founders of the Freedmen's Aid Society, B. F. Crary, assailed Haven for not "[taking] his own medicine." "No man ever had a better field," he maintained. "The Bishops offered him one of the best positions in the South, and he did not go. We do not accept of any possible excuse . . . [for] we believe that Bro. Haven ought to have gone to Vicksburg if certain death stared him in the face." Those who did go South, Crary continued, "will not now be much affected by his advice." Haven only "[declaimed] against caste at a safe distance" instead of working where he would "have to bear the odium" of practical action that aided the blacks.[160]

In a rejoinder Haven wrote a full account of his side of the controversy with church officials. He disputed Crary's claim that he was offering advice to southern missionaries. "I have simply and *solely* sought to bring *the church* to this position [against caste]," he wrote. "I sympathize with these brethren in their services and sacrifices, and only wish that the church would so direct their work that it should be altogether right and enduring." He also denied Crary's contention that Massachusetts was "a safer place for the utterance of these truths than St. Louis or the South." Proving that he practiced what he preached, Haven reported that he had spoken freely on racial topics in both of his visits to the South (Maryland and Virginia in 1861 and Nashville in 1866) and that he carried on a constant war against caste in Boston. At the North Russell Street Church one of his class leaders had been Brother Freeman, a Negro. He concluded with a typical expression

159. *Northwestern Christian Advocate*, Nov. 7, 1866. See also Haven's two essays in the *New York Christian Advocate*, Dec. 13, 27, 1866.
160. *Central Christian Advocate*, Nov. 14, 1866.

of confidence that his cause would ultimately triumph. "It is winning its way in the state," he declared, "it will yet, and, though I regret unspeakably to say it, I fear it will *afterward,* triumph in the church." That it should be so ought to be "a source of infinite mortification," but the church "did not abolish slavery till it had been done by the state. She will not, I fear, abolish its spirit and soul, caste and separations based professedly on the tint of a man's face." But Haven's response failed to convince Crary. "We beg our very dear Boston brother," he replied, "to remember that we are a set of intense abolitionists so far ahead of him that we practice what he preaches." [161]

If "A Plea to the Missionary Board" invoked the personal criticism that Haven expected from certain quarters in his own church, it also provided the occasion for black churchmen to commend him openly for his "masterly article." The official paper of the African Methodists, the *Christian Recorder,* reprinted the complete appeal to which James Lynch, the editor, appended a note, expressing disappointment that only the *Northwestern Christian Advocate* of Methodist Episcopal papers had the courage to publish the piece. "We expected it to appear in the *Advocate* of New York," he remarked, criticizing Daniel Curry for its omission. Another contributor compared Haven with Charles Sumner and praised them both for being "true to right principles and views." Because Haven had "faced the storm of opposition," his testimony was all the more authentic. "If every man, professing to be a Methodist," the writer declared, "would continue to feel as he felt, when God, for the sake of his Son, spoke the life-giving word in his soul, there would be no proscriptions on account of color, in the Church." [162] Three months later the most distinguished African Methodist Episcopal leader in the country, Bishop Daniel A. Payne, added his endorsement of Haven's anti-caste effort. "It will be a glorious day in the history of the venerable [Methodist Episcopal] Church . . . ," he wrote, "when she will leap upon and stand on the elevated and elevating platform erected by Rev. Gilbert Haven, who seems to be the apostle of the movement for demonstrating the oneness of apostolic Christianity, which recognized no distinctions among believers on account of race or color." [163]

In his return to the public forum through the religious press, Haven also wrote extensively about the political aspects of the national racial situation. He saw grave threats to the cause of equal rights. In the summer of 1866, riots in Memphis and New Orleans ended in massacres of Negroes and

---

161. Haven's essay and Crary's reply are in *ibid.,* Jan. 9, 1867. Haven recounted his efforts to get the official board and congregation at North Russell Street to accept Brother Freeman in *Zion's Herald,* May 7, 1868. See also a reference to Freeman in *Christian Advocate and Journal,* Nov. 30, 1865.

162. Both the reprint of Haven's "Plea," Lynch's note, and the commentary, signed "W." (probably Elisha Weaver), are in the *Christian Recorder,* Dec. 22, 1866.

163. See Payne's letter on "Relations of the African Methodist Episcopal Church to the Methodist Episcopal Church and the Methodist Episcopal Church, South," in the *Western Christian Advocate,* Mar. 13, 20, 1867. His tribute to Haven appeared in the second installment.

white northern sympathizers who had moved to the South. The Democratic victory in Kentucky and threats to the Republican cause in Maryland, Tennessee, and Missouri became ominous political signs of a backlash against Reconstruction. Many freedmen were reduced to a state of serfdom not unlike the slavery they had recently escaped, when infamous "Black Codes" were enacted in the southern states. Haven particularly attacked the treachery of President Johnson, whose policy had put ex-Confederates back into power while denying blacks any voice in the new governments. Late in 1865, fifteen representatives and seven senators, all of whom were former rebel military and political leaders and including Alexander H. Stephens, asked for admittance to the Thirty-ninth Congress. They had been elected under Johnson's scheme for reunion. Fortunately, in Haven's view, Congress refused to recognize the new state governments which they represented and began the reconstruction process anew. The President exerted every effort, however, to block the congressional program for the South, vetoing the Freedmen's Bureau Act and the Civil Rights Act of 1866. When Congress overrode the vetoes, Haven was pleased, but he did not spare the legislators when they failed to provide for universal suffrage as a remedy to the national crisis.[164]

To Haven "the renewal of the South" depended upon the concurrent action of the Congress and the church. "To make this vast region peaceful and loyal," he wrote, "is the mighty task placed by Providence upon the Congress of the nation." The first requirement was to impeach the President. Congress could make no real progress in Reconstruction until the executive branch of government worked harmoniously with the legislature. Haven believed that a delay to accomplish needed changes until the elections of 1868 would be disastrous. Before then the South would be reconstructed on some basis. Congress had to insure that its plan effected the "permanent and righteous reorganization" of the nation.[165]

The second task for Congress was to guarantee *"loyal manhood suffrage"* for the South. Haven warned that some safeguards had to be placed on the franchise in order to deny political participation to disloyalists. His recommendations were similar to the policy of the radical Republicans in Congress, though Haven was more insistent than were most politicians that whatever standard applied in the South must also be adopted for the North. He also believed that no territory which barred Negroes from voting should be admitted to statehood. He proposed that "Congress . . . annul all the rebel governments that . . . have taken the place of rebel armies"; keep their successors "in a territorial condition" until they have proved their loyalty; oust the Presi-

164. Franklin, *Reconstruction*, pp. 32-68; *New York Christian Advocate*, Aug. 30, 1866. He also admonished Congress for failing to enact impartial suffrage for the District of Columbia, *ibid.*, Oct. 4, 1866.

165. *The Independent*, Sept. 6, Dec. 13, 20, 1866; Jan. 10, 1867. "By the fall of 1866 several abolitionists were calling for the impeachment of President Johnson" (McPherson, *The Struggle for Equality*, p. 369).

dent, "who will prevent, as long as he remains in power, a peaceful and righteous settlement of affairs"; protect the ballot for "every loyal man" and deny it to "every disloyal man"; and reorganize the army with "Northern soldiers . . . combined with the loyal white and black militia of the section." [166] Haven also called upon the Supreme Court to declare racially based suffrage to be unconstitutional as another way to insure "democratic institutions and constitutional blessings" in the South.[167]

When he discussed the duty of the church in social reconstruction, Haven reiterated a familiar theme. "Political equality every conscience and voice demand," he wrote. "But political fraternity is no more the duty of the State than is ecclesiastical fraternity of the Church." He exposed the northern denominations which had already accepted a pattern of racial separation in their southern work. He ridiculed segregation which place in "colored schools" students whose skin complexions were lighter than some of their "white" teachers. The church, he demanded, should cease to use words like "freedman," "colored," and "white," and recognize only "men and brethren." "She must elevate in all her churches those who are fitted for office-bearers to their true position, irrespective of any obsolescent outward distinctions," he declared. "She must preach and practice, in the parlor no less than in the pew, in the store and street as well as in the prayer-room, this only gospel, and thus strengthen the hands and inspire the hearts of our statesmen in their hardly lower or less important work." To "take any lower ground [would] harm rather than help the true work of reconstruction." [168]

With his series of essays on political and church reconstruction, which appeared during the winter of 1866-67, Haven had reentered the public discussion of the nation's responsibility for racial justice. He presented a comprehensive program of racial reform for the church and for American society to move beyond emancipation to racial equality. Early the following spring he was given a unique opportunity to promote his program and affect public opinion more directly to join the struggle against caste.

166. *The Independent*, Jan. 10, 1867.
167. *Ibid.*, Jan. 24, 1867; *New York Christian Advocate*, Mar. 7, 1867.
168. *The Independent*, Jan. 24, 1867.

V

Crusade Against Caste

In March, 1867, the Boston Wesleyan Association unanimously elected Gilbert Haven to succeed Nelson E. Cobleigh, retiring editor of *Zion's Herald*. As its publications board, the association pledged to help make the *Herald* the leading religious newspaper in New England. Haven accepted that pledge and the offer of the position, despite the fact that, as he wrote in his journal, he had done "no steady and responsible work since November, 1865, almost a year and a half." [1] But if he questioned whether he was capable of handling the job, there were others who certainly did not share his doubts. *The Independent* praised the choice, saying that the Methodists had "promoted themselves in promoting [Haven]—the most prominent representative of Christian radicalism in their church." James Lynch of the *Christian Recorder* likewise rejoiced in the selection of such "an ideal man in Christianity, patriotism and scholarship [who was] by nature a Reformer [and who stood] unmoved amid the fiercest opposition of error." Not everyone agreed, however, to the wisdom of Haven's election. The *Pittsburgh Christian Advocate* complained sarcastically that the *Herald* now had "a thoroughly one-idead editor." [2]

As he launched an editorial career which lasted for the next five years, Haven immediately inaugurated measures to make the *Herald* more appealing to readers. He secured articles from leading churchmen outside, as well as within, his own denomination, and he published the work of some of the popular women writers of the day, Augusta Moore, Anna Warner, Mrs. H. C. Gardiner. He established, each with an editorial supervisor, "Children's, Home, Commercial, Agricultural, Foreign, Political, and Religious" departments for the paper. Subscriptions increased to more than sixteen thousand as the journal became one of the best known Methodist weeklies in the country. [3]

The paper's success under Haven depended not alone upon his creative management. His own writing on diverse religious and social topics as well helped to establish its distinctive identity. At one time or another between 1867 and 1872, practically every significant reform movement in America received some notice in the *Herald*. The issues varied from coeducational schools and the cooperation of labor and capital to the legal recognition of Christianity in the federal constitution. Haven argued for a more just national

1. Quoted in Prentice, *Life*, pp. 334-35; *New York Christian Advocate*, Mar. 21 and 28, 1867.
2. *The Independent*, Mar. 21, 1867; *Christian Recorder*, Mar. 23, Apr. 20, 1867; *Pittsburgh Christian Advocate*, Aug. 17, 1867. For another commentary on Haven's election, see *Central Christian Advocate*, Mar. 27, 1867.
3. See advertisements for the *Herald* in the *New York Christian Advocate*, Nov. 26, 1868; Dec. 21, 1871; *Geo. P. Rowell & Co's American Newspaper Directory* (New York, 1869), p. 44. For examples of the prospectus for the paper and Haven's conception of religious journalism, see *Zion's Herald*, Apr. 10, Aug. 22, Oct. 17, 1867; Jan. 2, Sept. 24, 1868; July 1, 1869; June 27, 1872.

policy toward American Indians and attacked lotteries, the theater, more liberal divorce laws, and capital punishment. He also wrote about the problems of the cities whose slums and immigrant population were expanding.

The woman suffrage and prohibition movement were among Haven's special concerns. In 1868 he had an important role in organizing the New England Woman Suffrage Association, which, in turn, gave rise to a national organization. A few years later he served as president of the American Woman Suffrage Association, and he often shared the platform with leading women's rights spokesmen, like Lucy Stone, Julia Ward Howe, Abby Kelly Foster, and Wendell Phillips.[4] Throughout his editorship, Haven also carried on a constant war against the advocates of legalized liquor. The issue had political implications in Massachusetts. Finally Haven became so disillusioned with "rum Republicans" that he eventually joined the Prohibition Party. Sometimes he tried to make a case that linked prohibition with the ballot for women, arguing that legal control of the consumption of alcoholic beverages could be more easily won with the support of women voters.[5]

Agitation for specific ecclesiastical reforms was also a common practice in Haven's paper. He had supported lay representation in the annual and general conferences of Methodism since 1864. In the *Herald* and within the councils of the denomination, he continued to urge that lay members be given the vote on ecclesiastical questions.[6] A related matter both to women's rights and lay representation was Haven's move to provide an equal voice in church affairs to women members. He even commended the practice of ordaining women to the ministry. For example, he enthusiastically endorsed the evangelistic work of Mrs. Maggie Newton Van Cott, the first of her sex licensed to preach in the Methodist Episcopal Church.[7]

These social and ecclesiastical reforms reflected Haven's broad interests, but they were always secondary to the crusade for racial justice and brotherhood. Even the women's suffrage and temperance causes, he discovered, were

4. *Zion's Herald*, June 17, 1869; *National Antislavery Standard*, June 5, 19, 1869; *New York Christian Advocate*, Nov. 12, 1874; *Southwestern Christian Advocate*, Jan. 27, 1876. See Harriet H. Robinson, *Massachusetts in the Woman Suffrage Movement* (Boston, 1881), pp. 48, 53, 55, 68, 147, 220. Further examples of Haven's editorializing on women's rights are in *Zion's Herald*, Apr. 24, 1867; Feb. 6, Mar. 19, Apr. 16, 1868; Dec. 23, 1869; Jan. 13, May 26, June 16, 1870; May 18, July 13, Sept. 7, 1871.

5. Among numerous articles and editorial notes in *Zion's Herald*, see issues for Apr. 17, May 8, June 26, Nov. 14, 1867; Sept. 24, 1868; Nov. 24, 1870; Mar. 16, May 25, Oct. 5, 1871; *The Independent*, Sept. 28, 1871; Feb. 29, 1872. See also Haven's letters to Governor William Claflin, Sept. 23, Oct. 2, 1869; Oct. 6, 1870, William Claflin Papers, Rutherford B. Hayes Library. The last letter is quoted in Prentice, *Life*, pp. 312-15.

6. Besides his pamphlet, *Lay Representation in the Methodist Episcopal Church*, which was originally serialized in *The Methodist* between July 23 and Sept. 10, 1864, see *Christian Advocate and Journal*, Apr. 14, May 4, 1864; Aug. 31, 1865; *The Methodist*, Oct. 14, 1865; *New York Christian Advocate*, June 11, 1868; *Zion's Herald*, June 11, 1868.

7. *Zion's Herald*, Apr. 29, July 8, 1869; Mar. 31, July 7, 1870; Records of the Boston Methodist Preachers' Meeting, Sept. 13, 1869; Oct. 24, 1870; Jan. 1, 15, February 5, 19, 1872. Haven wrote the introduction to John O. Foster's *Life and Labors of Mrs. Maggie Newton Van Cott* (Cincinnati, 1872), pp. xiii-xxviii.

infected with white racism. In 1869 feminists divided over whether to support the Fifteenth Amendment which enfranchised black men but left all women without the vote. The segment of the movement to which Haven was linked was willing to back the voting rights amendment, since it represented an extension of suffrage to a portion of the population which, like women, had been disfranchised. The National Division of the Sons of Temperance, in Haven's view, likewise conceded to racial prejudice in adopting a policy of localism which left membership standards up to state organizations. The action virtually insured racially segregated temperance societies.[8]

Because Haven did not abandon the cause of black freedom and racial equality after the war, as did some antebellum reformers, he wrote more articles on this question in its political, social, and ecclesiastical aspects than on all other reforms combined. His first issue indicated what his readers could expect. On page one, column one, Haven published an appeal by the New England Conference to its churches. The title of the article, composed by him and approved by the conference, was a motto of the *Herald* for the next five years—"No Caste in the Church of God." The conclusion was an even clearer summary of the scope of Haven's commitment "to purge the church, and society of this unrighteous leaven, and hasten forward the kingdom of our Saviour and Father, whose love embraceth all in equal ardor, patience and perfection." [9]

I

At the time that Haven took his editorial post, he was optimistic about the political prospects for racial reform in the country. Congress had thwarted President Andrew Johnson's scheme of national reunion. A civil rights act had been passed and the Freedmen's Bureau sustained. The basic congressional Reconstruction program had just been enacted. The army was preparing to insure the reformation of state governments in the South in conformity with the Fourteenth Amendment, providing for black political participation and disfranchising those ex-Confederates who were barred from holding office by the amendment. Even though Johnson had vetoed the Reconstruction acts, including two measures designed to curtail his power, many politicians hoped that he would still administer the new legislation without executive obstruction.[10]

Generally Haven was pleased with the congressional plan for Reconstruc-

8. James M. McPherson, "Abolitionists, Woman Suffrage, and the Negro, 1865-1869," *Mid-America*, 47 (January, 1965), 40-47; *Zion's Herald*, July 22, 1869; see also Sept. 14, 1871.

9. *Zion's Herald*, Apr. 10, 1867. The piece also appeared in the *Central Christian Advocate*, May 8, 1867.

10. See Haven's survey of the national situation in *Zion's Herald*, Apr. 24, 1867. For the Reconstruction acts and Johnson's veto messages, see Edward McPherson, *The Political History of the United States of America during the Period of Reconstruction*, 2nd ed. (Washington, 1875), pp. 166-81, 191-94.

tion, but he considered its greatest shortcoming to be the failure to protect Negro suffrage in the South. He argued that enfranchisement of blacks was both morally and politically necessary. As long as the question was left up to the states, voting rights for Negroes could not be guaranteed. "Once back into the Union," he warned, "the rebels might, if not nominally, at least in fact, disfranchise so large a portion of the blacks that their former supremacy could be established within their respective States." To remedy this omission, he called on Congress "to embody the principle of impartial suffrage in an amendment to the Constitution." [11]

Developments in northern states during 1867 further exhibited the need for a national standard for voting. In the spring Connecticut again turned down Negro suffrage, although the Republican leadership did not fail, as it had in 1865, to back the proposal. Haven condemned the rejection as a "wicked" act, but he praised the political leaders who had supported the unsuccessful measure. "Better a thousand fold be defeated with impartial suffrage in the platform," he declared, "than be victorious without it." [12]

In the fall attempts to establish equal suffrage in Ohio, Minnesota, and Kansas were also defeated. [13] As Haven recognized, nine times, between 1865 and 1867, northern electors had voted against Negro suffrage. In five other states Republicans had refused to submit the issue to a referendum. Only Wisconsin, by a court decision, and Nebraska, where Congress required legislative adoption of impartial suffrage before statehood was approved, had added equal suffrage in the North. Tennessee was the first reconstructed southern state to remove racial restrictions from voting.[14] Because of these results Haven began to fear that the Republican Party was in danger of "sacrificing the rights of man to the lusts of man." In an editorial at Thanksgiving, he reflected upon "the shameful recreancy of mere politicians" and upon the "general backsliding" throughout the country from "the highest ideas of civil and eternal righteousness." "The political revival is seemingly at an end," he wrote. "The people are getting tired of being virtuous. They are forgetting their vows made under the lash of God's wrath, and [are] going back as our Saviour so forcibly declares to the detestable vomit they were compelled in that hour of sickness to disgorge." [15]

11. *Zion's Herald*, Apr. 24, June 26, 1867; J. McPherson, *Struggle for Equality*, p. 376.

12. *Zion's Herald*, Apr. 17, 1867. The vote in 1867 was considerably closer than in 1865. The amendment lost by a thousand votes compared to 6,200 in the first attempt. E. McPherson, *History of Reconstruction*, pp. 120, 353-54.

13. Ohio rejected a new franchise law by a majority of nearly forty thousand votes. Minnesota turned down impartial suffrage by 1,300 votes, and Kansas also refused to strike the word "white" from voting requirements. E. McPherson, *History of Reconstruction*, pp. 257-58, 353-54. Haven commented on these results in *Zion's Herald*, Oct. 17, Nov. 28, Dec. 12, 1867.

14. Haven's "All hail, Tennessee!" was in the *New York Christian Advocate*, Mar. 7, 1867. On the same subject see *Zion's Herald*, Sept. 12, 1867. See also Leslie H. Fishel, Jr., "Northern Prejudice and Negro Suffrage, 1865-1870," *Journal of Negro History*, 39 (1954), 13-14, 19-22; William Gillette, *The Right to Vote: Politics and the Passage of the Fifteenth Amendment* (Baltimore: Johns Hopkins Press, 1965), pp. 25-26, 28; E. McPherson, *History of Reconstruction*, pp. 257, 353-54.

15. *Zion's Herald*, Oct. 17, Nov. 28, 1867.

As congressional Reconstruction proceeded, the southern scene provided an ironic contrast to the North. All the southern state constitutional conventions which met in the fall and winter of 1867 included significant Negro representation.[16] Impressed by southern progress toward political equality, Haven declared that the freedman was the "corner-stone" of the new South.[17] Under congressional Reconstruction, southern Negroes were winning political rights more rapidly than blacks in any part of the North, except New England. Haven was disturbed by the contrast of "Southern freedom and Northern restrictiveness."

Here in Massachusetts we may congratulate ourselves that we are not behind our Southern neighbors. We had two respectable colored men in the House of Representatives, and we have negro jurymen and justices of the peace. But Connecticut still refuses the colored man the ballot, and so do New York and Pennsylvania and the Western States, except Wisconsin. . . . When we look southward, we see the city of Washington revolutionized by colored voters, and we hear authentic accounts of preparations made in various parts of the South to elect colored men to the constitutional conventions and to the Legislature, and to Congress. This contrast must not much longer be allowed to offend the public eye and the public sense.[18]

A national law or constitutional amendment establishing equal suffrage would guarantee the right to vote in the South and extend it where it was still restricted in the North. Haven thought that the middle and western states would eventually vote for an impartial franchise, but, he wrote, "we cannot afford to wait." In Kentucky and Maryland, "free suffrage" would have to be enforced by law, he predicted, or it would not be established for another twenty-five years. Because "existing constitutions, usages, traditions and prejudices obstruct the good work of reform," Haven asked for a national solution. "Congress has already done well"; he contended, "let it lay the people under new obligations, and entitle itself anew to the respect of the friends of popular government throughout the world by passing an act or adopting a constitutional provision, which shall sweep away all distinctions of color in suffrage and government." [19]

The movement for national equal suffrage was partially diverted in late 1867, when Congress made the unprecedented attempt to impeach President Johnson. Haven had not called for impeachment between January and June, but when the President interfered with federal commanders in the South, he renewed his attack. Because of the problem of presidential succession,

16. Franklin, *Reconstruction After the Civil War*, p. 102. Blacks dominated only one convention, however, and except for Louisiana, Florida, and South Carolina, their representation was never more than 20 percent of the total.

17. *Zion's Herald*, Aug. 8, Sept. 12, 1867; Jan. 30, Feb. 20, 1868. Nelson Cobleigh, who had become the president of East Tennessee Wesleyan University, later warned Haven not to be overly optimistic about the southern situation. He predicted the conservative reaction in Tennessee which subsequently spelled the end of Reconstruction there. *Zion's Herald*, Apr. 2, 1868; Aug. 26, 1869.

18. *Ibid.*, June 26, 1867.

19. *Ibid.*

however, he still doubted that an impeachment could be won.[20] In August when Johnson suspended Secretary of War Edwin M. Stanton for his complicity in congressional Reconstruction operations, and removed two southern commanders, Philip Sheridan and Daniel Sickles, because they supported Congress, Haven lambasted the chief executive as the "Traitorous President." He severely chastised Congress for adjourning without having acted against Johnson. "It should have proceeded," he exclaimed, "in the strength and majesty with which the Constitution has clothed it to calmly investigate the charges against the President, to arraign him, try him, and if found guilty, to remove him." [21] Moderate Republicans who had blocked the impeachment proceeding earned Haven's special censure. They were inconsistent, he observed, to approve half-constitutional "limitations of the President's prerogative" while refusing "to do what the Constitution most clearly permits and requires." [22]

Unquestionably impeachment was the major political issue for the 1867-68 session of Congress. The first attempt in the House failed on December 7, even though a majority of the Judiciary Committee had recommended Johnson's removal.[23] Writing on the congressional debate, Haven disputed those who claimed that Johnson's "crimes and misdemeanors" were not "indictable by statute or common law." To him, and to other abolitionists, impeachment was a political, not a legal action—"a process for getting rid of a bad and dangerous public officer" and "not a trial for the punishment of a criminal." [24] Congressional Republicans realized, however, that the Constitution made impeachment a judicial procedure. They doubted whether they could win a legal case against Johnson. Haven seemed to recognize that problem when he spoke of Johnson's retirement and anticipated the election in 1868 of an executive "who shall represent radical ideas." [25]

The first attempt to impeach had failed, but President Johnson did not seem anxious to see his battle with Congress end. In his annual message of December, 1867, he launched a withering attack against his opposition. He contended that the Reconstruction effort to provide political equality for blacks was doomed. The paper was full of references to "negro domination" and to the evils of "clothing the negro race with political privileges torn from white men." Johnson did not believe a racially equalitarian society was possible. The inferior or the superior race—the black or the white—must dominate. "The great difference between the two races in physical, mental, and moral characteristics," the President stated,

20. *Ibid.* Since Johnson had become president after Lincoln's death, Ben Wade in the Senate would have been his constitutional successor.
21. *Zion's Herald*, Aug. 22, 1867.
22. *Ibid.*
23. E. McPherson, *History of Reconstruction*, p. 264; J. McPherson, *Struggle for Equality*, p. 383.
24. *Zion's Herald*, Dec. 12, 1867; J. McPherson, *Struggle for Equality*, p. 384.
25. *Zion's Herald*, Dec. 12, 1867.

will prevent an amalgamation or fusion of them together in one homogeneous mass. If the inferior obtains the ascendency over the other, it will govern with reference only to its own interests—for it will recognize no common interest—and create such a tyranny as this continent has never yet witnessed. . . . Of all the dangers which our nation has yet encountered, none are equal to those which must result from the success of the effort now making to Africanize the half of our country.[26]

Johnson's "atrocious message," Haven wrote in an extensive evaluation, was "interfused and interpenetrated with the very essence of diabolism." He refuted the President's charges against the congressional Reconstruction program, which, though not "a perfect one," had been "as successful as the country had any right to expect. Mr. Johnson states what is utterly false," Haven charged, "when he says it was designed to place the white people of the South in subjection to the negroes. It was designed to bring about what the South has never yet seen, the reign of equality and justice. And to a very large degree it has had this result." Quoting the *New York Tribune,* Haven pointed out that "in six of the ten States which [were] subject to the plan of reconstruction a majority of the registered voters [were] *whites"* who accepted the state of affairs. But "Presidential treachery" and "Northern political cowardice and defection" gave "the malcontents new courage and opportunities for mischief" in those states. "The troubles of the South, financial and industrial, and social and religious, are sore enough," he maintained,

but politically there is but slight complaint from that section. Yet here comes the President of the United States, with an incendiary and revolutionary appeal to Congress to undo all its work, to take away from the black man the suffrage he has just begun to exercise so wisely, to remand him again into the control of his white master, in whose hands, so far as all political and civil rights are concerned except perhaps the mere right to live and work, he will be as powerless as he was before the era of emancipation dawned upon him.[27]

During the next few weeks Johnson further antagonized his opponents, many of whom, by this time, were his former associates from the moderate wing of the Republican Party. Before Christmas he publicly approved the action of General Winfield Hancock who sanctioned the existing provisional governments in Louisiana and Texas with an authority that directly defied congressional legislation.[28] Shortly thereafter, the President removed two more commanding generals in the South, John Pope and E. O. C. Ord, and appointed conservative replacements. In editorial notes Haven followed the congressional reaction to Johnson's moves, particularly in the dispute between

26. Johnson's message is in James D. Richardson, *A Compilation of the Messages and Papers of the Presidents 1789-1897* ([Washington], 1912), vol. V, pp. 3756-79, esp. pp. 3759-64.

27. *Zion's Herald,* Dec. 12, 1867.

28. Eric L. McKitrick, *Andrew Johnson and Reconstruction* (Chicago: University of Chicago Press, Phoenix Books, 1964), pp. 499-500.

General U. S. Grant, acting secretary of war, and the President. Grant did not want to be caught between Johnson and Congress, so he resigned as soon as the Senate reinstated Stanton.[29] Johnson's most provocative act, which Haven designated the "Presidential Suicide," came on February 21, 1868, when he appointed Lorenzo Thomas to replace Stanton. On February 24, for the first time in American history, the House of Representatives voted to impeach the President. The legislators accused Johnson of "high crimes and misdemeanors in office." [30]

From the first Haven was confident that the Senate would also convict Johnson. He went to Washington to cover the opening of the trial, which continued for more than two months. His accounts of the proceedings were filled with abusive descriptions of Johnson. "There never was a Pharaoh in history blinder or more obstinate," he wrote. "There never was a President with so black a political record. . . . Worse than all, there never was a king of England, within modern times, with a personal history so utterly foul. Since his accession to the pure chambers of Abraham Lincoln, the White House has been the political dismal swamp and infected region of our country." The attack on Johnson's personal life was unwarranted. For all his obstinacy and indiscretion, the President's integrity was not suspect. But Haven's real objection was buried beneath his excessive rhetoric. The fundamental difference between the two men was a conflict in racial philosophy which applied not only to the sectional problem but also to the broader issue of the place of the Negro in American life. Haven opposed Johnson's persistent refusal to approve even the most modest efforts to give civil and political protection to southern freedmen. "The American President," he contended, "has defied popular ideas, the spirit of the age and the constitution of the State, all in the interest of a base prejudice and baser nature." [31]

Either the intractable President did not realize, or he did not care, but he was at odds with Congress, with avowed racial equalitarians like Haven, and with the majority of northern public opinion. Even though they were unwilling to support universal Negro suffrage at the time, most northerners felt a moral responsibility to protect the civil rights of the freedmen. That feeling arose after the war, partly as a vague assumption by victorious Yankees, partly as a conscious commitment in the Republican Party. After the Johnsonian state legislatures enacted "Black Codes" in 1865, and ex-Confederate politicians and army officers showed up in Washington to be admitted to Congress, northern public opinion began to show alarm that the South

29. Zion's Herald, Feb. 6, 13, 1868; J. McPherson, Struggle for Equality, p. 383.
30. Zion's Herald, Feb. 27, 1868; McKitrick, Andrew Johnson and Reconstruction, pp. 504-5; E. McPherson, History of Reconstruction, pp. 265-66.
31. All quotations are from an article in Zion's Herald, Mar. 5, 1868. See also issues for Mar. 26, Apr. 2, 9, 1868. Two recent studies explore Johnson's racial views: LaWanda Cox and John H. Cox, Politics, Principle, and Prejudice 1865-1866, Dilemma of Reconstruction America (New York: Free Press, 1963), esp. ch. 8; Kenneth Stampp, The Era of Reconstruction 1865-1877 (New York: Alfred A. Knopf, 1965), ch. 3.

was returning to the *status quo antebellum*. Then Johnson vetoed all civil rights legislation in 1866 and refused to cooperate at any point with the Congress to provide federal protection for the freedmen. Thereafter, standard Republican policy became "radical" on the southern question, reflecting a growing sentiment of many Northerners.[32]

The President's final defiance of Congress, Haven hoped, would initiate a new commitment to the Negro's political rights. The government crisis was a "fortunate one" since it would clear up many of the unsolved postwar issues. He believed "it [would] teach Presidents, as the execution of Charles I. taught kings, that they must obey the laws or be punished by them . . . [and] permanently establish the doctrine that Congress is the legitimate representative of the National will."' Moreover, "the unsubdued Rebels [could be made] to understand that the victorious North [was] absolute master of the situation." If the crisis turned out as he expected, Haven trusted that it would serve to "assure protection to every loyal man in every part of the rebellious States" and to "set at rest in the country forever the fears of patriots who foresaw in the boldness of Johnson and the timidity of Congress a new source of danger to the Constitution." His deepest hope was in a new affirmation of "the great principles of liberty, equality and fraternity, without which," Haven wrote, "the war would have been a failure, and the triumph of the nation a misfortune to the cause of Christian civilization." [33]

While the impeachment trial was in process, Haven took an active role to rally support for Congress at two ecclesiastical gatherings. On March 29, the New England Conference endorsed a report on the "State of the Country" which reflected Haven's basic position. The paper praised Congress for "carrying forward the work of national regeneration," regretted "the constant and violent hostility of the President," and "heartily and solemnly" approved his indictment by the House. The report singled out General Grant and Secretary Stanton for special tribute, because of their stands against Johnson.[34]

On May 13, at the General Conference of the Methodist Episcopal Church, meeting in Chicago, Haven offered a series of resolutions that asked the body to hold a special prayer service on the day before the final vote on impeachment. Even though he remarked on presenting the document, "You will notice that there is not in the resolution any ultimatum of anything as to what end shall be reached, and for which we shall pray," its internal content made clear what verdict Haven expected to receive divine aid. The preamble stated that "the failure of the impeachment . . . [would] subject

32. See Cox and Cox, *Politics, Principle, and Prejudice*, pp. 195-232.
33. *Zion's Herald*, Mar. 5, 1868.
34. *Minutes of the New England Conference*, 1868, pp. 33-34; *The Independent*, Apr. 2, 1868. Copies of the report were to be sent to Stanton, Grant, Chief Justice Salmon P. Chase, the Speaker of the House, and the President of the Senate. Stanton acknowledged receiving the report, with appreciation, in a letter which appeared in *Zion's Herald*, Apr. 16, 1868.

the greatest of our generals, and all under his authority, to the power of an infuriated Executive, who has opposed every law that has been made to heal the nation on the only true and permanent basis of equal rights to loyal men." To release Johnson, the preamble concluded, would "reanimate the dying embers of rebellion throughout all the South, sacrifice the lives of many of our fellow-citizens, and thus cast all that region into terror, distress, and danger." The resolution asked the general conference to invoke divine guidance upon the Senate "that tyrannical usurpation [might] be rebuked, the authority of the law [might] be maintained against the most dangerous hostility of an Executive who avows his irresponsibility to its obligation, and that the peace and safety of our fellow-citizens in all the South [might] be secured." [35]

The delegates debated the propriety of ecclesiastical action on such a delicate political matter. The conference finally laid Haven's motion on the table, accepting a compromise that called merely for a special meeting "for prayer for our country." On the next day, however, Bishop Matthew Simpson reintroduced the question in a successful substitute motion that embodied Haven's basic intention in less direct language. [36]

Despite the national Methodist prayer meeting in Chicago the day before, the Senate failed by one vote on May 16 to obtain the requisite two-thirds majority in order to convict Andrew Johnson. A government crisis had been averted, but the President's effective leadership had been destroyed. Most Americans were disgusted over the whole affair. The verdict greatly agitated Haven. He entitled his editorial of May 28, "Darkness Over All the Land." He singled out those Republicans who voted for acquittal, especially Senators William Pitt Fessenden of Maine and Lyman Trumbull of Illinois. He indulged in absurd remarks like "Andrew Johnson is king" and "Congress is no more a Parliament." After he calmed down, he urged new efforts to prevent setbacks in the South, and he looked ahead to the coming election. [37]

In the same hectic month of May, the Republican national convention in Chicago nominated General Grant for the presidency. As the North's great military hero, his selection was a foregone conclusion. The support which might have gone to Chief Justice Salmon P. Chase crumbled in the end, due to the way he handled the impeachment proceedings and because of his attempt to get the nomination of the rival Democrats.

For several months many abolitionists had ridiculed Grant's potential ability to lead the country, but Haven did not adopt that view. During Grant's controversy with Johnson, Haven praised the general for adhering to principle. He predicted then that Grant would soon have "popular favor

35. *Journal of the General Conference of the Methodist Episcopal Church*, 1868, p. 152; *Daily Christian Advocate*, May 14, 1868.
36. *Daily Christian Advocate*, May 15, 1868; *Zion's Herald*, May 21, 1868.
37. *Zion's Herald*, May 28, 1868.

and national immortality" equal to George Washington, "our first General and President." After the nomination he made the same comparison. "No man since Washington has been nominated to the Presidency by such universal acclaim," he wrote.[38] Specifically Haven believed that only Grant could restore order to the South where the Ku Klux Klan was conducting a campaign of violence and terror. The country also needed a president who could cooperate with Congress. Haven thought that Grant was the man, therefore, to bring national unity and harmony and to exert firm executive leadership.[39]

The election of 1868 was an important test for the congressional Reconstruction program and for the national movement for Negro suffrage. In February, Haven made the forecast that manhood suffrage would enter as "the chief element in the tremendous political battle of the coming summer." [40] A Democratic victory in the fall, he recognized, would overturn radical Reconstruction and bury the possibility of a racially impartial standard for suffrage in the country. The Democrats, who had made sizable gains in the elections of 1867, nominated Horatio Seymour, ex-governor of New York, for their candidate. His vice-presidential running mate was Francis P. Blair, Jr., one of the more outspoken northern politicians on racial matters. His letter of acceptance revealed a violent opposition to Negro suffrage. Blair referred to the "host of ignorant negroes" in the South as "an alien race of semi-barbarous men" whose enfranchisement stripped "the white race of their birthright." [41] These views harmonized with the statement of the Democratic platform which called the Reconstruction acts "usurpations and unconstitutional, revolutionary, and void" and which advocated the immediate restoration of the southern states without equal suffrage. The Democrats geared their campaign along the lines of the platform, opposing "all political instrumentalities designed to secure negro supremacy." [42]

As Haven saw it, the Democrats had turned down a golden opportunity to challenge the Republicans. Chief Justice Chase offered himself as a compromise candidate who favored conciliation toward the South, but with impartial suffrage throughout the nation. But the Democrats, whom Haven called "once the great party of all that was equal, human and Christian in politics," refused the chance to outmaneuver the Republicans. The outcome in November, he thought, was inevitable.[43]

Although he enthusiastically supported General Grant, Haven was dis-

38. *Ibid.,* Feb. 13, May 28, 1868; J. McPherson, *Struggle for Equality,* pp. 417-19.

39. For Haven's editorials exposing Klan atrocities in the South, see *Zion's Herald,* Apr. 23, Aug. 20, Oct. 1, 15, 1868.

40. *Zion's Herald,* Feb. 20, 1868.

41. E. McPherson, *History of Reconstruction,* pp. 369-70. For other evidence of the racist views of the Blairs, father and son, see Cox and Cox, *Politics, Principle, and Prejudice,* pp. 55-56, 195-96.

42. E. McPherson, *History of Reconstruction,* pp. 367-68.

43. *Zion's Herald,* July 16, 1868. At first Haven condemned Chase for his part in acquitting Johnson, and he questioned the motives for his attempt to get the Democratic nomination. Later he defended the Chief Justice and praised him for trying to convert the Democrats to an equalitarian position. See *Zion's Herald,* July 23, Sept. 10, 1868.

turbed over the plank on suffrage in the Republican platform. A month before the national convention, Michigan had solidly turned down a new constitution which included impartial suffrage. The instance was a frank example of northern racism. "The odium against man because of his color," Haven wrote, "yet holds the mastery in the hearts of the great majority of the Northern people." But he still called for Republicans to come out for manhood suffrage in May.[44] Conservatives and moderates, however, took a mediating position which, to Haven, was a double standard. Equal suffrage was demanded for "all loyal men at the South," while the question in the North was left with the states. This display of expediency and inconsistency, Haven charged, found Republicans endorsing the states' rights doctrine of the Democrats.[45]

But disagreement with the platform was hardly sufficient grounds for Haven to refuse to support Grant. He considered the real issue of the campaign to be the present and future role of the Negro in the nation. The general had agreed to go along with the present Reconstruction program, although neither he nor Schuyler Colfax, the vice-presidential nominee, had distinguished himself in the cause of Negro rights. The nation also needed strong leadership to quell the widespread disorders in the South. The act of the Georgia legislature in September, 1868, was good evidence that Negro rights there were not secure. White legislators expelled all thirty-two black members. The old Confederacy was far from subdued. Perhaps Grant, the president, could do politically, Haven reasoned, what Grant, the general, had done in military conflict.[46]

Haven was overjoyed with the election results. "The great victory is the humanitizing [sic] of the nation," he wrote in the Herald.[47] On Thanksgiving Day he preached at Medford, Massachusetts on the meaning of the election. First, he claimed that the Republican victory would bring peace and order to the nation. No longer would ex-rebels be encouraged by a sympathetic president to defy Reconstruction. Grant's triumph also assured "the universality of suffrage and the equality of legal and civil rights." Confident that political equality would soon be accomplished, Haven looked forward to the end of racial discrimination in all of American life. He portrayed his familiar millennial vision of universal brotherhood, encompassing not only the social equality of all races but also including women's rights.[48]

The Republican victory must not, Haven insisted, be a signal to rest upon

44. *Ibid.*, Apr. 23, 1868.
45. *Ibid.*, July 23, 1868. See J. McPherson, *Struggle for Equality*, pp. 419-21, and C. Vann Woodward, "Seeds of Failure in Radical Race Policy," in *American Counterpoint: Slavery and Racism in the North-South Dialogue* (Boston: Little, Brown, 1971), p. 176.
46. *Zion's Herald*, June 25, Sept. 10, 24, Oct. 1, Nov. 12, 1868. Haven's report of the action in Georgia listed only twenty-five Negroes. See also Franklin, *Reconstruction After the Civil War*, pp. 130-32.
47. *Zion's Herald*, Nov. 12, 1868.
48. The sermon, entitled "America's Past and Future," appeared first in *The Independent*, Jan. 14, 1869. It was reprinted in *National Sermons*, pp. 603-30.

past laurels. Every facet of his interpretation of the election had a future reference. Turning immediately to the issue of Negro enfranchisement, he announced that "the first duty of Congress" was "Universal Manhood Suffrage." The continued failure in the North to enact equal suffrage on the state level proved that only Congress could solve the problem. "The intensity of prejudice would to-day make almost every State vote for Grant," Haven wrote, "where this suffrage does not exist, vote against its bestowal." He pointed to Missouri, which supported Grant but rejected impartial suffrage by nineteen thousand votes.[49] The nation's inconsistency, by requiring Negro suffrage in the South and rejecting it in the North, Haven contended, was no longer tolerable. "It is the worse sore in the Southern heart today that they are required to receive what the North will not give itself. We have no moral right to impose an obligation on one part of the land which the rest will not accept. We can have no peace until this right is made national."[50]

During January and February, 1869, there were long and complex congressional debates over different versions of what was to be the Fifteenth Amendment to the Constitution. Agreeing with the position of Charles Sumner, Haven believed that Congress already had power under the provisions of the Fourteenth Amendment to enact universal suffrage. He doubted whether confirmation of a constitutional change could be secured.[51] Most politicians recognized the risk of submitting the controversial question to the states, but they also realized that a simple law imposing Negro suffrage, as Sumner advocated, could easily be repealed by a future Congress.[52]

For some reason Haven did not bother to analyze the various versions of the proposed amendment. Most other abolitionists favored the prohibition of literacy and property qualifications, as well as the end of racial restrictions. At one time during the discussion in Congress, it appeared that the amendment would also remove racial bars to office-holding. After the Senate and the House deadlocked, however, a compromise bill passed which only forbade the denial of voting rights "by reason of race, or color, or previous condition of slavery." Otherwise the states had full power to determine standards for voting. Various devices could still be, and in fact they were, employed to disfranchise blacks.[53]

49. Haven did praise Iowa and Minnesota for abolishing racial restrictions in their voting laws, but neither victory was a clear endorsement of equal rights. Iowa continued to prohibit blacks from running for Congress, and the Minnesota amendment had to be vaguely worded in order to be passed. *Zion's Herald*, Nov. 12, 19, Dec. 10, 1868; *The Independent*, Jan. 14, 1869; Fishel, "Northern Prejudice and Negro Suffrage," pp. 23-24.
50. *Zion's Herald*, Dec. 10, 1868; *The Independent*, Jan. 14, 1869 (*National Sermons*, pp. 620-21).
51. *Zion's Herald*, Dec. 10, 1868; David Donald, *Charles Sumner and the Rights of Man* (New York: Alfred A. Knopf, 1970), pp. 352-54.
52. Gillette, *The Right to Vote*, pp. 44, 80. By the time ratification began, twenty states, including ten reconstructed southern states, permitted Negroes to vote.
53. See Gillette's extensive account of the debates and the reaction of the press to the amendment, in *The Right to Vote*, pp. 46-78. See Woodward, *American Counterpoint*, pp. 177-78. On abolitionist involvement see J. McPherson, *Struggle for Equality*, pp. 417-28.

Apparently Haven was not concerned at this point with the continuing legal and extra-legal methods which could be used to circumvent the intent of the amendment. He greeted the passage of the first House version as "the last political act in the great warfare against Slavery." He conceded that ratification would require the support of "the yet unreconstructed States of Virginia, Texas, Mississippi and Georgia." His forecast proved to be accurate, for after thirteen months and a difficult fight, ratification was obtained, but only after Congress had forced four states to approve the amendment before being readmitted to the Union. In April, 1870, Haven rejoiced that the amendment had been successful, and he printed in the *Herald* Grant's special message proclaiming its ratification.[54]

With the passage of the Fifteenth Amendment, the political crusade for Negro equality and the organizational history of the abolitionist movement came to an end. The American Anti-Slavery Society disbanded, and abolitionists like Wendell Phillips and Theodore Tilton predicted that the Negro question would henceforth be taken out of politics.[55] Haven shared the sense of achievement, of having reached a major goal in the crusade for equality. He felt, for example, that the mission of the Republican Party was fulfilled, and that new reforms, like prohibition and women's suffrage, should be advocated. But at the same time he was disturbed over what appeared to be a withdrawal on the part of the old antislavery vanguard. "It is a question whether the time for the dissolution of the Anti-Slavery Society is fully come," he observed. Realistically he knew that the battle against racism was far from over. Therefore, he endorsed the sentiments of Charles Sumner and published the senator's letter to the American Anti-Slavery Society. "I do not think the work finished," Sumner wrote, "so long as the word 'white' is allowed to play any part in legislation; so long as it constrains the courts in naturalization; so long as it rules public conveyances, steamboats, and railroads; so long as it bars the doors of houses bound by law to receive people for food and lodging, and licensed as places of amusement; so long as it is inscribed on our common schools."[56] The senator believed that political action could still be employed to protect and defend equal rights to all citizens in the nation. Undaunted in the face of an increasingly apathetic northern public opinion, he led such a movement for further legislation, and Haven strongly supported him.[57]

II

With the achievement, at least potentially, of voting rights for blacks, Haven sensed that the battle against caste had to move in new directions. No sooner

54. *Zion's Herald*, Feb. 11, 1869; Apr. 7, 1870. See also Gillette, *The Right to Vote*, pp. 79-91.
55. J. McPherson, *Struggle for Equality*, pp. 427-30.
56. Quoted in *Zion's Herald*, Apr. 21, 1870.
57. Donald, *Charles Sumner* (1970), pp. 421-25, 450.

had Grant taken office, however, than it was clear that enforcement of the Fourteenth and Fifteenth amendments and of other Reconstruction legislation was going to be a major task for the new administration. Right after he made enthusiastic prognostications at the time of the inauguration, Haven issued his first criticism of the new President for not acting to quell southern violence.[58] He reported Ku Klux Klan activity in Warren County, Georgia, and racially connected disturbances in Texas and other places in the South. "Where is the President?" he asked sarcastically, demanding that Grant "let the office-seekers go, and save these loyal lives." Johnson had refused federal protection, he charged, but "there can be no excuse now for such outrages." [59] Along with this sort of censure Haven added a warning against the federal government's "first act . . . leaving the South to herself" in Virginia and Tennessee. A counterreconstruction movement there seized power from black and white loyalists and returned control of state governments to southern conservatives. The turn of events held dark portents for the future of Reconstruction. If he did not sense the full implication of what was happening, Haven at least understood its dangers to the congressional program in the South.[60]

Aside from these instances, however, Haven commented less and less on the political aspects of Reconstruction from 1869 until the election of 1872. He did review annual presidential messages, and he criticized Grant's firing of two cabinet officers because they refused to make appointments for political reasons, or as Haven put it, "they will not do mean things at the dictation of those slimy creatures, which now, as in Eden, tempt the upright man to his ruin." He was so alarmed at the time that he even wrote that "President Grant has done more harm to the nation by this last act, than Johnson by his continued wrong-doing." [61] The only important new Reconstruction legislation during this period was a series of enforcement acts in 1870 and 1871, which further protected Negro suffrage and drove the Klan underground. Haven commented only on the first of the three acts, but he praised it more because it would reform corrupt voting practices in the North than for its particular application to Negro rights. When Klan violence emerged again in the spring of 1871, Haven did call for government suppression and cry out, almost in despair, "How long, O Lord, how long!" [62]

58. For examples of Haven's optimism and of his account of the inauguration, and of the prayer meeting which he helped to organize just prior to the cermony, see *Zion's Herald*, Nov. 12, 1868; Mar. 4, 11, 18, 1869; *The Independent*, Mar. 11, 1869. See also A. W. Wayman, *My Recollections of African M. E. Ministers* (Philadelphia, 1882), p. 162.

59. *Zion's Herald*, Mar. 25, Apr. 22, 29, May 20, 1869. Further criticism of "the terrible intermeddling of myriads of office begging sovereigns" is in the issue of Apr. 8, 1869.

60. *Zion's Herald*, Aug. 26, 1869.

61. *Zion's Herald*, Nov. 10, 1870. On Grant's annual messages see issues for Dec. 16, 1869; Dec. 15, 1870; Dec. 14, 1871. For texts of these papers see E. McPherson, *History of Reconstruction*, pp. 533-40 and his *A Handbook of Politics for 1872* (Washington, 1872), pp. 16-27.

62. *Zion's Herald*, June 16, 1870; Apr. 13, May 18, 1871. The texts of these bills are in E. McPherson, *History of Reconstruction*, pp. 546-50; and *A Handbook of Politics*, pp. 3-8, 85-87.

There was one other exception to Haven's general nonchalance after 1869 about southern matters. Early in 1871, Haven did join with his old friend, Sojourner Truth, in a petition campaign asking Congress to set aside public lands in the West for southern freedmen. On Emancipation Day in Boston that year he discussed the emigration scheme at a celebration sponsored by the National Association for the Spread of Temperance and Night Schools among the Freed People of the South. President of the association was William Wells Brown. The plan had grown out of Sojourner Truth's desire to give freedmen a new start outside the South. Its rationale was the frontier myth which assumed that blacks could become independent and successful farmers in the virgin West. Unfortunately, the proposal never made much progress, despite Sojourner Truth's speaking tour in its behalf. It represented, on the other hand, Haven's only significant effort to provide freedmen with an economic base to accompany fundamental political rights. He had sometimes spoken of the need for freedmen to become property owners but, other than a general request for confiscation, he had little grasp how that end could be achieved.[63]

The dominant factor in Haven's relative unconcern about Reconstruction issues and the southern scene after mid-1869 was a shift in emphasis in his crusade against caste. The social barriers to interracial brotherhood, he believed, had to be overcome. His understanding of racial justice always embraced social equality, but the emphasis, practically speaking, had been secondary, first to the elimination of slavery and then to the removal of legal and political disabilities that obstructed citizenship for Negroes. But Haven knew well that both "chattel slavery" and "political slavery" originated in the same source. He was uniquely prepared, therefore, to comprehend the way that "social slavery still [prevailed]" in the land. "Despite the mighty panorama of divine events that has passed before this people, their hearts are hardened toward those for whom God has wrought such great deliverance," he wrote in the introduction to his volume of *National Sermons,* issued in 1869. "We are still cursed with a curse" that prevented "the aspiring and competent [black] youth" from opportunity in "trade," closed pulpits "to the accredited and popular ministers of Jesus Christ" who were Negroes, and poisoned "society" generally. "Aversion thus defiles the whole national heart," Haven asserted. "The victims of our contempt feel the yoke of bondage with which we still burden their souls. The liberties they have won only makes these chains the more galling. Not until every such fetter is broken will God's controversy with America come to an end." [64]

63. *Zion's Herald,* May 15, 1867; Jan. 5, Feb. 23, Nov. 2, 1871; *National Standard,* Mar. 4, 1871; [Mrs. Frances W. Titus and Olive Gilbert], *Narrative of Sojourner Truth* (Battle Creek, Michigan, 1884), pp. 209-12, 238.

64. *National Sermons,* xi-xii. Note Haven's distinction between physical, legal-political, and social bondage in *Zion's Herald,* Aug. 8, 1867. For reviews of the *National Sermons,* see one by Abel Stevens in the *New York Christian Advocate,* Dec. 20, 1869; "Politics and the Pulpit" by Haven's old

Much of Haven's writing focused on ways to break the social and psychological barriers to interracial unity. He recognized that social acceptance was the most difficult aspect of the fight against racism. No external compulsion could finally force men to regard each other as brothers. Without disavowing the importance of the civil rights and Reconstruction legislation which had been passed since 1865, he knew that it alone could not insure an end to racial prejudice. "I am aware," he said in the sermon on Grant's election, "that this evil cannot be utterly abolished by any enactments. The leprosy lies deep within. It dwells in our churches, in our souls, in our education, in society. . . . It still leads us to erect barriers between us and our kindred." [65]

In his editorial crusade against racial prejudice Haven intended "to build up the right ideas," which was his definition of "the true work of reform." [66] He seized every possible occasion to praise the accomplishments of Negroes in education, politics, and agriculture. When blacks were accepted into the bricklayers and printers unions and into a medical society in Washington, he pointed out the significance of the actions.[67] Repeatedly Haven requested the national government to appoint Frederick Douglass to some distinguished position, both because he deserved the honor and for its symbolic impact. Once he asked Harvard and his alma mater, Wesleyan, to bring distinction to themselves by giving an honorary doctorate of laws to Douglass.[68] As southern states began to send Negroes to Congress, he urged his readers to help elect able blacks in the North as their representatives. He refused to believe Horace Greeley's more realistic prediction that few Negroes would, in fact, become prominent national leaders.[69]

Another of Haven's tactics against racial prejudice was to expose the racist assumptions which many whites held. When the Methodist related Female College of Pittsburgh refused to allow a student to remain in school after the administration discovered that, despite her light complexion, she was Negro, he wrote a satirical editorial which asked "What Is the Test of African Blood?" Pretending to ask seriously how the girl's racial origins were discovered, Haven showed the absurdity of the whole affair. He first thought "that the college authorities must have become experts in this line through a course of very nice studies in color," but he ruled that out because Pittsburgh's air was so polluted, with its "hundred iron furnaces," as "to preclude the application of that test." He continued to ridicule. "Again, since the New

colleague, Daniel Steele, in the *Methodist Quarterly Review*, 52 (1870), 189-240; another by George Prentice in *the Ladies' Repository*, 30 (1870), 401-6; and a book notice in *Western Christian Advocate*, Nov. 3, 1869. In 1969 Arno Press and the *New York Times* reprinted *National Sermons* in their series, "The Anti-Slavery Crusade in America."

65. *The Independent*, Jan. 14, 1869 (*National Sermons*, p. 622).
66. *Zion's Herald*, Mar. 31, 1870.
67. *Ibid.*, July 23, Oct. 1, 15, 1868; July 8, 1869; July 20, 27, 1871.
68. *Ibid.*, June 25, 1868; Apr. 15, 29, 1869; *The Independent*, Jan. 14, 1869 (*National Sermons*, p. 622); *Western Christian Advocate*, Mar. 24, 1869.
69. *Zion's Herald*, Dec. 10, 1868; Feb. 11, Mar. 11, Apr. 15, 1869; Mar. 17, 24, 1870.

York *World,* the oracle of American negrophobia," he wrote, "has recently declared that the odor of that African who notices the virtue next to godliness is not peculiar, that criterion can no longer be considered infallible." Then he inquired, humorously,

Do the Pittsburg Methodists resort to the easy test of the quondam slave traders of the Old Dominion, namely: the application of a rule to the chin and the tip of the nose, and pronounce all whose lips touch the rule to be of African blood [?]. Or do they use a Kentucky Senator's standard and inspect the footprints of the young ladies to see if "the hollow of the foot makes a hole in the ground?" Or is every candidate for admission now required to submit her arm to the phlebotomist for the purpose of extracting a sample of her blood to be subjected to a sanguinometer, if the scientific laboratory of the college comprises such an instrument? Or has the institution a standing committee on ethnology who apply the microscope to each young lady's hair to detect the African crinkle in its articulated structure? Or are all candidates required to bring in their trunks their genealogical registers—
    "long and dark
    Drawn from the mouldy rolls of Noah's Ark?"
Probably they found in this "roll" the proof of her connection with Ham.[70]

Occasionally Haven devoted his attention to prevailing scientific and historical theories of race. Once he disputed the ethnological findings of an explorer, Paul Belloni Du Chaillu, who was well known for his accounts of equatorial Africa.[71] In a lecture at the Boston Lyceum the traveler had claimed that an inferior race could not be elevated in status, even by association with a superior race. The Caucasian was the master race of the world, he contended, so that all inferior types, including the Negro, would eventually disappear. To Haven, Du Chaillu was inconsistent to argue that mixture within the same racial family would produce a higher type of man, while insisting that the blending of different racial families violated "the law of nature." "Now, Du Chaillu's theory of the extinction of 'inferior' races," he wrote in the *Herald,* "is only the family pride of the old houses of Europe extended to a type of mankind. It is quite absurd . . . to place the negro outside the fold of races that are to be physically saved. This predestination in science is quite as faulty as predestination in theology. Men are not created by races but by individuals." [72] In addition, as he previously observed, "in the earliest times," quoting Charles Brace, "when Turanian, Semite and Aryan were nomadic tribes . . . the Hamitic race was the instructor and leader of the human family." To underscore the point he interrupted the quotation to

70. *Zion's Herald,* Apr. 10, 1867.
71. See Du Chaillu's *Explorations and Adventures in Equatorial Africa* (New York, 1861) and *A Journey to Ashango-Land* (London, 1867). In the latter volume Du Chaillu made the prediction that Negroid people were doomed to extinction. See pp. 435 ff.
72. *Zion's Herald,* Mar. 18, 1869.

add, "Aryan, remember my dear, turning-up-the-nose-at-the 'nigger'-Yankee, means Caucasian and you." [73]

Another approach which Haven used to combat racism was to reveal examples of unjust treatment of Negroes in public life. He attacked the Jim Crow policy of a boat line in Fall River, Massachusetts, which excluded from its dining room the black pastor of Joy Street Church in Boston.[74] When the first black cadet at West Point was unduly intimidated by his classmates because of his race, Haven helped to create sympathy for him.[75] After the refusal of the Revere Coffee House in Boston to serve four "well-dressed and well-behaved" Negroes, Haven commented, in an editorial note, that "all true men" should "treat this house as it treats these men, until it publicly repents this misdemeanor." [76] He likewise publicized the discriminatory treatment which Frederick Douglass received at hotels in Meriden, Connecticut, and in St. Louis.[77]

Because he advocated equal access to public facilities regardless of race, Haven supported Charles Sumner's unsuccessful bid during 1871 and 1872 to secure new civil rights legislation. The senator's original bill would have compelled "all inns, public halls, places of amusements, schools, and churches, to abolish the hateful distinctions of caste." The move, Haven said, was "the best and bravest deed of all the good and brave ones Charles Sumner has done." It was needed, he claimed, to complete the long series of enactments connected with the abolition of slavery. "We want Mr. Sumner's bill for Boston and the Revere House," Haven wrote, referring to the coffeehouse which was across the street from Sumner's residence.[78]

A controversy between Sumner and President Grant, however, complicated Haven's endorsement of the senator's civil rights measure. The clash was over the proposed annexation of Santo Domingo, which Grant greatly desired but which Sumner, who was chairman of the Senate Foreign Relations Committee, opposed. Haven sided with Grant and accused Sumner, rather curiously, of believing in a "separation of the races" because he held that "the West Indies shall be reserved for the Negro race." On the basis of "a manifest destiny that necessitates annexation," Haven went so far as to include Haiti with "Dominica" in his expansionist claims, saying that both "ought to be in one government, and that the government of the United States." [79] Privately he explained to Sumner that he wished to "have states in our Union largely black, so that the white element may be counterbalanced." Black senators and representatives from the West Indies would, he wrote in the *Herald*,

73. See Haven's review of Brace's *The Races of the Old World* in *ibid.*, Aug. 12, 1863.
74. *Zion's Herald*, Dec. 8, 1870.
75. *Ibid.*, Aug. 4, 1870; Feb. 9, 1871.
76. *Ibid.*, Apr. 27, June 8, 1871.
77. *Ibid.*, Feb. 13, 27, 1868; Feb. 15, 1872.
78. *Ibid.*, Apr. 27, June 8, Nov. 23, 1871; Feb. 8, 22, 1872.
79. *Ibid.*, Jan. 26, Mar. 23, Apr. 6, 1871.

help to thwart the design of "our Gulf States . . . to reduce the black man to vassalage." Both in his letter to Sumner and publicly through his paper, Haven tried to heal the breach between Grant and the legislator whose career he had followed closely and with deep admiration for two decades. He appealed for the two men to agree "on this policy" and continue to work together on southern strategy "for the peace and liberty of the country and the continent." [80] A few months later he had become more sympathetic to Sumner's side of the dispute with Grant, perhaps because he was aware of the vindictive measures which the President had taken against the senator for effectively blocking the annexation. By April, 1872, Haven still grieved over Sumner's attitude toward Grant, but he acknowledged that the President had been "the aggressor." For this reason Haven was willing to say that "if [Sumner] could and should utterly block the wheels of Government with his Civil Rights Bill, posterity would bless him for the act." [81]

Primarily Haven was concerned to prevent American society from establishing a rigid color line. He argued against the social segregation of races. "A divided people is a weakened people," he wrote. "The population of the South is too poor and sparse, and that of the North too homogeneous to maintain two sets of literary or religious institutions, one for each race; and were the financial difficulties obviated, the separation would be productive of evil, and only evil, and that continually." On this basis he commended Sumner's bill for insisting on "no separation in the common schools, North or South." The equalitarian doctrine of the Declaration of Independence was denied, he contended, "if a child may be refused from school on account of color. There is an 'order of nobility' if the money of a man born of certain parents will entitle him to a privilege which is denied to the son of another man." He denied "that a city could, by a constitutional law, build two schoolhouses, furnish one with piano, carpet, and able teacher, with money from the taxes of a man whose children are sent to the other because they trace their ancestry to Africa instead of Normandy." The racial discrimination "against which Mr. Sumner is fighting," he maintained, "is as impolitic as it is unconstitutional, wicked, and repugnant to the spirit of our independence." [82]

Haven's advocacy of racial equality in the public arena constantly provoked attacks from other editors. His fellow Methodists did not spare him, especially when Haven sought to instruct them concerning their responsibility to rebuke racial caste. The editor of the *Pittsburgh Advocate*. S. H. Nesbit, took up the cudgels after Haven's barrage against the administration of the city's Female College for suspending its Negro student. Nesbit thought that no one had a

80. Haven to Charles Sumner, Boston, Mar. 30, 1871, Charles Sumner Papers, Harvard University; *Zion's Herald*, Apr. 6, 1871.

81. *Zion's Herald*, Apr. 4, 1872; Donald, *Charles Sumner* (1970), pp. 433-97.

82. *Zion's Herald*, Apr. 4, 1872, and the issue for Nov. 23, 1871. See Alfred H. Kelly, "The Congressional Controversy over School Segregation, 1867-1875," *American Historical Review*, 64 (1959), 543-49.

right to demand a private school to accept any student, white or black. "Social rights and courtesies are not determinable by act of Congress or the General Assembly," he stated, quoting the views of the *Pittsburgh Gazette*. "If Mr. [Theodore] Tilton and other gentlement see proper to educate their daughters in a private school, in company with black girls, that is their privilege, provided they build and endow the school; but it is sheer impertinence for them to insist that gentlemen whose tastes lead them to adopt a different plan shall not do as they will with their own." [83]

A similar dispute over integrated education arose between Haven and S. M. Merrill, editor of the *Western Advocate*. When he discovered that an able Negro boy had been denied admission to an academy at Belpere, Ohio, Haven asked Merrill to condemn "the spirit of *caste*" evidenced by the school. "If the trustees admitted the boy, and outside pressure excluded him," Merrill replied, "the facts indicate a state of things not favorable to the mixed school system." In both instances Haven did not dispute the logic or facts of his opponents. To Nesbit, he simply argued against the bad principle of "admitting a young lady, keeping her for a time and then expelling her, for no cause except her complexion." Against the *Western Advocate* he said "it is its business, as a Christian journal, to denounce this 'state of things' as most unchristian; not to give it the shelter of its sacred protection." [84]

As a constant target for those who bitterly disagreed with his racial views, Haven was sometimes subjected to personal abuse. Late in 1867, there circulated among Methodists a rumor that Haven had refused to share the same room at annual conference with "Father" Mars, his black ministerial associate. The charge was completely false, but it spread to a number of papers, including Nesbit's *Advocate,* which would not publish Haven's reply. By inducing Haven to acknowledge that he had had Negro guests in his home for meals and lodging, and that he had shared overnight accommodations on occasion with them, however, his opponents accomplished what they intended by the story. The personal nature of the rumor especially perturbed Haven. After he directed one of his comments on the matter at the *Western Advocate* which had first published the story, the editor at the time, John M. Reid, apologized for publishing the piece. "We had much rather occupy the same room and bed with a gentleman of [Mars'] complexion, though we have no especial liking for such double-bedded arrangements," Haven wrote to Reid, "than with any white man, however exalted in the State of Ohio who refused to give [blacks] the right of suffrage. That would be an ignominy we should find it hard to endure." In his apology Reid saluted Haven's consistency, even though he did not share such "tastes and opinions." [85]

83. Quoted in the *Pittsburgh Christian Advocate*, June 15, 1867; *Zion's Herald*, June 26, 1867.
84. *Western Christian Advocate*, Jan. 27, 1869; *Zion's Herald*, June 26, 1867; Jan. 14, Feb. 11, 1869.
85. *Western Christian Advocate*, Oct. 30, Nov. 13, 1867; *Zion's Herald*, Nov. 7, Dec. 26, 1867; Jan. 16, 1868. The story made the rounds in the southern religious press where it was remembered

The *Springfield Union* (Massachusetts) was a daily paper which disagreed with Haven's equalitarian views. Responding to one of Haven's frequent pleas for an end to caste, its editor wrote:

We confess we cannot see the connection between equality of rights and this social miscegenation, and we use it in no offensive sense. Equality of rights does not necessarily imply intellectual or social equality; and social equality does not imply the obliteration of those characteristics that distinguish one race from another, or the sundering of those natural ties that bind us to our own kindred or race.

We are a conglomerated nation, made up of every race and people under heaven, and are of necessity brought into contact with these different nationalities. Yet we rarely mingle socially, from choice, with those of another race or nation. There are mental and social characteristics that distinguish one race from another, that renders their society more agreeable to each other than to those of another race. . . . It is only the working of a natural law, which neither reason or religion can subvert.[86]

No individual of foreign nativity, Haven answered, was socially proscribed like the black American. The immigrants of various European nationalities had mixed in the country's melting pot, he admitted, but the Negro had not been assimilated. Social equality was a step toward that assimilation. "Our greatest folly to-day is the attempt to shelter this prejudice with the pretty prattle that social equality does not mean fraternity and unity," he declared. "It can mean nothing else." [87]

Unlike some of his contemporaries who advocated equal rights, Haven did not fail to deal explicitly with the most controversial aspects of the issue of social equality—racial mixture and interracial marriage. In his sermon on Grant's election he urged Americans to change their "feelings of aversion" toward Negroes to "feelings of regard." He believed that a mutual attraction between the races would develop like the inclination of opposite forces to unite. "The light complexioned turns to the dark, and the dark to the light, as day to night and night to day," he explained. "The tall seek the short, and the short the tall; the small the large, and the large the small." This attraction of opposites, he confessed, was "the Creator's mode of compelling the race to overleap the narrow boundaries of families and tribes, into which blood, so called, invariably degenerates." Becoming more explicit, Haven spoke of "the illegal but divinely implanted admiration of Southern Solomons for black but comely maidens." He praised dark complexion for its "velvety softness," "fineness of fiber," and "richness of tone." For his authority he cited the description of the beauty of black skin and of facial and body features of Negroes which Frances Ann Kemble had written in her *Journal*

as late as 1873. See *Baltimore Episcopal Methodist*, Nov. 30, 1867; *Baltimore Christian Advocate*, July 30, 1870; *Christian Neighbor*, July 4, 1872; *New Orleans Christian Advocate*, May 1, 1873.
86. Quoted in *Zion's Herald*, Feb. 27, 1868.
87. *Ibid.*

of a Residence on a Georgia Plantation in 1838-9.[88] Looking ahead to the time when interracial marriage would be a fully acceptable social practice, Haven announced that "the hour is not far off when the white-hued husband shall boast of the dusky beauty of his wife, and the Caucassian [*sic*] wife shall admire the sun-kissed countenance of her husband as deeply and as unconscious of the present ruling abhorrence as is his admiration of her lighter tint." The statement, which was one of the most widely quoted remarks Haven ever made, concluded with the assertion that "Amalgamation is God's word, declaring the oneness of man, and ordaining its universal recognition." [89]

This endorsement of amalgamation gave Haven the reputation as one of the most radical equalitarians in the country. It was not the first time that he had been driven by his religious belief in the unity of the human race to this conclusion. As early as 1854, before he had achieved anything more than a local prominence as an obscure Methodist preacher in western Massachusetts, he had declared these sentiments.[90] In 1865 he had claimed that "God was the first amalgamationist" and that interracial mixture was "the embodiment of the unity and brotherhood of man." [91] But if amalgamation seemed the natural outcome to Haven of Judeo-Christian doctrines of creation and of the unity of humanity, the view was extravagant to most other people. One Methodist editor called Haven's position "wild and foolish talk." Another writer, in a review of his volume of sermons, dubbed him a "radical" who betrayed considerable "indifference to the sensibilities of his fellow-citizens." "If any Christian minister should be guilty of seriously perpetrating such nonsense," another editor declared, "we should take it as the clearest evidence of his fitness for the mad-house." [92]

Southern editors took particular delight in ridiculing Haven's radicalism, erroneously contending that his "negrophilist proclivities" were representative of the views of the majority of northern Methodists. Edward H. Myers of the *Southern Christian Advocate* called him "the great advocate of miscegenation . . . who has lauded negro blood, and predicted such great things of Africo-America, when Saxon blood shall be thoroughly 'warmed' up by the African infusion, that Dr. [Thomas E.] Bond was led to suppose [Haven] regretted his

88. Haven had reviewed this book in *ibid.*, Nov. 4, 1863, where he commented that Mrs. Kemble's writings would cure "our anti-amalgamation humbug." For the controversy over Haven's statement in this sermon that the complexion of Mary and Jesus was of the same "despised hue" which suffered from American caste, see *National Sermons*, pp. 622, 655-56 (n. 22); *The Methodist*, Jan. 23, 30, Feb. 6, 1869; and two letters written from Boston by Haven to George R. Crooks, Jan. 23, 25, 1869, Crooks Papers, Drew University.

89. *The Independent*, Jan. 14, 1869 (slightly revised in *National Sermons*, pp. 622-26).

90. *National Sermons*, pp. 137-38, 146-49.

91. *Christian Advocate and Journal*, Oct. 12, 1865.

92. The first criticism was by George R. Crooks in *The Methodist*, Jan. 23, 1869; the second by an anonymous reviewer in the *Western Christian Advocate*, Nov. 3, 1869; the last by Erasmus Q. Fuller in the *Methodist Advocate*, Feb. 10, 1869.

mother was not a negress." [93] Bond, an antagonist from prewar days who had left northern for Southern Methodism, was Haven's favorite opponent in editorial battles that often involved excessive language, but which was over-laden with considerable good humor on both sides. Haven knew that any hint of Negro equality provoked a most passionate response from Bond who thought that Haven was "either mad, or only saved from madness by a natural impossibility to lose his senses." Thus, he enjoyed asking Bond to notice inter-racial social events like the dinner at the "elegant club house" of J. B. Smith, the black caterer of Boston, which Charles Sumner, Edward Atkinson (manufacturer, economic theorist, and editor), and a number of eminent clergymen attended.[94] His standard reply to Bond's tirades was to refer to racial mixture during slavery, to chastise southern whites for not acknowl-edging their offspring born from these illegitimate unions and to urge southern churchmen to see interracial brotherhood as a foretaste of "a heavenly amalgamation." [95]

There was abundant evidence that most Americans of the time were more sympathetic with Haven's opponents than with his equalitarian ideas. The "Negro question" was, by 1870, a tiresome political issue in many quarters. Postwar idealism had been drained out at least by the time the Fifteenth Amendment passed. The ranks of the reformers were thinning out, by death, disinterest, and diversion to other than racial issues. A reaction against new civil rights legislation was underway. Reconstruction was deteriorating from within and losing support outside the South. The whole of American society had entered an era of apathy and accommodation.

Haven was not unaffected by these developments. Although he expanded his reform activity and attacked caste as vigorously as ever, he found it difficult to discern where to go next, politically and socially, in the crusade against racism. He turned back to the only institutional base he ever had for any reform, the church, and tried to build a plan for ecclesiastical integration. He expected the battle to continue in the church, no matter what happened in the surrounding society. In 1870 he spoke of "social equality" as "the next duty" of the nation and of his hope that the church would "lead in this re-form." With organized abolitionism breaking up, he wrote of "the difference between the Church and a reformatory Society." While "the Anti-Slavery Society disbands," *"The Liberator* stops," and *"The Anti-Slavery Standard* drops its chief title," the work of the church—"to abolish slavery and sin everywhere"—continues. "Its aim," he confessed, was "the liberation, eleva-tion, sanctification of all men." In that mission "she will never rest until every

93. *Southern Christian Advocate,* June 11, 1869. See also *Richmond Christian Advocate,* Feb. 11, 1869. Myers referred to Bond's editorial which Haven answered in *Zion's Herald,* Dec. 3, 1868.

94. *Zion's Herald,* Oct. 15, Dec. 3, 1868; Dec. 8, 1870. Examples of Bond's reactions can be found in the *Baltimore Christian Advocate,* Jan. 15, 29, Apr. 16, May 28, June 18, 1870.

95. *Zion's Herald,* Dec. 3, 1868; see also Dec. 12, 1867; April 2, May 28, July 2, Sept. 17, 1868; Feb. 18, May 6, June 3, July 15, Dec. 23, 1869; Jan. 13, June 16, 1870; Jan. 26, 1871; Sept. 19, 1872.

child of man is redeemed unto Christ, and all nations, tongues, and persons are made free and fraternal in Christ Jesus." [96]

III

Most of Haven's hopes for racial change within and through the church were frustrated by the same failure of will which characterized the nation's refusal to bring about racial equality. Haven sensed that failure in February, 1868, when he wrote, "The Christians of America (Methodists included) have not yet grown in grace sufficiently enough to even be agitated as to their duty to receive their brethren, without regard to color, to their churches, families, and pulpits." [97] The most devastating aspects of that failure was the inability of the churches to transcend racial distinctions in their own membership. But Haven labored feverishly to overcome that flaw, to stem the tide of further racial separation and to realize some measure of interracial brotherhood in his own denomination.

There were various degrees of racial separation in the Methodist Episcopal Church when Haven took over *Zion's Herald* in 1867. Two annual conferences, Washington and Delaware, had entirely black clergy and churches. The other northern conferences had either wholly or predominantly white constituencies. In no situation was a Negro minister the regular pastor of a white congregation, and there was very little racial integration in local churches. In its southern mission work, only the South Carolina Conference had an explicit policy against racial caste at all levels of the ministry and membership. Even there, significant integration was difficult to accomplish, and the conference tended more and more to become an exclusively black body with a few white missionaries. In other areas, like Kentucky, Missouri, and Tennessee, the annual conferences were racially inclusive, but there were divisions according to race in districts and local churches. A white presiding elder supervised white pastors and churches, and a Negro presiding elder administered the work among blacks. A slight variation of this pattern was practiced in the lower South, in Mississippi and Louisiana, where white and black pastors belonged to the same district under one presiding elder, but again nearly all local churches were racially segregated. [98]

One of Haven's strategies toward breaking down caste distinctions was to seek to attract black leaders to the idea, and in some cases, to induce them to leave their independent Negro churches and join with him in campaigning for an integrated denomination. The most important man whom Haven influenced in this direction was James Lynch, ex-chaplain in the Union army, former missionary to the freedmen and, at the time they met, editor of the

96. *Ibid.,* Apr. 14, 1870.
97. *Ibid.,* Feb. 20, 1868.
98. *Northwestern Christian Advocate,* Nov. 7, 1866; *Zion's Herald,* Oct. 17, 1867. Tennessee adopted the Mississippi and Louisiana pattern in the fall of 1867. *Zion's Herald,* Oct. 24, 31, 1867.

Christian Recorder in Philadelphia, the official paper of African Methodism. In February, 1867, Haven invited Lynch to be a guest at the next session of the New England Conference. He introduced Lynch to the conference and to Bishop Levi Scott and printed the black editor's promise that he would join the Methodist Episcopal Church when all caste was removed.[99] Apparently Lynch was so attracted by the sincerity of Haven and some of his conference associates, who had adopted the position paper on "No Caste in the Church of God," that within two months he had decided to resign from the African Methodist Episcopal Church and join "the old Mother Church." His valedictory editorial in June explained the compulsion under which he made his decision. Answering why he was resigning, he wrote of "convictions of duty to [his] race as deep as [his] own soul." "They impel me," Lynch explained, "to go to a Southern state and unite my destiny with that of my people, to live with them, suffer, sorrow, rejoice, and die with them." He believed that he could "do more for [his] race, religiously and politically, by working in the South than remaining at [his] present post." [100]

A few months later, after he had moved to Mississippi to begin an ecclesiastical and political career, Lynch gave a fuller explanation why he had chosen to join a predominantly white church. He remarked that African Methodism did not have "the ability to carry on the great work of Methodist reconstruction in the South" and that "its mission as a separate organization [was] near a close." On the other hand, he contended, "The M.E. Church is dotting the South with temples, where white and black can meet as equals around God's altar, while its biblical institutes, institutions of learning, the common schools which follow in its wake, its numerous periodicals, pleading for our religious, civil, and political equality, these make me believe that it is God's chosen power to lift up my race from degradation." [101] During the next five years Lynch became one of the most prominent black leaders in Mississippi, serving as its secretary of state, organizing churches, and editing the *Colored Citizen's Monthly.* His correspondence with Haven provided important information, much of which appeared in the *Herald,* concerning denominational developments and the political struggle of black Mississippians.[102]

Though the Methodist Episcopal Church did lure other black ministers from the two independent Negro denominations especially for work in the South, there were few who were Lynch's equal in capacities for leadership.

99. *Christian Recorder,* Apr. 20, 1867; *Zion's Herald,* Apr. 10, 1867.

100. *Christian Recorder,* June 8, 1867, quoted in the *New York Christian Advocate,* June 13, 1867. See also the *Advocate,* Jan. 23, 1868.

101. Quoted from the *New Orleans Advocate* (forerunner of the *Southwestern Christian Advocate*) in the *New York Christian Advocate,* Nov. 14, 1867.

102. *Zion's Herald,* Jan. 9, 16, Nov. 5, 1868; Mar. 25, Apr. 15, 22, Dec. 23, 1869; Jan. 27, 1870; Apr. 27, May 4, 1871; Jan. 11, May 2, June 6, 1872. See also William B. Gravely, "A Black Methodist on Reconstruction in Mississippi: Three Letters by James Lynch in 1868-1869," *Methodist History,* 11 (July, 1973), forthcoming.

The event was certainly the most successful effort in which Haven was involved to bring about, at least symbolically, a model of racially integrated Christianity. At the same time he worked diligently at trying to alter the racially exclusive patterns of New England Methodism through a union of the African and Zion Methodists of the region with his own denomination. He announced in the *Herald* that ministers from the two black churches were willing to join the New England Conference, if they could be received as equal brethren. He pled with local churches to speak out against racial caste and to state their willingness to receive a Negro pastor. He realized that New England Methodists could not consistently urge a policy against caste, unless they were willing to practice it. "One deed is worth a thousand declarations," he wrote.[103] His rationale touched the religious roots of his anticaste commitment. "We may not make every one a personal friend," he declared, "but we must regard as socially our equals all who are of our church or any church of Christ. The Lord Jesus administered to his disciples the most scathing rebuke he ever gave them for their attempt to create social inequality among themselves, and in his last hours enforced this fundamental principle of his gospel in the most expressive act of washing their feet." [104]

Most black Methodists in Massachusetts belonged to the African and Zion denominations, but there was one all-Negro church, Revere Street in Boston, which was related to the New England Conference.[105] In the summer of 1867, following the death of the pastor of the church, Haven challenged white Methodists to take into their communion the members of the Revere Street society. "It is time," he wrote, "that these brethren and sisters were invited back to the fold. They are devoted Christians who will bless the churches they shall join. They will open the way for the reception of all their color into these larger congregations. Such a deed will greatly cheer and strengthen the church here and everywhere. It will be hailed throughout the land as a conquest of prejudices that happily prefigures the future oneness of believers." The official boards of four white churches responded to the appeal and invited the blacks to unite with them. The experiment was nothing but a symbolic gesture toward ecclesiastical integration, however, for most Negro Methodists preferred to remain in their own church.[106]

There was some integration as a result of Haven's efforts. Wherever blacks and whites worshiped together, he saluted the achievement of transracial Christian fellowship. Early in 1868, he described "a union love feast in Grace Church" where "all hearts were melted into a living, holy, joyful unity." One

103. *Zion's Herald*, Aug. 22, 1867; Jan. 30, 1868.
104. *Ibid.*, Feb. 27, 1868.
105. In 1868, the African Methodist Episcopal Church reported 616 members, including local preachers and exhorters, and the Zion Methodists, 609 members, for the state. See *ibid.*, Nov. 24, 1870.
106. *Ibid.*, June 5, 1867; see also Apr. 10, 1867; Jan. 30, 1868. The Revere Street charge remained on the list of appointments in 1868. *Minutes of the New England Conference*, 1868, p. 78.

barrier that had not been surmounted, except in a token sense at revivals and camp meetings, however, was the possibility of having black preachers for white congregations. Certainly there was no thought of a free assignment of pastors to churches without regard to race. Haven entreated his fellow Methodists "to cooperate in this most important duty" by asking for Negro pastors for their appointments. "If any Quarterly Conference will say to their Presiding Elder," he maintained, " 'Send us Bro. Mars, or Bro. [William T.] Butler,' . . . —or any other such brother; or if they will say, 'If such an one is sent he will not be refused,' the path is opened to the inevitable and glorious goal. Those churches will stand forth in our history crowned with chiefest honor." [107]

Once again Haven wanted New England to "lead in the new path." "She must raise her sacred mace against this last idol, break it in pieces, and scatter its foul dust forever. She will do it," he wrote confidently. "We hope to see colored men receiving appointments with their white brethren at our next session." [108] The issue of assigning Negro pastors to white congregations did emerge at the annual conference in March, but not in the way Haven anticipated. On the concluding day of the session, Bishop Edward R. Ames, Haven's nemesis during the controversy over racial policy for missions back in 1865, announced his intention to transfer "from ten to twelve colored brethren" to the New England Conference during the next year. Immediately Haven offered resolutions approving the transfer, but he soon faced considerable opposition to his move. Some clergymen stated that "not one church could be found willing to accept colored men as pastors." Though other delegates denied that assertion, the conference only passed a compromise resolution which stated that the transfers would be welcome where they could be stationed "acceptably to the churches." The amendment did request the quarterly conferences to endorse the transfers, and the ministers promised to "do all in their power to secure such acceptance." [109]

The opposition among Haven's clerical colleagues showed that there was no overwhelming impulse for racial integration in the New England Conference. Haven's campaign had not greatly affected the racial attitudes of many white Methodists. He was left in a dilemma, for there was no way to justify the compromise without equivocating with his own convictions. Hoping that an integrated policy could still be put into practice, he finally defended the conference action, and urged the ministers to fulfill their promise to recommend that Negro pastors be accepted. To critics, he pointed out that by appealing to its churches to receive pastors without distinction of color, the New England Conference was doing more than any other group in the church to combat caste. He also acknowledged that Bishop Ames' move was "a very novel act,"

107. *Zion's Herald,* Jan. 30, 1868.
108. *Ibid.*
109. *Minutes of the New England Conference,* 1868, p. 12; *Zion's Herald,* Apr. 9, 30, May 7, 1868.

since New England Methodists had long opposed the practice of transferring ministers into their conference. But Haven's defense could not get around the fact that there was considerable opposition in the region to church integration. Once again Bishop Ames had taken action which placed him in the embarrassing situation of having to deal with the practical reality of racial prejudice which even his friends and associates demonstrated.[110]

Reluctantly, Haven conceded that the church was, perhaps, powerless to force its own members to act against their wishes. He was not willing to impose by hierarchical authority racial integration on his conference. His solution was to advocate a policy for the church like the congressional Reconstruction program on Negro suffrage, to "forbid new Conferences from recognizing [caste]," even if the older ones in the North still placed "more importance on the color of a Christian's skin than on the state of his heart." He declared, "If we cannot yet have manhood suffrage in the old States, we at least need not allow the contrary sort in those newly reconstructed. Congress had proceeded on this wise course. It refuses to allow any distinction where it has the power. It urges its abolition where its power is limited. So should the church." [111]

Because there was a fundamental difference between the congressional Reconstruction program and the southern mission work of the Methodist Episcopal Church, however, Haven's analogy was misleading. His denomination never officially established racial inclusiveness as the norm for new conferences in the South, as the Congress had required political equality of the reconstructed states. From the beginning the patterns of racial separation emerged because, as Haven had warned so persistently in 1864 and 1865, there was no policy against segregation. Unless the church was willing to begin anew and set an explicit standard against caste, segregation would go virtually unchallenged in the church in the South except for individual protests.

A further blow to Haven's hopes for racial integration came a month after the controversy in his conference. At the General Conference of 1868, the Kentucky Annual Conference obtained permission to divide and form a separate Negro organization. Haven fought the move, but his amendment, which allowed those colored members who wished to remain in the Kentucky Conference, was tabled.[112] In addition, the general conference gave a blanket permission "to divide [annual] Conferences which are already formed in the South, provided that two thirds of the members of such Conference or Conferences shall concur in such division." Haven had tried unsuccessfully to have the two existing colored conferences dissolved and provide for their absorption by the white conferences in the same areas. Instead the church extended the separatist policy of the previous general conference. Ironically,

110. *Zion's Herald,* Apr. 9, May 7, 1868.
111. *Ibid.,* May 7, 1868.
112. *Journal of the General Conference,* 1868, pp. 116, 307, 318.

Haven did not even have the support of the Negro delegates of the Washington and Delaware conferences, who asked to continue their racially separate bodies as organized. The predominantly black Mississippi Conference, on the other hand, petitioned the general church that no more colored conferences be organized.[113]

The action to divide the Kentucky Conference, Haven described as wrong in principle. "It was a step backward," he wrote, "and will, if it is carried out, yet breed harm to both Church and State. It creates Conference caste in the most wicked State of the Union." The policy, he feared, would undercut what little ecclesiastical integration had been achieved in the South. "It approves of the Washington and Delaware plan more than that of South Carolina and Mississippi," he complained. "It tempts all the Conferences below to conform to this standard." Since the proposed separation needed the bishops' consent, Haven begged the episcopal board to delay approval.[114] But he was fighting a losing battle. The next year the separation took place as scheduled. "The Kentucky Conference has succeeded in getting rid of its colored associates," he lamented. "We presume all of them are dismissed, though several of them did not ask for the favor, as would none of them, had they been treated as brothers and equals. . . . It is a sad sight, for our Church to present to a State so hostile, such a divided front." [115]

There were other signs of erosion of principle in the South. In Georgia there was a movement for separation in 1869. Since the Virginia and North Carolina conferences paid little attention to missions among Negroes, they continued to be almost entirely white organizations.[116] In the leading cities of the South, like Atlanta and New Orleans, the Methodist Episcopal Church was building large churches exclusively for white members.[117] Except for support in Mississippi and South Carolina, Haven's appeals against caste in the southern work went unheeded.[118] Most of his fellow churchmen complained that Haven's radical views, in fact, hindered the success of the denomination's efforts.[119]

Still another disappointment to Haven in 1868 was the dissolution of two independent Methodist papers in the South which Louisiana and South Carolina churchmen had supported at New Orleans and Charleston since their formation in 1865 and 1867. Both papers championed equal rights for Negroes in church and society. Haven sought to get the general conference to adopt them as official church periodicals. Limited support was authorized,

113. *Ibid.*, pp. 171, 186, 197, 308, 318-19.
114. *Zion's Herald,* July 9, Oct. 1, 1868.
115. *Ibid.*, Mar. 25, 1869.
116. See Haven's criticism, *ibid.,* Mar. 18, May 27, 1869; Apr. 21, 1870.
117. *Ibid.,* Mar. 12, Apr. 23, 1868; May 18, 1871.
118. For example, see James Lynch's commendation of Haven's stand against the racial separation of the Kentucky Conference, *ibid.,* Apr. 22, 1869.
119. *Western Chirstian Advocate,* Sept. 16, 1868; Feb. 10, Nov. 3, 1869; *Methodist Advocate,* June 30, 1869; *Zion's Herald,* May 21, 1868; July 1, 1869.

but when the general conference simultaneously established another paper in Georgia, its publishing committee decided that only one paper for the South could be afforded. The new *Methodist Advocate* in Atlanta got the nod.[120] The strong equalitarian positions taken by the Charleston and New Orleans papers, Haven suspected, influenced the decision. He was afraid that the Atlanta paper would fail to give the same leadership to the crusade against caste in the South. His fears were not unfounded.[121]

Almost from the first issue of the Atlanta paper, its editor, Erasmus Q. Fuller, and Haven were at odds. It was soon quite evident that Fuller, a midwesterner, did not intend to jeopardize the future of his journal by challenging racial separation.[122] By the summer of 1869, the two men were involved in an editorial duel.

When the Supreme Court of Georgia ruled interracial marriage illegal, Fuller wrote of the decision, "We know of no one who will feel personally afflicted by the opinion of the Court save the parties in the case and perhaps the editor of Zion's Herald, of Boston." His criticism grew harsher as he continued. "Still, as this brother has already refused to do anything but 'blow' for the people for whom he professes such unmeasured admiration," he remarked caustically, "we doubt whether the race will materially suffer through him from this cause, unless it be from sympathy for his sorrow. But if the sorrow is measured by the affection, neither party will be heavy losers." Then Fuller added a comment which harkened back to Haven's refusal to come to Vicksburg as a missionary in 1865. Quoting the *Nashville Advocate,* Southern Methodism's official paper, he said that the court decision would "bar [Haven] from taking work in our State. But here, again, are providential compensations," Fuller wrote, "for, firstly, he *won't* work in our colored missions, and, secondly, it would be a serious damage for the cause if he did. He does much harm where he is, but in the field would do immeasurably more. His weekly aims at us are simply firing rockets at the moon. If he were to point at nearer objects he might frighten, though he never hit. In a national museum," the Atlanta editor concluded, "he serves admirably as a curiosity, in practical work here the case would be very different." [123]

Ignoring the personal invective, Haven replied that the assault was consistent with Fuller's treatment of the question, "Shall the Church, and through it, society in the South, be built on the corner-stone of humanity, a stone planted by God, the Father and Brother of man, or on that of a cursed and cruel caste?" Fuller was more disposed to fraternize with the Methodist Epis-

120. *Journal of the General Conference,* 1868, pp. 267-68; *Zion's Herald,* Feb. 11, Apr. 1, 1869; *Western Christian Advocate,* Feb. 24, 1869.
121. *Zion's Herald,* Dec. 3, 1868; Jan. 14, 1869. See criticism of the Charleston and New Orleans *Advocates* for endorsing local and national Republican candidates in their columns, *Western Christian Advocate,* July 22, 1868.
122. *Zion's Herald,* Feb. 25, Mar. 25, Apr. 15, 22, 1869; *Methodist Advocate,* Mar. 10, 1869.
123. *Methodist Advocate,* June 30, 1869. A similar attack is in the issue of July 19, 1871.

copal Church, South, Haven noted, than to defend the right racial policy. "If our Church fails to flourish and triumph in the South," he warned, "if it sinks into a powerless fragment, or becomes helplessly absorbed in an unrepenting Southern Church, that fatality will be due almost entirely to the only official journal we publish there." [124]

Fuller was not the only Methodist editor who locked horns with Haven over church policy. In a more involved controversy Haven and S. M. Merrill again confronted each other. "It is useless to talk about ignoring all distinctions of color in the Church," Merrill declared in one of his first editorials after becoming editor of the *Western Advocate*. "This is simply an impossibility. Practical men, white or black," he argued, "do not look for such a thing. A plain recognition of the fact that black men are black, is a necessity, and it violates no law of humanity or Christianity." Despite the contentions of "impracticable theorists," Merrill stated, with an eye to Haven, "we are just matter-of-fact enough to believe that it is best in this particular to obey the laws of affinity; and, therefore, we believe in keeping up churches, circuits, stations, districts, and conferences, for our colored brethren." [125]

During a subsequent debate Merrill gave the two basic arguments of Methodist racial separationists. First, he maintained that Negroes desired separate church organizations, and that to prohibit their formation was to deny them their rights. "Whether the preference of colored people for their own associations be an instinct of nature, a mere prejudice, or the result of inhuman treatment from the whites, it is a *fact* which we can not ignore;" he wrote, "and to undertake to force them to have white pastors, and mingle in white congregations, . . . would be a species of ecclesiastical tyranny not to be tolerated in the Church of Christ." Expediency was the ground for Merrill's second argument. There could be no success, especially among whites in the South and on the border, he declared, if Negroes were given ecclesiastical equality. Directing his remarks again quite pointedly in Haven's direction, he wrote, "Our whole life has not been spent in the safe retreats and quiet atmosphere of the North, studying abstract principles of social science, and indulging in airy flights of rhetoric in regard to Southern antagonisms." Based on "personal observation," he charged that "the ultraisms of the few who denounce caste the most flippantly, and contend not only for equal rights—as we all do—but for social equality, even to the extent of amalgamation . . . form the greatest barriers to our success, and at this very time are jeopardizing our whole interests in the South." [126]

Upholding the principle of racial inclusiveness in the church, Haven admonished Merrill for having fallen "into the usual error of the times in treating this question. That error," he explained, "is an attempt to fasten on the colored

124. *Zion's Herald*, July 22, 1869; see also Apr. 22, May 13, 1869.
125. *Western Christian Advocate*, July 15, 1868. D. D. Whedon, influential editor of the *Methodist Quarterly Review*, 50 (1868), 632-33, expressed similar sentiments.
126. *Western Christian Advocate*, Sept. 16, 1868; see also Aug. 12, 1868.

people our own iniquity. They want to be separate. Why refuse them their wish?" Merrill had inquired whether Haven would deny a request by Negro churchmen for a separate organization. "We answer, yes," Haven replied. "Greeks and Jew [sic] might have desired to worship separately, but the greatest of the apostles allowed no such walls to be erected in the church of Christ." Only "in very rare cases," he added, did blacks want to separate, and then "on very good ground," arising "from our refusal to allow them to worship with us, and to accept their ministers as our ministers, as we ought to do, *must* do, and WILL yet do." [127]

Merrill's second argument for racial separation was more difficult to counter, for Haven was aware of the practical difficulty that resulted because most whites refused to attend integrated churches. Sometimes he ignored this problem, declaring that success awaited the church which openly denounced caste and integrated its membership and ministry. He even blamed the financial difficulties of the missionary board on its failure to announce a no-caste policy.[128] But with the development in his own conference over Bishop Ames' transfer plan and upon reports from the South that integrated congregations did not prosper, Haven had to acknowledge that his transracial ideal might not work. But, he advised, "Throw open our doors to all. If the 'all' are black, Amen. If a few whites mingle with them, rejoice over that too. Pay no regard to color, but to souls." [129] Unlike Merrill, Haven refused to capitulate to the facts of white prejudice, for he believed that it was the duty of the church to overcome, rather than to accept racism. "The struggle is great in the South," he observed soberly. "That we concede. The prejudices are greater; that, we are ashamed to say, is the truth, and regret that *The Western* never rebukes them. They have not died out in New England. Many a Christian heart still harbors this leaven of malice and unrighteousness. But, God helping us," Haven said, stating his heartfelt convictions, "wherever He places our lot, in the little breathing spell left us on this earth, we shall uplift our voice against this unchristian and inhuman cruelty." He knew from experience that "no prejudice wears out," but that "every devil must be *driven out.*" [130]

Looking ahead to the General Conference of 1872, Haven predicted that an attempt would be made there "to erect colored Conferences all over the South." He was determined to block that movement. In 1870 he developed a new argument when the Methodist Episcopal Church, South, completed the organization of its Negro members and preachers into a separate denomination, the Colored Methodist Episcopal Church. "If we do the same, what do we more than they?" he asked his readers. "Why distract these brethren by a distinction without a difference? Let [all blacks] go together, if we have not Christianity enough to rise to a higher plane of grace and Godhood." He

127. *Zion's Herald*, Sept. 3, 1868; see also Oct. 1, 1868.
128. *Ibid.*, Oct. 15, 1868.
129. *Ibid.*, Apr. 23, 1868.
130. *Ibid.*, Sept. 24, 1868; Apr. 8, 1869; Aug. 11, 1870.

predicted that if the theory of separation prevailed, "the Church South will surpass ours. It ought to," he insisted. "Let it have a monopoly of this iniquity, and let us continue powerless until we can do our work right." [131] In anticipation of the coming debate Haven advised the church to "Choose the Right, and Stick"—to ignore caste, rather than foster it—to "practice the wholly right" rather than "the half right, which is almost always the wholly wrong." [132]

As a further objective in his plan for racial inclusiveness in American Methodism, Haven hoped that a union could come about by 1872 between one or both of the African Methodist denominations and the Methodist Episcopal Church. Little progress toward a union with the African Methodist Episcopal Church had been made, largely because of considerable competition and controversy between the two denominations over southern missions among the freedmen. In 1866 a delegation from the black denomination went to the General Conference of the Methodist Episcopal Church, South, and openly attacked white Northerners for invading the region. The move was partly designed by the Negro churchmen to secure property rights to buildings being used by the freedmen, but which legally belonged to the Southern Methodists from their prewar missions among the slaves. Even though Daniel A. Payne, the senior bishop of the African Methodists, severely chastised the delegation for assuming "a servile attitude" toward southern whites, the deed strained relations between his church and Haven's denomination.[133]

One other issue threatened any realistic chance for an organic merger between the two churches. In 1867 New England Unitarians agreed to send teachers and provide funds for African Methodist Episcopal schools and missions in the South. Warning that cooperation with Unitarians was dangerous because of their unevangelical theology, Haven denounced the plan. He predicted that the association would destroy some of the developing sentiment toward the union of the Methodist Episcopal and African Methodist churches. In this case he let his religious dogmatism reign over his humanitarian concerns, and the Boston Unitarians took him to task for his attitude.[134]

The possibility for union with the Zion Methodists was considerably better. At the General Conference of 1868, Haven engineered the appointment of an official commission to discuss a merger with the black church. He did not succeed in persuading the conference to empower the commission to conclude the union, but it was ordered to negotiate and report back in 1872.

131. *Ibid.*, Jan. 6, 1870; see also Nov. 19, 1868.

132. *Ibid.*, Apr. 8, 1869.

133. *Ibid.*, Oct. 10, 1867. B. F. Crary proposed a plan of union between the two denominations in September, 1866, but no official steps were taken in response. Payne wrote his reaction to the idea in *Western Christian Advocate*, Mar. 13, 20, 1867. See also Payne's address, *The African M.E. Church in its Relations to the Freedmen* (Xenia, Ohio, [1868]); and *Christian Recorder*, Feb. 9, Apr. 6, June 1, Sept. 21, 1867.

134. *Zion's Herald*, Oct. 10, 1867; Jan. 30, Feb. 6, 20, 27, June 25, 1868; Feb. 11, Mar. 11, 1869.

Haven greeted the action hopefully and prophesied that the merger would be consummated without difficulty.[135]

In some quarters, however, the idea of a merger with either Negro church was received coldly. For example, Merrill proposed that the Methodist Episcopal Church should give its influence to a union of all black Methodists in the country into a separate denomination, rather than to an organic merger with the Zion Church.[136] Haven bitterly criticized the idea and Merrill's "pious patronizing" spirit. "Others see some difference," he exclaimed, "if the *Advocate* does not, between driving off our own children and marrying others into our family." He had no sympathy for the suggestion that Negroes, then in separate conferences in his own denomination, be "invited . . . to leave their life-long communion, and form with other bodies a great Black Methodist Church." Merrill had said that northern Methodists could "afford to be magnanimous" and "give up all the [Negro] members we have" to the proposed denomination. "Magnanimity is great-souledness," Haven told Merrill. "It is a total expulsion of the devil of caste from our own soul, a complete 'ignoring of all distinctions of color in the church,' a cessation of all such patronage . . . , a manly and brotherly meeting of the manly and brotherly offer of the Zion's Church, meeting it soon, too, meeting it so all the church and the world shall see that we have conquered through Christ all our prejudice." [137]

The controversy between the two editors quieted down in the fall of 1868, but two years later Merrill once more raised the idea in a slightly different form. He commended the formation of the Colored Methodist Episcopal Church in 1870 as "the beginning of the consolidation of all organizations of colored Methodism." [138] Again, Haven blasted the proposal as "foreign to Methodism and Americanism, as it is from Christ and the Bible." The "quarter of a million of [black] members," most of whom had come into the Methodist Episcopal Church since the end of the war, "will not go," Haven argued, despite "the coldness of *The Western,* and its attempts to put them out." He believed that his own denomination, "in some of its movements, [was] much nearer expressing the purpose of God. When it puts all its members together, and sets a pastor over them, regardless of color;" he wrote, "when it puts all the ministers in the same territory into the same Conference, irrespective of color; it is on the track of God and the nation." [139]

All during this time conservatives in the Methodist Episcopal Church were pushing, as they had done since 1865, for a reunion with Southern Methodism,

135. *Journal of the General Conference,* 1868, pp. 114-15, 199-200, 206, 227, 237-38, 472-76; *Zion's Herald,* June 4, 11, 1868. See also David Henry Bradley, Sr., *A History of the A.M.E. Zion Church,* pt. I, 1796-1872 (Nashville, 1956), pp. 154-55.

136. *Western Christian Advocate,* July 15, 1868.

137. *Ibid.; Zion's Herald,* Aug. 6, 1868.

138. *Western Christian Advocate,* June 15, 1870.

139. *Zion's Herald,* July 7, 1870.

rather than with any of the Negro churches.[140] The episcopal board reflected this disposition when they sought to open fraternal communications with the Methodist Episcopal Church, South, in the spring of 1869. Haven censured the bishops for making "advances" to southern whites which they were not willing to make toward the black denominations.[141] In any reunion with Southern Methodists, he warned, "the negro would be crushed out." Then, he placed his opposition in the context of his millennial hope for the nation. "If God means one thing more than another concerning America, as an earthly result," he wrote, "it is the consummation here of the brotherhood of man. Everybody here feels that this is her mission." But, he continued,

Against this result, the M.E. Church, South, has set itself. It will be converted yet, and be the most zealous in advocating and practising this duty. But to-day it is fostering its opposite. It loathes (officially) the negro. It puts him in churches and Conferences by himself. It refuses any recognition of his brotherhood. Bring us together, and the act of the Kentucky Conference, so dishonorable to us as Christians, will be renewed over all the South.[142]

While the advocates of reunion with the southern church awaited official action by its general conference in 1870, the commission of the Methodist Episcopal and Zion churches met in Philadelphia in November, 1869. Meanwhile, a new threat to the union had developed in the Negro denomination. Many of its leaders in the South resented the treatment which they were receiving from white ministers and members of the Methodist Episcopal Church. In addition, there were some Zion churchmen who saw the merger merely as an absorption by the larger body. They feared that they would not receive equal rights and representation after the union.[143]

Despite opposing forces in each church, the commissions held a cordial conference, discussed terms of merger and agreed to meet again at or before the 1872 sessions of their respective general conferences. The official report stated that "unless some unforeseen hinderances shall arise it will not be found impossible at their future meeting to satisfactorily arrange all the terms of union, and to bring the two bodies into one, by the concurrent action of the two General Conferences." [144]

In 1870 the general conference of the Methodist Episcopal Church, South, rebuffed the overtures of its northern counterpart, which had once again become a national denomination through its southern missions, and refused to appoint a commission on union. Since Haven had opposed the initiative

140. *Ibid.*, Dec. 16, 1869. Haven explicitly criticized George R. Crooks and his paper, *The Methodist*, for supporting union with the Methodist Episcopal Church, South, in place of the merger with the Zion Church.
141. *Zion's Herald*, Aug. 12, 1869. See issue of May 27, 1869 for the official correspondence between northern and Southern Methodists.
142. *Ibid.*, Aug. 19, 1869.
143. Haven was aware of these difficulties. See *ibid.*, Dec. 17, 1868; Nov. 4, 1869.
144. *New York Christian Advocate*, Dec. 9, 1869.

in the first place, he welcomed the southern decision. He believed that the proposed union with the Zion Church now had a better chance of being approved. In New England he worked to relieve suspicions among members of the Negro denomination, by visiting their annual conferences and conferring with their ministers and bishops. He also continued to rally support for the merger among white Methodists of the region, fully expecting that the union would be realized in 1872.[145]

Besides preventing further racial separation in conferences and arranging for the union of the Methodist Episcopal with the Zion churches, there was one further goal for which Haven aimed in ecclesiastical reform. He wanted his church to have a black bishop. As early as October, 1867, he had suggested the easiest way in which it could be done. John Wright Roberts, a Negro missionary bishop in Liberia, could be given full episcopal powers and returned to America. The General Conference of 1856 had provided for the election of a missionary bishop for the Liberia Conference, but the office's episcopal functions were limited to Africa. Roberts, a native of Virginia, was consecrated in 1866 to replace the late Francis Burns who first held the post. Haven questioned the constitutionality of the office of missionary bishop, which, he contended, was contrary to the basic Methodist understanding of the general superintendency. He pointed out that the limitations against Bishop Roberts resulted both from a too narrow understanding of the church and from "the prejudice against color." [146] After getting New England Methodists to petition that Roberts be given equal rank in the episcopacy and permitted to preside over American conferences, Haven expected the General Conference of 1868 to deal with the matter, but no action was taken.[147]

Two years later, he brought up the question again. In opposition to Haven, the editor of the *New York Advocate,* Daniel Curry, stated that Roberts was "no more a 'Bishop of the Methodist Episcopal Church,' in the specific and legal sense of that phrase, than is any other travelling Elder." Thus, he had no authority to exercise his episcopal office in America. Strictly speaking, Haven conceded, Curry was right, but he claimed that Roberts was a bishop "in a moral, and formal, and potent sense, far more 'than any other travelling Elder.' " He requested the General Conference of 1872 to remove the "unjust, and unbrotherly, and unwise restrictions" from Roberts' office.[148] He also tried to exploit the significance of Roberts' case with reference to the proposed union with the Zion Church. "We thus begin the work of true unification at the head, where it ought to begin," he advised. "We offset the move-

145. *Zion's Herald,* May 26, June 16, 1870; Apr. 13, Sept. 21, 1871; *Minutes of the New England Conference,* 1870, pp. 31-33. See also an undated (but probably 1871) manuscript address from the New England Conference of the A.M.E. Zion Church, New England Conference Papers.
146. *Zion's Herald,* Oct. 17, 1867.
147. *Ibid.,* Feb. 13, May 7, 1868.
148. *New York Christian Advocate,* July 7, 1870; *Zion's Herald,* Aug. 4, 1870.

ment of the Church South, . . . and plant a Bishop of our own creating, created in the place of his predecessor twenty years ago, among his peers, their complete and beloved equal and associate. We open the way for the admission of the Bishops or Bishop elected by the Zion's Church and its over a hundred thousand members." To have already a black bishop functioning in the Methodist Episcopal Church would assist the union effort, Haven believed, precisely in an area of controversy. The African Methodist Episcopal Zion denomination had four bishops, a considerably higher ratio to its membership than Haven's denomination, in which seven bishops served 1,400,000 members. Likewise, the black church elected bishops only for four-year, not life-time, terms.[149]

In the months prior to the General Conference of 1872, a lively debate over the "colored bishop" question was carried on in the Methodist press. Haven was determined that there should be a Negro bishop. "In some way, either from our own ranks, or by union with the Zion's Church, or by making Bishop Roberts full Bishop, must we have in our General Superintendency a man of color."[150] Once again, S. M. Merrill was the first editor to come out against Haven. He charged that his Boston colleague was making "the color of the skin" into "a passport to promotion." Pointing out that although blacks comprised "about one fifth" of the church's "members and ministers," Haven answered Merrill that it was impossible for even "the ablest and lightest colored of these brethren [to occupy] any desirable pulpit in the Church." Negroes, he declared, "are no better than whites, but they are as good, and they must be represented." Specifically, as potential episcopal candidates, he mentioned James Lynch, who, Haven claimed, "[was] as competent as the editor of *The Western*," William Butler of New York, C. O. Fisher of Savannah, Georgia, and the unnamed "pastor of the Clark Street Church in Nashville."[151]

The major debate, however, on this question occurred between Haven and Daniel Wise, secretary of Sunday school and tract publications for the denomination, who decried agitation of the issue. He said that he had hoped that the Negro would "be quietly left to work out his destiny without further controversy." In recommending that a colored bishop be elected, the Negro's "friends have begun to torment him with the baited hook of ecclesiastical ambition."[152]

Wise claimed that few black Methodists actually desired the election of one of their race to the episcopacy. He also doubted whether any Negro was "fitted for this high office." Then his final point touched the real objection,

149. *Zion's Herald*, Dec. 29, 1870; see also Aug. 18, 1870.
150. *Ibid.*, Aug. 10, 1871.
151. *Ibid.*; see *Western Christian Advocate*, Aug. 16, 1871. Haven earlier suggested Lynch, but thought his preference to continue as a political leader in Mississippi would probably prevent his consideration. *Zion's Herald*, Jan. 27, 1870; see also June 6, 1872.
152. *Zion's Herald*, Feb. 8, 1872, in response to Haven's editorial of Jan. 18, 1872.

"the conventional prejudice against color." Wise wrote of its "living power in society," which fact affected "the expediency of electing a colored Bishop." He reminded Haven that "a colored Bishop would be a *general* superintendent" who should not be "limited to colored conferences," but who would "preside in turn at Boston and Baltimore, as well as in Charleston and New Orleans." He would ordain "white neophites" and appoint "white preachers" and "as a bishop . . . share the hospitalities due to his office, and be admitted to the tables of white laymen of wealth and cultivation." Because he was a bishop, "social recognition in the best circles of the Church [would] be his due." Frankly, Wise queried, "Is the Church yet prepared to yield its remaining prejudice against color to this extent?" He answered his own question. "Surely no man at all acquainted with what is called good society will say that it is." His recommendation, therefore, was to delay such a matter until "society" was prepared to give a black bishop proper recognition.[153]

On every point Haven disagreed with Wise. Though he admitted that blacks had not agreed on "their man," he denied that they did not desire a bishop of their race. "They are afraid this deed is to be used as an entering wedge to drive them from the Church," he wrote, "and this is their chief objection. Convince them that it is a pledge of closer unity, as it is, and they will adjust the matter of the candidate without trouble." Haven also disputed Wise's contention that there were no Negroes capable enough to be bishop. He commended the ability of the bishops of the two African Methodist denominations and suggested another name, Benjamin Brown of the Washington Conference, as a potential nominee among blacks in the Methodist Episcopal Church.[154]

Initially Haven discounted Wise's statement that white Methodists would not receive a Negro bishop. "Men of wealth in many places will honor themselves by honoring him," he commented. More realistically he had to admit that hospitality might be withheld, but he maintained that "there are plenty of poor and 'cultivated' laymen who [would] gladly receive him as their guest, and it would be well if such brethren had the privilege more frequently of entertaining the chief representatives of our Church." To insure acceptance, he suggested that one of the veteran bishops could accompany the new black bishop on his first round of conferences.[155] On a practical level, Haven understood that the selection of a Negro bishop would be a great blow against racial separation. "A colored bishop, therefore, traveling our country, accepted in our Conferences as a president, making appointments, ordaining ministers, talking to candidates, dedicating churches, he will be a fact that settles forever all controversy."[156] Characteristically, Haven

153. *Ibid.*, Feb. 29, 1872. Both of Wise's articles were widely reprinted throughout the church. See *New York Christian Advocate*, Feb. 8, 22, 1872; *Methodist Advocate*, Feb. 21, Mar. 6, 1872.
154. *Zion's Herald*, Feb. 29, 1872.
155. *Ibid.*
156. *Ibid.*, Jan. 18, 1872.

could not resist portraying the ultimate significance of the action, which he saw as a divine opportunity. "We believe the new era has fully come," he wrote in the *Herald,* "and that the disabilities under which men have labored in this country on account of a God-given and God-approved complexion, should utterly cease. We believe the Church should deal it a death-blow. This death-blow is given when one of that color is chosen among its general superintendents." [157]

At the General Conference of 1872 in Brooklyn, Haven hoped to score a major victory against racial segregation in the church. Besides New England he could count support in the South, especially in Louisiana and South Carolina, whose conference delegates drew up position papers against caste in the church and in behalf of a Negro bishop.[158] The opposing forces, however, were not without organization and strategy. One of Haven's opponents, E. Q. Fuller of Atlanta, just before the conference, altered his earlier advocacy of a Negro bishop, declaring that no colored man could preside over whites. In his paper he likewise attacked the equalitarian arguments of the "Louisiana Platform" and what he called the "South Carolina Manifesto." He was also the leading figure in the movement for racial division in the Georgia Conference.[159]

One objective in Haven's program for racial reform went down to defeat early in the session. Across town the Zion General Conference adjourned after meeting only three days. Opponents of union, led by Bishop Joseph Jackson Clinton, ruled the meeting and threatened to divide the denomination if the merger was approved. In a letter to the Methodist Episcopal General Conference, Bishop Singleton T. Jones, who had spearheaded the union movement, asked "that further negotiations may be stayed until pending efforts with a view to harmony within our own ranks shall have been exhausted, or developments shall warrant further action." [160] The position of the Zion Church, therefore, prevented the controversial question of union from ever coming before the Methodist Episcopal conference. Haven held out hope that the northern wing of the Negro body would still favor union, but there was little chance for that. Except where members and ministers acted individually, organic union was dead.[161] Years later, Bishop James W. Hood, historian for the Zion Church, reflected back upon the ill-fated venture.

157. *Ibid.,* Feb. 8, 1872.
158. See *ibid.,* Apr. 4, 1872, for the "Louisiana Platform," written by veteran abolitionist, L. C. Matlack, who had become a missionary in New Orleans. He also wrote eloquent essays on the "colored bishop" question and the issue of colored conferences, which see in *ibid.,* Mar. 7, 1872; *New York Christian Advocate,* Apr. 4, 1872. On the South Carolina Conference petition, see *Zion's Herald,* May 2, 1872.
159. *Zion's Herald,* Mar. 7, Apr. 25, May 2, 1872; *Methodist Advocate,* Mar. 13, Apr. 10, 17, 24, May 1, 1872.
160. *Journal of the General Conference of the Methodist Episcopal Church,* 1872, pp. 534-35, *Zion's Herald,* Apr. 25, 1872.
161. *Zion's Herald,* May 9, 1872; *Daily Christian Advocate,* May 4, 1872; Bradley, *A History of the A.M.E. Zion Church,* pt. II, 1872-1968 (Nashville, 1970), pp. 41-45.

"Gilbert Haven was perfectly honest," he wrote, "and thought he could manage it," but sentiment against ecclesiastical equality was too strong. "Some of us fully understood the meaning of this;" Hood continued, "we could see from the newspaper reports that there was no hope of what Gilbert Haven and others held out to us. They were anxious to do it, but the odds were against them; many of us, therefore, made up our minds to pursue the matter no further." [162]

Haven was no more successful in his project to elect a Negro bishop. The conference deferred, without further action, a resolution to remove the restrictions on Bishop Roberts. Even though eight new bishops were elected, no Negro churchman was seriously considered. Behind the scenes, Haven worked to nominate blacks for several other general church positions of leadership, but again without success. The general conference did rule that "there is nothing in race, color, or former condition that is a bar to an election to the Episcopacy," but the policy statement made little difference in the practical matter of giving black Methodists serious consideration. An even more comprehensive standard was adopted, declaring that "There is no word 'white' to discriminate against race or color known in our legislation; and being of African descent does not prevent membership with white men in Annual Conferences, nor ordination at the same altars, nor appointment to Presiding Elders, nor election to the General Conference, nor eligibility to the highest offices in the Church." But again, the principle could be, as it was, violated on the basis of custom without formal legal backing. The norm, moreover, was difficult to reconcile with the actual existence of three colored conferences.[163]

The support which might have gone to a qualified Negro in the episcopal elections went instead to Haven himself. He attracted votes from some of the southern, and all of the Negro, delegates. Most conferences in the Northeast backed him as a candidate, because no bishop had come from New England since 1852. Other delegates, however, worked against Haven's election, distributing handbills which quoted his most controversial statements on race. Some of his own friends, in fact, feared that it would not be best for him to be chosen as a bishop.[164] Despite opposition and because so many bishops were needed, Haven's supporters somehow gained sufficient strength to elect him on the third ballot, the seventh of eight new episcopal leaders who were named. His selection did not mean, necessarily, that the church was endorsing his racial views, since his leading antagonist, S. M. Merrill, and another conservative who promoted reunion with Southern Methodism, Randolph S. Foster, were also elected to the superintendency. In any event black Methodists had one man on the episcopal board who

162. James W. Hood, *One Hundred Years of the African Methodist Episcopal Zion Church; or, The Centennial of African Methodism* (New York, 1895), pp. 98-99.

163. *Journal of the General Conference*, 1872, pp. 58, 253, 330, 373.

164. Daniels, *Memorials of Gilbert Haven*, pp. 82-83, 147, 182-83.

defended their right to equality in the church, even if no Negro had been seriously considered.[165]

By the time the issue of racially separate conferences got to the floor for action, Haven, as a presiding officer, could not participate in the debates. The Georgia and Alabama conferences brought petitions, some of which came from Negro Methodists, requesting a racial separation. Fuller of Atlanta made a motion asking permission to divide the two conferences during the next four years, but two black delegates, Joseph Middleton of South Carolina and Lynch of Mississippi, made such impressive speeches in opposition that the general conference tabled the request.[166] The action was "the death-blow," Haven wrote, "to this caste legislation." The general conference also struck the word "colored" from the official titles of the three all-black conferences—a move hardly adequate to alter the facts of the situation. What looked like a victory for integrationists was in reality only a stalemate.[167]

By the spring of 1872, racial separation in the Methodist Episcopal Church was even more a settled pattern than it had been five years before when Haven first began his editorial crusade. A few more of the northern conferences had Negro clerical members, but they continued to be employed exclusively as pastors for black churches.[168] Three of the sourthern conferences had no Negro members. There was one more colored conference, Lexington in Kentucky, than there had been in 1867.[169] Haven's own New England Conference could hardly boast that its lone Negro minister continued to be "Father" Mars who had transferred back to the area to take the Revere Street appointment in 1869.[170]

Of Haven's three objectives, two failed outright. The proposal for a Negro bishop was not dead after 1872, but it was nearly a half-century before Haven's idea was realized.[171] A union with either of the African Methodist denominations was less and less likely in a society where the color line was destined to be drawn more rigidly than ever. The third objective—to halt the movement for racially separate conferences—was only temporarily successful, and it would become the issue that caused Haven's most severe disappointment as a bishop. But with that minor achievement in 1872, he was closer to the realization of his goals for racial reform in the church than he would ever be again. His crusade against caste had made no great progress on any front; yet the failure was less his than that of a generation which could not share his dream of interracial brotherhood.

165. *Journal of the General Conference*, 1872, p. 306.
166. *Ibid.*, pp. 90, 92-93, 109, 417.
167. *Ibid.*, p. 435; *Zion's Herald*, June 13, 1872.
168. *Zion's Herald*, Apr. 1, 1869; Aug. 18, 1870; July 6, Sept. 21, 1871.
169. *Ibid.*, Mar. 28, 1872.
170. *Minutes of the New England Conference*, 1869, p. 49.
171. See the article, "A Prophet and His Dreams," *Zion's Herald*, Jan. 5, 1921, commemorating the centennial of Haven's birth and reporting the story of the first Negro bishop presiding over an annual conference in the Methodist Episcopal Church.

VI

Prophet Without Honor

To many Methodists the selection of Gilbert Haven to the episcopacy in 1872 was not merely a surprise. The wisdom of the action, in their view, was questionable at best, entirely injudicious at worst. They immediately cautioned Haven that the conservative nature of the episcopal office would force him "to abate some of his zeal for the social equality of the black man, and confine himself to purely religious questions." Even his fellow bishops urged him to guard the dignity of his position by restraining himself from publishing his opinions abroad on certain controversial matters. They reminded him that his editorial custom of freely expressing his views on any subject was inappropriate, now that he was one of the chief officials of the church.[1]

From the beginning, however, Haven showed that he clearly intended to set his own style and to champion, as always, the cause of equal rights. The African Methodist editor, Benjamin T. Tanner, predicted as much when he wrote with "tongue in cheek" that "the M.E. General Conference [tried] to put a stop to [Haven's] radical career" by "[putting] a crown on [him]," but it would not succeed. "It is our thought," he said confidently, "that *Gilbert* Haven, will be greater than *Bishop* Haven," that the new occupant of the episcopacy would be faithful to his lifelong commitments.[2] Haven was true to form, therefore, when, before the general conference in Brooklyn had ended, he published a letter of protest in the *New York Tribune* deploring the discriminatory treatment which a black ministerial delegate had received at a "well-known oyster house in Fulton Market." He recommended a boycott of the establishment until the proprietors issued a public apology for the insult. If they refused, Haven wrote, "Mr. Sumner's [civil rights] bill will soon make its repetition impossible there and everywhere else." [3]

Two months later Haven revealed even more dramatically his indisposition, as one writer afterwards noted, "to compromise his opinions for the exigencies of his new ecclesiastical position." [4] In an article for *The Independent* he thrust himself squarely into the national political debate between disaffected Republicans, who joined with moderate Democrats to sponsor the candidacy of Horace Greeley, and party loyalists, who backed incumbent president U. S. Grant. The chief issue of the campaign was sectional reconciliation, generally, and Grant's southern policy, in particular. By proposing universal amnesty to all Confederates and "home rule" for the South, the Liberal Republicans, as the Greeleyites called themselves, attacked the basic formula

1. Daniels, *Memorials of Gilbert Haven*, pp. 82-85.
2. *Christian Recorder*, June 29, 1872.
3. *New York Tribune*, May 31, 1872.
4. *Methodist*, Aug. 3, 1872.

of federal intervention and protection of civil rights, which racial equalitarians like Haven had supported since 1865.[5]

Earlier in the year as editor of *Zion's Herald,* Haven had come out against the Greeley movement, calling it "the defection of men once zealous for the truth from its demands and duties." He warned then that the triumph of Liberal Republicanism would be "the victory of all unrepentant slaveholder's [*sic*] views and feelings." [6] The purpose of his article in *The Independent* was more specific. He hoped to prevent Charles Sumner's support of Greeley. The piece was an open appeal to the senator, employing arguments which Haven had already privately urged upon Sumner.[7]

President Grant had mistreated Sumner during the previous four years, especially in maneuvering the senator's removal from the chairmanship of the Senate Foreign Relations Committee. Haven knew that, but he still thought that the points of disagreement between the two men were "petty considerations" compared with the overriding issue on which they were united —the necessity for the national protection of equal rights. He charged that promises of "equality and fraternity with the negro" made by the Liberal Republicans were insincere. The real power behind the Greeley campaign lay with ex-Confederates, not with the advocates of equal rights. A victory for Greeley, Haven was convinced, would bring disaster to the cause of racial justice. "The negro of the South will have to hide himself from his murderous foe," he wrote, "or crouch at his feet in revived servility and a more hideous slavery." On this ground Haven advised the famous legislator to put aside his personal antagonism toward Grant in order to support the party which would "keep faith with the loyal men of the South." "We entreat Mr. Sumner to give pause," he warned in his appeal. "Let him dislike and disavow the chief nominee, if he chooses; but not disavow, for any reasons, the principles of the party which are in him represented." [8] Four days after Haven's public letter appeared, Sumner endorsed Greeley.[9]

As expected, the Methodist press rebuked Haven for giving open support to Grant. Though the *Northern Christian Advocate* agreed with his sentiments, its editor doubted whether a Methodist bishop should have written such an article.[10] "We think it is wise," George R. Crooks of *The Methodist* advised, "for our bishops to refrain from public participation in party strife." [11] The loudest outcry came from editors of the Southern Methodist

5. McPherson, "Grant or Greeley? The Abolitionist Dilemma in the Election of 1872." *American Historical Review,* 71 (1965), 43-61.

6. *Zion's Herald,* Apr. 25, May 9, 16, 30, June 6, 13, 27, 1872.

7. An account of Haven's visit to Sumner contained in his private journal is quoted in Prentice, *Life,* pp. 398-400.

8. *The Independent,* July 25, 1872; *New York Times,* July 28, 1872; *Christian Recorder,* Aug. 3, 1872.

9. J. McPherson, "Grant or Greeley? The Abolitionist Dilemma," p. 56; Donald, *Charles Sumner* (1970), pp. 544-55.

10. As quoted in *Nashville Christian Advocate,* Sept. 7, 1872.

11. Aug. 3, 1872.

church papers, who seized upon Haven's stand as conclusive evidence that its sister Methodism was indeed a "politico-ecclesiastical organization." [12] These writers had already begun to taunt their Methodist competitors as soon as they learned that Haven's official residence was to be Atlanta. The *Southern Christian Advocate* had greeted Haven's appointment by saying, "Zion's Herald is bereaved, let us hope that its loss, will be some gain to the Race which has been so successfully ridden by the Bishop to his present eminence." [13] From Nashville, Thomas O. Summers had commented in a similar vein, "It will be warm for Bishop Haven in Atlanta;" he wrote, "but as he is fond of rich, dark complexion, the Sunny South may impart it to him." [14]

Haven's denominational associates in the South, therefore, were already on the defensive before the controversy over his article in *The Independent*. Some leaders were unwilling to accept the fact that Haven was to be their resident bishop, hoping that an alteration could somehow be made in the arrangement. J. C. Kimball, a leading layman who had moved to Atlanta after the war, privately advised Bishop Matthew Simpson that "the location of Bishop Haven in our midst, as the chief Pastor of our Southern work, would seriously embarrass our white work in [Georgia] if not in the entire South." Haven's appointment, Kimball warned, would threaten to destroy the bases for understanding which Northerners who had migrated South had been able to establish. "The mere fact of placing in charge of our Southern work," he stated, "a man of such extreme and boldly declared views, upon questions that have deeply agitated the Southern mind, would instantly renew with increased intensity all the old antagonisms that we have been trying for years—and with some success—to *live down*." [15] The presiding elder of the Knoxville [Tennessee] District, John F. Spence, was equally blunt in his protest to Simpson. "Our people know you and love you," he wrote. "But they repudiate Bishop Haven. We are sorry he is to be sent to the Southern work. Can there not be a change? Any member of the board but G[ilbert] Haven will be heartily rec'd. Our people I fear will not receive him." [16]

Since they were already sensitive about Haven's assignment, churchmen like Kimball and Spence were all the more disturbed when his controversial article about Sumner was publicized. Nelson Cobleigh, who had just left the presidency of East Tennessee Wesleyan University to return to the editorial chair, this time in Atlanta, reflected their sentiments. "We are sorry," he

12. *Nashville Christian Advocate*, Aug. 17, Sept. 28, Oct. 5, 1872; *Southern Christian Advocate*, Aug. 14, 1872; *New Orleans Christian Advocate*, Aug. 15, 1872.
13. June 12, 1872.
14. *Nashville Christian Advocate*, June 29, 1872. Further examples of such sarcasm in the Southern Methodist press may be found in *New Orleans Christian Advocate*, June 6, 1872; *Southern Christian Advocate*, July 17, 1872; *Nashville Christian Advocate*, June 1, 8, 22, 1872; *The Christian Neighbor*, June 27, July 4, 1872; *Texas Christian Advocate*, as quoted in *Zion's Herald*, July 11, 1872.
15. Kimball to Simpson, June 17, 1872, Simpson Papers, Library of Congress.
16. Spence to Simpson, Sept. 3, 1872, Simpson Papers, Library of Congress.

said, "that Bishop Haven has been so indiscreet as to give the enemies of our Church in the South any opportunity to inflame the prejudices of the people against our Church. He evidently does not understand the situation." [17]

During his initial year as bishop, Haven had his first opportunities to learn what the situation was in the South. He did not, however, come immediately to Atlanta. His delay touched off speculation that he might, after all, choose not to take the post assigned by the general conference. He admitted some disappointment at not being able to remain in New England, but after the decision to send him to Atlanta was made public it was well nigh impossible for him to refuse.[18] The specter of the crisis of 1865 over his Vicksburg appointment was still too vivid for anyone to forget, least of all Haven. As late as the year before, for example, Erasmus Q. Fuller, while he was still editor of the Atlanta *Advocate,* had reminded his southern readers that Haven had refused "to preach to the colored people" when he had the opportunity. Moreover, he accused Haven of having "kept out of the treasury of the Church by his misstatements" support that amounted to "thousands of dollars." "Is it not time," Fuller asked, "that he should cease seeking to atone for his own deliquencies by misrepresenting others?" [19] Because of such attitudes Haven knew that "it would be charged upon [him] instantly in all the papers as a cowardly desertion, if [he] should change [his] field." [20]

In late June Haven began to allay the doubts of those who wondered whether he would accept his assignment. He announced to the Boston Methodist preachers that he intended "to conquer the South in the name of Christ and Methodism." [21] A month later, however, protests from churchmen like Kimball had reached the denominational leader Matthew Simpson, who wrote to Haven that a change from Atlanta might be in everyone's best interests. Haven disagreed. "I was glad," he replied to Simpson, "when I lost New England, which of course I preferred, as no one was more elected from & by & for his section, that Atlanta was left open for me. I preferred it to any other point. I do yet." He assured Simpson that he "[did] not expect to encounter any opposition," and that he "[had] no fear of difficulty with the Ch[urch] So[uth]." "I don't value the fraternizing idea very highly," he declared, "& especially the Union [of the Methodist Episcopal with the Southern Methodist church], at least before we have a colored bishop, would

17. *Methodist Advocate,* Aug. 21, 1872. See also *Christian Recorder,* Aug. 31, 1872.
18. *Zion's Herald,* June 20, 1872; *Methodist Advocate,* July 3, 10, 1872; *The Methodist,* July 13, 1872. The General Conference of 1872 had made the first attempt in the Methodist Episcopal Church to establish official residences for its bishops. They were determined, however, that this arrangement not lead to a diocesan conception of the episcopacy, so that every bishop still itinerated and presided over conferences throughout the country.
19. *Methodist Advocate,* July 19, 1871.
20. Haven to Simpson, Aug. 16, 1872, Simpson Papers, Library of Congress.
21. Records of the Methodist Preacher's Meeting for Boston and Vicinity, June 24, 1872.

be a great mistake & wrong, but I shall be on good terms with them not-withstanding." Then Haven defined how he understood his mission.

I shall go to assist in building up our church in the right manner. The South needs N[ew] E[ngland] money & will get it more than the N[orth] W[est]. It also needs N[ew] E[ngland] ideas more, & I hope will get them. With a colored man nominated for Governor of Louisiana, it will never do for us to affiliate too warmly with those who dislike us & to ignore or treat with disrespect those who are fast rising to top of Southern society.[22]

I

After a busy summer and fall holding conferences, preaching, and traveling in New England and the Midwest, Haven finally arrived in Atlanta and was welcomed by church leaders, including his critics, Kimball, Cobleigh, and Fuller. When he showed up at a reception in his honor accompanied by a Negro churchman who had not received an invitation, Haven made clear that he was going to act upon his racial views in the South as elsewhere.[23] This first visit to Atlanta, however, was very brief, for the new bishop was on his way to Mexico to inaugurate Methodist mission work in the early months of 1873.[24]

Despite an episcopal itinerary which covered twenty thousand miles, by the end of his first year Haven had met most of the leaders of the Methodist Episcopal Church in the region. He spent only a total of seven days in Atlanta during the entire period, but he managed to visit every southern state except two and to get "a bird's eye view" of his work.[25] Wherever he traveled, he found potential subjects for his letters to the religious press. Into these accounts of the South, Haven injected a number of statements against racial caste. In the Atlanta *Advocate,* he made a particular appeal for others to join in lifting up the ideal of a racially inclusive church. "The only way to break to pieces this abominable folly of caste is to live it to pieces by action," he wrote. "Come and act as though it does not exist, and it will not. Never recognize it in any shape, and it will soon die. It is a ghost of a dead power," he entreated, which ought to be expelled "from our church, instantly and utterly." [26]

22. Haven to Simpson, Aug. 16, 1872. The letter from Simpson to which Haven was replying, is not extant, but the internal contents of this letter make clear what Simpson's suggestions had been.
23. *Methodist Advocate,* Jan. 1, 1873; Daniels, *Memorials of Gilbert Haven,* pp. 85-86.
24. During the first six months of 1873, Haven published quite a number of articles in *Zion's Herald, Methodist Advocate,* and *The Independent,* describing his experiences in Mexico. They were republished with other material in his, *Our Next-Door Neighbor: A Winter in Mexico.* See also John Wesley Butler, *History of the Methodist Episcopal Church in Mexico* (New York, 1918), pp. 21, 38, 41, 63, and several letters from Haven in the Simpson Papers, Library of Congress, and in the Skilton Family Papers, Collection of Regional History and University Archives, Cornell University. Archives, Cornell University.
25. For criticism of Haven for not spending more time in Atlanta, see *New York Christian Advocate,* May 15, July 31, 1873. Haven defended himself in *The Methodist,* June 28, 1873.
26. *Methodist Advocate,* Apr. 23, 1873. Other references to Haven's hope for a church without

Haven did not have to wait long for a response to his appeals against racial separation in Methodism. His remarks ignited a heated discussion of the question, and he soon discovered the actual state of opinion among some of his constituents. One pastor from western Tennessee forthrightly declared, "We can never subscribe to the published opinion of our good Bishop Haven, and other ultramontanes of the church." Another Tennessee preacher described three instances of distinct failure in local situations where Methodists sought to overcome caste by "living it to pieces," as Haven had advised. He regretted that the bishop had "decided on the proper course of action for our Southern conferences" on this controversial matter, without having consulted with the ministers and members. W. C. Graves, another Tennessean, anticipated attacks upon the church because of Haven's views. "We acknowledge that he is at least fifty years ahead of the age in which he lives," Graves observed, "at least so far as the South is concerned." [27]

The actual debate focused on the church's racial policy at the annual conference level. The union of white and black preachers in the same conference was the only remaining concrete symbol in Methodism of the ideal of an integrated church. There was significant opposition to that union, especially among white Methodists in Tennessee, Georgia, and Alabama. They had not laid aside the issue, even though the General Conference of 1872 had failed to approve additional separate conferences. Before Haven arrived in the South, the Georgia and Alabama clergy had made new requests for racial division.[28] After all sides of the question were aired during the spring and summer of 1873, the stage was set for Haven's first direct confrontation with the conflicting parties in the annual conferences themselves.[29]

Before Haven met the southern conferences in the fall, he came under fire because of his racial views from outside his own denomination. Southern Methodist editors, especially R. N. Price of the *Holston Methodist,* made sure that Haven's fellow churchmen knew about the bishop's correspondence in *Zion's Herald* which contained some of his choicest statements on amalgamation. One of these letters entitled "The Tinted Venuses," which described the mulatto women whom Haven had observed in Charleston, South Carolina, made the rounds in most of the southern papers. "I can pardon a little to the devil of slavery when I see what fine specimens of humanity it produced," the bishop had written.

caste appear in his correspondence from Mexico, which see in *Methodist Advocate,* Feb. 12, Mar. 12, 26, 1873; *New York Christian Advocate,* Jan. 23, 1873; *Zion's Herald,* Jan. 23, 30, February 6, 1873.

27. *Methodist Advocate,* Mar. 19, Apr. 9, May 21, 1873.

28. Minutes of the Georgia Annual Conference of the Methodist Episcopal Church, 1872, pp. 120-21; Minutes of the Alabama Conference of the M.E. Church, 1872, pp. 9-10 [typed copies at the Duke Divinity School Library]. See also *New York Christian Advocate,* Nov. 21, 1872.

29. The debate can be followed in *Methodist Advocate,* Mar. 19, Apr. 9, 23, 30, May 7, 14, 21, 28, June 11, July 9, 1873.

If you want to see the coming race in all its virile perfection, come to this city. Here is amalgamation made perfect. . . . What exquisite tints of delicate brown; what handsome features; what beautiful eyes; what graceful forms! No boorish, Hanoverian blood here, but the best Plantagenet. Here are your Pinckneys and McGills. I have met these very names in these handsome forms and faces. Here are your Rhetts, Barnwells, and Calhouns, and all other lordly bloods. The best old Beacon Street wine of humanity is theirs, and soars to the rich quality that flashes in these eyes and veins and figures.

Haven went on to commend legal interracial marriage in contrast to immoral sexual relationships which existed between whites and blacks outside the marriage bond. "Let the white gentleman make the less white lady his wife," he wrote, "and let her not degrade herself by any voluntary associations of sin." [30]

The editor of the *Holston Methodist* immediately published these quotations, adding spicy commentary. In response Haven defended his letters as a "rebuke of the anti-Christian and anti-human falsehood of caste." His long epistle, which Price printed in full, included a summation of the religious basis for Haven's racial views. "It is simply and solely whether the Bible doctrine of the absolute oneness of the human race is true or not;" he argued,

whether Christ is the Elder Brother of all humanity, or only a Brother of a proud and petty portion thereof; whether or no all came from our father and mother who lived in Eden and another father and mother who were saved in the ark. For whether we be of Ham, Japhet [*sic*], or Shem—the reputed order of their birth—it matters not, if we be all of the family of Noah. We are still cousins at the second remove, and no one is averse to that kindred as such, but the contrary rather. We are brothers in the higher relation and One in the highest.

The result of "the unity of the race" was "common, perfect and indissoluble brotherhood," Haven claimed. "We can not accept the histories of Adam and of Noah as verities, and not accept the negro as being as completely our brother as the Englishman. We can not be Christians, and not adopt, with all our hearts, this truth of truths." [31]

In addition Haven explained to Price that his letters were not written in order to condemn the South but to rebuke racial prejudice in general. "The faces of the Northern Whites, as a general fact," he admitted, "are as hard against their brothers and sisters as any in the South, and even harder." Haven granted that blacks had greater access to certain privileges in the North than in the South. There was little or no discrimination in trains and

30. *Zion's Herald*, July 24, 1873. For reactions to these statements in the papers of the Methodist Episcopal Church, South, see *Nashville Christian Advocate*, Sept. 13, Nov. 29, 1873 (as quoted in *Southwestern Christian Advocate*, Jan. 1, 1874); *New Orleans Christian Advocate*, Oct. 2, 1873; *Christian Neighbor*, Sept. 4, 1873.

31. *Holston Methodist*, Aug. 30, 1873 as quoted in *Southwestern Christian Advocate*, Sept. 4, 1873. Part of the original article, entitled "A Few Facts and Principles," is in Prentice, *Life*, pp. 420-22.

streetcars and, at least in New England, the schools were "equally impartial." But, because "most of the forms in which this evil exhibits itself are as potent in our part of the land as in the other," Haven wrote, "the North is the seat of the sin of caste as the South was the seat of the sin of slavery." He conceded that there was within the system of slavery "social intimacy without social equality" that caused some Southerners, under "the law of *'noblesse oblige' "* to treat their servants kindly and to overcome, through deep personal attachment, their racial antipathy. Haven hoped to convince Price that he was not sparing "the Northerner, especially of the Middle and Western States" whose racism was "often deeper and [was] always more detestable than that which [prevailed] in the South." [32]

By the time he began his official tour of the conferences, knowledge of Haven's racial sentiments had become so widespread that many of his fellow churchmen feared that there would be an explosion over the issue. In Tennessee the two Southern Church papers added fuel to the fire in their campaign to discredit Haven before he arrived there to meet his first conference.[33] Nevertheless, Haven refused to be intimidated, and he proceeded as he had planned. At the Holston Conference he set the pattern for the succeeding meetings. "I had concluded before these Conferences began that I would proceed impartially, as I had done in the North," he recorded in his journal. "There was great fear that I should destroy somebody or something, so I proceeded to first administer the sacrament. . . . [asking] all the presiding elders forward to assist . . . , two of [whom] were colored."

I gave them the elements before taking them myself [the account continued], so that none should say that I was not willing to do as I would have others do. The next table was all whites, the next of both sorts, and the next of ladies and others. The ice was broken at the start. The Church South ministers ridiculed our men for partaking of the sacrament with niggers, but our men defended themselves. One said, "You have taken food after niggers have chewed it, and yet you ridicule us for partaking of the Lord's Supper together."

Haven added that he cancelled "separate services" for "the colored brethren," so that worship was integrated, with the blacks occupying "one of the amen corners." At the conclusion of the conference he ordained the deacons and elders on an "alphabetical" basis, rather than separating the white from the black candidates. "A bitter caste man called them, confessing himself it was right," Haven wrote. Recognizing that this act was "a great change within a few years," he was gratified with the cooperation which he received. But Haven made few converts. The official minutes of the conference, when published, did not abandon, for example, its distinction between "members" and

---

32. *Ibid.*

33. The *Nashville Christian Advocate* joined the *Holston Methodist* in this effort. See *Methodist Advocate*, Aug. 6, Dec. 3, 1873; *Nashville Christian Advocate*, Sept. 13, 20, Oct. 4, 1873.

"colored members," despite a general conference prohibition against racial designations in official reports and statistics.[34]

At the Tennessee Conference a week later, Haven repeated the same concrete acts of ecclesiastical equality. During the meeting there were tense moments connected with his administration. An ex-slaveholder, Marion Bell, who had lived with his Negro mistress for twenty years and had fathered eight children by her, had been converted. He had taken her to Mississippi to be wed, when, after returning to Tennessee, they were prosecuted for violating state law against interracial marriage. Before the court case was tried, Bell's wife died. He joined the church, felt called to preach, and was now seeking admission to the annual conference as a ministerial member on trial. The sensitivity of most white people on the issues of amalgamation and intermarriage connected with the case made Haven's position a difficult one. Since John Braden, president of Central Tennessee College, was willing to sponsor Bell, however, Haven agreed to ask the conference to approve the application. Several of the regular members threatened to resign over the matter. The bishop told them that he would, if necessary, fill their places with someone else. Bell's opponents tabled the motion to receive him as a candidate, but Haven still gave him a supply pastorate under a Negro presiding elder. The opposition party replied that an appeal would be sent to other bishops about the action. Despite this difficulty, Haven felt that under the circumstances he got along quite well with most white ministers and that his experiment had been accepted, if reluctantly.[35]

Word of Haven's strategy preceded his visit to the Georgia Conference in Atlanta, his next stop. The white local preachers and supply pastors boycotted the sacramental service by refusing to go to the altar, by walking out, or by remaining outside. "Brother P. sat chief and stiffest through it all," Haven recorded in his journal. "It was a fearful exposure of this sin of caste in its depths. I felt it keenly, but the elders felt it worse than I. I arranged to ask Brother P. to lead the morning prayer-meeting next day, and then put him on a committee with a colored minister as chairman. He grew in grace every day, and so did the others. The house was well filled, and in the middle seats blacks and whites got badly mixed up." [36] The body adopted a report which partially approved colored conferences, though the resolution explicitly denied that the move excluded "any individual on the ground of race, color or previous condition." The actual sentiment of the white membership, how-

34. Haven's journal is quoted in Prentice, *Life*, pp. 414-15. See also his description of this conference in the *New York Christian Advocate*, Dec. 11, 1873; *Minutes of the Ninth Session of the Holston Annual Conference of the Methodist Episcopal Church, Held at Knoxville, Tenn.*, October 1st, 1873, pp. 7-8; *Methodist Advocate*, Oct. 8, 15, 1873.

35. See Haven's own account of this episode in his journal as quoted in Prentice, *Life*, pp. 415-16 and in Daniels, *Memorials of Gilbert Haven*, p. 90. His article about the conference is in *New York Christian Advocate*, Nov. 13, 1873. See also *Methodist Advocate*, Oct. 15, 1873.

36. Quoted in Prentice, *Life*, p. 416.

ever, was not that ambiguous. The conference approved the arrangement of district work according to race. The move was taken as a concession to local prejudice that had caused a decline in membership following the refusal of the general conference the previous year to grant Georgia's request for racial division. Furthermore, when C. O. Fisher, a black presiding elder, asked the members to ignore race "in conference sittings," the white clergy tabled the resolution. Responding to Haven's racial views, the Georgia Methodists also declared "that in all our conference and church relations the question of the social relation of the races, is *outside of our jurisdiction*." Clearly, as Haven noted in his journal, "caste is yet here." [37]

Of all the conferences Haven found the greatest prejudice in Alabama. Throughout his stay he was in constant disagreement with his host, a Mr. Hoge, who objected to having in his home black ministers who came to confer with the bishop. For the most part, however, Haven kept his good humor, and once turned the tables on Hoge and his family when they interrupted a mission committee meeting in the tent where the conference was being held. In jest Haven insisted that they were not allowed inside because the members were "very particular" about what company they kept. In the ordination service Haven had one of the darkest complexioned Negro ministers to assist him. Afterwards he was told that his administration had given a new dignity and confidence to the black members of the body.[38] In his published report of the conference he called attention to the significance of what had happened. "A full house attended its last session, and drank in the novel spectacle, n [sic] this country, of all men being treated as equals," he wrote.

There is yet something to be learned of this truth in the North as well as the South, and it is not unlikely the South will get her lesson learned first and best. These ordinations, in their alphabetical and proper order, assisted by all the brethren in the presiding eldership, are no small sign of a return to the first Scriptural ordination—that which separated Paul and Barnabus for their life work, in which, by direction of the Holy Ghost, one of the impositionists was "Simeon called Niger" (the "i" is pronounced short and "g" hard here, after the true classic fashion).[39]

With the Alabama Conference, Haven concluded the first part of his tour. He had gone through the middle South where there was the most tension over racial mixture in the church. In all these conferences the membership was more nearly balanced racially than elsewhere. The organization of white Methodist Episcopal churches, therefore, had been more successful in these

37. In two years the total membership of the Georgia Conference had dropped from 18,725 in 1871 to 14,676 in 1873. See Minutes of the Georgia Conference of the M.E. Church, 1871, p. 101; 1873, pp. 13, 19, 31-32. Haven's journal is quoted in Prentice, *Life*, p. 416. See also his editorial letter in *Zion's Herald*, Nov. 20, 1873.

38. See his journal as quoted in Prentice, *Life*, pp. 416-17.

39. *The Methodist*, Nov. 29, 1873; see also the previous issue, Nov. 22, 1873. Haven's biblical reference is Acts 13:1.

areas than in Florida, South Carolina, North Carolina, Louisiana, and Mississippi. If Haven could win his point in the four conferences over which he presided in the fall of 1873, his plan of ecclesiastical integration in the South had a chance. Before he completed his tour, he reflected back upon his recent experience. "I have had a great time on these four conferences," he observed in his journal.

Holston got it (that is, negro equality) before they knew it. Tennessee was mad, fearfully, but will get over it. Georgia took it easier, but not easily; and Alabama was stunned. The idea of negro equality had never got in there. They looked on them as pious mules. But I put through my alphabetic ordinations, and asking black presiding elders to assist in ordaining white ministers; and it was like an electric shock to an ox—he don't know why, or where, or what, except he is immensely stirred up.[40]

Actually, Haven was a little surprised that the reaction to his impartial administration was not more severe. "There have been some amusing instances of fears lest the whole social fabric would be turned topsy-turvy if any variation from the dead letter of the past caste was indulged in," he commented in his report from Alabama. " 'Strange horrors seized them, and pangs unfelt before,' at this dread possibility. But nobody found any chance to indulge the fears he feared, and the Church moves on her way, meeting all together in love and labor and life." [41]

Meanwhile, during the fall conference sessions, Nelson Cobleigh had been busy writing in his Atlanta paper to calm some of the more nervous churchmen who imagined the worst consequences of Haven's actions. He took pains to declare that "the Methodist Episcopal Church does not propose to meddle with either social or political questions in the South or elsewhere when no moral or religious principles are involved." He referred particularly to the issue of amalgamation, which had been emphasized so consistently by Southern Methodist papers. In answer, Cobleigh stated the covert feelings of most white Methodists, though there was not, nor had there ever been, any explicit church legislation on the matter. "The Methodist Episcopal Church," he asserted, "has always, both in theory and practice, been opposed to 'amalgamation,' as talked about by the M.E. Church, South." Apparently Cobleigh did not sense that he was violating his own principle of neutrality by giving this opinion as if it was the official position of his denomination.[42]

In November, Cobleigh breathed a sigh of relief that the conferences had proceeded peaceably and that dire predictions of a gigantic disruption in the church had proved false. He gave a candid report of Haven's work and reaction to it, denying that the bishop was "such a firebrand as our enemies have represented him."

40. Quoted in Daniels, *Memorials of Gilbert Haven*, p. 91.
41. *The Methodist*, Nov. 29, 1873.
42. *Methodist Advocate*, Oct. 15, 1873. See Haven's exchange with Cobleigh over the nature of the mission of the Methodist Episcopal Church in the South in issues for Oct. 1, 8, 1873.

He is genial and approachable, ready to hear all sides and to decide all questions according to his best judgment under the circumstances. He has decided opinions, and thorough convictions on all the vital questions at issue in our work. He does not disguise his sentiments, but on all suitable occasions frankly avows them. He does not attempt, however, to force his opinions upon any person who may differ from him. As he claims the right to hold and speak freely his own convictions, so, as a Christian gentleman, he accords the same right to others. This he has always done, this he will ever do. None need to fear his presence, nor dread his authority. Like the rest of his brethren, he seeks the good of the church, knowing as well as any other one that "united we stand, divided we fall."

Before he finished his editorial, on the other hand, Cobleigh reiterated his earlier assertion that the Methodist Episcopal Church had no calling "to dabble in politics or to intermeddle with social questions." He chose his words carefully, for he intended as much to warn Haven as to calm some of the dissenters against the new anticaste policy. He reminded everyone, including the bishop, that the *Discipline* of the church was the guide for all policy, and he cautioned against "new departures except in an increase of zeal and diligence, of devotion and love for the divine Master and his holy cause." [43]

But to request Haven to isolate his religious concerns from the social and political aspects of the race problem was to ask him to surrender the fundamental commitment of his whole life. He did not respond directly to Cobleigh's statements, but not long afterwards he wrote of his dedication to "ethical Christianity" in a way that revealed, by implication at least, his essential disagreement with the Atlanta editor. He criticized exclusive concern for either "the post-mortem salvation" or "the ante-mortem," since "both belong together." He emphasized the historical responsibility of the church, "to renew the earth as well as to people Heaven. Every true reform, therefore," he argued, "should have its most powerful advocates in the Church, and the Church journals should be their foremost supporters." But Haven knew how great the resistance to such a view was. "When one speaks of such reform," he wrote, "immediately some journal of ecclesiasticism more than of Christ . . . cries out: 'That is ahead of the age.' 'That is for the millennial times, but not for these.' 'That is disturbing church and community with radicalism.'" Against this timid conservatism and complacency Haven was scornful. "As if radicalism in righteousness is not meant to disturb communities," he asserted, "and as if it was not our duty to bring on the millennial age, and to be ahead of this age as we lead to that." From his now-familiar millennial faith, then, he continued to press for closer interracial harmony in the Methodist Episcopal Church in the South and to call for Christian devotion to work for equal rights and brotherhood through all possible means. [44]

43. *Methodist Advocate*, Nov. 5, 1873.
44. *The Independent*, Feb. 26, 1874.

The sessions of the Florida and the two Carolina conferences at which Haven presided early in 1874 went off without incident.[45] At the same time reaction among whites in his denomination against an equalitarian policy became more and more vocal. The editorial war conducted in the papers of the Methodist Episcopal Church, South, was taking its toll. Southern Bishop John C. Keener, for example, viewed with some satisfaction the tensions within the Methodist Episcopal Church in Tennessee after Haven's experiment in ecclesiastical integration. He thanked the Holston editor, Price, for his part in keeping the issues before the people. "The affiliation of our Northern brethren with that rare ebony, mahogany and chocolate-colored civilization, and which so enthuses the Boston bishop, is not shared very heartily by his less ardent Anglo-Saxon co-laborers," Keener remarked with cynical sarcasm. "The Holston *Methodist* is doing a work here that other church papers do not seem equal to. It is full of live issues, and the editor is not afraid to call things by their right names, which to me is always a comfort. It will limit and define the range of the Methodist Episcopal Church as illustrated by its representatives in eastern Tennessee." [46] Price himself made no pretensions about why he attacked Haven. "Our Northern Methodist friends are pretty certain to have trouble on this question [of racial equality]," he wrote. "Let all of them who desire to have peace come over to the Methodist Episcopal Church, South where there will probably be no trouble on the subject." [47] A Southern Methodist from Alabama, Anson West, likewise predicted the demise of the Methodist Episcopal conference in that territory if Haven kept insisting on his "theory of social equality and amalgamation." [48]

During the six months after Haven's southern excursion, the volume of the reaction against racial mixture in the church signified that the bishop had very little support for his views. Most of those who endorsed his no-caste position were black Methodists or whites who worked among Negroes. Of the church press, only the *Southwestern Christian Advocate* in New Orleans and the short-lived *Southeastern Christian Advocate* in Orangeburg, South Carolina, consistently backed Haven.[49] The Atlanta *Advocate,* placed again under the supervision of Erasmus Fuller following the death of Nelson Cobleigh early in 1874, reported the various viewpoints, but, as before,

45. *New York Christian Advocate,* Feb. 5, 19, 26, Mar. 5, 1874; see Haven's accounts of these conferences in *The Methodist,* Feb. 21, 1874; *Zion's Herald,* Mar. 12, 19, 1874. William George Matton, a white presiding elder in the North Carolina Conference, has a record of Haven's administration at the 1874 session in his manuscript memoirs, ch. 10, pp. 2-4, Matton Papers, Duke University Library. See also, *Methodist Advocate,* Jan. 21, 28, 1874.
46. *New Orleans Christian Advocate,* Nov. 6, 1873.
47. Quoted in *Zion's Herald,* Oct. 9, 1873; see also *Methodist Advocate,* Dec. 10, 1873; Jan. 21, 1874.
48. *Nashville Christian Advocate,* Nov. 15, 1873; see also Dec. 6, 1873; Jan. 10, 1874; *Methodist Advocate,* Dec. 10, 1873.
49. *Southwestern Christian Advocate,* Sept. 4, Nov. 20, 1873; Jan. 1, July 2, 1874. No extant issues of the *Southeastern Christian Advocate* have been found, but see *ibid.,* Nov. 5, 1874.

its editor had no sympathy with Haven's position. Arguing that the attempt to mix churches and conferences was "a complete failure," he gave details of losses among white members who believed rumors, based on Haven's published statements, that Negro preachers would be appointed to white congregations. As a solution Fuller called for local option to settle racial policy in the churches throughout the South.[50]

A few of Haven's fellow Methodists in the South refused to believe that he really held the views which were attributed to him.[51] Some of his opponents who were openly hostile defected from the denomination. Of those who disagreed with him, however, the majority remained, saluted Haven's abilities, and agreed to follow his leadership in all other respects; but they openly disavowed his racial views. They insisted that Haven's position was merely his individual opinion and was not representative of the denomination. In one of his frequent discussions of racial policy in the church, W. C. Graves stated that Haven knew and acknowledged that his views "[were] not entertained by the Methodist Episcopal Church in the North" and that "in the South there [was] scarcely a man, woman, or child in the Methodist Episcopal Church that would subscribe to some of his singular notions."[52]

There was a more subtle form of dissent from Haven's radicalism. James Mitchell, for example, defended the bishop's call for legal marriage in place of illicit relationships between the two races. In the process, however, he declared that "the religion of Christ" did not intend "to enforce any carnal assimilation of races." "It is the impure and unholy that have produced mixed races," Mitchell argued, and "in the sections of the land where there is a pure Christian morality, and the greatest freedom of choice, the white and colored races do not mix." His presupposition of the superiority of "pure" to mixed races was quite different from Haven's continued appeal to "the unity of the human race."[53]

In a number of ways Haven tried to overcome the prejudices which his colleagues in the South held against him. He exerted himself considerably to visit all parts of the episcopal area, despite his responsibility to hold conferences in other, sometimes distant sections of the country. As a guest in white as well as Negro schools, he commended the work and urged their support, though he often added a passing remark that he hoped for a time when all schools would recognize no distinction of color.[54] In personal relations Haven's sense of humor and genial personality often won the af-

50. *Methodist Advocate,* May 13, 1874. Other Methodists made the same argument in that issue and the one for June 10, 1874.

51. For two examples see *ibid.,* Feb. 18, 1874.

52. *Ibid.,* Jan. 7, 1874. For similar statements see issues for Dec. 10, 1873; June 17, Sept. 2, 1874; *New York Christian Advocate,* Feb. 5, 1874.

53. *Methodist Advocate,* Apr. 22, 1874. Nonetheless, Mitchell wrote a perceptive article on "the pride of race" the following week, Apr. 29, 1874.

54. *Ibid.,* Feb. 11, Mar. 11, June 3, July 22, 1874; June 9, Dec. 29, 1875; Mar. 15, 1876; *Zion's Herald,* July 16, 1874.

fection of his most outspoken opponents, even though they rarely altered their racial views.[55] As he traveled about, dedicating churches and schools, visiting camp meetings and district conferences, preaching and lecturing, Haven won the praise of the southern secular press as well as the regard of his own people so long as he refrained from touching the sensitive issue.[56] Because he would not compromise in act or word on that question, he continued to be an embarrassment to many of his fellow churchmen even as they honored his capacities and appreciated his labors in their behalf.

II

Besides his beliefs and actions concerning racial relations in the church, Haven's public stance on civil rights and Reconstruction became an additional source of contention within his denomination and throughout the South. His correspondence to the religious press provided a running commentary on southern racial affairs. He told his readers of the practical effects of the "color line" which operated in much of southern society. His extensive travels gave him firsthand acquaintance with colored passenger rooms in Chattanooga and Danville and with the "colored car" on railroads in Virginia, North Carolina, and Georgia. Sometimes he had to separate, for instance, from a black traveling companion like C. O. Fisher, the presiding elder from Savannah. On such occasions Haven had to ask permission from the conductor to visit his ministerial colleague. Once he was forced out of the Jim Crow car where he was conversing with a friend. After the incident, Haven wrote, "I vowed to the Lord that I would not rest till that brother could come and ride by me." He was especially incensed when the "colored car" was used as a smoker by the whites and when Negroes were crowded into a separate car despite empty seats in the white section of the train.[57]

In some southern hotels and restaurants Haven found the same evidence of caste. He noted in Vicksburg, Mississippi, "the foolish attempt to avoid civil rights by putting 'Private Boarding' over the door of hotels, and 'Private Parlor' over ice cream saloons." [58] In the Mississippi state capital he broke the "color line" in a hotel dining room, though not without some difficulty. The waiter prepared to serve Haven and his black clerical companion, but at the sideboard rather than in the regular dining room. After the bishop insisted on being treated like the other customers, the proprietor ordered

55. *Methodist Advocate*, Jan. 21, Feb. 18, Mar. 18, Apr. 15, June 17, 1874; Mar. 24, July 28, 1875; *New York Christian Advocate*, Mar. 19, 1874.
56. *Atlanta Constitution*, Mar. 9, 1873; *Atlanta Daily Herald*, June 11, June 12, 1873; Feb. 16, 1875 as quoted in *Methodist Advocate*, Mar. 3, 1875; *Chattanooga Commercial* as quoted in *Zion's Herald*, Oct. 9, 1873; *Knoxville Whig and Chronicle* as quoted in *Methodist Advocate*, June 23, 1875. See also *New York Christian Advocate*, June 26, 1873; Feb. 26, 1874; *Methodist Advocate*, Oct. 15, 1873; Mar. 11, 25, July 22, 1874; Feb. 3, Mar. 3, 1875.
57. *Zion's Herald*, Jan. 23, 1873; Aug. 6, 1874; *New York Christian Advocate*, June 19, 1873; *The Independent*, Mar. 26, Aug. 13, 1874; *Methodist Advocate*, Apr. 22, 1874; Prentice, *Life*, p. 445.
58. *Zion's Herald*, July 3, 1873; *The Independent*, Mar. 26, 1874.

regular service for the two guests.[59] In his discussion of such incidents Haven usually seized the occasion to make a point to his fellow Methodists by linking racial discrimination in society to the spirit of caste so evident in the church.[60]

Haven's accounts of discrimination in public accommodations in the South coincided with the congressional reconsideration of a national civil rights bill. In December, 1873, as he had done insistently since May, 1870, Charles Sumner introduced such a measure, though because of poor health that foreshadowed his death, he was not able to give much leadership toward passage of the legislation. The possibilities of some kind of bill were better than ever, particularly after President Grant suggested in his annual message for 1873 the need of "a law to better secure the civil rights which freedom should secure, but has not effectively secured, to the enfranchised slave." Blacks and the old-guard abolitionists likewise called for congressional action to meet that need.[61]

Haven hoped that two leaders from his native state, Benjamin Butler in the House, and Senator Sumner, despite his feeble health, would champion the civil rights bill. He had long ago forgiven Sumner for not backing Grant in 1872, especially after he had not himself voted for the Republican, but for the Prohibition, party candidates.[62] But Sumner died on March 11, 1874, pleading from his deathbed that the civil rights bill be passed.[63] At the time Haven was in the South where he joined blacks who mourned the senator's passing. He attended, for example, one service at a black school, Shaw University in Raleigh, North Carolina. Later that summer he delivered a eulogy for Sumner at a gathering in Boston, which effort was one of his more effective public addresses.[64] With others Haven asked that the senator be honored by "the passage of the [civil rights] bill making the declaration of Jefferson complete in the legislation of Sumner—the Equality of all men before the Law [which] phrase was his watchword through life." In an article for *The Independent,* he asked rhetorically,

Will we rear [Sumner's] true monument? Enact civil rights. Will we carve his perfect statue? Enact civil rights. He was himself careful to get provisions into the amendments that covered this power, so that no court, nor state, nor statesman

59. Prentice, *Life*, pp. 444-45; *Methodist Advocate*, May 19, 1875.

60. For one of many examples, see *Methodist Advocate*, Apr. 22, 1874.

61. Richardson, ed., *Messages and Papers of the Presidents* (1912), vol. VI, p. 4209; J. McPherson, "Abolitionists and the Civil Rights Act of 1875," *Journal of American History*, 52 (1965), 504; L. E. Murphy, "The Civil Rights Law of 1875," *Journal of Negro History*, 12, (1927), 114, 117; Donald, *Charles Sumner* (1970), pp. 531-40, 562-63, 579-80.

62. *The Independent*, Feb. 26, 1874; *Springfield Daily Republican* (Mass.), Dec. 15, 1875. Apparently Haven was not fully aware of the considerable tensions that existed between Sumner and Butler. See Donald, *Charles Sumner* (1970), pp. 565-77, 581-83.

63. Donald, *Charles Sumner* (1970), pp. 586-87.

64. *Methodist Advocate*, Apr. 22, Aug. 26, 1874; *Zion's Herald*, Apr. 23, 1874; *The Independent*, Mar. 26, 1874; Jan. 31, 1878; William George Matton's memoirs, ch. 10, p. 3. Haven's "The Very Chiefest of Our Statesmen," his eulogy for Sumner, is in William M. Cornell, ed., *Charles Sumner: Memoir and Eulogies* (Boston, 1874), pp. 41-83.

should presume to question it. But he did not live to see it wrought into a statute. Shall he live in that statute? Only thus will he perfectly live.[65]

For the first time since he began to write for the paper twelve years before, Haven found himself disagreeing over the pending legislation with *The Independent's* editor and publisher, Henry C. Bowen. Adopting essentially a states' rights position, Bowen insisted that he favored racial integration, but he believed that the federal government had no constitutional power to prevent individuals from discriminating against Negroes. In a commentary on Haven's articles which cited the need of civil rights for southern blacks, he wrote of "the unwise and unconstitutional attempt to relieve their wrongs by national legislation." [66] Against Bowen, Haven appealed to the Declaration of Independence and insisted that advocates of equal rights could not wait upon persuasion to influence the separate states to abolish "unequal legislation." He wrote, "Law alone abolishes a seated evil. Moral suasion never killed so much as a mosquito sin." [67]

From the opening of the discussion Haven called for a national law, citing the need for its application in New York and Ohio as well as in the South. He attacked the Ohio Supreme Court for its unanimous decision declaring "separate but equal" school facilities constitutional, and thus denying the right of a child to go to the school of the parent's choice.[68] Most of his examples of the need for new legislation, however, came out of his southern experience. He pointed to some of the absurd situations to which Negroes were subjected because of differences in civil rights laws among the various states. In railroad travel, for example, black passengers could remain in integrated cars in states which had equal rights legislation like Florida, South Carolina, Mississippi, Louisiana. But as soon as the train crossed over into states where no civil rights law was in force, as in Georgia, North Carolina, and Tennessee, they had to go to the "colored cars." [69]

The part of the civil rights bill which came under greatest attack in the South was the section which prohibited segregated schools. Southern educators declared that the law would destroy the system of public education which had grown up in the region after the war. The underlying cause of southern sentiment was clear. It was the view that the legislation attempted to force the social equality of the races. On this matter Bowen and Haven clashed again. The editor maintained that prejudice could not be corrected by legislative coercion, and that Congress had no right to assume jurisdiction over

65. *The Independent*, Mar. 26, 1874.
66. *Ibid.*, Aug. 13, 1874. See also Feb. 5, 19, 26, June 4, 1874; McPherson, "Abolitionists and the Civil Rights Act of 1875," pp. 504-5.
67. *The Independent*, Feb. 26, 1874. Benjamin T. Tanner saluted "the glorious Bishop Haven" for his articles exposing segregation in public places and in transportation and for his support of the civil rights bill. See *Christian Recorder*, Feb. 26, Mar. 5, 1874.
68. *New York Christian Advocate*, Dec. 11, 1873; *The Independent*, Feb. 26, 1874.
69. *The Independent*, Feb. 26, Aug. 13, 1874.

the public schools.[70] Haven's Atlanta colleague, Fuller, took a similar stand, claiming that separate schools were better than no schools at all. His long-standing disagreement with Haven over racial equality emerged in his discussion of the issue. "We do not hesitate to say that we believe it would be better for every public school in the South to be discontinued forever than that the children of both races should be thus thrown promiscuously together through all the land at this time," he wrote.

If the moral and elevating forces now in operation can continue for a generation or two, with both races as separate as is practicable to keep them, another state of things will be brought about. . . . This is not a question of color, or caste, or prejudice, but of propriety, or more, of morals, and he who thinks only of "color" or prejudice in the case is as far from an apprehension of the underlying philosophy of these embarrassments as an impracticable, abstract idea well can be from a practicable good.[71]

Haven did not believe that the southern threat to close all public schools would be carried out, though he added, "Perhaps they had better be ruined than perpetually to train little children and youth to abhor each other who have no natural antipathies." [72] He praised the integrated school system in New Orleans where "that terrible bugaboo of mixed schools is practically settled." The Louisiana school law, he claimed, had ended friction in that state. "Now, if no harm can come of such a law in New Orleans, how can it elsewhere?" he asked Fuller and Bowen.

There never was a more foolish fear than that which dreads the education of all the children in the same school. They are utterly without prejudice. No child even dreams of this devil existing even, much less of tempting him. Every Southern child, in the old times as well as the new, is thus born free from caste. Separate schools enslave them. May that cruel yoke be broken from our children's necks! [73]

Once again Haven had taken a minority point of view. The Civil Rights Act, passed in 1875 by a lame duck session of Congress, made no mention of discrimination in education. That provision was forced out so that the law could be enacted.[74] Despite the "very cowardly" concession, Haven was glad to have "the Civil Rights Bill in part," even though the law was virtually a dead letter from the first.[75] Eight years later the United States Supreme Court ruled its major provisions to be unconstitutional. Upon its

70. *Ibid.*, June 4, 1874.
71. *Methodist Advocate*, June 3, 1874; see also Apr. 29, May 20, June 10, Sept. 16, 1874. George R. Crooks of *The Methodist* (June 20, 1874) agreed with Fuller, but Joseph C. Hartzell of the *Southwestern Advocate* (May 7, June 18, 1874) argued vigorously in behalf of equal rights. See also Tanner's debate over civil rights with Fuller in *Christian Recorder*, July 2, 23, Aug. 27, 1874.
72. *The Independent,* Feb. 26, 1874.
73. *New York Christian Advocate*, July 2, 1874. The *Atlanta Constitution* (July 5, 1874) attacked Haven for this essay.
74. *Methodist Advocate*, June 24, 1874. See McPherson, "Abolitionists and the Civil Rights Act of 1875," pp. 507-8; Kelly, "The Congressional Controversy over School Segregation," pp. 537-63.
75. Prentice, *Life*, p. 441.

passage, Fuller assured his readers that he had not come over to Haven's side, even though he had talked as if he supported the bill without the school clause. Commenting on the violence of a white mob which expelled a Negro from an Atlanta theater, he wrote that "the social equality scare is consummate nonsense. No one is so stupid as to wish to regulate social affairs by law. The law ought to protect all, however, in the enjoyment of their rights. This it must do, leaving social relations to regulate themselves." [76]

But Haven's refusal to let social relations regulate themselves was the chief issue being contended between his white Methodist associates and himself. He was consistent in that he did not ask others to practice what he refused to do. His ecclesiastical business brought him into homes of Negroes as a guest, and he welcomed and publicly complimented their entertainment.[77] One occasion of a racially integrated social affair was widely reported, after the *Atlanta Constitution* featured the story. Haven and his daughter Mary were dinner guests of Dr. Badger, a distinguished Negro dentist, who afterward took the couple for a drive in the city. The Atlanta paper interviewed the host to confirm the account, and perhaps also to warn Badger against another such breach of the etiquette of southern segregation. Its story appeared replete with five separate headlines:

NOTABLE INAUGURATION OF THE SOCIAL FEATURE.

Living up to Principle, or, Reducing
Theory to Practice.

The Glory and Bliss of an Atlanta Darkey.

A Methodist Bishop and Daughter Dine
with a Colored Family at their Residence.

A Sumptuous Affair, Generous Entertainment,
Conversations, Incidents, A Ride, Etc.

Despite the obvious sarcasm of the headlines and in the content of the article, the reporter actually paid tribute to Haven for his consistency. "The Bishop has evidently eclipsed his Northern rivals," he wrote. "He is far ahead of the most rabid of the social equality howlers, or civil righters,

76. *Methodist Advocate*, Mar. 17, 1875.
77. *Ibid.*, Apr. 23, 1873; July 14, 1875; *Zion's Herald*, Oct. 16, 1873; Aug. 6, 20, 1874; *New York Christian Advocate*, July 2, 1874; Feb. 17, 24, 1876.

which means almost the same, but who are fonder of preaching than practicing. The Bishop has shown his faith by his works." [78] More than a year later the southern secular press was still referring to Haven as "the old rapscallion who preaches in Atlanta and allows his daughters [sic] to ride out with buck niggers." [79]

Haven's equalitarian views and practices were such disturbing elements in his own denomination that one layman inquired whether there was not "a new test of membership" for the church. The writer reported that many of his friends had gotten the impression that they should leave the Methodist Episcopal Church because they were not willing to associate "with the colored people in school and Church gatherings." Fuller replied to the inquirer that there was no such test, and to express his evident weariness of controversy which Haven kept stirring up, he wrote, "All who love God and keep his commandments may be received into the Methodist Episcopal Church without respect to their particular notions on any outside questions, and the sooner we understand the Church has no control over one's social relations or his opinions concerning them, the better." [80]

Late in 1874, the first organized opposition to Haven's views and actions began to emerge. The Morristown District of the Holston Conference adopted a resolution, a part of which was aimed specifically at the bishop. It stated that the "Conference [denied] any intention of favoring the doctrine of social equality with the colored people, . . . [believing] that the most sensible portion of the colored people [did not] desire any such thing." With Haven in mind the churchmen also announced, "we can not indorse [sic] the views of any man, whatever his official position may be in our Church, who would or does advocate the mixing up of white and colored people, either in their worshiping assemblies or in the schools of our country." [81] Even though the annual conference was still stalemated in 1874 about the viability of continuing on a "mixed" basis, Georgia Methodists likewise repeated their disavowal of Haven's equal rights philosophy which had passed the previous session, disclaiming "jurisdiction" on "the question of the social relation of the races." [82]

Closely connected with Haven's civil rights position was his public defense of radical Reconstruction and his persistent warning to the North that Dixie politicians were making a power play to recover at the ballot box what they had lost on the battlefield. Haven's political views, therefore, further prevented his acceptance in the South. The outcry against him was not so

78. *Atlanta Constitution*, June 16, 1874. See also June 21, July 5, 1874; and Prentice, *Life*, pp. 431-33; *Zion's Herald*, July 2, 1874; *New York Christian Advocate*, July 2, 1874; *Nashville Christian Advocate*, July 11, 1874; *Southwestern Christian Advocate*, July 2, 1874.
79. *Savannah News* as quoted in *Methodist Advocate*, Aug. 18, 1875.
80. *Methodist Advocate*, Oct. 7, 1874.
81. *Ibid.*, Dec. 2, 1874.
82. *Ibid.*, Oct. 28, 1874.

much within his own denomination, however, since many members of the Methodist Episcopal Church were loyal Republicans. But whatever was lacking in criticism from his own constituents was compensated for by a constant barrage against Haven in the southern secular and religious press. The papers seemed to complete to see which could villify the bishop the most thoroughly. He earned such epithets as "a rancid old ecclesiastical goatherd," "a red mouth, miscegenating, ranting, howling hypocrite," and a "hell-roaring, bloodhound of Zion, the great negro-squeezing Bishop Haven." The *Atlanta Daily Constitution* once called him an "old negro-affiliating political preacher and shameless propagandist of every radicalism." Even southern Baptist and Presbyterian denominational journals joined the onslaught.[83]

During the first two years of his southern residence, Haven visited several of the state legislatures, including Louisiana and South Carolina where the last of the radical governments were still in power.[84] They had become the chief focal points of the continuing Reconstruction controversy. In Louisiana he met publicized Governor P. B. S. Pinchback whose character, Haven acknowledged, was "much" and "justly debated." Even as he saluted the governor's ability, the bishop admitted that the charges of corruption against him and the legislature could probably be substantiated. Nonetheless he offered a defense of Louisiana reconstruction, declaring that the opposition of "the New Orleans old *regime* [was] not at all corruption." The real bone of contention was "because 'the nigger' in this political wrestle is atop." The current political corruption was "bad enough," Haven recognized, but not worse than that of the former Democratic administrations in the state. The blacks had "the votes" and "the offices," and they did "some swindling." "But," Haven explained, "they had been swindled out of all their wages, their wives, their children, themselves, for all their lives, and from the inherited wealth which they would have had but for a like swindling of their fathers and father's fathers. They know that the men that robbed them would rerob them today, had they the power." Moreover, the blacks were willing to cooperate with "their former masters, but they [would] not. They oppose them at every turn," Haven claimed.

83. Daniels, *Memorials of Gilbert Haven*, pp. 87-88, 96; Prentice, *Life*, p. 442; *Zion's Herald*, Jan. 6, 1876. See also *Rome Courier* (Ga.), as quoted in *New York Herald*, Dec. 19, 1875; *Atlanta Constitution*, June 19, 22, Dec. 29, 1875; *Macon Messenger* (Ga.) as quoted in *Methodist Advocate*, July 14, 1875; *Savannah News* as quoted in *Zion's Herald*, Sept. 2, 1875; *Atlanta Herald*, Sept. 1, 1874; *Gadsden Times* (Ala.), as quoted in *Methodist Advocate*, Dec. 9, 1874; *Southern Christian Advocate*, Feb. 4, 18, Sept. 30, 1874; *Richmond Christian Advocate*, Feb. 26, 1874; *Nashville Christian Advocate*, June 8, 22, 1872; Sept. 13, Oct. 4, 25, Nov. 1, Dec. 6, 1873; Jan. 10, June 27, Sept. 26, Oct. 10, 1874; Feb. 27, Nov. 20, 1875; *New Orleans Christian Advocate*, Sept. 3, Oct. 29, 1874; Feb. 25, 1875; *Alabama Baptist*, Sept. 8, Nov. 17, 1874; Feb. 9, 1875; *Christian Index*, Oct. 29, 1874; *Methodist Advocate*, Sept. 30, 1874; July 7, 1875; *Presbyterian* as quoted in *The Independent*, Sept. 9, 1875.

84. He also visited the Virginia legislature in the latter part of 1872. *Zion's Herald*, Jan. 9, 1873.

They will not grant them an ounce more than the law compels. They will not allow them all that, if they can help it. They refuse to let their children enter the high school, though required to do so by law. They grant them no seats in their churches, no entrance into halls and hotels and restaurants, when they can yet keep them out. They still persist in the old feelings, without any of the old power that accompanied it. They abuse the government of the nation and fill the leading papers of the city with their cries.[85]

Haven's opinion of the South Carolina reconstruction program was an even more enthusiastic endorsement than his defense of Louisiana. Writing just as leading northern journalists had stepped up a campaign to expose the "Negro-Carpetbag" regimes of the South, Haven spoke of South Carolina as "the observed state." He defended the radical government there because of its fundamental commitment to equal rights. He believed that South Carolina in 1874 was "the first state in the Union in the three-fold essentials for human progress—life, liberty, and rightful opportunity." He vigorously denied that it was "the prostrate state," as charged by James Shepherd Pike, whose book by that title played such an influential role in convincing the North of the injustice of radical Reconstruction.[86] "True, the men of color rule;" Haven wrote,

but does that make it prostrate? True, taxes are heavy, trade and production is low, thieves in the government circles exist; but all these together do not prostrate a state. Only one of them can—political dishonesty. But was New York a prostrate state, if Tweed ruled from Albany? Did some shrewd writer and journals, that had brought on the party sovereignty that had broke out in this one grievous sore, demand the over-throw of that party because of that burden? There is a vital difference between pruning a rotten branch and cutting up a tree by the roots.

There was no way to convince Haven that for all the problems of South Carolina reconstructionism, "this tree of emancipation [was] rotten," and that counterrevolution was the only remedy. "Is South Carolina a proof of the folly, if not the wickedness, of all the preaching and praying and voting and fighting for human rights and personal liberty, that God has heard and helped in this last generation?" he asked. "It is, if these dolorous doomsmen [like Pike] are authority."[87]

The crucial factor in Haven's defense of South Carolina Republican rule was the improved status of the Negro. He called attention to the marked contrast "in the manner and spirit of the colored men" in that state compared with Georgia, where the southern Democrats had ended Reconstruction

85. *The Independent*, Jan. 23, 1873. Another account of this visit is in *Methodist Advocate*, Jan. 15, 1873. For a reaction of the Southern Methodist paper in Louisiana, see *New Orleans Christian Advocate*, Feb. 6, 1873. See also *New York Christian Advocate*, Jan. 23, 1873.
86. James S. Pike, *The Prostrate State. South Carolina under Negro Government* (New York, 1874). See also Robert Franklin Durden, *James Shepherd Pike. Republicanism and the American Negro, 1850-1882* (Durham: Duke University Press, 1957).
87. *The Independent*, Mar. 12, 1874; *Zion's Herald*, Mar. 12, 1874.

in 1871.[88] "In the one [state] he moves as if depressed and timid and scared; in the other as if free," the bishop wrote. In South Carolina there were better educational and business opportunities for blacks, greater free speech and broader political participation, as well as more equal public accommodations. Neither did South Carolina Negroes, Haven observed, enjoy these freedoms in order to insult their white neighbors. "The man of color does not prevent his whiter brother [from] enjoying every privilege he himself possesses," he wrote. For all these reasons Haven differed with the critics of the radical government. "From much observation in many parts of this commonwealth, and much conversation with many leaders in church and state," he confessed, "I am still ready to defend the ideas which are here bearing their best fruit." To northern readers, he pleaded, "Believe, then, in South Carolina." "This state," he declared, "is right side up, if it is bottom side up, and only needs a purification in its present direction, as all States always do, even if right in aim, and not a substitution of opposing elements that are more corrupt in principle, and not less so in practice." [89]

Of the rest of the South, politically, Haven had few words of praise. He considered only South Carolina and Louisiana, and to a lesser extent, Florida, Alabama, and Mississippi, the only remaining "free states" in Dixie.[90] The return of former rebels to leadership in other states, in Haven's view, was a dangerous threat to the security of the nation. He decried the crusade in the northern press against South Carolina and Louisiana, calling its tendency "the general surrender in whole or in part of the Northern mind to the Georgia [that is, Democratic] domination," which, he warned, would "bring forth fatal fruit." Haven predicted, "It may lead to a recapture by the captured of the whole result of the war. It is the set purpose of the old South to recover what it has lost—the government of the nation; and to recover this without any more surrender of their old claims than is possible." [91] On another occasion Haven was more specific about the designs of southern Democrats, offering a domino theory of the failure of Reconstruction. "They must first reconquer their own territory," he declared in *The Independent.*

This is two-thirds done. Texas and Arkansas have just surrendered. The last was evenly divided a year ago; now it rolls up over seventy thousand on the old side. Is there such a change? No; but the negroes and the [white] Union men dare not vote. Tennessee is gone; North Carolina will make no such fight this year as

88. For Haven's criticism of the overthrow of Reconstruction in Georgia, see *Zion's Herald,* Nov. 13, 1873; Aug. 6, 1874.

89. *The Methodist,* Feb. 21, 1874; *The Independent,* Mar. 12, Aug. 6, 13, 1874.

90. *The Independent,* Mar. 26, Aug. 6, 1874; *The Methodist,* June 28, 1873.

91. *The Independent,* Aug. 6, 1874; *Zion's Herald,* Feb. 18, 1875; Mar. 2, 1876. On the changing public opinion in the North about Reconstruction see James M. McPherson, "Coercion or Conciliation? Abolitionists Debate President Hayes's Southern Policy," *New England Quarterly,* 39 (1966), 475-78; and "The Antislavery Legacy: From Reconstruction to the NAACP," in Barton Bernstein, ed., *Towards a New Past: Dissenting Essays in American History* (New York: Random House, 1968), pp. 128-37.

last. It will fall. Virginia has disappeared. They are determined to conquer the rest, and then they will proceed, as of old, to split the North and rule and ruin afresh the country for they mean nothing else.[92]

As he looked ahead to the elections of 1874 and 1876, Haven believed that a showdown between the conflicting factions in the South was imminent. It was imperative, he complained bitterly, "to awaken the North to a sense of the perils in her Southern section" and cease "crying peace, hugging her defiant enemies to her breast and heaping up epithets against those who are her true and faithful friends." He attacked those who spoke of "ignorant suffrage" in the South as if blacks were the only ones who could not read, and as if voting for the preservation of "the Union and her liberties" were not more important than literacy. Desperately he hoped that at least South Carolina could be saved and become the new base for a fresh effort in Reconstruction. "Let her be purged of her errors without destroying her truths," he argued. "If she sinks, there is a dark and awful night to all this region. If she stands all will be raised up to her lofty level." [93]

When outbreaks of mob violence and increased intimidation of Negroes brought the South to the brink of anarchy in 1874 and 1875, Haven was more than ever concerned for the future of the radical governments. Southern whites, banding together in politico-military movements known by various titles, were determined to restore Democratic rule whatever the cost. A number of bloody battles against blacks and their white sympathizers paved the way for a political take-over. Major conflicts occurred in New Orleans (August–September, 1873), in Vicksburg (December, 1874, and July, 1875), and in two other Mississippi towns, Yazoo City and Clinton (September, 1875). Conservatives in Mississippi gained an upper hand through a most effective technique of political violence called the "Shotgun Plan" that drove the last Republicans from office and became a model for later conservative counterreconstruction movements in South Carolina and Louisiana.[94] The southern Democratic press featured every indication of racial conflict in apocalyptic terms, spreading huge headlines on their front pages about "The War of Races," "The Negro War," "The Race War," and the like.[95] One South Carolina paper, late in 1875, put the alternatives bluntly. "There is no more room for soft talk in this matter," its editor announced. "We must say to the colored race: Give way or die!" [96] The papers also supported economic repression in order to subject Negroes to a state of serfdom. Atlanta's leading daily, for instance, endorsed a plan to hire only white laborers for all jobs except the most menial, in order to drive the blacks back to "their old ante-

92. *The Independent,* Aug. 13, 1874.
93. *Ibid.*
94. Otis A. Singletary, *Negro Militia and Reconstruction* (New York: McGraw-Hill Book Co., 1963), pp. 74-79, 81-99, 129-44.
95. For examples see *Atlanta Constitution* in the summer and fall of 1874.
96. *Greenville News* (S.C.), as quoted in the *Atlanta Constitution,* Dec. 22, 1875.

bellum employments, in which they would be comparatively harmless." [97]

The southern situation greatly troubled Haven. Almost in despair he sighed, "How slow [are] the steps of liberty!" [98] During the summer of 1874 from Columbia, South Carolina, he wrote, "The air is full of blood. If the North drifts as she does now, then blood will come. You ought to see the rabidness of the press. It is awful. And it is all based on 'anti-nigger.' " [99] Later the same year from Atlanta he spoke of the "very dark times here this summer." "The South means secession," he explained to Julius A. Skilton, the American counsul-general of Mexico with whom he had worked closely in the Methodist mission project there in 1873. "Georgia is the worst lot of the whole. There is no liberty here of speech or of press, except in a few centers like this. Hundreds of men have been killed this year & thousands would have been but for the submission of the blacks, and their declining to vote. It is death to them." [100] In the same month Haven repeated his alarm to another correspondent, "Horrible times in Mississippi; worse in Georgia. Only Grant will save us." [101]

President Grant did intervene by sending federal troops into Louisiana, but his leadership in the waning months of his second term could hardly be called aggressive. Nevertheless, Haven was still captivated by the mystique surrounding "the man on horseback" who, as a military hero, symbolized northern victory in the Civil War. Although many of his actions had been ineffective, he had, as chief executive, permitted, if he never fully supported, radical Reconstruction. To Haven he remained "the only instrumentality that [could] control the mad and blinded disunion element of this country, and bring order and beauty out of confusion." [102] There was a further reason for Haven's loyalty to Grant. W. S. Robinson, longtime newspaperman, neighbor to the Havens in Malden and a famous writer of "pen-portraits" by "Warrington" for the *Springfield Republican,* diagnosed it. "Haven is 'a Grant man,' " he wrote, "because the black man is for Grant. He believes in the negro, not in Grant." [103]

References to Grant's possible renomination in 1876 as a way to keep alive the hope of a reconstructed South began to creep into Haven's articles. By this time the bishop had come to know the President personally. He had visited the White House to report on his trip to Mexico in 1873. The next summer the President and first lady came to Martha's Vineyard, Massachu-

97. *Atlanta Constitution,* Aug. 21, 1874.
98. Quoted from his journal in Prentice, *Life,* p. 440.
99. Haven to an unidentified correspondent, July 8, 1874, as quoted in Daniels, *Memorials of Gilbert Haven,* p. 92.
100. Haven to Skilton, Oct. 31, 1874, from Atlanta.
101. Unidentified letter quoted in Daniels, *Memorials of Gilbert Haven,* p. 93.
102. From an unfinished essay as quoted in Prentice, *Life,* pp. 443-44.
103. Mrs. W. S. Robinson, ed., *"Warrington" Pen-Portraits, Reminiscences,* p. 493.

setts, stayed in Haven's cottage and heard him preach.[104] A year later Haven privately analyzed the chances for a third term presidency. "Politics are getting ready to boil," he wrote Julius Skilton. "I think the inside lines are with Grant yet. But there is no knowing. Politicians pronounce against the Third Term, but not the people. The South is deadly quiet, waiting for the capture of Washington next year. Then Mexico will be preferrable to Georgia." [105]

Late in the year Haven's support of Grant suddenly emerged as a national issue. On December 6 before his old friends in the Boston Methodist Preachers' Meeting, Haven made a short speech, later magnified in one account to have been a two-hour address, in which he discussed the southern scene. The *Boston Globe* summarized his remarks:

Bishop Haven said that there is to be a tremendous political battle this year, beginning with the election of a democratic speaker of the national house of representatives. He said that the ministers of Boston are in the field of battle; their words are reported and the southern papers comment on them.[106] The question is, "Shall the northern people rule the nation?" "Shall the Puritan or the Cavalier be the ruler?" "Shall Boston or Charleston be the center?" The Methodist Episcopal church is the only institution in the south to-day that represents the American nation. You must, he said, stand by your church. There are in the south nearly 300,000 members of the Methodist Episcopal church, who know what they believe just as well as the people of New England, and better. They appreciate liberty and those who gave it to them; they never will be betrayers, and let the people of the north never betray them. The malcontents of the south know that they were defeated by one man; that man is President Grant, and if the people throw him over at the command of politicians they will rue it. Pray brethren, that President Grant may be reelected.[107]

As the report of the meeting made the rounds in the nation's newspapers, some editors thought that they saw in Haven's speech signs of a larger movement promoting the renomination of Grant. The bishop's remarks had, after all, coincided with a recent statement by the President in which he had not disclaimed the possibility of accepting another term. As a result some of the facts of the original story of Haven's speech were twisted and magnified. The Preachers' Meeting, which, having ceased to be merely a private ministerial association, was open to the public, became "a Methodist convention." The call for the audience to pray for Grant's return to office became a formal

104. *Zion's Herald,* Feb. 4, Aug. 12, 1875; *New York Christian Advocate,* Sept. 3, 1874; *The Methodist,* Sept. 12, 1874; Haven to Julius A. Skilton, Nov. 27, 1873. See also Ralph E. Morrow, *Northern Methodism and Reconstruction* (East Lansing: Michigan State University Press, 1956), p. 231, n. 56; and Prentice, *Life,* p. 443.

105. Haven to Skilton, June 5, 1875, from Atlanta.

106. Earlier in the year the Preachers' Meeting had adopted a series of controversial resolutions commending President Grant and General Philip Sheridan for quelling violence in Louisiana. Haven endorsed those resolutions in *Zion's Herald,* Feb. 4, 1875. See Records of the Boston Methodist Preacher's Meetings, Jan. 18, Feb. 22, Mar. 8, Sept. 27, Nov. 1, 1875; *Nashville Christian Advocate,* Feb. 27, 1875.

107. *Boston Globe,* Dec. 7, 1875, as quoted in *Atlanta Constitution,* Dec. 14, 1875; Records of the Boston Methodist Preachers' Meeting, Dec. 6, 1875; Prentice, *Life,* pp. 433-35.

address with an explicit statement of nomination. A resolution of thanks, voted by the meeting after the speech, became a rousing hurrah from the ministers, seconding, with one voice, the nomination.[108] In Washington the excitement which was created by the publicity was so great that the Democratic-controlled House of Representatives passed a resolution declaring any notion of a third term "unwise, unpatriotic and fraught with peril to our institutions." [109]

If he did not already know, Haven soon discovered that the state of opinion in the country was decidedly against a third term. Ironically, his remarks in Boston helped to bury the idea. Some of the Republican papers even joined the antiadministration press to decry the alleged ecclesiastical attempt to influence politics. Others, like the *New York Tribune,* murmured, "There are a great many excellent people in the country who would have been able to reconcile themselves to almost any afflictive dispensation whereby Bishop Haven's tongue should ave [*sic*] been tied for ever, rather than have had it wag so loosely on that fatal day in Boston." [110]

The outburst against Haven and the third-term idea indicated a widely held feeling in the North that new political leadership was necessary. A financial panic in 1873, political corruption throughout the administration, and weariness with the southern problem made the voters in both parties restless for a change. No appeals, like Haven's, to the critical state of affairs in the South convinced any significant number of people that Grant's election could alone protect southern loyalists, white and black. *Harper's Weekly* explicitly denied that the nation was in such a dangerous situation as Haven depicted. "He can not compare himself with the preachers of the Revolution nor with the antislavery preachers of twenty years ago," its editorial said, "because he can not plead any urgent, threatening moral peril for which the re-election of the President is the plain and necessary remedy." [111] After Haven expressed his determination "to go on praying and preaching for the re-election of Grant," the *Springfield Daily Republican* commented wryly, "Reconstructing Brother Haven is more of a job than reconstructing the South." [112]

Charles Nordhoff, the *New York Herald's* correspondent in Washington, went further and stated frankly that Haven himself was one of the causes of sectional irritation. In an earlier series of articles Nordhoff, a Methodist layman, had attacked Haven's racial views. This time he charged the bishop with having failed to create good relations with Southern Methodists which had damaged, rather than strengthened, "the bond of brotherhood between the

108. *Springfield Daily Republican,* Dec. 15, 1875; *Philadelphia Item* as quoted in the *New York Tribune,* Dec. 10, 1875. Haven has an explanatory article in the *Tribune,* Dec. 15, 1875.

109. *New York Herald,* Dec. 16, 1875. This Democratic daily ran stories on Haven's speech and editorialized freely on the dangers of the third term idea for most of the month.

110. *New York Tribune,* Dec. 13, 1875; see also Dec. 8, 1875; *Hartford Courant* (Conn.) as quoted in *Springfield Daily Republican,* Dec. 14, 1875; *Harper's Weekly,* Dec. 25, 1875.

111. Dec. 25, 1875.

112. Dec. 16, 1875.

sections." Haven was given "this task of reconciliation," but he had, instead, "done a great deal to widen the breach. He is detested all over the South," Nordhoff contended,

for public expressions in favor of an amalgamation of the negro and white races, and I became satisfied he has done a great deal to keep up and even embitter wherever he labored, not only race prejudices, but the feelings naturally remaining from the war. When he comes to the North he industriously spreads tales of the "disloyalty" of the Southern whites and of the wrongs suffered by the "poor negroes" and of the danger to their future. In fact, he talks of the South precisely like the average political carpetbagger, and the final clause of his argument, like that of the political carpetbagger, is always, "We must re-elect General Grant to keep down the rebels and protect the negroes." [113]

The African Methodist editor, B. T. Tanner, agreed with Nordhoff's essential point, that "the mortal offense" was not the request to pray for Grant's reelection but his racial views, particularly his rousing article from the previous summer in which he had written, "The word for America of to-day is not Abolition, but Amalgamation." [114] The third-term issue was "a Godsend . . . to the enemies of Bishop Haven," he wrote.

His advocacy of mixed churches, and mixed schools, and mixed conferences, was to be endured; but when he proclaimed for *mixed families* . . . , both his tongue and his pen became too intolerable to be borne. To let him know how hateful he was, was what all who are now croaking, waited for. Of course, they could not come out, and attack him directly on his abolition and amalgamation proclivities. That would not do. But they bode their time, which came doubtless sooner than they expected. [115]

In the aftermath of the controversy Haven was deeply hurt by the censure of some of his fellow Methodists. Preachers' meetings in Philadelphia, Baltimore, and Salt Lake City publicly disapproved his stand, and Daniel Curry of the *New York Advocate* criticized the impropriety of the speech. Some papers defended the bishop's right to state his opinion, but Arthur Edwards of the *Northwestern Advocate* was the only denominational editor to agree with Haven that the nation was indeed in danger at the South. Most of his support, Haven wrote to a friend, had come "from colored brethren" like Tanner who prayed "that the faith of this Christian hero may fail not." [116]

113. See Nordhoff's *The Cotton States in the Spring and Sumner of 1875* (New York, 1876) for his original attack on Haven, and *New York Herald*, Dec. 27, 1875 for the above quoted passage.
114. Haven's piece, entitled "Ding-Dong," appeared in *The Independent*, Aug. 26, 1875. For Benjamin T. Tanner's comment on the article, see *Christian Recorder*, Sept. 2, 1875.
115. *Christian Recorder*, Dec. 23, 1875.
116. *Ibid.*; an undated, unidentified letter as quoted in Daniels, *Memorials of Gilbert Haven*, p. 95. On Methodist opposition to Haven see *New York Tribune*, Dec. 13, 14, 1875; *New York Herald*, Dec. 12, 16, 18, 19, 22, 1875; *New York Christian Advocate*, Dec. 16, 1875; *Zion's Herald*, Dec. 16, 23, 30, 1875; *Methodist Advocate*, Dec. 29, 1875; *Northwestern Christian Advocate*, Dec. 22, 1875, as quoted in *New York Christian Advocate*, Dec. 30, 1875; *Southwestern Christian Advocate*, Dec. 16, 30, 1875; Jan. 27, 1876; *Christian Recorder*, Dec. 16, 1875.

Despite his discouragements Haven never wavered in his convictions. The mood of the country merely confirmed his fears that northern concessiveness was going to provide the key to a successful counterrevolution in the South. He saw again that he was standing with a small minority against an overwhelming tide of reaction to Reconstruction and equal rights. Nevertheless, he still hoped that his "call to prayer [would] yet strike deep into the Christian heart," and he pledged himself to cry out anew against the injustices being perpetrated at the South. He denied that "drunken wine-bibbers at Philadelphia" or "politicans at Washington" were going "to settle this greatest of problems, how to save our poor brothers at the South." Haven wrote privately,

The key of this whole question is the oppressed and hated man of color. It is the four or five millions of such, whom we all cruelly hate and despise, who are left to their pursuers to do with them as seemeth good or evil in their eyes. God, the Lord Jesus Christ, who loves them more than he loves all the rest of us to-day, will compel this nation to do justice, or will scourge us yet more with bloody rods. . . . I shall say so still, and everywhere, by the help of God.[117]

III

By this time in Haven's career he had realized, in one sense, his boyhood goal to achieve national prominence. He had carved out a distinctive place in American social and ecclesiastical life, not, however, on the basis of how effective he was or what practical results he had caused, but through a determined and consistent avowal of human rights and the ideal of interracial brotherhood. He had always been primarily an agitator concerned initially with what was desirable, what ought to be, rather than with the politician's measure of what was possible or workable. It was this stubborn disregard for "the proprieties of his [episcopal] office" and seeming nonchalance over whether his "manner of handling things" was acceptable to others that drove Methodist conservatives to conclude that Haven was no longer "safe for himself or the church." [118] Because he had chosen the role of prophet, however, Haven never counted on having majority support. On one level, therefore, he should have been prepared for the repudiation of his dream of racial equality which came in politics and in the church during 1876, the centennial year of national independence. But on a deeper plane, those defeats to his hopes were particularly bitter to swallow because of what they finally represented.

The first and greatest disappointment came in his denomination. As the

117. Undated and unidentified letter as quoted in Daniels, *Memorials of Gilbert Haven*, pp. 94-95.
118. These are the sentiments of denominational conservative, David H. Wheeler of *The Methodist*, quoted in the *Springfield Daily Republican*, Dec. 15, 1875.

General Conference of 1876 neared, there was considerable evidence that it would have to decide not only the question of future racial policy in the church but also whether or not to give Haven's episcopal leadership a vote of confidence. His no-caste administration in the South and the third-term fiasco had precipitated much contention and unrest. According to one report, "What on earth the M.E. Church is to do with the Bishop," was being seriously asked in denominational circles. "No possible conception of Episcopal proprieties, will allow him to sacrifice the rights and the privileges of Colored people," Benjamin Tanner continued. Referring to the editor of *The Methodist,* he wrote, "It is the pain of Dr. [David H.] Wheeler's soul that he will not be dignified; that 'Gil' Haven will not surrender to Bishop Haven. The fact that such surrender is impossible seems never to enter the mind of this class of gentlemen. Why, don't they know that God made 'Gil' Haven, while the Methodist General Conference made the Bishop; and they might just as well expect the Alps to surrender to the Pyramids?" [119]

In the months preceding the general conference, Haven had demonstrated that Tanner's analysis was not far from the mark. He explicitly refused to modify his position in order to pacify dissenters, and he continued to push for racial mixture in the church at all levels. One after another of his attempts failed. In Atlanta, for example, he had encouraged black Methodists from the Clark Chapel congregation to merge with the Loyd Street Church. The effort backfired. Some whites at Loyd Street even left the denomination; others formed a new congregation for whites only, the Marietta Street Church. When *The Independent* called on Haven to "rebuke the spirit of the Marietta street movement," he made no public response, since his decision to merge the two races in one church had touched off the white walkout.[120] His silence provoked a rare criticism from Tanner who declared that it was "utterly impossible for any white man to feel about caste as does a colored man. It is the burnt child that dreads fire," he went on to explain. "We have often wished that we could make Gilbert Haven black for a month. With the experience that would give him, we think his stammering tongue would be cut loose." [121]

At about the same time as the controversy in the Loyd Street Church Haven directly entered the debate in the denominational press over racial division in the annual conferences. He chided an Alabama Methodist who urged separation "on the color line" as recommending "a return to the dark

119. *Christian Recorder,* Dec. 23, 1875. Earlier Tanner had commended Haven's anticaste faithfulness, but he also warned of the difficulties that the bishop was bringing upon himself. See issues for Oct. 30, Nov. 6, Dec. 11, 1873; Mar. 5, July 30, 1874; Mar. 18, Aug. 26, Sept. 2, 1875.

120. Edmund Jordan Hammond, *The Methodist Episcopal Church in Georgia* (n.p., 1935), pp. 131, 137-39; *Methodist Advocate,* May 19, June 2, 9, 16, 1875; *The Independent,* May 27, June 10, 1875; Joel Chandler Harris, *Life of Henry W. Grady Including His Writings and Speeches* (New York, [1890]), pp. 290-91; George W. Cable, *The Negro Question* (Garden City, N.Y., 1958), pp. 104-8.

121. *Christian Recorder,* Feb. 10, 1876; see Haven's allusion to this statement in *Methodist Advocate,* Oct. 22, 1879. Tanner's comments on the Marietta Street project are in *Christian Recorder,* May 27, June 3, 10, 17, 1875.

days of slavery." He pleaded with his brethren in the Alabama Conference to be true to anticaste principles. But the southern pastor did not let Haven's "cut" go unchallenged. He charged that the bishop knew less about what was possible on this question than the preachers out in the field. "The 'devil of caste' is not so easily cast out as Bishop Haven seems to think," he retorted.[122]

Dissent against his views, however, did not deter Haven. He continued to appeal to the church, North and South, to overcome racial separation. Although he was a firm believer in the efficacy of revivals, he especially decried the evidence of caste in evangelistic meetings. "The great and terrible barrier sin erects (and Satan) between saved souls still stands," he wrote concerning "a great revival [that was] spreading over all this section."

Brothers cannot approach the same altar yet. Should a brother of low degree and dusky hue dare to enter one of these most crowded, intense, and seemly perfectly free meetings, and either ask for prayers or give his testimony, it would instantly be met with a universal and unspeakable resentment. The whole multitude would rise and expel the intruder, or rise and leave him alone to his prayers and testimony.[123]

Haven's charge was not an overstatement. When his friend, the female revivalist, Maggie Newton Van Cott, came to New Orleans in 1874, the official board and pastor of the all-white Ames Church voted to exclude Negroes from seats except in the gallery. The stated purpose of the move was to insure a greater receptivity of the revival among the white people of the city.[124] A similar situation occurred two years later when students at Fisk University in Nashville were refused admission to the revivals held by Major Whittle and Dwight L. Moody.[125] Haven turned away in disgust from such spurious piety which did not overcome caste nor issue in ethical action and social service. "Not sanctification raptures in Northern campgrounds and Churches, but devotion to these Christ's children in captivity and contumely is," he exclaimed, "to be the real test in that day of the Christ-like condition of the believer." [126]

In spite of Haven's presistent efforts to stem the tide of segregation, he saw that little progress was being made in the denomination. Less than a year prior to the general conference he noticed that within the discontent and

122. *Methodist Advocate*, Mar. 24, May 19, June 2, 1875.
123. *Zion's Herald*, Aug. 12, 1875; see also *Christian Recorder*, Aug. 26, 1875; *Zion's Herald*, May 2, 1878.
124. *Southwestern Christian Advocate*, Apr. 9, 1874; *Zion's Herald*, Apr. 23, 1874; *Central Christian Advocate* as quoted in *Southwestern Christian Advocate*, May 7, 1874; *Christian Recorder*, May 28, June 11, July 23, 1874. See also J. C. Hartsell's letter to Bishop Matthew Simpson, Apr. 2, 1874, from New Orleans, Simpson Papers, Library of Congress.
125. *The Independent*, July 20, 1876.
126. *New York Christian Advocate*, Nov. 18, 1875; *Eighth Annual Report of the Freedmen's Aid Society of the Methodist Episcopal Church* (Cincinnati, 1875), p. 23.

cries for reform, which always sounded as the quadrennial legislature of
Methodism approached, there were attempts being made "to cut our Southern
Conferences in twain on the color line, and so to reproduce the old state
of antebellum iniquity by the voice and power of the Church." [127] He
warned of what was happening and reiterated an opinion which he had held
for a long time. "If we run our Church on caste lines," he asserted, "we had
far better leave the field. We are not called to that bondage. There is enough
of that here already. Only by clinging to Christ and human brotherhood shall
we win or deserve to win." [128]

Reaction to racial mixture in the church which began in 1874 gained
momentum during the remaining months before the general conference. White
Methodists in Tennessee, Georgia, and Alabama made their argument first
in district conferences, which adopted official resolutions calling for racially
separate annual conferences.[129] Then they took their case to the mixed
annual conferences. Racial tensions mounted in 1875 as the fall sessions for
those conferences approached. In Alabama, where the membership of twelve
thousand was almost equally divided between whites and blacks, the ministers
unanimously passed a resolution asking for a division of the conference. Of
the whites, only O. L. Franklin, an ex-slaveholder and a presiding elder
among blacks, dissented.[130] In Georgia the issue was not so easily settled.
Black Methodists outnumbered their white brethren three to one. When they
defeated the motion asking for a racial division, an exciting controversy
ensued. The Negro members caused further racial disharmony when they
caucused to try to gain control of both seats in the lay delegation to the
general conference. Cool heads prevailed, and a compromise was reached on
both issues. The conference asked for "a geographical division," if deemed
necessary. But before that request was granted, the opponents of division
forced the adoption of an explicit statement disavowing "any movement which
looks to the separation of our work into a white and colored conference."
The result, therefore, was ambiguous. White Methodists seeking separation
interpreted the geographical division to be the way to have racial division.
Black Methodists argued that the conference was on record against any such
separation.[131]

In the two Tennessee conferences quite similar developments took place.
Like Alabama, the Holston Conference voted to establish a separate organization for its struggling Negro minority.[132] The Tennessee Conference in the

127. *Zion's Herald*, June 17, 1875.
128. *New York Christian Advocate*, July 1, 1875.
129. *Methodist Advocate*, Feb. 17, 24, Aug. 25, Sept. 22, Oct. 20, Dec. 15, 1875.
130. Minutes of the Alabama Conference of the M.E. Church, 1875, p. 5. See *Methodist Advocate,*
Feb. 23, Mar. 22, Apr. 12, 19, 1876; *Southwestern Christian Advocate*, Jan. 27, Mar. 9, Apr. 6, 1876.
131. *New York Christian Advocate*, Nov. 18, 1875; *Methodist Advocate*, Jan. 12, 1876; Minutes of
the Georgia Annual Conference of the Methodist Episcopal Church, 1875, pp. 14-15.
132. The actual separation was postponed until 1879. There were 19,447 whites to 3,973 Negroes in
the conference. *Minutes of the Eleventh Session of the Holston Annual Conference, of the Methodist
Episcopal Church, Held at Greeneville, Tenn., September 29, 1875*, pp. 23, 25-26.

western part of the state, however, got embroiled in controversy that was even more bitter than that of its Georgia counterpart. The racial constituency of the conference was almost exactly equal in membership and ministers, but there was sufficient support among white teachers and preachers who worked among blacks to defeat the request for separate conferences. The separationists grew very hostile when the same coalition defeated the effort to elect one of their number as a general conference delegate. After the conference the two sides exchanged verbal assaults in the church press.[133]

Though he was not the presiding officer, Haven was present at the Georgia and Tennessee conferences. Afterwards he commended the stand of the integrationists, but he passed over the ambiguity of the actions and the ill feeling within both organizations. In the Atlanta *Advocate,* he merely re-entered his plea against racial division, reminding his readers that more than eighty ex-Confederates in the national House of Representatives sat and voted on a level of equality with seven Negro congressmen. He wrote that "to go back to the dark age of separating brethren on account of color, would be a barbarism that God would most assuredly condemn. It is anti-Christianity of the worst sort." But the best Haven could hope for was to hold on to the status quo in the face of the strength of the sentiment for division.[134]

The prevention of further racial separation, however, was plainly not going to be possible. The defeated white minorities in Georgia and Tennessee did not intend for the movement for division to be thwarted. A churchman from the latter state, John W. Ramsey, stated their case. "Resolutions against a division of a conference into white and colored, and instructions to delegates can only delay, but can not prevent that which the white laymen of the South are determined to have," he wrote. "No enthusiasm about the 'brotherhood of man' can change their purpose, for that is not the issue." [135] Other members of the separationist party filled the church press with familiar arguments in favor of division. They cited Haven's failure in mixing churches, circuits, districts, and conferences.[136] They also claimed that black Methodists really wanted their own conferences. When representative black leaders came out against division, they charged that "a few zealous but misguided white brethren," teaching and preaching among Negroes, were responsible for the opposition. "Many of the colored, when not under the eye of such leaders

133. *Minutes of the Tenth Session of the Tennessee Conference of the Methodist Episcopal Church, October, 1875,* pp. 11, 14-15. See *Methodist Advocate,* Jan. 12, Mar. 8, 15, 22, 29; Apr. 5, 12, 19, 26, 1876; *Western Christian Advocate,* Feb. 23, Apr. 5, 19, 26, 1876.

134. *Methodist Advocate,* Dec. 29, 1875.

135. *Ibid.,* Jan. 12, 1876.

136. The most important articles are in *Methodist Advocate* between January and April, 1876 and in *Western Christian Advocate,* Feb. 23, Mar. 22, Apr. 19, 26, 1876.

232

as Bishop Haven, Mr. Lansing and a few other theorists, desire division," one influential separatist wrote.[137]

White Methodists in Tennessee and Georgia adopted other strategies to make their feelings known to the church. They gathered in special conventions in each state, which drew up official papers and resolutions to the general conference requesting racial division. The leading figure in this movement in Georgia was Erasmus Fuller, who endorsed the convention idea but warned that the general church would require good grounds for separation. "If we want a school, or circuit, or conference for white people especially, we must ask that because we believe that more souls could be saved by that means," he explained. He also hinted that if there were enough requests for division before the general conference, the church could hardly ignore the issue.[138] Taking the cue from Fuller, the Ellijay (Georgia) Convention, which met on March 22 and 23, 1876, declared that the end sought by division was not "the gratification of personal opinions, or preferences, either as individuals, or as a body, but the glory of God in the greater advancement of his cause as connected with our work." The memorial to the general conference defined the request so as to assure Methodists that the church would be forced to grant division or abandon work among whites in the South. The convention's real sentiments were clear when it openly condemned a series of articles, entitled "Church Without Color," by Professor I. J. Lansing of Clark University, calling them "the speculations of a theorizing imagination" which represented a position so "extreme as to demand the obliteration of distinctions which God himself instituted." [139]

The Tennessee Conference Convention, held April 4, took a similar stand. Since the regular conference delegation to the general conference was against separation, the members appointed a representative to go to Baltimore as a lobbyist in behalf of the convention.[140] In a long paper setting forth reasons for division, the Tennesseans were not reluctant to air in public their differences with their southern bishop. They sought to dispel the notion "that the distinctive and only mission of the M.E. Church in this section, is to attack the social customs of the country in relation to the two races." The paper protested that "erroneous impression" which "[diverted] the minds of the people from our real object—'to spread Scriptural Holiness over these

137. *Methodist Advocate*, Jan. 12, 1876. For opinions of Negro Methodists on division see Sept. 29, 1875; Mar. 1, 29, Apr. 26, 1876; *Southwestern Christian Advocate*, May 4, 1876. See also *Methodist Advocate*, Apr. 5, 1876; *Western Christian Advocate*, Apr. 19, 1876. The Mr. Lansing referred to in the quotation was either I. J. Lansing, a teacher at Clark University and vigorous supporter of Haven; or his brother, John A. Lansing, a northern pastor who had answered Haven's call to go South and minister to the freedmen in Tennessee. See his "My Call to Our Southern Work," *Zion's Herald*, Nov. 5, 1874.

138. *Methodist Advocate*, Jan. 12, Feb. 2, 1876.

139. *Ibid.*, Apr. 5, 1876. Lansing's series ran in the *Advocate*, Feb. 9, 16, Mar. 1, 8, Apr. 5, 1876.

140. See J. E. Cole's complaint against the two regular delegates in *Western Christian Advocate*, Feb. 23, 1876.

lands.' " The convention had Haven in view in damning "certain persons" whose "expressed opinions upon this subject [were] repugnant to our people," and in disclaiming "any mission to this or any other country to unify the races." [141]

Prior to the general conference, there was still some support for Haven's position against separation in the North Carolina, South Carolina, Louisiana, Mississippi, and West Texas conferences. In all, however, there were large Negro majorities and so few white societies that separate conferences were impracticable. Furthermore, the separationist party in the middle South had argued its case effectively. The denominational press, except *Zion's Herald,* either favored or tolerated the idea of racial division. Daniel Curry of the *New York Advocate* approved the policy of local option. *The Methodist* attacked the fanatical policy of "the mixers of races," and likewise commended "the policy of local liberty." Even the *Northwestern Advocate* conceded that further separation was inevitable, and only asked to what degree the color line would be drawn. Only the *Western Advocate* stood up for the present "law and usage of our Church," but Erasmus Fuller took care of that argument. "So we believe," he wrote, "and are therefore unable to see why the 'law and usage' in Indiana, Ohio and Kentucky should be denied to Tennessee, Alabama and Georgia, if the people there think they can best serve the ends of the Church by that policy." The separationists had fully convinced most of their northern coreligionists that they had no right to require racial integration in the South when they did not practice it in the North.[142]

In addition it was clear that none of Haven's episcopal colleagues supported a no-caste plan. Early in 1875, Bishop Randolph S. Foster had refused to side with integrationists. He admonished dissident black Methodists in Louisiana who had complained about being separated in special sections in Ames Church "to abide quietly in their own churches." Foster defended the rights of local congregations to decide who may be kept out and where attendants may sit. "The pews in the churches are the people's," he said.[143] Likewise, Bishop Thomas Bowman backed the separationists in Georgia and Tennessee. He interpreted the plan for geographical division in Georgia to be an endorsement of racial separation, thus agreeing with the white minority there. Shortly before the general conference opened, he also wrote an account of the all-black Washington Conference as a way to commend the success of racial

141. *Methodist Advocate,* Apr. 12, 1876; *New York Christian Advocate,* Apr. 20, 1876.

142. *New York Christian Advocate,* Mar. 4, 1875; *The Methodist* as quoted in *New Orleans Christian Advocate,* Sept. 30, 1875; *Northwestern Christian Advocate* as quoted in *Methodist Advocate,* Apr. 19, 1876; *Western Christian Advocate* as quoted in *Methodist Advocate,* Apr. 12, 1876.

143. *Southwestern Christian Advocate,* Jan. 14, 1875; see also issues for Mar. 11, Apr. 8, 1875; *New York Christian Advocate,* Mar. 4, 1875; *The Independent,* Feb. 18, Apr. 1, 15, 22, 1875; *Zion's Herald,* Feb. 25, May 13, 1875; *Christian Recorder,* Feb. 11, Mar. 11, May 13, 27, 1875; Mar. 9, 1876; Morrow, *Northern Methodism and Reconstruction,* p. 188.

separation in Maryland and vicinity.[144] Of the remainder of the episcopal board, none came to Haven's rescue in the controversy in the South. Such an action would have been uncharacteristic of at least five of the bishops, including Foster, who were at the time standing vice-presidents of the American Colonization Society which aimed to take blacks back to Africa.[145]

One further factor complicated the general conference's consideration of the problem of racial policy. It was the developing fraternal relationship between the two major sectional branches of American Methodism. When the two denominations exchanged greetings in Louisville, Kentucky in 1874, one of the most formidable obstacles to the establishment of "formal fraternity" was the racial stance of the Methodist Episcopal Church. The policy pursued by the Methodist Episcopal Church, South, in 1870, in setting up a separate organization for its Negro members, stood in contrast to the northern-based denomination's arrangement. "They have mixed Conferences, mixed congregations, and mixed schools," the official report of the Southern General Conference stated. "We do not ask them to adopt our plan. We could not adopt theirs." Despite that and other problems in the path of fraternity, the Southern Church appointed a commission to meet with the Methodist Episcopal Church whose General Conference of 1876 was charged with the responsibility of providing for a similar commission.[146]

The Southern Methodist press had repeatedly made clear with reference to Haven's acts and sentiments that the racial problem was a chief source of irritation between the two denominations. Numerous writers explained that Southern Methodists could not associate with Haven. Charles W. Miller, a member of the committee on fraternity in the Southern General Conference of 1874, put it crudely. "What wonder, then, if, when the negrophilistic Haven comes into our midst as one of their 'representatives,' showing only the spirit of an Inquisitor-general in his bearings toward 'the Church, South,' and illustrating more of the licentious spirit of Dean Swift in his delineations of the voluptuous beauty of negro damsels, than the chaste and pure sentiment of a Christian bishop," Miller exclaimed, "what wonder, I repeat, if 'the Church, South,' lets him *severely* alone?" [147] As long as the Methodist Episcopal

144. *Methodist Advocate*, Dec. 1, 22, 1875; *Zion's Herald*, July 27, 1876; *Central Christian Advocate* as quoted in *Methodist Advocate*, Apr. 19, 1876.

145. The bishops were Edmund S. Janes, Matthew Simpson, Levi Scott, Edward R. Ames, and Foster. See *Fifty-ninth Annual Report of the American Colonization Society* (Washington, 1876), p. 3.

146. *Formal Fraternity. Proceedings of the General Conferences of the Methodist Episcopal Church and of the Methodist Episcopal Church, South, in 1872, 1874, and 1876, and of the Joint Commission of the Two Churches on Fraternal Relations, at Cape May, New Jersey, August 16-23, 1876* (New York, n.d.), pp. 19-40.

147. *Nashville Christian Advocate*, May 22, 1875; see also June 27, Oct. 10, 1874; *Richmond Christian Advocate*, Feb. 26, 1874. Southern Methodist antagonism toward Haven is amply illustrated in Hunter Dickinson Farish's *The Circuit-Rider Dismounts: A Social History of Southern Methodism 1865-1900* (Richmond: The Dietz Press, 1938), pp. 110-11, 152, 159, 189, 198, 211-14, 218-20. Because he dwelt on Haven's antagonism toward the white South and saw the bishop's racial stance as the especially offensive feature of his life and thought, Farish erroneously considered Haven's radicalism as typical of northern Methodist sentiment.

Church had conferences "organized on the Haven fashion," fraternalism, according to the consensus of the southern church, was impossible.[148]

Those northern Methodists who were anxious for fraternization with the southern church agreed. Among the editors, David H. Wheeler of *The Methodist* was the foremost exponent of fraternity. He ridiculed "Bishop Haven's amalgamation moonshine," and assured Southerners that the majority of both churches had the same racial views. "We really recognize the color line," he declared. Wheeler, and for a time, Gilbert's cousin, Otis, backed the resurrected proposal for a union of all Negro Methodists as a step toward fraternal relations with the southern church.[149]

Southern editors took advantage of such sympathy at the North. Six weeks before the northern general conference got underway, T. O. Summers plainly stated the best way for the two sectional churches to have harmonious ties. "Let this unification take place among colored Methodists, and fraternization will be comparatively easy with the white Methodists, North and South." [150] The *New Orleans Advocate* coolly predicted the outcome of the racial controversy between the two denominations. In a hypothetical dialogue, "One Way to Fraternity," a "Southern Methodist" spoke candidly and prophetically to a "Northern Methodist." "The negro free, as well as the negro slave, has been an occasion of difference between us," the Southerner said.

This would have continued so long as you were at a distance, theorizing, and we, on the spot, dealing practically with the case. Now you are in contact with the problem; full of hope, full of plans. Gradually you will come over to where we stand. . . . In the last few years you have moved toward our position. The tendencies to further movement in this direction are evident. The poetry is wearing off. Your Annual Conferences in the South will divide on the color line, and ultimately you will see and acknowledge that the best service you can do for the negroes is to help them to organize a separate and independent church, receiving your friendly aid.[151]

By an overwhelming vote the General Conference of 1876 moved precisely in the direction predicted by the "Southern Methodist." It enacted a policy of local option in regard to racial separation, setting in motion a process that ultimately destroyed the last vestiges of ecclesiastical integration in the Methodist Episcopal Church. Since Bishop Haven could take no part in the debate,

148. *Nashville Christian Advocate*, July 11, 1874; Nov. 27, 1875; *Christian Neighbor*, May 20, 1875; *New Orleans Christian Advocate*, Oct. 22, 1874.

149. *The Methodist* as quoted in *Southern Christian Advocate*, Oct. 13, 1875; see also *Zion's Herald*, Oct. 7, 1875; *New Orleans Christian Advocate*, Sept. 30, 1875; *Methodist Advocate*, Aug. 11, 1875; *Nashville Christian Advocate*, Nov. 6, 1875; *New York Christian Advocate*, Oct. 14, 1875; *Southwestern Christian Advocate*, Dec. 16, 1875; *Christian Recorder*, Oct. 21, Nov. 25, Dec. 2, 1875; Morrow, *Northern Methodism and Reconstruction*, pp. 195-96.

150. *Nashville Christian Advocate*, Mar. 11, 1876; *Southern Christian Advocate*, Apr. 26, 1876; *New Orleans Christian Advocate*, June 15, 1876.

151. *New Orleans Christian Advocate*, Feb. 17, 1876.

Lucius C. Matlack, the veteran abolitionist and missionary among the freed-men, made the pleas for the outnumbered minority.[152] Otis Haven was the chairman of the committee which brought in the majority report. After summarizing the basic arguments of both sides of the question, the committee made a special point to show that there had been a significant loss of membership in the three annual conferences most affected by the problem. Acting immediately upon passage of the report, Erasmus Fuller secured approval for explicit racial separation in Alabama and geographical division in Georgia. When the committee on boundaries reported, there were two conferences outlined for both states.[153] The process of division was yet to be worked out in the other parts of the South, including Tennessee, but the die was cast. The decision was at least consistent with the church's practice elsewhere, for the general conference also refused to permit the all-black St. Mark's church in New York city to join the New York Conference, rather than to be part of the Delaware (colored) Conference.[154]

The action on racial division was the crucial issue of the conference for Haven. The decision of his fellow churchmen was, in effect, a repudiation of his episcopal administration in the South and a fulfillment of the worst fears which he had entertained. The Methodist Episcopal Church had, as Benjamin Tanner predicted in 1874, "finally [succeeded] in appeasing the South." [155] The way for fraternity with the Methodist Episcopal Church, South, was clear.

But that defeat did not end Haven's miseries. He also had to bear further odium, when the Minnesota Conference petitioned the national church to remind "our General Superintendents" not "to publicly attempt to lead political movements, or to shape the nominations for important offices of State," and "to avoid unnecessarily exciting popular prejudice." [156] Further, the general conference put aside several petitions which Haven had supported for the election of a black minister to the episcopacy.[157] As a concession, Hiram Revels, former U.S. Senator from Mississippi and a black presiding elder in the conference upon his retirement from politics, was selected to edit the *Southwestern Christian Advocate* in place of J. C. Hartzell, who had been one of Haven's strong supporters. But Revels' election was less a compliment to him, than it was part of a movement to eject Hartzell. When he discovered the facts of the case, he resigned and Hartzell resumed his post.[158]

152. See Matlack's speech in *Southwestern Christian Advocate*, June 15, 1876.

153. *Journal of the General Conference of the Methodist Episcopal Church*, 1876, pp. 326-32, 369-70, 372, 377.

154. *Ibid.*, pp. 124-25, 368-69, 371.

155. *Christian Recorder*, June 11, 1874; see also May 8, 1873; Jan. 7, Apr. 1, 15, 1875. The extent to which Haven's own denomination disavowed his leadership in racial reform is the missing dimension in Ralph E. Morrow's otherwise penetrating analysis of the northern Methodist postwar invasion of the south. See his *Northern Methodism and Reconstruction*, pp. 181-202.

156. *Journal of the General Conference*, 1876, p. 237.

157. *Ibid.*, pp. 158, 187-88, 195, 244, 353.

158. *Ibid.*, pp. 301, 304; *Southwestern Christian Advocate*, June 1, Aug. 31, Sept. 28, 1876; *New York Christian Advocate*, Sept. 21, 1876; *Methodist Advocate*, June 28, Oct. 4, 1876. See

A final blow to Haven was the decision by the senior bishops to leave him without a regular appointment for the entire next year and to arrange for him to visit the Liberian Mission Conference in Africa.[159] The year before, Haven had expressed himself rather pointedly about that African country. "I am not one of those who have much faith in Liberia," he wrote. "Our Liberia is in our own land—five millions here, fifty thousand there. Make these free indeed, and we shall best liberate Africa." [160] The assignment was difficult to accept, for it meant that Haven would have to be out of the country during the crucial presidential election, over which he was so greatly concerned. But he had to reconcile himself to his fate. Finally he was able to say, "As to Africa, I like the idea more and more. I may make a good thing of it for the church. I would not give it up now." [161]

A few days after the general conference adjourned, Haven was headed south in the company of his traditional opponent, the Atlanta *Advocate* editor. "Dr. Fuller is my companion," he wrote to a friend, "and the General Conference battles are rebattled. He whipped me on the color line, but we will conquer yet." [162] His mood, however, was more sober in his correspondence to *Zion's Herald* in July. He referred to "graver themes" which "arise out of the new and painfully altered status of our Church in the Southern central regions." The church, he said frankly, was tending "against the very cause and [of?] Christ." He feared that "all our work here may be worse than lost," and that it would "have to be done over again" on the right basis. "We have fallen apart, and are on deceitful and dangerous ground," he confessed of the denomination. "Let New England Methodists, most of whom stood so grandly by the right at Baltimore, and all who sympathize with them, labor and pray, the last first, but not alone, for the recovery of the lost principle, and its advancement to the front over all our territory, and through all forms of religious and social being." [163]

Before he left on his foreign voyage, Haven toured parts of his old episcopal region where his constituency, except among the blacks, had been alienated from his effective influence. At Florence, South Carolina, he visited a national cemetery which had been a Civil War prison camp. As he walked among the graves of the Union dead, he mused with himself, "Is the cause victorious for which these youthful martyrs perished?" In one sense, he reasoned, there had been progress. Hardly more than a decade before, the man who accompanied him on the tour of the graveyard "could not once have ventured to own his

Gravely, ed., "Hiram Revels Protests Racial Separation in the Methodist Episcopal Church (1876)," *Methodist History*, 8 (1970), 13- 20.
159. See Haven's complaints to Bishop Simpson for being left without episcopal assignment for both the fall of 1876 and the spring of 1877 in letters to Simpson, Oct. 13, 24, 1876, Simpson Papers, Historical Society of the Philadelphia Annual Conference of The United Methodist Church.
160. *Zion's Herald*, Aug. 19, 1875; Daniels, *Memorials of Gilbert Haven*, p. 97.
161. Unidentified letter in Daniels, *Memorials of Gilbert Haven*, p. 98.
162. Unidentified letter in *ibid.*, p. 91.
163. *Zion's Herald*, July 13, 1876.

horse and house and wife." But, in a more profound sense, the victory over racism had not come. "Though a gentleman of birth and breeding," Haven continued, referring again to his companion, "he is an outcast yet from Southern and Northern society; though no one would dare to feel it in his presence." Then Haven drew an analogy from the dead-line, the boundary in prisoner of war camps beyond which one dared cross only at the risk of being shot. "The terrible Dead-Line of Caste runs through the social, civil, and ecclesiastical camp," he wrote. "It is called 'The Color Line'; but it is as imperceptible to sight as the one which was drawn across the stockade." Sadly he reviewed the extent to which caste still corrupted American life. It was to be found everywhere, in fraternal orders, temperance societies, the Young Men's Christian Association, and "every church, Protestant and Catholic." Because of its pervasive influence, Haven wrote, "No one can throw stones at his neighbor for this American offense and sin. No church can do it, not even the Quakers. They are not without blemish." [164]

As he had done twenty years before, Haven was tempted to be a perfectionist alternative, to leave the "church or party because of this backsliding." But he refused. "Defeat must only make us work the more earnestly and steadily for victory," he told himself and the readers of *The Independent*. "The sufferings of these martyrs of Florence will never be complete until there shall be no more distinction among the living than there is now among these holy dead." Attempting to emerge from his somber mood, Haven asked, "What is our duty?" He answered as if he hoped to begin the crusade all over again. " 'To create'—as a gentleman said to me in Columbia—'to create an American conscience.' We had no American conscience on slavery. We had to create it. So must we that on caste. The churches here and in the North, the large ones and the small, the more influential and the less, must be stirred to their depths by the Spirit of Christ, the Holy Ghost brooding on these now sunless abysses and creating a 'soul under these ribs of death.' " [165]

But the era of crusades on the race problem in America was over, at least for the nineteenth century. Haven would not again rouse any significant group of people, in church or in society, to the banner of racial justice. After 1876, he was left to go on almost alone, to be a bishop without the support of his church. But in the national cemetery at Florence, Haven transcended his present despair and renewed his faith so that he could leave for his unrequested African mission at peace with himself.

IV

The outcome of the election of 1876 was as disheartening to Haven as the setbacks had been which he experienced at the Methodist General Con-

---

164. *The Independent*, Aug. 24, 1876.
165. *Ibid.*; *Southwestern Christian Advocate*, Apr. 19, 1877.

ference in June. Because of his trip to Liberia, however, he did not learn for some time the results of the election. With a number of black emigrants who were leaving the country with the aid of the American Colonization Society, he had sailed just prior to voting day in early November.[166] Upon his arrival a month later, he found only an English paper which referred to a recount of ballots in Louisiana without hinting which candidate was leading. From that reference Haven assumed that the Democratic bid for power, about which he had warned, had been partly, if not wholly, successful.[167]

On December 30, Haven finally discovered the basic facts concerning the election in which both Republican Rutherford B. Hayes and his challenger, Samuel J. Tilden, claimed victory. He still hoped that three southern states where the results were in doubt, Florida, Louisiana, and South Carolina, could provide the margin for a narrow Republican victory. He did not know how much intricate political manipulation and compromise was underway in both parties to save the nation from an explosive governmental crisis.[168] Before his return to the states, as he found out further details, Haven commended the agreement to submit the disputed contest to a bipartisan electoral commission for settlement.[169]

After meeting the Liberian Conference and visiting schools and churches in the region, Haven cut short a proposed trip around the African coast and returned home in order to see just what had taken place during his absence.[170] He arrived in time to attend the New England Conference in April, where he gave a speech on his African experience. By this time he knew the full story of the political bargain which the Republicans had made a few weeks before. In order to retain the presidency, the incumbent party's leaders agreed to allow southern Democrats to take over the last two radical state governments, South Carolina and Louisiana, in exchange for their electoral support of Hayes. Democrats in the two states promised to defend the basic political rights of all citizens, including the freedmen. The new President, in turn, was to remove all federal troops from the South, thus ending that symbol of the post-Civil War commitment of the Republican Party to the national enforcement of equal rights. By April, 1877, conservatives had assumed power in all southern states, and the withdrawal of federal forces was in progress. Reconstruction was officially over.[171]

166. *New York Christian Advocate*, Oct. 26, 1876.

167. *Zion's Herald*, Feb. 22, 1877.

168. *Methodist Advocate*, Mar. 7, 1877. The article was dated Dec. 30, 1876.

169. *New York Christian Advocate*, Apr. 12, 1877. The article was written before Haven left Liberia.

170. Haven's letters from Africa are in *New York Christian Advocate, Zion's Herald, Methodist Advocate, Northwestern Christian Advocate,* and *The Independent* during the period from February through May, 1877.

171. See C. Vann Woodward, *Reunion and Reaction: The Compromise of 1877 and the End of Reconstruction*, 2nd rev. ed. (Garden City, N.Y.: Doubleday Anchor Books, 1956).

Since he was a visitor and not the presiding officer at the New England Conference, Haven took sides with the delegates who sought to pass resolutions censuring President Hayes' "southern policy." The full conference rejected the move and took a conciliatory stance, expressing confidence in the new President's promise "to secure to all classes of our citizens the full and free exercise of all their rights and privileges." [172] The decision was hardly an endorsement of Haven's sentiments. A few days later he delineated his views in full to Henry J. Fox, a professor and president of the University of South Carolina until ousted by the Democratic regime. He complained that "nobody yet wants to strike Hayes." Concerning the political situation in South Carolina, the bishop condemned "this surrender of Hayes & the North." He confessed that he "[had] no faith in these new measures," and insisted that he could not understand why they were deemed necessary. "I can't run Politics, & never could, & never tried," he wrote. "I only speak the truth. Great or small is the company that work it out." He also asked sarcastically whether a new church, recently organized in Columbia, had yet been "hayes'd out of existence." [173]

In a more somber mood later in the letter to Fox, Haven reflected on the implications of the end of Reconstruction in the South. He believed that a national racial crisis was imminent. "I can't see any light ahead, except in God & in Him is no darkness at all," he remarked. Still trying to hold on to his dream, Haven mused with himself, "He will bring it to pass, in our day, perhaps. What if not? I don't expect everything to be done in my day." The confession was a tacit acknowledgment of defeat to which Haven added the dire prediction that "this deep, wide, awful detestation of color, will only be washed out in blood." He anticipated that emigration would have a new appeal to American Negroes. He spoke of having heard from Richard Greener, a Harvard-educated Negro also on the faculty of South Carolina University, who asked for aid in getting a post in Haiti. Likewise, Alonzo Webster, who had come South as an educator and minister among the freedmen after the war, had written to Haven about Africa and "about our folks going there." But colonization was no solution. "A vessel or two a year," Haven wrote Fox, was not nearly sufficient for "so many." The necessary capital was lacking. Moreover, he had discovered that Liberia did not need any emigrants "except young men who will live off the land," or "men of business & industrious habits." Realistically, he admitted, "Only a few can go. The Problem must

172. *Minutes of the New England Conference*, 1877, pp. 17-18. Earlier drafts of the resolutions are in the Conference Papers. See also *Southwestern Christian Advocate*, Apr. 19, 1877; *New York Christian Advocate*, Apr. 12, 1877.

173. Gilbert Haven to [Henry J. Fox], Apr. 24, 1877 from Malden, Massachusetts, Methodist Historical Library, Perkins School of Theology, Southern Methodist University. The identification of Fox as Haven's correspondent has been made on the basis of the internal contents of the letter, which include Haven's response to Fox's request to be transferred to the New England Conference. The transfer occurred in the summer of 1877. See *Zion's Herald*, July 12, 1877; *The Independent*, Aug. 6, 1874.

be wrought out in this country. It can't be anywhere else. Africa will be of help, but not much." [174] Later the same year writing for the *North American Review* Haven repeated his opinion. "There is no possibility that this great and growing portion of our population will be deported to Africa," he declared. "As well expect the Anglo-American to be deported to Great Britain." [175]

For the major part of the year following his return from Liberia, poor health prevented Haven from devoting much energy to halting the expansion of segregation and continuing racial oppression in America. He brought back from Africa a severe case of malaria which was to plague him throughout the remainder of his life. From the spring of 1877 to January, 1878, he was in and out of hospitals and rest homes in Philadelphia, New York City, Boston, Saratoga and Clifton Springs, New York. He was able to go South only once during the period for a hurried ten-day visit. In the late summer of 1877, he did meet four conferences, but in Cincinnati he was stricken and forced back into convalescence.[176]

On his brief southern trip Haven got definite impressions about the new state of affairs in "the solid South." In *Zion's Herald* he contrasted his earlier visits to South Carolina with his latest. "It was a deep, lung-filling breath we had been accustomed to draw when we crossed into this State—the breath of liberty," he said. "Here, at last, man to man had brother become. All were free, all equal, and almost all fraternal." What had been true for a decade, however, had ended, and "a change had come over the famous State." "Dangers stood thick through all the ground to push us to the tomb," he declared. "It was not fierce diseases so much as fierce enmities, hatred of brother and sister, of one's own flesh and blood, of his real wife, son and daughter; this was in all the air." Sounding forth a theme that he repeated incessantly during the remaining months of his life, Haven cursed the acquiescence of the national government and the North's "unbrotherly surrender of its own brothers and sisters" in allowing the rights of southern blacks to be wantonly violated.[177]

Early in 1878, Haven had recovered from the worst effects of malaria and returned to active work. For the first time in a decade he was a persistent critic of a Republican administration on the southern question. He severely reprimanded President Hayes for failing to keep his campaign promise to protect the rights of the freedmen. Because of the bargain of 1877, he never

174. Haven to [Fox], Apr. 24, 1877.

175. "America in Africa," *North American Review*, 125 (July, 1877), 152-53. See also his concluding essay in the November issue, pp. 517-28 and *Zion's Herald*, May 2, 1878.

176. *New York Christian Advocate*, Aug. 9, 16, Sept. 20, 1877; Jan. 17, Feb. 28, 1878; *Zion's Herald*, Aug. 2, 9, 23, 1877; Feb. 21, 1878. See also Haven's letters to Bishop Simpson, July 31, 1877 from Malden, Simpson Papers, Library of Congress; June 22, 1877 from Wynnewood [Pa.]; June 23, 1877 from Middletown, Conn.; July 11, 1877 from Saratoga; July 26, 1877 from Boston; Dec. 3, 1877 from Malden, Simpson Papers, Philadelphia.

177. *Zion's Herald*, Aug. 9, 1877.

forgave Hayes, even when the President publicly admitted that his policy was
"a failure." [178] In the church press he predicted that Hayes would "suffer
for that betrayal from the American people a worse contempt and detestation
than has stamped the names of even [Benedict] Arnold and Jefferson Davis."
Privately he wrote to Charles H. Fowler about Hayes. "What a weakness is
he," stated Haven. "My stomach heaves at the lukewarm water. He's the
bottom of the American Presidency as Grant was the top." [179] But Haven not
only attacked Hayes. He likewise excoriated the President's party for failing to
guard the right to vote in the South and for surrendering the blacks to a new
political and economic serfdom. Because of the Republicans' "treason to God
and their fellow-man," as Haven put it, the Methodist Episcopal Church remained the only unionist and national institution in the South. In its policies,
however, the church had already gone the way of the politicians, by compromising with southern social patterns. Haven's faith in the influence of his
denomination, therefore, seemed hardly justified.[180]

During 1878 and 1879, Haven joined the old warhorses of the abolitionist
movement, William Lloyd Garrison and Wendell Phillips, in an effort to
reassert the dead issue of Reconstruction and to renew the crusade for equal
rights. They spoke out against southern violence and earned reputations, even
among fellow Northerners, of being defamers of the South who kept alive
sectional tensions by taunting the old Confederates, or, as that practice was
called, by waving "the bloody shirt" to evoke memories of the war.[181] To
Haven, however, the end of Reconstruction had virtually reversed the outcome of the war. The South had regained political power in the nation on the
basis of its old antebellum doctrine of states' rights. Hence, he was impatient
with many former antislavery activists, who, unlike Garrison and Phillips, did
not see that the very cause which they had championed was being destroyed
by a combination of northern concessiveness and southern political sagacity.
In the face of oppression and injustice in the South, he could not abide the
silence of those voices which had, in another day, been so zealous for freedom. Looking about, he asked Frank Sanborn, one of John Brown's cohorts,
to speak through his editorial columns in the *Springfield Republican*. He
ridiculed Thomas Wentworth Higginson's claim that the South, from what he

178. McPherson, "Coercion or Conciliation?" pp. 494-96; *Methodist Advocate*, June 4, 1879.
179. *Zion's Herald*, May 2, 1878; *Atlanta Constitution*, May 7, 1878; Haven to Fowler, March 1, 1878 from Atlanta, Fowler Papers, Drew University.
180. *Zion's Herald*, Apr. 18, July 18, 1878; *The Independent*, Oct. 10, 1878; Stanley P. Hirshson, *Farewell to the Bloody Shirt: Northern Republicans and the Southern Negro, 1877-1893* (Blooming-ton: Indiana University Press, 1962), pp. 21-62.
181. For an example of public criticism of Haven when he spoke on the South in New Hampshire, see *Methodist Advocate*, Nov. 5, 1879. Haven praised Garrison and Phillips for their courageous witness in *The Independent*, Oct. 10, 1878. He spoke of reading Henry J. Fox's letter on the South Carolina situation to Phillips, in his reply to the former, Apr. 24, 1877. He tried unsuccessfully to hold a memorial service for Garrison in the state capitol in Atlanta in the summer of 1879. See his tributes to Garrison in *Zion's Herald*, June 19, 26, 1879. *Methodist Advocate*, June 18, 1879; *New York Christian Advocate*, June 26, 1879; *Southwestern Christian Advocate*, June 26, 1879.

could tell on a visit there, was basically peaceful. Haven asked the former officer of one of the early black units in the Union Army to "look a little deeper, in his next tour, and find what the legal and political rights of his late soldiers are to-day." He called on *Harper's Weekly* to "rekindle its editorial torch" and have George William Curtis and the cartoonist, Thomas Nast, "once more" combine "in favor of human rights, of equality and fraternity, of union and brotherhood." The effort was futile, for Haven aroused no one, least of all Sanborn, Higginson, and Curtis, who were conspicuous for their conciliatory views toward the new southern regimes.[182]

Haven's rallying cry only served to alienate public opinion. He became known throughout the country for his attacks on the South and his exposure of the plight of blacks and white supporters of equal rights. In May, 1878, his oration, "Murder for Opinion's Sake," was widely reprinted in both the religious and the secular press. It was a memorial address delivered in Washington for a northern judge, his son, and his daughter, all of whom had been slain by a mob in Mississippi.[183] His public letter sent to Henry C. Bowen's nationally famous Independence Day gathering that summer enforced Haven's public reputation as an agitator of the southern question. In a piece, consciously modelled after one of Charles Sumner's addresses, "Are We a Nation?" he argued passionately against the states' rights theory that had been restored to prominence in the New South. But the application of national enforcement of equal rights, he recognized, was needed in the North as well as the South. He explicitly condemned Rhode Island's refusal to repeal its law against interracial marriage and Connecticut's rejection of blacks from the state militia.[184]

In February and May of the next year Haven attacked the Hayes administration for not using the sovereign power of the federal government to suppress violence in Texas and Louisiana and for not insuring fair trials throughout the South. He recounted the sordid facts of one incident of racial violence in which "the murderers were white men, and the murdered, 'niggers.' " The nation's apathetic response, he wrote bitterly, was to go on as usual, to eat "her Christmas dinners and [wipe] her smooth face, and [say]:

182. *Zion's Herald*, July 18, 1878; J. McPherson, "Coercion or Conciliation?" p. 489, and "The Antislavery Legacy," pp. 134-35.

183. *New York Christian Advocate*, May 30, 1878; *Zion's Herald*, June 13, 1878; *Northwestern Christian Advocate*, June 12, 1878; *Southwestern Christian Advocate*, June 13, 1878; *The Independent*, June 27, 1878; *Methodist Advocate*, June 5, 1878; *Christian Recorder*, June 20, 1878; *Boston Daily Globe*, May 20, 1878; *Daily Evening Traveller*, May 21, June 4, 1878; Haven to Charles H. Fowler, May 20, 1878 from Washington. On the story of these murders and the unsuccessful effort to convict any one for the crime, see *Zion's Herald*, May 24, 1877; *Southwestern Christian Advocate*, May 10, 31, 1877; *Methodist Advocate*, May 23, June 25, Dec. 26, 1877; June 12, 1878; *New York Christian Advocate*, June 7, 14, 1877; Sept. 18, 1879; *The Independent*, Sept. 18, 1879. For a defense of the mob's action, see James D. Lynch, *Kemper County Vindicated, and a Peep at Radical Rule in Mississippi* (New York, 1879).

184. *New York Times*, July 5, 1878; *Methodist Advocate*, Aug. 7, 1878.

'It can't be helped'; 'It is the outcome of the war'; 'It will adjust itself'; 'We have deprived ourselves of all power of constitutional intervention.' " [185] At a public meeting at Faneuil Hall in late April, Haven repreated these charges in an impassioned speech. He told the Boston audience "that not one-millionth part of the negroes' sufferings and wrongs [had been] told." [186]

On July 4, 1879, Haven was present at Bowen's Woodstock, Connecticut, rally which he had been unable to attend the previous year. There he made his last major public speech, culminating eighteen months of feverish activity in which he and others had tried to resurrect Reconstruction. In the long address Haven brought together the themes of his career in racial reform, including extravagant praise for ex-President Grant's "marvelous career." He traced the ideals of equality and union through American history, lifted up the heroes of the war and Reconstruction, and called for a new attack on racial discrimination, *"national supervision of national matters,"* and a constitutional amendment making Christianity the official religion of the republic. He added at the end an expression of manifest destiny which portrayed a national empire comprising the whole of North America, and perhaps, even, the entire earth. The speech, therefore, combined all the elements of Haven's version of a Christian America, but the press only emphasized his "unstinted laudation" of the Grant administration. One paper wrote that Haven "celebrated America and Grant in the flappiest spread-eagleism," comparing the ex-president with "the transfigured saints." The *Springfield Republican* did admit, nonetheless, that "it is as consistent as could be expected that Bishop Haven when he 'comes to the 'rousements' should lay down as the first duty of citizenship that *'we should conquer our prejudices.'* " [187]

The Woodstock address on the last Independence Day of Haven's life was a fitting summary of the vision which had empowered him for more than thirty years. He had not come to the end of his long battle against racism without some sense of accomplishment. Yet, on that July afternoon in 1879, as he set forth his ideals one final time, he revealed poignantly how far out of step with his own generation he had drifted as well as how much remained to be done in order to fulfill his hope for a racially just society. In the end, however, he was doing what he always did best—donning the mantle of prophet, discerning the signs of the times and calling others to share his vision of what should be.

185. *The Independent*, Feb. 13, May 15, 1879; *Zion's Herald*, Feb. 20, 1879. See also *Southern Christian Advocate*, Mar. 1, 1879; *Richmond Christian Advocate*, Feb. 6, 1879; *Methodist Advocate*, June 4, 1879.

186. *Methodist Advocate*, May 7, 1879.

187. *New York Times*, July 5, 1879; *Springfield Republican*, July 5, 1879; *The Independent*, July 10, 1879; *Daily Evening Traveller*, July 5, 8, 1879; *Boston Herald*, July 8, 1879. See also Haven to Bowen, June 30, 1879 from Malden, Special Collections, Emory University Library. An important earlier address on the theme of the Christian republic is Haven's "God's Purpose for America," *Ladies' Repository*, 36 (December, 1876), 522-33.

V

In the last months of his life, Haven had to face not only the failure of Reconstruction, the reassertion of white supremacy, and the establishment of the color line in American society. He also had to work as a bishop within racially segregated structures in the Methodist Episcopal Church. He did not officiate in any of the southern conferences between January, 1876, and November, 1878, for he was not given assignments within the region. Other members of the council of bishops took the responsibility for implementing the legislation of the General Conference of 1876 which adjusted the southern conferences along racial lines. They approved divisions in Alabama, Georgia, and West Texas in 1876, and in Tennessee in 1877. The senior bishops never asked Haven to be a party to action of which he disapproved so emphatically. They perhaps understood that he would not willingly give his official sanction for a conference to divide, so that having him preside outside the South, as his health permitted, prevented needless controversy.[188]

Occasionally, and rather half-heartedly, Haven voiced his objections to the pattern of racial segregation in the church. In November, 1878, before the general missionary committee he saluted the Holston Conference for standing by "the old style" and ignoring "the color line." A year later, however, that conference also succumbed to racial division when the whites concluded that the two thousand black Methodists in the area could finally support a separate organization.[189] After that Haven had no more examples of ecclesiastical integration to point out, for one by one the remaining mixed conferences divided. Separation occurred in Arkansas in 1878 and in North Carolina in 1879. In the latter instance there were only eight white ministers in the conference, but all but one of them still asked for a division.[190] When Bishop Jesse T. Peck approved it, he summed up the various justifications for separate conferences, as reported in *Zion's Herald:*

1. It seems to be the policy of the Church, there being an equal number of white and colored Conferences in the South. 2. It seems to be ordained in the providence of God that white Churches should have white preachers, and colored Churches colored pastors. He hoped they would soon have a colored bishop when they could find a good one. 3. The colored men can live on less money than the whites, and

188. *Southwestern Christian Advocate,* Nov. 9, 23, Dec. 21, 1876; Aug. 30, Oct. 18, 1877; *Methodist Advocate,* Aug. 2, Sept. 20, Oct. 18, Nov. 8, 1876; *The Independent,* Nov. 23, Dec. 28, 1876; Jan. 18, Nov. 8, 1877. In West Texas thirteen black members voted against the division to no avail. *Journal and Minutes of the Fourth Session of the West Texas Annual Conference of the Methodist Episcopal Church Held at San Antonio, Texas. November 29th, 1876,* pp. 8-11.

189. *New York Christian Advocate,* Nov. 14, 1878; *Methodist Advocate,* Jan. 22, May 21, 1879. *Minutes of the Fifteenth Session of the Holston Annual Conference of the Methodist Episcopal Church, Held at Knoxville, Tennessee, October 15, 1879.* This conference approved division in 1875, but delayed because the Negro membership was too small for a separate body.

190. *Southwestern Christian Advocate,* Dec. 4, 1878; Jan. 23, Apr. 3, 1879; *Methodist Advocate,* Feb. 12, 1879. A majority of the blacks were adamant against division. See William George Matton's *Memoirs,* ch. 11, pp. 7-9.

hence the missionary appropriation will go farther. 4. They will be sure of a colored delegate to General Conference. 5. They will grow faster, being thrown on their own resources.[191]

Peck's statement, complete with its theological rationale for racial division, expressed a growing consensus in the church that sounded the final death knell to Haven's hopes for ecclesiastical integration. Late in 1878, he found himself presiding over separate white and colored conferences in Texas.[192]

With racial segregation institutionalized in the structures of the Methodist Episcopal Church, the greatest obstacle to harmony with Southern Methodism had been removed. Again, Haven dissented from the majority opinion in his denomination. He was highly critical of "formal fraternity" which had been established between the two Methodisms in the fall of 1876, for he was keenly aware at what cost of principle in racial policy the relationship required.[193]

Haven's perspective was obviously colored by the treatment which he had received from ministers and members of the Methodist Episcopal Church, South. A year before his death he stated that no preacher of any church but his own and no Southerner of any prominence had ever come to his residence in Atlanta during the seven years of his stay there.[194] Yet Haven had treated Southern Methodists cordially when they visited the North. He had endorsed their ecumenical Methodist project, to build a Wesley Memorial Church in Savanah, despite the fact that he was told that he would never be allowed into its pulpit. He had written letters to northern politicians to support the claims of Southern Methodism against the government for war damages to its publishing house in Nashville.[195] But, when Haven visited the Southern General Conference in Atlanta in 1878, he was purposely ignored by the presiding officers, some of whom he had entertained at his northern summer residence. Their refusal to introduce him as a fraternal guest sparked a brief controversy between the two denominations in which some of Haven's opponents in his own church acknowledged that the Southerners had erred. The office of bishop was due respect, they contended, whatever one thought of the man who occupied it. David Wheeler of *The Methodist*, on the other hand, accused Haven of having provoked the incident, in that he had no business at the conference.[196] Some southern church editors defended the discourtesy with superficial excuses, but others, like Atticus G. Haygood, frankly wrote that Haven was "an unsuitable person to be introduced to the General Conference." Most writers confessed that the real issue involved in fraternizing with Haven was the racial problem.

---

191. *Zion's Herald*, Feb. 20, 1879.
192. *New York Christian Advocate*, Apr. 10, 1879; *Zion's Herald*, Feb. 27, 1879.
193. *Formal Fraternity*, pp. 59-84.
194. Daniels, *Memorials of Gilbert Haven*, p. 89; *Zion's Herald*, Feb. 20, July 24, 1879.
195. *Methodist Advocate*, July 3, 24, 1878.
196. Quoted in *Zion's Herald*, Aug. 22, 1878.

His intolerable views on that subject ostracized him as one who, the *Texas Christian Advocate* insisted, was "not fit to sit at meat with Christian and truthful people." [197]

Naturally Haven was cynical about a fraternity which did not include him. Sarcastically he wrote of the Southerners, "What pleasant brethren they are, out of conference! They are very sociable when they cease to be official." His criticism of "formal fraternity" was, however, based on more than purely personal differences. He refused, for example, to accept the pretense that Southern Methodism was not "a political church." Its denominational press, he knew well, constantly supported the Democratic Party and glorified the Confederacy's lost cause. He claimed, therefore, that "the Church South [was] the most political church in the country except one—its corival. It represents its section to-day in every heart throb," he charged. "Its papers are a unit, active and potent, as no other religious journals of the South are in opposing all National reconstruction based on National ideas of unity, civil rights, and [a] free and untrammeled ballot." [198] By its silence if not explicitly, he argued, Southern Methodism "feeds the fires of rebellion, sustains the Ku-klux outrages, [and] hates, despises, chains, murders its own brother, if slightly colored." [199] He indicted southern religious leaders for failing to stand up for equal rights and racial justice and for refusing to condemn the violence that accompanied the end of radical rule. On these grounds he was convinced that "formal fraternity" represented the ecclesiastical counterpart of the political sellout by the North in 1877. To his death he bitterly protested what he called "a sham fraternity, a fighting fraternity, a murdering fraternity," but as, in the case of segregated conferences, he was otherwise powerless to prevent what was happening. [200]

Under these circumstances, there was little that Haven could do in a practical way to keep alive his dream of and commitment to racial equality in the church. His denomination's educational program in the South, however, gave him the needed outlet for energies which he had earlier devoted to ecclesiastical integration. He had always vigorously supported the establishment of schools as part of the church's mission in the South. As bishop he raised funds throughout the country, wrote appeals, and lectured in behalf

197. *Wesleyan Christian Advocate* as quoted in *Methodist Advocate*, Aug. 7, 1878; *Richmond Christian Advocate* as quoted in *New York Christian Advocate*, Aug. 22, 1878; *Baltimore Episcopal Methodist* as quoted in *New York Christian Advocate*, July 4, 1878; *Western Methodist* (Memphis) as quoted in *Methodist Advocate*, July 24, 1878 and in *Southwestern Christian Advocate*, July 18, 1878; *Northwestern Christian Advocate*, Aug. 7, 1878; *The Independent*, Sept. 5, 1878; *Texas Christian Advocate* as quoted in *Southwestern Christian Advocate*, Feb. 20, 1879; *Christian Recorder*, June 13, 1878. H. Shelton Smith, who sees Haven as a catalyst in the North-South dialogue between churchmen about racial matters, points out that Southerners like Charles W. Miller and Henry W. Grady continued to warn against "Gilbert Havenism" even after "the Amos of northern Methodism" had died. See *In His Image, But . . .* , pp. 233, 279, 292.
198. *Methodist Advocate*, July 24, 1878.
199. *Ibid.*, Sept. 10, 1879.
200. *Ibid.*, Oct. 22, 1879; *Southwestern Christian Advocate*, Nov. 6, 1879; Daniels, *Memorials of Gilbert Haven*, pp. 151-52.

of the cause.[201] After the disappointments of 1876, however, southern education took on added significance for Haven. It became tangible evidence that, despite failures in other matters, the ideals that guided the postwar crusade into the South had been at least partially vindicated.

Faced with general disillusionment throughout the North over racial and sectional issues, Haven was determined to convince his fellow churchmen there that, whatever ambiguities existed concerning religious reconstruction, its one unequivocal accomplishment was the creation of the network of Methodist schools across the South. He pressed home that fact time and again in his extensive correspondence to the church press. One such example was his report in the *New York Advocate* of a tour of schools in four states early in 1878. He commended the Freedmen's Aid Society, and its dedicated secretary, Richard S. Rust, for providing funds for various kinds of institutions, from grade schools to professional training centers, including some not officially connected with the church. He appealed for missionaries to continue to go South and serve both races. "Come, to make every church a school-house, as in our earlier days we made every school-house a church," he wrote. "Come to preach an ethical as well as a dogmatic gospel." [202] The bishop's own son, William, answered the call and taught at a black school in South Carolina during the interim between college and his theological education.[203]

In a racially divided church, Haven raised support for white as well as black institutions. Despite the defect of the color line he believed that his denomination was offering "a Union and Christian education" not otherwise available to white Southerners. Of East Tennessee Wesleyan University's curriculum he wrote, "No Aleck Stevens' [sic] 'History of the War Between the States' is used here, in which State Rights is faithfully taught." [204] Not surprisingly, however, Haven put more emphasis on Negro education. He rarely missed commencements at black schools, one of which at Waynesboro, Georgia was named in his honor.[205]

Haven recognized that in most states there were few if any public-supported schools for blacks above the primary level. After the resegregation of the

201. Besides numerous references in his regular correspondence in the church press see *An Appeal to Our People for Our People* (n.p., [1875]), which originally appeared in *New York Christian Advocate*, Feb. 18, Mar. 11, 1875; *Methodist Advocate*, Mar. 17, 1875.

202. *New York Christian Advocate*, Feb. 28, Apr. 11, 18, 1878. W. E. B. DuBois' *The Souls of Black Folk*, originally published in 1903, captures the spirit of missionary zeal and sacrifice that was part of the postwar crusade into the South. See especially chapters 2 and 6 in the reprint edition, *Three Negro Classics*, ed. John Hope Franklin (New York: Avon Books, 1965).

203. *Zion's Herald*, Sept. 27, 1877; *Methodist Advocate*, June 26, 1878.

204. *New York Christian Advocate*, Apr. 18, 1878; *Southwestern Christian Advocate*, June 6, 1878; *Methodist Advocate*, June 26, July 17, 31, 1878.

205. *New York Christian Advocate*, June 19, 26, July 3, 1873; Feb. 28, 1878; *The Methodist*, July 5, 1873; *Zion's Herald*, July 9, 1874; Aug. 2, 9, 1877; May 2, 1878; Feb. 27, 1879; *Methodist Advocate*, May 26, 1875; July 3, 31, 1878; Mar. 12, July 9, 1879; *Southwestern Christian Advocate*, June 6, 1878.

state university in 1877, for example, his denomination's Claflin University at Orangeburg, South Carolina was "the only institution of collegiate grade open to a majority of the youth of the State." In the summer of 1878 with the help of Secretary Rust, Haven prevented that school from being transferred to state control under Governor Wade Hampton in order that liberal arts as well as industrial education could be continued there.[206] He took special pride in the professional institutions that had been formed for Negroes. The Meharry Medical School in Nashville was connected with Central Tennessee University, of whose board of trustees Haven was president. Besides teaching training schools throughout the South, his church had also established a law school in Tennessee and another medical college in New Orleans.[207] In some situations Haven took charge personally of financial campaigns for new buildings and real estate. His most significant effort was the purchase of land and the raising of funds for endowment and for construction at Clark University in Atlanta, from which came, after his death, Gammon Theological Seminary. In 1889 the divinity school, whose first president was Haven's son-in-law and later a Methodist bishop himself, Wilbur P. Thiekield, remembered these labors by naming the library building in his memory. The aged reformer-poet, John Greenleaf Whittier, composed for the dedicatory ceremony some verses that became the motto for the school.[208]

In November, 1878, Haven delivered his last important speech on Negro education at the annual meeting of the Freedmen's Aid Society. The burden of the address, which he called "The Americo-African," was to contrast the plight of the freedmen in 1865 with their improvement and accomplishments, especially in education, thirteen years later. He described the location and condition of twenty Methodist schools, scattered over eleven states, in which three thousand students had matriculated the previous year. He related stories of the educational results of the church's benevolence which totalled more than $700,000 through the society since 1866.[209] At the close of the oration, Haven paid tribute to the Northerners who had gone South since the war, on an educational and moral crusade. He celebrated as "that grandest word of

206. *New York Christian Advocate*, Apr. 11, 1878; *Zion's Herald*, Apr. 18, 1878; *The Independent*, July 11, 1878; *Methodist Advocate*, July 17, 31, 1878. See Haven's letters to former Massachusetts governor, William Claflin, benefactor, with his father, of the school, June 24, Sept. 11, 1878, Claflin Papers.
207. *Methodist Advocate*, Mar. 12, June 4, 1879; *Eleventh Annual Report of the Freedmen's Aid Society of the Methodist Episcopal Church for 1878* (Cincinnati, 1879), pp. 6-7, 39.
208. *Tenth Annual Report of the Freedmen's Aid Society of the Methodist Episcopal Church* (Cincinnati, 1878), pp. 48-49; Prentice, *Life*, p. 463; *Zion's Herald*, Feb. 27, 1879. The *Atlanta Constitution* as quoted in *Methodist Advocate*, Dec. 10, 1879, credited Haven with having secured a gift of $50,000 from a wealthy churchwoman in the North to cover the cost of Chrisman Hall at Clark. On his last visit to Atlanta, he visited the grounds of the campus and surveyed the construction that was underway. He wrote to Bishop Simpson from his deathbed asking him to deliver the dedicatory address when the building was completed. He left provision in his estate to cover a pledge for $10,000 that he had promised to raise for the school. Haven to Simpson, written by Mary Michelle Haven, from Malden, Nov. 28, 1879, Simpson Papers, Library of Congress; *Methodist Advocate*, Jan. 14, 1880.
209. *Eleventh Annual Report of the Freedmen's Aid Society*, 1878, pp. 6-7, 21.

the age" the expletive by which they had been known—"the carpetbagger." He delineated the hardships which they had faced, and praised them particularly for identifying with "their emancipated brothers . . . [in that by accepting] their very name, they [were] 'nigger teachers,' 'nigger preachers,' niggers of niggers." Their missionary venture, he contended, was an expression of "the word of Christ and Christianity to-day." [210]

It was perfectly appropriate, and fully to be expected, for Haven to evoke the moral idealism of the past. As he stood at the end of nearly three decades of racial reform within the church, he could recall having been part of a successful, if belated, antislavery movement. He had been involved in some of the noteworthy achievements in Negro education and with the expansion of the Methodist Episcopal Church throughout the South among blacks and whites. Yet, in the end the results of his efforts were ambiguous. His hope that there would be a postwar crusade against caste in the church and in American society generally was constantly frustrated. His own attempts in ecclesiastical integration had consistently failed. Ironically, his radicalism probably hastened the very process of formal segregation which he so much wanted to prevent. At the time of his death, therefore, his dream of a casteless church and a racially equalitarian social order was almost as far from realization as it had been in 1850.

210. *Ibid.*, pp. 36-49. The address first appeared in *Zion's Herald*, Nov. 28, Dec. 5, 1878; *New York Christian Advocate*, Nov. 14, 1878; *Southwestern Christian Advocate*, Dec. 12, 19, 1878; *Northwestern Christian Advocate*, Nov. 20, 1878; *Methodist Advocate*, Nov. 27, Dec. 4, 1878. For reactions in the Southern Methodist press see *Southern Christian Advocate*, Nov. 23, 1878; *New Orleans Christian Advocate*, Jan. 9, 1879.

Epilogue
An Elusive Dream

On November 18, 1879, Gilbert Haven returned to his family home for his last stay. His health had been seriously impaired ever since his trip to Liberia. Nonetheless over the previous year and a half he had kept the same intensive schedule for work that had characterized his first term in the episcopacy. After a tour of conferences in the Pacific Northwest during the late summer of 1879, however, it was obvious that he was near physical exhaustion. He looked older than his fifty-eight years. Hampered by a limp caused by a cancerous hip bone, his step was less lively. His hands trembled visibly. Even his red hair and beard, which had always given him a distinctive appearance, had become less striking.[1]

The evidence of debilitation and accompanying pain perhaps warned Haven of the imminence of death. Since his collapse in 1866, he had occasionally wondered how long he would live. On the various anniversaries of his wife's birth and death and of their marriage he routinely expressed in his journal a wish to die and be reunited with her. Once he remarked, more seriously than in jest, that Mary would scold him if he came to heaven before Willie and Mamie were grown. Friends remembered him to say quite often that he anticipated the end of his earthly pilgrimage when he could rest his head in Mary's lap for a thousand years.[2]

Apparently Haven was afflicted with a number of diseases. According to one contemporary diagnosis, he suffered from "scrofula," "African malaria, the osteal fungus, Bright's disease," and eventually heart failure. His final bout was, therefore, against considerable odds. It began on November 23, when he was stricken at a worship service in the Malden Centre Church. After three weeks of confinement, his son wrote to Bishop William Harris that "there [were] still hopes for his recovery, though [the doctors had] little expectation of its being speedy." [3] For himself Haven did not count much on the prospect of recuperation, so reconciled was he to the inevitability of a fatal outcome. As best he could, given the doctor's orders for rest and quietness, he maintained an interest in politics. He quizzed his male nurse about what was being said in the papers concerning ex-president Grant's tour of the South and the results of a political tussle in Maine. He also kept up his typical "playfulness" and good humor, preventing his sickroom from becoming dismal. On one occasion when his mother, now in her ninety-third year, was grieving over the possibility of his death, he joked with her

1. *Methodist Advocate,* Oct. 30, 1878; Jan. 15, 1879; *Zion's Herald,* Mar. 28, 1878, and Haven's series, "From Boston to Portland," issues between Aug. 14 and Oct. 16, 1879; also Nov. 27, 1879; Daniels, *Memorials of Gilbert Haven,* pp. 103-4.
2. Daniels, *Memorials of Gilbert Haven,* p. 112; Prentice, *Life,* pp. 200-209, 486, 491, 496.
3. Prentice, *Life,* pp. 493-97; W. Ingraham Haven to Bishop Harris, December 13, 1879 from Malden, as quoted in *New York Christian Advocate,* Dec. 18, 1879.

about preparing, with her other "boys, [to] give [her] a royal welcome into heaven." [4]

In the sixth week of his struggle for life Haven's condition worsened. On the third day of the new year his doctor announced that the bishop would live no more than a few hours. Immediately upon receiving the news Haven directed that the house be opened so that he could see his friends and relations one last time. Throughout the day old acquaintances like Fales H. Newhall and Daniel Steele, of the Triangle from a score of years before, came and went. Only Bishop Randolph S. Foster of the episcopal board was near enough to attend the deathbed reunion. Haven was busy recollecting fond memories of the past with his visitors and dictating messages to his associates in ecclesiastical and reform circles.[5] To the suffragette, Harriet H. Robinson, for instance, he sent regards and told her "to take a whole Christ, a whole Bible—and if she will follow that track; we'll meet again." [6] When the exchange of greetings was over, the final scene in the classic format of nineteenth-century evangelical piety unfolded in a "happy death" in the company of his immediate family. Bidding farewells and affirming his faith, he came to his end about six o'clock in the evening, January 3, 1880. Soon after, the bells in the church next door began to toll, bearing the sad tidings that Gil Haven was no more.[7]

The response to Haven's death in the press, while it included occasional invective against the man, by and large discerned the distinguishing marks of his life's mission. One Boston paper lamented that his loss made "another gap" among "the already well-thinned ranks of the leaders in the conflict with Slavery." Placing him "in the temple of American honor" along with William Lloyd Garrison and Wendell Phillips, the editor wrote, "He was a firm abolitionist before the war, and a staunch friend of the colored race, whose cause probably no man in this country has more earnestly advocated." [8] The *New York Times* called him "an opponent and vigorous hater of every form of caste and a thorough believer of the fundamental truths laid down by the Declaration of Independence." Its columnist focused on Haven's defense of "the persecuted freedmen" during "the dark days of the reconstruction period and afterward." "He believed," the writer maintained,

that the results of the war gave the National Government the legal and moral right to protect the negro in all the rights that that struggle had conferred upon him. . . . He was not vindictive by nature, but he loathed and abhorred the barbarities by which the White League and Kuklux sought to re-enslave the

4. Prentice, *Life*, pp. 497-500; Daniels, *Memorials of Gilbert Haven*, pp. 105-6.
5. Prentice, *Life*, pp. 501-7; Daniels, *Memorials of Gilbert Haven*, pp. 106-11.
6. Message from Gilbert Haven from his deathbed to H. H. R[obinson], January, 1880, Robinson Papers, Schlesinger Library, Radcliffe College. Mrs. Robinson, who did not share Haven's Methodist faith, added at the bottom of the sheet: "And if she does not?"
7. Prentice, *Life*, pp. 508-10; *Methodist Advocate*, Jan. 14, 1880.
8. *Evening Traveller*, Jan. 5, 1880; undated article as quoted in *Methodist Advocate*, Jan. 14, 1880.

newly-enfranchised race. His moral nature revolted at the tyranny and torture inflicted on his dark-skinned brethren, and in season and out of season his voice was raised in denunciation of the wrong.[9]

Bishop Foster's eulogy at the funeral in Malden touched on the "strange contradiction" in Haven's character that made him "a radical of the radicals, a conservative of the conservatives." Acknowledging that his sentiments were "in advance of his times, and extravagant," the bishop explained that Haven took "the extremest views" and "the most radical forms of expression and action in matters in which human interests were at stake, where justice revolted, and interposed itself against oppression and cruelty." His convervatism lay in his "fixed" principles, so that "in all his views of truth and righteousness he was established upon firm and unchangeable foundations." These principles, Foster declared, gave Haven "a sense of fairness, a sense of right, that sent him into the defense of the defenseless, and made him strong in the cause of the oppressed." [10] In a memorial sermon before the Boston Methodist Preachers' Meeting, George M. Steele, another of Haven's Triangle colleagues, picked up the same theme. "He was anchored to the eternal verities," Steele asserted. "It was this that gave him security when venturing out where other men have lost themselves; and it was this which rendered his ideas and projects safe, which in the hands of others have been either doubtful or disastrous." [11]

Nearly every commentator remarked on the loss which Haven's death brought to his church. His style was so unique, a denominational editor declared, that "his place will never be filled again by one man." [12] A journal that had freely criticized Haven, the *Springfield Republican,* added, "The nearer one gets to the primitive church the more does he find bishops like Gilbert Haven. He was also, be it remembered, a kind of missionary ecclesiastic,—a bishop *in partibus infidelium,* who must keep testifying against his own diocese as well as trying to convert it." [13]

The most common practice of Methodist speakers and writers was to express gratitude that, in the words of Bishop Foster, Haven had "lived for eight years to demonstrate the wisdom of [the] action" in 1872 which made him a bishop. Now that he had passed from the scene, *Zion's Herald* noted, ministers and members from all parts of the country, some of whom "stood aghast when his election to the episcopacy was announced," had come forward with "a series of unqualified lamentations over his bier, and expressions of high and tender appreciation of his character and ability." [14] Perhaps it

9. *New York Times,* Jan. 4, 1880.
10. Prentice, *Life,* pp. 516-25; Daniels, *Memorials of Gilbert Haven,* pp. 117-28; *Zion's Herald,* Jan. 15, 1880.
11. Daniels, *Memorials of Gilbert Haven,* p. 133.
12. *National Repository,* n.s. 7 (March, 1880), 288. The article is signed J. H. W., who is probably J. H. Walden.
13. *Springfield Daily Republican,* Jan. 5, 1880.
14. Prentice, *Life,* p. 520; *Zion's Herald,* Jan. 22, 1880.

was to be expected that old hostilities and disagreements would be obscured in this manner and that Haven's enemies in life would be able to praise him in death. The tendency went so far with Abel Stevens that four years later he was prepared to sanction amalgamation and declare Haven "not merely an apostolic bishop, whose humanitarianism was worthy of the highest ethics of his religion, but as a heroic prophet in our national Israel." A more realistic picture, however, would have required candor of the sort Haven's old teacher from Wesleyan University and Methodist editor, Daniel D. Whedon, demonstrated when he stated the deeper truth with which the departed had had to reckon. "We did not feel, as he very well knew," Whedon wrote in a review, "our own views, or the views of the Church, to be truly represented by his positions." [15]

Among his deathbed instructions Haven had asked that "Father" Mars, now an old man, speak at his funeral and that another black preacher, T. B. Snowden (pastor of the Revere Street Church) be on the platform. In this way Haven intended to symbolize his long devotion to the cause of black people. In his last hours he also told W. F. Mallalieu of the New England Conference, "Stand by the colored man, when I am gone. I know," he added, "the Lord will not find fault with me for my work in the South." [16] Of all his fellow churchmen, therefore, black Methodists were the ones most keenly affected by Haven's death. Throughout the South—in Georgia, Louisiana, Mississippi, the Carolinas—black congregations and conferences held solemn memorial services in his honor.[17] "Oh! what a defender of right and of our race is gone!" confessed E. M. Pinckney, presiding elder of the Orangeburg District in South Carolina. "The living words of our dying Bishop will ever be cherished by us, as well as his public acts, private counsels, and earnest toil in behalf of a long-oppressed and still-wronged people." A committee of the Mississippi Conference, chaired by Hiram Revels, stated in its tribute that Haven "lived not for himself, but for the glory of God in the intellectual, social, moral and religious elevation of his fellow-men." Speaking at a memorial service in Cincinnati, Marshall W. Taylor of the Lexington Conference acknowledged the loss of Haven to the nation and the church, but to "the colored people," he claimed, "much more is he our dead." [18]

Such were the sentiments of other black churchmen. "In his death," Ben-

15. Stevens, "The Problem of our African Population," *Methodist Quarterly Review*, 66 (January, 1884), 117-19; Whedon's review of E[rastus] Wentworth's *Gilbert Haven: A Monograph* in the *Quarterly Review*, 62 (October, 1880) 783.

16. Prentice, *Life*, pp. 503-4; Daniels, *Memorials of Gilbert Haven*, p. 109.

17. *Methodist Advocate*, Jan. 14, Feb. 4, 1880; *Zion's Herald*, Jan. 22, 29, 1880. *Journal of the Louisiana Annual Conference. Methodist Episcopal Church. Twelfth Session. Held at New Orleans, January 21-25, 1880*, pp. 32-33.

18. *Zion's Herald*, Jan. 22, 1880; Daniels, *Memorials of Gilbert Haven*, pp. 210-14; *Journal of the Twelfth Session of the Mississippi Annual Conference, of the Methodist Episcopal Church, Held at Macon, Mississippi, January 14-19, 1880*, pp. 38-40.

jamin T. Tanner of the *Christian Recorder* argued, ". . . American Christianity [has lost] one of the finest representatives of its best phase." Then he offered a most penetrating analysis of Haven's character and career.

He was of the few that made public opinion instead of following it; and happily for mankind, like the great Master he loved, he made it on the side of the poor, the bond, and the ostracised. We have spoken of him as the finest type of our American religion—a religion that, to a large extent, sanctioned slavery in the past and both sanctions and practices caste in the present. But the great soul of Gilbert Haven was against both.

He was the one man of his Church that dared treat the "negro question" other than in a sentimental way. For much of the legislation of 1876, at Baltimore, he blushed. Separate Conferences and separate churches were alike hateful to him, and to him, their corollary, a separate God and a separate heaven, was blasphemous. Nor did the idea of separate parlours fare any better at his hands. In his eyes the social ostracism of the colored men of the North was but a species of bull-dozing as murderous (for he that hateth his brother is a murderer) in its tendency as were the rifles of the South. Nor could he be charmed from his conviction, "charm they never so wisely." Whether in the North or in the South his was always a certain sound. . . . His voice yesterday was his voice today. What he said in the North, he repeated in the South.[19]

At the end of his editorial Tanner stated that his sense of loss was "assuaged by the conviction that [Haven's] seed [would] be multiplied in the land." The post–Reconstruction Era, however, was not good ground for the growth of such sentiments and commitments as Haven held. Among white churchmen no one took his place. A decade later the *Christian Recorder,* under B. F. Lee's editorship, recognized the fact in speaking of Haven as "the only man whom the [Methodist Episcopal] church has elevated that could fellowship all men, . . . and his seed seems to have died with him." [20] The proponents of social Christianity of the next generation largely left the racial issue undisturbed, finding a new cause in economic injustice and urban problems. Some social gospel leaders, like Washington Gladden, even deemed it necessary to disavow the sentiments of "Gil" Haven and to speak of "the foolishness of reconstruction" in which "the natural order of society" was inverted in "the attempt to establish negro supremacy." [21]

Nearly another century filled with traumatic and tragic moments in race relations passed before an American churchman championed as forcefully as did Gilbert Haven the cause of Negro freedom and equality. Like Haven, he articulated the Christian faith and national ideals in terms of a dream of human brotherhood. Like Haven, he was a clergyman who rose to national (and international) prominence, and his work brought him into the company of the presidents and senators of his time. Unlike Haven, he was a black man

19. *Christian Recorder*, Jan. 8, 1880.
20. *Ibid.;* Sept. 24, 1891.
21. Gladden, *Recollections* (Boston, 1909), pp. 176-81, 189-90, 366-76.

who led a movement of other black men and women. And unlike Haven, he did not enjoy the luxury of dying in his own bed. In the life, teachings, and death of Martin Luther King, Jr., the dream of Gilbert Haven was distinctively embodied for our time. Because the crisis in black and white continues, as does the tradition of *racial* Christianity in America, that dream remains unfulfilled.

Selected Bibliography

I. Unpublished Letters and Papers of Gilbert Haven

"Camp Life at the Relay," manuscript of an article which was published in revised form (see below). In private possession of George A. Wood, Jr., South Lincoln, Mass.

"The Identity of Philosophy," the philosophical oration at commencement exercises, Wesleyan University, Aug. 5, 1846. Archives of Olin Library, Wesleyan University, Middletown, Conn.

Journal, May 1, 1861–July 25, 1861 (52 unnumbered pages). In private possession of George A. Wood, Jr., South Lincoln, Mass.

Letters: Boston Public Library, William Lloyd Garrison Papers (1 letter).

Cornell University Library, Skilton Family Papers (20 letters).

Duke University Library, J. E. Bryant Papers (2 letters).

Drew University Library, George R. Crooks Papers (11 letters); Charles H. Fowler Papers (19 letters); Miscellaneous collections (3 letters).

Emory University Library, Special Collections Department (2 letters).

Garrett Theological Seminary Library, John Davies Collection (1 letter).

Harvard University Library, Ralph Waldo Emerson Papers (1 letter); Henry Wadsworth Longfellow Papers (1 letter); Charles Sumner Papers (1 letter).

Historical Society of Pennsylvania, Simon Gratz Autograph Collection (2 letters).

Library of the Boston Athenaeum (1 letter).

Library of Congress, Nathaniel P. Banks Papers (1 letter); Matthew Simpson Papers (43 letters).

Lovely Lane Museum of the Baltimore Conference Historical Society (1 letter).

Michigan Historical Collections, Alexander Winchell Papers (15 letters).

New England Methodist Historical Society Library, Boston University (16 letters).

Philadelphia Conference Historical Society, United Methodist Church. Matthew Simpson Papers (18 letters).

Radcliffe College, Arthur and Elizabeth Schlesinger Library on the History of Women in America. Harriet H. Robinson Papers (1 letter).

Rutherford B. Hayes Library, Fremont, Ohio. Mary Clemmer Ames Papers (2 letters); William Claflin Papers (16 letters).

Southern Methodist University, Perkins School of Theology, Methodist Historical Library (6 letters).

Syracuse University, George Arents Research Library. Gerrit Smith Papers (1 letter).

University of Michigan, William L. Clements Library. Theodore Dwight Weld Papers (1 letter).

University of North Carolina, Chapel Hill. Albion W. Tourgee Papers (on microfilm, 1 letter).

II. Other Unpublished Material

Cornell University Library, Skilton Family Papers (3 letters).

Library of Congress, Matthew Simpson Papers (7 letters).

Malden, Mass. Public Library. Papers for Haven family anniversaries.

Michigan Historical Collections, Erastus Otis Haven Papers (2 letters).

New England Methodist Historical Society Library, Boston University. Harvard Street Methodist Church, Cambridge, Quarterly Conference Records, 1845-69; Papers of the New England Conference; Records of the Methodist Preachers' Meeting for Boston and Vicinity, 1857-80.

Newhall, Fales Henry. Journal and Commonplace Book, 1854-80. In private possession of Dr. Jannette Newhall, Boston.

Wesleyan Academy, Wilbraham, Mass. Union Philosophical Society program, 1839.

Wesleyan University, Middletown, Conn. Commencement papers, 1846.

III. Newspapers

(A bracketed date indicates an incomplete survey of the paper. An unbracketed date refers to a full inventory of all issues of a particular year.)

a. Methodist Episcopal Church

Central Christian Advocate (St. Louis), [1866-68]; *Christian Advocate and Journal* (New York), [1846-51], 1861-65; *Daily Christian Advocate* for the General Conferences of 1864, 1868, 1872, 1876; *The Methodist* (New York), [1860-74]; *Methodist Advocate* (Atlanta), 1869-80; *New York Christian Advocate*, 1866-79, [1880]; *Northwestern Christian Advocate* (Chicago), [1866-68, 1877-80]; *Pittsburgh Christian Advocate*, [1867]; *Southwestern Christian Advocate* (New Orleans), [1872-80]; *Western Christian Advocate* (Cincinnati), [1865-80]; *Zion's Herald*, 1850-79, [1880, 1921].

b. Methodist Episcopal Church, South

Baltimore Christian Advocate [1870]; *Christian Neighbor* (Columbia, S. C.), [1872-80]; *Episcopal Methodist* (Baltimore), [1865-67]; *Nashville Christian Advocate*, [1869-80]; *New Orleans Christian Advocate*, [1872-77, 1879-80]; *Richmond Christian Advocate*, [1865-80]; *Southern Christian Advocate* (Augusta, Ga.; Charleston, S. C.), [1869-80].

c. Other

Alabama Baptist (Montgomery), [1874-75]; *Atlanta Constitution*, [1873-76, 1878]; *Atlanta Daily Herald*, [1872-75]; *Boston Globe*, [1872, 1875, 1878-80]; *Boston Herald*, [1879]; *Boston Transcript*, [1875, 1879-80]; *Boston Traveller*, [1859-60, 1863-65, 1872, 1874-75, 1878-80]; *Christian Index* (Atlanta), [1874]; *Christian Recorder* (Philadelphia), [1867-78, 1880, 1891]; *Harper's Weekly* (New York), [1866, 1875]; *The Independent* (New York), [1854-80]; *The Liberator* (Boston), [1846, 1850, 1855, 1857-65]; *National Anti-Slavery Standard* (New York), [1857, 1869]; *National Standard* (New York), [1871]; *New York Herald* [1875]; *New York Times* [1872, 1878-80] *New York Tribune*, [1872, 1875-76]; *Northampton Courier* (Mass.), [1851-53]; *Springfield Republican* (Mass.), [1875, 1879-80]; *Westfield News Letter* (Mass.), [1856].

IV. Articles and Books by Gilbert Haven

"American in Africa." *North American Review,* 125 (1877), 147-58, 517-28.

"The Americo-African." In *The Eleventh Annual Report of the Freedmen's Aid Society of the Methodist Episcopal Church for 1878,* pp. 36-49. Cincinnati: Western Methodist Book Concern, 1879.

An Appeal to Our People for Our People [pamphlet distributed by the Freedmen's Aid Society of the Methodist Episcopal Church]. N.p., n.d.

"Armageddon and After. Part VIII. The Reverend Gilbert Haven Glimpses the Millennium (1863)." In John L. Thomas, ed., *Slavery Attacked: The Abolitionist Crusade,* pp. 172-74. Englewood Cliffs, N. J.: Prentice-Hall, Inc., 1965.

"The Beginning of the End of American Slavery, a Sermon Preached at Harvard St. M. E. Church, Cambridge, Mass., Nov. 6, 1859." In James Redpath, ed., *Echoes of Harper's Ferry,* pp. 125-40. Boston: Thayer and Eldridge, 1860. [Reprinted New York: Arno Press and the *New York Times,* 1969.]

"Camp Life at the Relay." *Harper's New Monthly Magazine* 24 (1862), 628-33.

"The Character and Career of Theodore Parker." In *Parkerism: Three Discourses delivered on the occasion of the death of Theodore Parker* by William F. Warren, Fales H. Newhall, and Gilbert Haven, pp. 77-115. New York: Carlton & Porter, 1860.

Christus Consolator or Comfortable Words for Burdened Hearts. Edited by William I. Haven. New York: Hunt & Eaton, 1893.

Education and Religion Essential to the Perfection of Character. A Discourse Delivered at Amenia Seminary, March 16th, 1851, on Resigning the Office of Principal. New York: Wm. C. Bryant & Co., 1851.

"Exegesis of Romans, IX, 3." *Methodist Quarterly Review* 45 (1863), 420-34.

"The Exodus." In *An Autobiography of the Rev. Josiah Henson (Mrs. Harriet Beecher*

Stowe's "Uncle Tom"), From 1789 to 1879. With a Preface by Mrs. Harriet Beecher Stowe, Introductory Notes by Wendell Phillips and John G. Whittier, As an Appendix on the Exodus by Bishop Gilbert Haven, pp. 333-36. Boston: B. B. Russell & Co., 1879.

Father Taylor, the Sailor Preacher. Incidents and Anecdotes of Rev. Edward T. Taylor, for over Forty Years Pastor of the Seaman's Bethel. With Hon. Thomas Russell. New York: Hunt & Eaton, 1871.

"God's Purpose for America." Ladies' Repository 36 (1876), 522-33.

"The Great Election." Methodist Quarterly Review, 47 (1865), 253-75.

"Havenisms" [selections from published writings]. In William Haven Daniels, ed., Memorials of Gilbert Haven, Bishop of the Methodist Episcopal Church, pp. 241-359. Boston: B. B. Russell & Co., 1880.

"Infant Baptism and Church Membership." Methodist Quarterly Review 41 (1859), 5-26.

Introduction. In John O. Foster, Life and Labors of Mrs. Maggie Newton Van Cott, The First Lady Licensed to Preach in the Methodist Episcopal Church in the United States, xiii-xxviii. Cincinnati: Hitchcock & Walden, 1872.

"Isaac Rich." Ladies' Repository 28 (1868), 321-24.

"John Ruskin." Methodist Quarterly Review 42 (1860), 533-54.

Lay Representation in the Methodist Episcopal Church: Its Justice and Expediency. Boston: James P. Magee, 1864.

The Mission of America: A Discourse Delivered before the New England M. E. Conference, at the High Street Church, Charleston, Ms., on the Occasion of the Annual State Fast, April 2d, 1863. Boston: J. P. Magee, 1863.

"Murder for Opinion's Sake." In James M. Wells, The Chisolm Massacre: A Picture of "Home Rule" in Mississippi, pp. 305-15. Chicago: Chisolm Monumental Fund, 1877.

National Sermons. Sermons, Speeches and Letters on Slavery and Its War: From the Passage of the Fugitive Slave Bill to the Election of President Grant. 1869. Reprinted New York: Arno Press and the New York Times, 1969.

Our Next-Door Neighbor: A Winter in Mexico. New York: Harper & Brothers, 1875.

"Pictures of Travel. Lake Geneva." Ladies' Repository 23 (1863), 27-33.

The Pilgrim's Wallet; or, Scraps of Travel gathered in England, France, and Germany. Boston: E. P. Dutton and Company, 1866.

"A Poem Delivered at Malden, on the Two Hundredth Anniversary of the Incorporation of the Town, May 23, 1849." In The Bi-Centennial Book of Malden. Containing the Two Hundredth Anniversary of the Incorporation of the Town, May 23, 1849; with Other Proceedings of That Day; and Matters Pertaining to the History of the Place, pp. 61-82. Boston: Geo. C. Rand & Co., 1850.

"Te Deum Laudamus." The Cause and the Consequence of the Election of Abraham Lincoln; A Thanksgiving Sermon Delivered in the Harvard St. M. E. Church, Cambridge, Sunday Evening, Nov. 11, 1860. Boston: J. M. Hewes, 1860.

The Uniter and Liberator of America. A Memorial Discourse on the Character and Career of Abraham Lincoln: Delivered in the North Russell Street M. E. Church, Boston, Sunday, April 23, 1865. Boston: James P. Magee, 1865.

"The Very Chiefest of Our Statesmen." In William M. Cornell, ed. Charles Sumner: Memoir and Eulogies, pp. 41-83. Boston: James H. Earle, 1874.

"Wordsworth." Methodist Quarterly Review 39 (1857), 362-81.

V. Secondary Sources on Gilbert Haven

Adams, Josiah. The Genealogy of the Descendants of Richard Haven, of Lynn. Boston: Elias Howe, 1849.

Alumni Record of Wesleyan University. 3rd ed. Hartford: n.p., 1883. Bibliography of Rev. Gilbert Haven, pp. 580-81.

Benton, Joel, ed. Amenia Seminary Reunion August 22d, 1906. New York: Broadway Publishing Company [1907].

Bucke, Emory Stevens, ed. *The History of American Methodism.* 3 vols. Nashville: Abingdon Press, 1964.

Butler, John Wesley. *History of the Methodist Episcopal Church in Mexico.* New York: The Methodist Book Concern, 1918.

Cable, George Washington. *The Negro Question. A Selection of Writings on Civil Rights in the South.* Edited by Arlin Turner. Garden City, N. Y.: Doubleday & Co., 1958.

Cameron, Richard M. *Methodism and Society in Historical Perspective.* Nashville: Abingdon Press, 1961.

Cooper, V. A. *A Tribute to Bishop Gilbert Haven, January 11, 1880.* Lynn, Mass.: Leech, Lewis & Parker, 1880.

Cuyler, Theodore Ledyard. *Recollections of a Long Life. An Autobiography.* New York: The Baker and Taylor Co. [1902].

Daniels, William Haven. *The Illustrated History of Methodism in Britain and America, from the Days of the Wesleys to the Present Time.* New York: Phillips & Hunt, 1879.
————, ed. *Memorials of Gilbert Haven, Bishop of the Methodist Episcopal Church.* Boston: B. B. Russell & Co., 1880.

Dunham, Chester Forrester. *The Attitude of the Northern Clergy Toward the South 1860-1865.* Toledo: Gray Co., Publishers, 1942.

Duren, William Larkin. *Charles Betts Galloway, Orator, Preacher, and "Prince of Christian Chivalry."* Emory University [Atlanta], Ga.: Banner Press [1932].

Farish, Hunter Dickinson. *The Circuit-Rider Dismounts: A Social History of Southern Methodism 1865-1900.* Richmond: The Dietz Press, 1938.

Flood, Theodore L. "Gilbert Haven." In Theodore L. Flood and John W. Hamilton, eds. *Lives of Methodist Bishops,* pp. 483-98. New York: Phillips & Hunt, 1882.

Fredrickson, George M. *The Black Image in the White Mind: The Debate on Afro-American Character and Destiny, 1817-1914.* New York: Harper & Row, 1971.

"Gilbert Haven." In *The National Cyclopaedia of American Biography.* Vol. XIII, pp. 261-62. New York: James T. White & Co., 1906.

"Gilbert Haven." In James Grant Wilson and John Fiske, eds. *Appleton's Cyclopaedia of American Biography.* Vol. III, pp. 117-18. New York: D. Appleton & Company, 1888.

Gravely, William B. "Methodist Preachers, Slavery and Caste: Types of Social Concern in Antebellum America." *The Duke Divinity School Review* 34 (1969), 209-29.

Hammond, Edmund Jordan. *The Methodist Episcopal Church in Georgia.* N.p., 1935.

Handy, Robert T. *A Christian America. Protestant Hopes and Historical Realities.* New York: Oxford University Press, 1971.

Harris, Joel Chandler. *Life of Henry W. Grady Including His Writings and Speeches. A Memorial Volume.* New York: Cassell Publishing Co. [1890].

Hood, J. W. *One Hundred Years of the African Methodist Episcopal Zion Church; or, The Centennial of African Methodism.* New York: AME Zion Book Concern, 1895.

Hughes, Edwin Holt. *I Was Made a Minister. An Autobiography.* Nashville: Abingdon Cokesbury, 1943.

Hurst, John Fletcher. *The History of Methodism: American Methodism.* Vol. III. New York: Eaton & Mains, 1903.

Hyde, A. B. *The Story of Methodism throughout the World.* Rev. ed. Springfield, Mass.: Willey & Co., 1889.

Jones, Donald Gene. "The Moral, Social, and Political Ideas of the Methodist Episcopal Church from the Closing Years of the Civil War through Reconstruction 1864-1876." Ph.D. dissertation, Drew University, 1963.

Jones, J. Lloyd. *Bishop Haven: An Elegy.* Cazenovia, N.Y.: F. M. Taylor, Book and Job Printer, 1880.

Joy, James R. "Gilbert Haven." In Allen Johnson, ed. *The Dictionary of American Biography.* Vol. VIII, pp. 407-8. New York: Charles Scribner's Sons, 1928.

Keller, Ralph Alan. "Northern Protestant Churches and the Fugitive Slave Law of 1850." Ph.D. dissertation, University of Wisconsin, 1969.

261

Kellogg, Amherst W., ed. *A Concise History of Methodism in England and America of Its Origin, Founders, Development and Institutions.* Milwaukee, Wisc.: H. O. Brown & Company, 1897.

Lee, James W.; Luccock, Naphtali; and Dixon, James Main. *The Illustrated History of Methodism.* St. Louis: The Methodist Magazine Publishing Co., 1900.

Leete, Frederick Deland. *Methodist Bishops.* Nashville: Parthenon Press, 1948.

McPherson, James M. "Abolitionists and the Civil Rights Act of 1875." *Journal of American History* 52 (1965), 493-510.

————. "Coercion or Conciliation? Abolitionists Debate President Hayes's Southern Policy." *New England Quarterly* 39 (1966), 474-96.

————. *The Struggle for Equality: Abolitionists and the Negro in the Civil War and Reconstruction.* Princeton: Princeton University Press, 1964.

Massachusetts, Commonwealth of. Adjutant-General's Office. *Massachusetts Soldiers, Sailors and Marines in the Civil War.* Vol. I. Norwood, Mass.: Norwood Press, 1931-1937.

Matlack, Lucius C. *The Antislavery Struggle and Triumph in the Methodist Episcopal Church.* New York: Phillips & Hunt, 1881.

Morrow, Ralph E. *Northern Methodism and Reconstruction.* East Lansing, Mich.: Michigan State University Press, 1956.

Mudge, James. *History of the New England Conference of the Methodist Episcopal Church, 1796-1910.* Boston: New England Conference, 1910.

Nicholson, Frank, ed. *Alumni Record of Wesleyan University, Middletown, Conn.* 4th ed. New Haven: The Tutter, Morehouse and Taylor Company, 1911.

Norton, L. Wesley. "The Religious Press and the Compromise of 1850: A Study of the Relationship of the Methodist, Baptist, and Presbyterian Press to the Slavery Controversy 1846-1851." Ph.D. dissertation, University of Illinois, 1959.

Osborn, Albert. *John Fletcher Hurst. A Biography.* New York: Eaton & Mains, 1905.

Powell, Milton Bryan. "The Abolitionist Controversy in the Methodist Episcopal Church, 1840-1864." Ph.D. dissertation, State University of Iowa, 1963.

Prentice, George. "Haven's National Sermons." *Ladies' Repository* 30 (1870), 401-6.

————. *The Life of Gilbert Haven, Bishop of the Methodist Episcopal Church.* New York: Phillips & Hunt, 1883.

[Rice, William North, and Rice, Charles Francis], eds. *William Rice: A Memorial.* Cambridge: Riverside Press, 1898.

Robinson, Harriet H. *Massachusetts in the Woman Suffrage Movement. A General, Political, Legal and Legislative History From 1774, to 1881.* Boston: Roberts Brothers, 1881.

Robinson, Mrs. W. S., ed. *"Warrington" Pen-Portraits: A Collection of Personal and Political Reminiscences from 1848 to 1876, from the Writings of William S. Robinson.* Boston: Rand, Avery and Co., 1877.

Sherman, David. *History of Wesleyan Academy, at Wilbraham, Mass. 1817-1890.* Boston: The McDonald & Gill Company, 1893.

Simpson, Matthew, ed. *Cyclopaedia of Methodism.* 5th rev. ed. Philadelphia: Louis H. Everts, 1883.

Smith, H. Shelton. *In His Image But . . . .: Racism in Southern Religion, 1780-1910.* Durham: Duke University Press, 1972.

Smith, Timothy L. *Revivalism and Social Reform in Mid-Nineteenth Century America.* New York: Abingdon Press, 1957.

Smylie, John Edwin. "Protestant Clergymen and American Destiny. II. Prelude to Imperialism: 1865-1900." *Harvard Theological Review* 56 (1963), 297-311.

Steele, Daniel. "Politics and the Pulpit" [review of Haven's *National Sermons*]. *Methodist Quarterly Review* 53 (1870), 189-204.

Stevens, Abel. "The Problem of Our African Population." *Methodist Quarterly Review* 66 (1884), 104-26.

Stowell, Jay S. *Methodist Adventures in Negro Education.* New York: Methodist Book Concern, 1922.

Stratton, C. C., ed. *Autobiography of Erastus O. Haven, D.D., LL.D., One of the Bishops of the Methodist Episcopal Church.* New York: Phillips & Hunt, 1883.

262

Swaney, Charles Baumer. *Episcopal Methodism and Slavery, with Sidelights on Ecclesiastical Politics.* Boston: Richard G. Badger, Publisher; The Gorham Press, 1926.

Sweet, William Warren. *The Methodist Episcopal Church and the Civil War.* Cincinnati: Western Book Concern Press, [1912].

————. "The Methodist Episcopal Church and Reconstruction." *Journal of the Illinois State Historical Society* 7 (1914), 147-65.

[Titus, Mrs. Frances W. and Gilbert, Olive]. *Narrative of Sojourner Truth; A Bondswoman of Olden Time.* Battle Creek, Mich.: Review and Herald Office, 1884.

Wayman, A. W. *My Recollections of African M. E. Ministers, or, Forty Years' Experience in the African Methodist Episcopal Church.* Philadelphia: A.M.E. Book Rooms, 1882.

Wentworth, Erastus. *Gilbert Haven: A Monograph. Delivered before the Troy Conference, April, 1880, and Published at Its Request.* New York: Phillips & Hunt, 1881.

Whedon, Daniel D. Review of *Gilbert Haven: A Monograph.* By Rev. E[rastus] Wentworth, D.D. *Methodist Quarterly Review* 62 (1880), 782-84.

————. Review of Gilbert Haven's Fast-Day Sermon [*"Te Deum Laudamus." The Cause and the Consequence of the Election of Abraham Lincoln.*] *Methodist Quarterly Review,* 43 (1861), 352-53.

————. Review of *The Pilgrim's Wallet; Or, Scraps of Travel Gathered in England, France, and Germany.* By Gilbert Haven. *Methodist Quarterly Review* 48 (1866), 302-5.

————. Review of *Report of the New England Annual Conference for 1865 on Church Reconstruction. Methodist Quarterly Review* 47 (1865), 479-83.

Winchell, Alexander. *Preadamites; or, A Demonstration of the Existence of Men before Adam; Together with a Study of Their Condition, Antiquity, Racial Affinities, and Progressive Dispersion over the Earth.* Chicago: S. C. Griggs and Company, 1888.

Index